Y0-ATD-819

MUSIC
ON THE AIR

BOOKS BY HAZEL GERTRUDE KINSCELLA
The Kinscella Readers in Musical Appreciation (Six Books)
Music and Romance for Youth

Music on the Air

BY

HAZEL GERTRUDE KINSCELLA

FOREWORD BY DR. WALTER DAMROSCH

INTRODUCTION BY DR. DANIEL GREGORY MASON

New York

THE VIKING PRESS

1934

MT
150
K56

Indexed in:
ESSAY INDEX

Copyright 1934 by Hazel Gertrude Kinscella
Published by The Viking Press, Inc.
Printed in the United States of America by The Vail-Ballou Press
Distributed in Canada by The Macmillan Company of Canada, Ltd.

TO MRS. EDWARD MacDOWELL

THIS BOOK IS AFFECTIONATELY DEDICATED

Acknowledgments

The author is deeply indebted to those kind and able friends who have given so freely of their knowledge in the special chapters contributed by them; is happy to acknowledge her gratitude to Dr. Walter Damrosch, Musical Counsel of the National Broadcasting Company, and to Dr. Daniel Gregory Mason, MacDowell Professor of Music at Columbia University, for their inspiring and valued contributions to the book; to Professor Douglas Stuart Moore and Mr. Paul Lang of Columbia University, and Dr. Carleton Sprague Smith, Chief of the Music Division of the New York Public Library, who have been so kind as to read in manuscript certain chapters of the book and make valuable suggestions; to *Musical Courier* for permission to reprint "Virginia Finds Her Folk Music," by John Powell; to *Musical America* and G. Schirmer, Inc., for the loan of pictures. To Mr. Ernest LaPrade, assistant to Dr. Damrosch at the National Broadcasting Company and friend of all good music, the writer expresses her obligation for many courtesies extended.

Credit for Photographs is Due as Follows:

Charles Wakefield Cadman. Courtesy of G. Schirmer.

John McCormack. Photo by Arnold Genthe. Courtesy of *Musical America*.

John Philip Sousa. Photo by Fred Hess & Son. Courtesy of *Musical America*.

Igor Stravinsky. Photo by Schede, Wiesbaden. Courtesy of *Musical America*.

Sergei Koussevitzky. Photo by Bachrach. Courtesy of *Musical America*.

The Gordon String Quartet. Courtesy of National Broadcasting Company.

John Alden Carpenter. Photo by Pirie MacDonald. Courtesy of G. Schirmer.

Sidney Homer. Photo by Mishkin.

The Oldest Piano; The Virginal; The Harpsichord. Courtesy of Metropolitan Museum.

Ancient Instruments. Courtesy of German Tourist Information Office.

Fritz Kreisler. Courtesy of Carl Fischer, Inc.

Lily Strickland. Photo by Townsend, N. Y.

John Powell. Courtesy of G. Schirmer.

Howard Brockway. Photo by Alice Boughton. Courtesy of G. Schirmer.

Howard Hanson. Photo by Pach Bros.

Charles Skilton. Photo by Maurice Seymour.

Seth Bingham. Photo by Bachrach.

George Gershwin. Photo by Mishkin.

From Microphone to Loudspeaker. Courtesy of National Broadcasting Company.

The Organ in St. Remiguns Church. Courtesy of German Tourist Information Office.

Bach's House. Courtesy of German Tourist Information Office.

Schloss Esterhazy at Eisenstadt. Courtesy of Austrian Tourist Office.

Johannes Brahms. Courtesy of German Tourist Information Office.

Brahms, His House; His Birthplace. Courtesy of German Tourist Information Office.

Maurice Ravel. Photo by Elliot & Fry, London. Courtesy of *Musical America*.

Frederick Stock. Photo by Underwood & Underwood.

Grieg's House. Courtesy of *The Mentor*.

FOREWORD

AN enormous amount of music is carried over the air by radio to millions of listeners. Some of this music is trash, which therefore deserves no recommendation or explanatory comment. But there is a constantly increasing quantity of real music which can be heard over the radio today, and as the greater number of listeners have never had an opportunity such as this before, it is important that their musical intelligence should be sharpened and their power of appreciation increased.

The book, *Music on the Air* by Hazel Gertrude Kinscella, is a real contribution in this direction. The writer occupies an honored place among musicians and has been active as an educator for many years. She has called to her aid some of her most noted colleagues who are specialists in the subjects of which they write. I prophesy a large distribution for this book, as it will fill a real need.

WALTER DAMROSCH

INTRODUCTION
MUSIC AS AN INTERNATIONAL LANGUAGE

THERE is a Russian edition of Rimsky-Korsakov's *Scheherazade,* a suite of pieces for orchestra founded on the Arabian Nights Entertainments, which flaunts as title-page a most gorgeously Oriental design of bright blues, reds, and greens, on a background of gold. It is strikingly handsome and quite barbaric, reminding one more than anything else of the wall decorations of Byzantine architecture. And the last touch of outlandishness is given by the text in those strange Russian letters which look, according to a whimsical friend of mine, "as English does when you have belladonna in your eyes." To see discerningly such a title-page, feeling the remoteness of the point of view that produced it from that of the Anglo-Saxon mind, and then to turn over the leaf and read, with a thrill of appreciation, the stirring melody with which the piece begins, is to gain a vivid sense of the universality of music, its power to bridge even such a chasm as that which separates East and West. A Russian and an American who stopped at the title-page might well feel a strangeness in each other, a sense of fundamental differences in racial memories, traditions, tastes, which would need only an occasion to manifest itself in active enmity. Yet if they once heard the music, witnessing each other's delight in it, they would feel underneath all this a bond of common human feeling uniting them already in potential friendship. However little sympathy they might have in other respects, the music at least would speak to both, by virtue of its unique power as the only language that requires no translation.

DANIEL GREGORY MASON

CONTENTS

Part I

The Voice of the People

In Our Own Time

Part II

ILLUSTRATIONS

Music on the Air
PART ONE

MUSIC ON THE AIR

THE STORY of radio broadcasting is a story of magic. It had its beginnings in mass communication and developed over a long period of years.

It is hard for anyone to realize the amazing achievements and developments of the past fifteen years. Communication during the World War took form in several fields, one of which was the development of radio transmission and reception, both telegraphic and telephonic.

I recall the thrill of the first broadcasting that I ever heard, a record of Sousa's "Stars and Stripes Forever" played in Sioux City, Iowa, and received by us in an amateur receiving station in an upper class room at the University of Nebraska at Lincoln—the amateur announcing, the winding of the phonograph, then the stirring melody. . . . Now, an hour ago, we were sitting in a service in historic old Trinity Church in Wall Street, New York City, and heard the chimes, just overhead, pealing out the melodies of Old World Christmas carols, to be synchronized with chimes playing the same carols from St. Dominiques in Quebec, Canada. . . . The wonder of the radio never ceases!

How many people heard this latest broadcast cannot be known, but there are, in the United States, according to the latest statistics, seventeen million receiving sets, and nearly twenty million homes wired for radio reception—nearly forty million places in the United States alone where people may gather to listen to music on the air!

That there is much music for them to hear is assured by the latest broadcasting reports, which state that over 67% of the total of all broadcasting done in the United States each twenty-four hours is music, bringing two million letters of radio applause to one large broadcasting office, alone, within the past ten months. Some of the letters bring commendation, some bring criticism, but many thousands bring questions, special phases of music and suggestions for better appreciation are discussed by different artists, each a specialist in his field. Ten chapters are devoted to as many fascinating aspects of music in America. Twentieth-century music is considered with special reference to its differences from earlier music. An outline of the history of music is included, as well as brief biographical sketches of outstanding composers together with stories, interpretations, and analyses of their most frequently performed and universally admired compositions.

EVERYBODY'S MUSIC

THERE is an old Russian legend which tells of a shepherd, in a far-off land, who made such sweet music upon his simple reed flute that all the other shepherds gathered about to hear him. "Our friend giveth such pleasure with his pipe," said one of them, "why should he spend his time guarding the sheep? Rather let us take care of his flock that he may play all day. Not all of us may play, but all may listen." And they divided his work among them, leaving him free to go about, playing not only for shepherds, but for cobblers and basket-makers, home-keepers, children, and kings in their palaces. And these, the old legend says, were the first concerts.

Music is, today, more than ever before, a universal possession, in which everyone may have a part, either as creator, performer, or listener. To appreciate one must first listen for something in particular, and it is, happily, possible for everyone to gain, through thoughtful listening and reading—and without burdening himself with a mass of technical language—general and sufficient information on all that contributes to the enjoyment of the grace and beauty of any real music, whatever its style.

Recently a list of two hundred of the best-known pieces of music of varied style was sent to five hundred people scattered throughout the country, only a few of whom were musicians, the others being selected from all walks of life. Each person was asked to mark the pieces in the order of his personal preference. The result of the "popularity" vote was an amazing one, for the votes for the first ten "favorites" were almost unanimous. The second ten (from eleven to twenty, inclusive) showed a more personal variation in taste, but the first group showed an almost universal reaction to the same general elements of beauty, which, aside

7

from individual mood and appeal, are rhythm, melody, harmony, and form.

It is seldom that any two people agree upon a single composition, but when five hundred agree upon ten pieces of music it is a fair test as to the type and quality of music that the general public likes best. The ten pieces in the order of their popularity are:

"Minuet in G"	Beethoven
"To a Wild Rose"	MacDowell
"Spring Song"	Mendelssohn
"Barcarolle" (*Tales of Hoffmann*)	Offenbach
"Melody in F"	Rubinstein
"Humoresque"	Dvořák
"Anitra's Dance" (*Peer Gynt*)	Grieg
"Träumerei"	Schumann
"Largo" (*New World Symphony*)	Dvořák
"Hallelujah Chorus" (*Messiah*)	Handel

The second ten pieces include:

Unfinished Symphony (First Movement)	Schubert
Fifth Symphony (*Andante con moto*)	Beethoven
"Serenade"	Schubert
"He Shall Feed His Flock" (*Messiah*)	Handel
"Deep River"	Negro Spiritual
"O Sole Mio"	di Capua
"Blue Danube Waltz"	Strauss
"Pilgrims' Chorus" (*Tannhäuser*)	Wagner
"Largo" (*Xerxes*)	Handel
"Cradle Song"	Brahms

A striking fact to be noticed in regard to the first ten chosen is that, with one exception, all of the compositions are instrumental rather than vocal. This one exception, the "Hallelujah Chorus," * has the added ap-

* The "Hallelujah Chorus" is the climax, though not the end, of the *Messiah,* which work, written in twenty-four days, had its first London performance (the proceeds of which went to charity) at Covent Garden, March 23, 1743. The audience became more

peal of being a dramatically religious work written as the result of concentrated and intense inspiration.

The general character of the first ten chosen is one of that same gracious simplicity (not to be confused with a commonplace "catchiness") which, in part, constitutes the age-old and universal appeal to the affections of such lyric gems as the folk songs "All Thro' the Night" and "Auld Lang Syne," and of such composed songs, folk-style in character, as Franz Gruber's "Silent Night" or Barnby's "Sweet and Low."

Rhythm, the oldest and most fundamental element of music, means the movement or swing of the music. This varies according to the rate of speed (tempo), or its time-measure, and the grouping of notes and rests of differing length. Some melodies achieve lasting popularity because of a clearly marked rhythm. This is true in many sturdy folk dances and singing games; in such folk songs as "Volga Boat Song" (also notable as an example of simple form, in which the same phrases are much repeated), or in such composed numbers as the "Barcarolle" from *Tales of Hoffmann,* and Tschaikowsky's cheerful "March" from the *Symphonie Pathétique.*

Melody (tune) is one of the greatest charms of music, and one of the most difficult to produce. As the human voice is really the foundation of all music, even an instrumental melody is best when—either consciously or unconsciously—its creator has so arranged its curves and climax, has so avoided over-repetitions of its highest tones, and so limited its range (distance between its highest and lowest tones), that it lies comfortably within the compass of the normal voice and is vocal in its nature. In other words, the deeply touching melody is usually singable, and the listener is instinctively intrigued into "humming a bit."

In the instrumental melody, added variety of mood is created by the characteristic voice qualities of the individual instruments, as in the popular "Humoresque" by Dvořák (most familiar as a violin solo); or in the eloquent melody first sung by the violas and 'cellos in the

stirred as the work progressed until finally, with the beginning of the celebrated chorus, the King, who was present, rose to his feet and remained standing until the number was ended. The audience, of course, joined him, and the custom of standing through the singing of this chorus has continued to this day.

Andante con moto from Beethoven's *Fifth Symphony,* one of the five or six most beautiful symphonic melodies of the world.

Harmony is the combination of two or more sounds at one time. In a folk song the harmonic setting is usually unimportant, possibly an afterthought; but many of the finest composed melodies are almost always associated with the colorful harmonies that surround them.

Form in music is created when the composer of a piece follows a definite plan in his writing so that the result is well-balanced and complete as it stands. When this is accomplished, the listener is at once aware of the shapeliness of the music. Such a quality is often displayed to perfection in even the simplest folk songs. To make such balance possible it is necessary that there shall be a certain amount of repetition in the melody, and enough contrast to give it an individual character. This idea of repetition and contrast is illustrated in the familiar round, "Three Blind Mice," * in which two extremely simple phrases are contrasted, both as to melody and rhythm, causing a delightful harmony when the tune is sung as a round.

In Schumann's "Träumerei," the form is elementary, as the whole piece is made up of the notes of a single chord, the lovely tune created from them being repeated without significant change, though transposed into another key.

"To a Wild Rose" by MacDowell—another of the "favorites"—is built upon a simple, questioning, three-note figure. This piece is also written in three "large parts," or distinctive sections, the first and last of which are almost exactly alike. A very short *coda,* or end-piece, is added.

Form may, therefore, be said to be a combination of *repetition* of certain material (usually the familiar tune or theme) and *variety* (use of new material) so balanced as to give a pleasing unified result. Sometimes, however, the composer wishes to create a definitely monotonous effect, as in the much-discussed *Bolero* by Maurice Ravel.

Bolero was composed for the use of Ida Rubinstein, in a ballet which she was creating for a Paris performance. In it Ravel wished to suggest the old folk-custom of Spain in regard to dances, in which the specta-

---

* See chapter on "Patterns and Styles," page 80.

tors are also performers, furnishing the rhythmic accompaniment by clapping of hands, snapping of fingers, stamping of feet, or strumming on the guitar. So, in his music, he used a single rhythmic figure which is repeated relentlessly and without variation for nearly twenty minutes. Only during the last two measures of the piece is there the slightest variation from it. At the beginning, only the beating of a drum is heard, done so softly that it is only a whispered suggestion of the bolero rhythm, and of the melody which follows. The tune used by Ravel as a theme is a very old one which has been sung for centuries in some of the Spanish provinces. The melody is first played by the flute, then is repeated by the clarinets. Over and over it is repeated, first by one wind instrument, then another, then by the different orchestral groups. The drum accompaniment, meanwhile, having been increased by addition of accents from the *pizzicato* strings, and the entrance of more drums. The whole piece is a constant crescendo of volume. Just before the end there is an abrupt modulation to another key, the brass and other percussion instruments join in, and the music ends in a tornado of sound. The *Bolero* is not a perversion of form, but a purposeful use of a single rhythm.

While the use of a singable tune may not seem to pervade all larger compositions, the careful listener will soon find, in a longer and more complex composition, as in the shorter and simpler ones, phrases easily comprehended and remembered, and the same essential elements of beauty. Repeated hearings will make the whole work clear and familiar. The melody is not always "on top" but is often interwoven with, and almost concealed by, its harmonies. A story is told of Purcell, an English composer of the seventeenth century, who wrote a piece of "birthday" music as a special tribute to Queen Mary II, his royal patron. In the bass of his accompaniment, Purcell inserted the tune of an old folk song of which the Queen was very fond. When the morning of performance came, the Queen listened attentively, the story goes, but only to the *top* line of the music, and so missed the main feature of the accompaniment, and also the delightful compliment of her devoted subject.

The Voice of the People

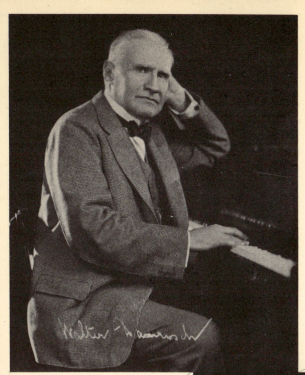

Walter Damrosch

Daniel Gregory Mason.

MRS. H. H. A. BEACH

DR. FRANCES ELLIOTT CLARK

VICTOR HERBERT   CHARLES WAKEFIELD CADMAN

FOLK MUSIC—SONGS AND
DANCES OF THE PEOPLE

FOLK MUSIC, the oldest type of song, is the unconscious work of a creator who seeks to give utterance to an emotion that fills his own heart and the hearts of many others, alike. The most marked characteristic of the folk song is its simplicity, and its most prominent musical elements are melody and rhythm. Harmony is not an essential feature of the folk song, as it has been sung, for centuries, without accompaniment.

Much of the oldest folk music, such as early Slavic song, owes its melodic character to the influence of modal church music or to pagan ceremonial songs. Mythology was the chief source of musical inspiration of the ancient Slavs, who chanted hymns to the gods of the sun, as is still done by some primitive peoples. When, toward the end of the tenth century, Christianity became the official religion, reference was still made to heathen gods in the words both of religious and secular songs. Every spring, at the "first ploughing," the clergy in many districts of Russia did, until recently, and in other Slav countries still do, join the members of the parish in a service at the outskirts of the village. Here prayers are made for a plentiful harvest, after which the young people indulge in gay and spirited round dances. The irregular rhythms, metric oddities, and unequal phrase-lengths of many of the old Russian folk dances, heard even today, owe their origin not only to the character of the language (as is the case in many countries) but to the violent and frequently distorted movements of the dancers.

One of the oldest forms of the folk song is the carol—usually an expression of great joy or praise—which takes its name from the old French word *carole*, meaning a circle dance accompanied by song; from the Latin *choraula*, and the Greek *choraules*. There were originally carols for every season of the year, but those now most familiar are the Easter and Christmas carols sung over all the earth at those joyous seasons. Through their universality of message, these have, through the years, become the property of the entire world, as illustrated by the gay "God Rest Ye Merry, Gentlemen," or the more stately "Adeste Fidelis." The term *wassail* (coming from the Old English words *wes hal,* a form of salutation meaning "Be hale" or "Be of good health") is given to many carols sung in England at the celebration of New Year's Eve and Twelfth Night. The French word used for Christmas carols is *nöel,* or *nowell,* meaning "news" and suggesting the "good tidings" of the Christmas season.

Certain basic characteristics peculiar to the folk music of any country include types of rhythm, scales or modes employed, general mood, and musical instruments familiarly used.

Ireland's claim to an ancient culture is borne out by its folk music, such as the appealing legendary air best known as "Londonderry Air" (modern settings of which include "Would God I Were a Tender Apple-Blossom" by Fisher, "Danny Boy" by Weatherly, and Percy Grainger's instrumental version known as "Irish Tune from County Derry") which, centuries ago, was identified with the pathetic Gaelic "Lament for Cucullain." The equally historic "Harp That Once Thro' Tara's Halls"—most familiar in connection with the words of Thomas Moore—refers to the bardic instruments of the fifth and sixth centuries and the annual contests of Irish harpers held in Tara Castle in County Meath until the year 565. These, together with "The Last Rose of Summer" and "Believe Me, If All Those Endearing Young Charms," illustrate the suavely flowing character of Irish song. The Irish jig, on the contrary—of which "The Irish Washerwoman" is a delightful example —is one of the liveliest folk dances in the world, and owes much of its peculiar effectiveness to its use of the pentatonic or five-toned scale, as well as a tendency to waver between the major and minor modes.

The use of this five-toned scale is further illustrated in "Auld Lang Syne," one of the oldest of Scotch songs, its extended use being thought by many scholars to be due in part to the character of the bagpipe, at one time a national instrument of Ireland, and later, of Scotland.

Scotch folk music, whether in song or dance, also frequently employs the unusual rhythmic pattern known as "Scotch snap," by which is meant a custom of uniting into one group two notes, the first of which, of short value, is followed by a dotted note having three times its value; or else the exact opposite. Sometimes the two rhythmic patterns are united, as in the melody of "Comin' Thro' the Rye." Scotch songs also make occasional use of the whole-tone scale.

Folk airs of Scandinavia often employ a scale in which, in a rising melody, the seventh tone becomes major, and on descending, is sung in minor mode, a peculiarity heard in the plaintive "Värmland," a song taking its name from a province which lies near the boundary between Norway and Sweden.

Spanish folk music owes its rich variety to the many climates and geographic aspects of the Spanish peninsula, and also to the invasions, during its history, by Asiatic, European, and African races, each of which brought its individual type of culture, tradition, and customs. In no country is dancing so interwoven with folk music, and many of the most popular airs are sung only when used as accompaniment to dancing. In Andalusia, to the south, the music has the colorful attributes of the song of Arabia, brought from Arabia by the invading Moors. Those of the Spanish folk songs which do not owe their form and manner to Arabic sources, have been influenced by early church music. The favored dances are the *solea*, the native *tango* (built upon a rhythm similar to that of the *habañera* but danced half again as fast), and the *seguidilla*. The latter is of three distinct types, the *seguidilla manchegas*, bright and happy in character; the *seguidilla boleras*, of a sedate character; and the *seguidilla gitanas*, with the romantic rhythms of the Spanish gypsies. In Galicia, to the northwest, near the Bay of Biscay, the people are descendants of a virile Celtic folk, their native music, even to the use of droning bagpipes, suggesting the melodies of Scotland.

In the Basque section, at the foot of the Pyrenees, the people display a rare talent for improvisation, and although the words of many popular songs may be "modern" (as they call the songs of the past hundred and fifty years) the tunes are usually very ancient, and sung without studied instrumental accompaniment.

In Aragon and Catalonia the influence of the songs of the troubadours is still felt. The Catalonian *sardaña* is performed in courteous manner to music of barbaric quality; and the *jota* of Aragon (which owes its name to Aben Jot, a Moor who originated it) is extremely popular. Other distinctly Spanish dances which influence scores of art works are the *pasodoble* (a lively air frequently played in the bull-ring), the *Morisco* (a burlesque Moorish dance which is an ancestor of the "mock morris" dances of England), the *fandango,* the *malagueña,* the *ball de bastones,* and the *ball del ciri.* The *ball de bastones* is done with sticks in the manner of a "mock morris"; and the *ball del ciri* is danced by groups of six couples each, the first two dancers carrying lighted tapers and a small jar of perfume which they sprinkle upon the bystanders. The *habañera,* thought of as a Spanish dance, was originally a Negro Creole dance, imported into Spain from Africa by way of Havana.

Spanish folk instruments are the castanets (taking their name from the chestnut—castaña—wood from which the clappers are made); and the guitar, a direct descendant of the lute, brought to Spain by the Crusaders returning from the East, and by the Moors.

Italy, with its songs of refinement, elegance, and light-hearted grace; France, with its centuries of dramatic and dignified song; Germany, with its rich heritage of song, created by the Minnesingers and Meistersingers; old Bohemia, from which come such vivid folk dances as the *polka* and *furiant;* and Russia, along whose highways still sound the balalaika and the gousli—all contribute brilliantly to the history of folk music.

NATIONAL CHARACTERISTICS
IN RUSSIAN ART MUSIC

THE FOLK music of a people forms a picture, truer than words, of its characteristics and environment. Geographic and climatic factors affect the timbre of a nation's song just as they do the ease or difficulty of its living conditions. Political developments and historical events exert a great influence upon it, and those who live in a balmy climate, and in peace, unconsciously sing a very different type of song from those who are constantly in the midst of privation, distress, or aggressive warfare. Social customs and beliefs are also molding influences upon the art music of various countries.

Many nations seek, consciously, to create a characteristic national type of art music, and of these the earliest was Russia, which may, therefore, be taken as a typical example of such use of its folk music. Its highly individual school of composition (by which is meant a general style or manner of writing peculiar to a certain group or nation), established in the nineteenth century and later imitated—especially in the twentieth century—by many other nations, owes much to the nation's rich sources of colorful folk lore and art, and to the devoted efforts of a few inspired leaders.

Russia's nearness to the Orient, its ancient trade-routes, and the annual fairs held since early centuries in some of its most important cities, brought it, at an early date, into close contact with the oldest civilizations of the world. Because of the country's great size, Russian folk melodies are varied to an unusual extent, but musical features almost universal are: the use of Oriental scales and ancient church modes; fiery, and often irregular rhythms, such as 5–4, 7–4, 3–16, or 9–8; much use of the minor mode, whether the dance or song be sad or gay; short melodies, with frequent repetitions of single phrases; frequent use of florid embellishments, due in part to the presence of wandering tribes of gypsies in the land from early days; and continued use of such stringed instruments as the balalaika (a form of guitar popular in Russia) and the gousli, which are small enough to be carried on horseback.

There are four different periods in the history of Russian music. During the first, beginning in pagan times and continuing for about a thousand years, countless folk songs heard even now in isolated parts of the land were created. The gousli, with its five or seven strings, was one of the favored instruments of those days.

The second period, lasting to about 1750, is dominated by the music of the early Greek Church at Byzantium, as the ancient city of Constantinople was then called, the quaint modal features of the liturgical music being imitated in the folk songs.

During the so-called third period, which lasted until about the opening of the nineteenth century, music from other parts of Europe, and especially Italy, found a warm welcome in Russia.

With the opening of the nineteenth century, the Russians became, gradually, interested in the possibilities of their own songs and folk lore, and in 1836, Mikhail Glinka, an ardent patriot, gave to the world an opera in which he made free use of both historical and traditional lore, and all the resources of folk song that the empire possessed. He was the first composer to exploit purely national Russian music, and his opera, *Life for a Tsar,* is the beginning of the Russian national "school."

Russian composers who followed his example include Tschaikowsky, who wrote, on one occasion: "I would like to have a Russian folksong sounding out through every one of my compositions"; and the "Five," an important group of composers which included Alexander Borodin (1834–1887), Modeste Moussorgsky (1835–1881), Mily Balakirev (1837–1910), Cesar Cui (1825–1891), and Nikolai Rimsky-Korsakov * (1844–1908). From this time on until shortly before the World War, Russia

---

* See also the story of *Scheherazade,* page 87.

produced a large amount of the most exotic and valuable contemporary music of the century.

Most of the plots used by these Russian composers in their operatic music are half fairytale and half history, the effect produced being something that can best be told only in music. As a plot for *Life for a Tsar,* Glinka used a heroic tale of seventeenth-century life in Russia which tells of the accession to the throne of Mikhail Romanov, in 1613. Ivan Susanin, a patriotic Russian peasant, is the hero. He and his daughter live in a small village where they are visited one day by a band of Polish soldiers who have lost their way while traveling to Moscow, where they hope to capture the future Tsar and prevent his coronation. Susanin, suspecting their treason, offers to guide them on their way, but, instead of taking them to the Tsar, leads them, under cover of the darkness, into a marshy forest. Meanwhile his daughter hurries to the hiding place of the future ruler and warns him of his danger. Susanin is suspected of treachery. During the night he argues with the Polish soldiers, but rather than betray his master, gives his own life. His strategy gives the Tsar time to escape to Moscow, where he is triumphantly crowned. Susanin's two principal arias, one sung as he offers himself as a guide, and the other as he realizes the hopelessness of his position, are among the most dramatic in operatic literature.

The first production of the opera, which not only uses the historic tale of a ruler, but also draws heavily upon national rhythms and folk airs, was in St. Petersburg in December 1836. Some of the nobility, sensing its popular appeal, and ignorant of the influence this work was to have upon the art of their land, laughed at it and called it "music of the coachmen." But they too, soon came to realize its dramatic force and great human reality, and to further Glinka's efforts.

Another Russian opera which is, in a way, parallel to *Life for a Tsar,* is *Boris Godunov* by Moussorgsky, with text by Alexander Pushkin, Russia's great national poet. Boris is a real character, the despotic regent who ruled Feodor, the weak-minded son of Ivan the Terrible. Gregory, false pretender to the throne, and the vagabond monks Varlaam and

Nussail, furnish some of the most dramatic moments. The entire texture of the music is interwoven with folk music characteristics, and some complete songs are used, as in the Coronation Scene. In Act II several colorful folk dance rhythms are introduced.

The libretto of Rimsky-Korsakov's fantastic opera-ballet, *The Golden Cockerel,* is based upon a *skazka,* a type of supernatural fairytale peculiar to Russia. Here a harassed King is presented, by his astrologer, with a golden cockerel which will always give him warning when danger is near. Local color of the nearby Orient was easily adapted to fill in the traditional flavor. The opera, completed in 1907, included many satirical reflections upon monarchy in general, and the Russian court was so displeased that its production was delayed two years. The "magic" of many of the scenes made it difficult of performance, and in 1912 it was arranged by Fokine as an opera-ballet. As presented in New York, the action is given to the ballet while the principal singers and chorus, clothed in dull red robes, are seated on terraces built upon each side of the stage. Each rôle thus has two representatives whose activities are closely synchronized. Folk melodies of Russia are introduced into the first and last acts; the King's humorous dance is accompanied by music of Oriental origin; and the popular "Hymn to the Sun" (sung by the Queen, accompanied by gousli players, Act II), with its exotic melody, florid arabesques and cadenza-like passages, and weird modulations, is one of the finest examples of the influence of folk material in art song.

Any review of Russian "national" opera must include mention of Borodin's colorful *Prince Igor,* begun in 1870, worked on for the remaining seventeen years of the composer's life, and finished by his friends, including Rimsky-Korsakov and Glazounov, who orchestrated and arranged the existing sketches, or set down from memory, sections they had often heard him play. The opera is based upon the life story of Igor, a historical personage of pagan days in old Russia, who led an expedition of Russian princes against marauding nomads called Polevetzians, in the twelfth century. Featured in the works are a series of Oriental dances which take place in the camp of Khan Konchak, who has captured Igor. These—a few of which are choral dances, accompanied by singing of dancers and onlookers as well as the orchestra—are a super-lative example of suave delicacy as contrasted with pagan Tatar sav-agery, and remarkable in their reflections of Russian rhythms, and melodies of the East which are frequently heard in Russia. They are often played as independent orchestral numbers.

ENJOYMENT OF SONG

BY MRS. H. H. A. BEACH, *American Composer*

THIS is an age of song. Even the air is full of song, but the art or concert song, as we know it, was not always known to the world. As singers, song writers, or listeners, we owe much to the folk song, and just now there is a return to and revival of it.

Even among our contemporaries there are many wonderful folk-singers. I have in mind a prairie picture from our own America, of an old Indian sitting, at dusk, before his simple home in the West, beating gently upon his tom-tom and singing softly to himself, the treasured song lore of his race—his memories taking on the form of a reverent soliloquy.

The entire life of the Labrador Eskimos is set to the accompaniment of song: primitive fragments with short, decided rhythms. A favorite song describes "The Returning Warrior," gives all his adventures, the games of the children dancing hand in hand around a ring, the weddings, and the funerals. The song is taught orally by one generation to another.

The Balkan region, too, is the background of wonderful folk tunes which have entered into the history of the people. Even a cry to Macedonia for help, repeating the one of Saint Paul's time, has come down through many centuries and forms the occasion for a superb melody.

In its evolution folk song was probably first a communication, then an improvisation or part of a ritual, a bit of primitive life, a scene from medieval pageantry, an element in the development of sacred plain-song, as well as an entity in itself.

The reason that the folk song lived is that it was so very simple that people learned and sang it unconsciously. The tune was at first unaccompanied, or else accompanied by the very simple rhythmic chords suggested through the dance and by the primitive instruments of the day. The song then grew gradually, the first singer expressing himself, possibly, with only a few notes. Each singer who repeated it expressed his own feelings also, and may have added a few more notes until, at last, the song achieved a completed form. It acquired balance of structure naturally, for people then did not demand drama, but only the depiction of each emotion. It acquired shape, as a rumor does, and finally became a complete and expressive communication to the world of an inner feeling.

The development of the art of printing made song universal as was not possible when it could only be perpetuated orally. The song maker of the folk became the song writer and music was now the product of an individual rather than of a people. Each song was now written to some particular poetic text, whether dramatic or lyric, and for the widest variety of accompaniment.

In writing a song the composer considers the voice as an instrument, and that the song shall be *singable* should be the fundamental principle underlying its creation. Many an otherwise magnificent work lies on the shelf, unused, because it is not suitable for the voice, being over-long, of awkward range, or having its idea overdeveloped. The music should be the poem translated into tone, with due care for every emotional detail.

It is of remarkable interest to see what a different reaction two composers of equally high standing—such as Robert Franz and Robert Schumann—will make to the same poem. To one it may seem infinitely sad, heart-breaking; to the other, the identical words may seem only a lovely suggestion of pathos. Another point of contrast is the almost infinite variety of interpretation given to the same song by singers of equal rank. Ten artists may sing the same song, each carrying out the composer's intentions with real exactness, but from a different viewpoint, and producing quite different results.

The best thing any person can do to further his own enjoyment of song—whether he considers himself a singer or not—is to sing many of the finest songs. If he really cannot sing the song he can still sing *at it* and thus help himself to become an appreciative listener as well as to build up for himself a mental library of song. To do this one may begin with the valuable old Scottish or Irish ballads sung in early days by wandering bards. In these is much repetition of the same little tune, whether the poem be one of tragedy, adventure, or comedy. Get the music, become acquainted with it, finger out the melody on the piano if you can do no more; say, learn, sing the words. Hum the tune. Learn the title in both languages if the song be written in a foreign tongue. Buy a record of it. Go to concerts where it is to be sung. Tune in on good radio concerts of song. All this will open up new vistas of delight.

In the published collections one finds many genuine treasures among songs so simple that they are seldom included in concert programs, yet bear the stamp of a master. One may gather, in the mind, the song treasures of many generations, beginning with such simple gems as Mozart's "Violet," the Haydn "Röslein," "Longing" (*Wonne der Wehmut*) by Beethoven, "For Music" by Robert Franz, songs by Schumann; and the exquisite "Lullaby," "Little Sandman," and "The Blacksmith" by Brahms. Fauré was the creator of many French art songs of great finesse, delicacy, lyric emotion, and subtle profundity. Cécile Chaminade has given us treasures in song which are not well enough known. Franz Schubert, who broke down the rigidity of song previous to his time, is, at his best, so fine that all other composers kneel at his feet, and there are so many of his songs which all should know— such as "The Wanderer," "Ave Maria," and "Serenade," that it is difficult to make a choice. Then there are the many splendid songs of our own American writers—Edward MacDowell and the many contemporary writers.

There is enjoyment in every contact with beautiful song—in writing, singing, playing, or even thinking of it—and it brings to the listener a sense of discovery of a world in which serenity and contentment still reign.

SONG AND THE ACCOMPANIMENT

BY FRANK LAFORGE, *American Composer and Teacher*

THE AIM of a singer is to make certain texts intelligible, and to impart to his declamation of them such human expression, imitation, or representation of certain emotions as to create, through the aid of the listener's imagination, a definite mood. The exact proportion that the song accompaniment plays in this creation, it is impossible to tell, but it is certain, because of its long and varied history, that the accompaniment to song—usually instrumental, though sometimes vocal —is one of the vital elements in its appeal.

Just as there have been many kinds of song, so have there been many kinds of accompaniment. The early folk song was usually unaccompanied, or, if used, in itself, as an accompaniment to folk dance, was embellished by beating of hands by the onlookers. Thus the first accompaniments were probably merely rhythmic, such as the monotonous but effective drum-beats still to be heard in the traditional songs of primitive peoples; or, as simple rhythmic chords played by the home musician, or by the itinerant bard upon his small lute or harp. Such supplementary rhythms inspired both singer and listener to greater endeavors, as has been seen repeatedly in times of danger or in the folk "working-songs." Percy Grainger says that "Rhythm is the thing called in to make people work harder than they naturally would."

The invention of printing encouraged the writing of longer and more complicated music, but, as much of this was inspired by sacred texts and intended to be performed in the church, it was sung unaccompanied. The exquisite many-voiced writing of Palestrina (1526–1594), whose beautiful music brought to a climax the composed church music of the sixteenth century, is an example of such a kind of song.

27

Toward the end of the sixteenth century, the remarkable development of secular song through songs of the minstrels, troubadours, and minnesingers brought into prominence the artistic possibilities of the vocal solo and of the instrumental accompaniment found desirable for its embellishment or background. The invention and elaboration of musical instruments were hastened by the desire of all fine singers for a more appropriate accompaniment.

The performances of the "first opera" in Florence in 1600, and of Monteverde's more elaborate operas *Orfeo* and *Arianne,* given a few years later, were impressive not only because of the dramatic stories they told, the alluring art of the singers, and the novelty of the entire form of presentation, but because of the spectacular size of the "string band," as the orchestra of the day was called, the Florentine accompaniment being written for harpsichord, lutes, and large viols.

Of *Arianne* only one number now remains, but this, the "Lament of Arianne," is said to have been the first dramatic aria ever created. To understand this wholly it is helpful to compare a bit of early plainchant of the church, after which many of the popular songs of the time were patterned with a phrase from the "Lament," in which the sentiment of the words is echoed in the broken and dramatically expressive character of the melody.

But even in those operas the accompaniment was very simple, and not until the rise of the *art song,* and the contemporary development of opera, did a song come to be composed throughout, by which is meant that it is written so that melody and accompaniment combined create a perfect unity, the music telling the story as completely as do the words, the finished composition being heard as the perfectly blended expression of one kind.

In the art songs of Franz Schubert, which include the familiar "Erl King," "Who is Sylvia," "Hark! Hark! the Lark," "Gretchen at the Spinning Wheel," "The Wanderer," and the entire cycle of the "Schöne Müllerin," are such glorious examples of the art of accompaniment writing as have never been surpassed by any song writer. Here the superb pictorial or descriptive effects and vividly rhythmic treatment of melody call for the most artistic performance on the parts of both singer and accompanist. Incidentally, the greater the artist, the more exact is the observance shown for the regular accents of the notes in singing. The better singers always secure their most striking effects with the least possible unsettling of the rhythm of the songs as set down by the composer, and take the fewest liberties with his music. Strict observance of rhythm is only a recognition on the part of the artist that singing has other demands besides those of sound. It is an acknowledgment of the composite character of every musical performance, even of one so simple as a song.

When the best results are obtained, all the elements are in perfect relation and balance, including time, tune, expression, tone color, and whatever else enters into the problem. In other words, music consists in the co-ordination of a number of things, each of which is just about as important as the other. The piano and voice parts should be considered together, as a unit. The piano, when used with the voice, requires a different touch from the piano when used as a solo instrument or in association with other instruments. Accompaniments played in soloistic style will never do, although in many of the Schubert, Schumann, and Brahms songs it has much independence and may be made as expressive as the player chooses. But it must not take attention from the voice. Good ensemble is one of the things for which there exists the highest popular appreciation. In the preludes and the postludes of the song, the accompanist becomes the soloist and should use a solo tone.

In the "Erl King," one of the greatest art songs ever written, the accompaniment supplies the main elements of the drama. The entire song was composed within an hour, Schubert having become wildly excited after reading the Goethe ballad of the terrified father's mad ride through the night, carrying his dying son in his arms, while beside him, singing alluring words of invitation to the child, travels the dread Erl King, a mythical character which, in the Middle Ages, represented Death. Here Schubert has written an entirely different and individual type of music to accompany each of the characters in the song drama, impersonating, in turn, the Narrator, the Father, the Child, and the Erl King.

In "Gretchen at the Spinning Wheel" the accompaniment depicts the incessant turning of the whirring wheel and helps to carry the tragic note of the maiden's lament through to its climax. Many listeners think that the accompaniment to "Wohin" (Schubert) is meant to suggest the murmuring of a brook, but this is not so. Here it is plainly a mill-wheel, turning upon its axis, that is depicted, the music being quite different from that of "Jealousy and Pride" (*Eifersucht und Stolz*) in which the rippling waters of a brook, moving now here, now there, and going all around, are pictured.

"Hark! Hark! the Lark" (text from Shakespeare's *Cymbeline*) expresses in its accompaniment, as well as in its vocal melody, the uplifting rapture of a morning in the spring of life, the music being a lovely mirrored reflection of the words. Schubert's "Who is Sylvia?" is another exquisite setting of a Shakespeare text. The unnumbered settings of Shakespeare's lyrics, incidentally, may be said to constitute a distinctive branch of song literature. The personality of no other poet so dominates the songs he has inspired or so unconditionally circumscribes and classifies them. The term "Shakespearean song" conveys even to the unmusical listener a highly definite impression, thus reversing ordinary conditions by emphasizing so very sharply the uppermost importance of the song's poetic foundation. But the Shakespearean songs which have touched the hearts of the multitudes have, largely, emanated from the pens of Englishmen and Americans. Only Franz Schubert is the great exception that proves the rule. One reason for this large proportion of successful Anglo-Saxon Shakespearean song is the fact that Shakespeare wrote a large number of his song poems in adaptation to the rhythms of old melodies already popular and firmly entrenched in the minds and hearts of dwellers in Great Britain.

Haydn wrote many descriptive accompaniments, for instance, his "Roaming in Foaming Billows" from the *Creation*. Handel was a master in expressing mood and grandeur through his aria accompaniments, as shown by the deeply devotional "I Know That My Redeemer Liveth," from the *Messiah,* in which complete conviction is expressed in even the first notes of the instrumental introduction.

Although the art song did not come to its full maturity until the time of Schubert and his associates, the composers of many of the oldest pastorales for the voice made their accompaniments contribute —so far as the instruments which were then available permitted—to the establishment of mood, or to description.

Speaking of old songs, I have never been able to see why artists think themselves bound to treat old sixteenth- and seventeenth-century airs like church music. When about to sing a love song like "Amarilli" by Caccini, many a singer lapses into a state of dreary solemnity and delivers the love song as though it were a hymn, and then tells us that it is a "matter of style." It is not. The people of that age were thoroughly as human as the ones of a more modern day, and their songs should be interpreted according to their human quality. Not to do so is to misinterpret them. It is as bad as the playing of certain Beethoven "specialists" who are so afraid of humor in music that they miss the whole spirit of Beethoven, the musician above all others in whose music humor runs rampant. It is no wonder to me that some persons have a dread of these old classics. But the fault is entirely with the "stylists."

Schumann, being a pianist, excelled, in his songs, in creation of atmosphere through the accompaniment, and many of the most telling accompaniments in existence are from the pen of Johannes Brahms. The exquisite atmosphere of romance and poetry which emanates from Brahms's "The Nightingale" is established by the hauntingly beautiful piano introduction. In his "Song of the Lark" the voice part is largely *recitative,* coming in between the "verses" of subtle rhythmic accompaniment.

It is amazing, when one considers, the influence which nature, and particularly the songs of birds—especially the cuckoo, lark, and nightingale—have on composed song. These three songsters have been given especial prominence since the days of John of Fornsete and his famous round, "Sumer Is Icumen In, Lhude Sing Cuccu." The cuckoo gained musical fame because of the character of its two-note song; the lark and the nightingale because of the variety and exquisite beauty of their songs.

In the Brahms songs, which number nearly three hundred, there are more than forty in which the texts make reference to birds, with the nightingale the most frequently mentioned. These poetic references are, naturally, reflected in the accompaniments to an astonishing degree. For instance, in the accompaniment of "Nightingales Are Winging" (*Nachtigallen Schwingen*), Brahms keeps mainly to an imitation of the twittering of birds. In "Rest Thee, My Dear One" (*Ruhe, Süssliebchen*), Opus 33, No. 9, syncopations in the accompaniment contribute to a portrayal of the stillness and mystery of nature at night. And toward the close of this song Brahms adds an extremely sympathetic and tender note through the inclusion of a brief phrase from the old German lullaby, "Schlaf, Kindchen, Schlaf."

The music of Brahms's "Death Is the Cooling Night" (*Der Tod, das ist die kühle Nacht*), Opus 96, No. 1—both melody and accompaniment—is more guided by the text than is the case in some others of the Brahms songs, in which his declamation was not entirely dictated by important words, his greater desire being to create an interesting musical profile. The nightingale, so favored in the Brahms texts, here appears again toward the close of the song where, at the words "over my couch," the rich arpeggiated harmonies suggest the bird's sweet song. It is heard again in the composer's "In Lonely Wood," Opus 85, No. 6, while "The Skylark's Song," Opus 70, No. 2, is unusual for its extreme constraint. In the yearning and utterly charming "Nightingale" Brahms used a melody which was evidently especially precious to him, as he had used it once before in a setting of "The Wanderer."

Other nature songs of Brahms—by which, just now, I mean nature as expressed by the music as well as by the words—though not expressive of bird music, include the extremely melodic "Longing at Rest," with its viola obbligato suggestive of the whispering winds; "To an Æolian Harp," in which Brahms makes a peculiar combination of

harp-like arpeggio and unequal rhythms to suggest the eerie tones of
a wind-swept Æolian (or wind) harp hanging in a garden; the ecstatic
"Wie bist du, meine Königin"; the colorful "Serenade," Opus 58, No. 8;
the realistic "While the Rain Falls," in which the staccato accompaniment suggesting the drops increases in strength as the rainfall grows
heavier; and the famous "Rain Song," in which the pianistic afterpiece,
or coda, is an artistic creation in itself, in the way it portrays the faltering raindrops as the storm dies away.

THE SINGER AND THE SONG

BY JOHN CHARLES THOMAS, *American Baritone,*
Metropolitan Opera

I T was William Byrde, that eminent composer of Queen Elizabeth's court, who so appreciated the beauty of the human voice that he wrote: "There is not any musicke of Instruments whatsoever, comparable to that which is made of the voyces of men, where the voyces are good, and the same well sorted and ordered."

I believe in spontaneity, the outpouring of the voice; one sings first, then learns the technique of singing. Songs which grow from the hearts of those who compose and sing them reach the hearts of those who hear them. Nothing is so impressive as simplicity and sincerity.

To me the first requirement for a good song is a good story (text), or a gorgeous melody, preferably both; and the story should always be descriptive rather than vague.

Needless to say, all the great songs are not written by the famous composers, although some snobbish folk look first at the name of the composer, then at the music, then at the words. ·

The words of the song should transmit a message, or suggest a definite mood or picture—these differing, of course, in effect, upon the individual hearer. *The first thing to listen for in a song is the message.* The singer's duty and privilege it therefore becomes to deliver that message.

Many of us speak glibly of the "art song." Just what *is* an art song? To me there are two distinct types: the first, *strophic,* in which the same music is repeated for each of the stanzas; and the *"through-composed"* (*durchkomponiert*) song, in which the composer writes new melody and new accompaniment constantly as the story progresses.

34

Of the first, a fine example is the charming "Heidenröslein" (Hedge Roses) by Schubert, in which a story is told of the small boy who found the thorns that always accompany a rose. Here each verse of the simple story is sung to the same lilting melody. Another is Schubert's setting of the old Scottish legend, "Edward." (There is also a setting by Loewe.) This is the gruesome tale of the cruel mother who inspired her son to kill his father, the king. When he returns to the castle in bloody clothing, she asks him what he has done. "What have you done, Edward, Edward?" At first he says that he has killed his hawk, then that it was his horse, and finally, that it was his father. Very appropriately, the same question has similar music in each of its repetitions. Here indeed the singer must serve as narrator, giving the tale in as simple and dramatic a telling as it doubtless had when carried from castle to castle by the minstrels of the olden days. In the strophic song one really reads the poem, accompanied by music, thus setting up the supreme importance of the text—an inheritance from the days of folk song.

In the "through-composed" art song the music is often of infinite variety. Schubert's "Erl King," in which the singer must impersonate, in turn, four characters, requires a versatile singer and a gifted accompanist for successful performance.

Each song has a personality as definite as that of a person, each its own definite and distinct style. For example, "Du bist die Ruh," with its flowing, sustained melody and slow crescendo, is a remarkable illustration of the expression of peace and mood. Meter and style of its piano accompaniment faithfully mirror the meter and style of the poem. Again the message of the song comes from the poem through the music. . . . And I have heard of songs being written before the poem had been chosen!

One of the finest contemporary songs to display special agreement between words and music is Mrs. Curran's "Nocturne," in which she has written both the words and the music, producing a real unit. "It is night, and stars are brightly shining"—a lovely musical picture of definite mood. Others are the setting of Joyce Kilmer's "Trees" by

Frank Tours, a description of a definite object; the idyllic "Phydile" of
Duparc; or the rollicking "Gypsy John" by Fred Clay. Contrast the
effects achieved by a single composer, such as John Alden Carpenter of
Chicago, in his "Sleep That Flits on Baby's Eyes" and his "Green
River," the latter song being a poetic description of a man who, in
his walk through field, by stream, flowers, and trees, communes with
Nature. In the first he is influenced by the text to write a delightful
description of slumber.

Much of the sincere dramatic value and artistic completeness of the
many gems by Schubert lies in the fact that a large part of his output
was written, not for the public, but for the sheer joy and necessity of
creating, and also sometimes to give pleasure to his friends. Some
modern composers, on the other hand, are thinking of the "effect" on
the public, all the while they are writing.

Sorry the artist who has no sense of humor (especially about himself). How else can he sing Beckmesser's grotesque serenade from *Die
Meistersinger;* Woolsley Charles's "Green-Eyed Dragon," which con-
jures up such a delightfully comic picture of the ogre which "on the
front doormat sat"; or Moussorgsky's satirical "Song of the Flea" (text
from Goethe's *Faust*), a most marvelous setting of an old Russian
legend?

How charmingly, and in how varied a manner have composers of different nationalities approached the composition of a serenade! There
is the "Serenade" of Järnefelt, a Finnish composer, a lovely song of
great depth but of equally great restraint, reflecting the characteristic
reserve of the composer's Northland. Contrast this with "Matinatta"
by Leoncavallo, a serenade filled with poignant rapture and with passionate Latin feeling. Dearest of all to the singer is Schubert's irresistible "Serenade," so calm and serene. It is told of its origin that
Anna Frölich, a teacher of the art of singing at the Vienna Conservatory,
wishing to celebrate a friend's birthday, begged from Franz Grill-
parzer, a Viennese poet, the words of this immortal song. She then
showed these to Schubert, who read them through quickly several
times, as he stood leaning against the piano, interrupting himself to

exclaim over their beauty. Suddenly he exclaimed, "I have it! It's done already." Three days later it was really finished, parts being provided for baritone solo and male chorus accompaniment.

A popular descriptive song of distinctly martial character and picturesque personality is "Au Pays" by Auguste Holmes. Here there is pictured the return of a soldier to his home town after an absence of some three years. Many and sundry thoughts pass through his mind, but uppermost, of course, is his Jeannette, his sweetheart. During his years at the front he has been through many battles and been promoted to top sergeant. His entire soliloquy is one of the finest pictures of pride I can recall. His chest is covered with medals of which he is very proud. No one is so proud as this top sergeant—he thinks he runs the army! "You have waited for me?" he asks Jeannette, as he sees her. But she replies that, instead, she has married the farmer who took her at the Fair.* His pride crumples in the dust. . . . But he is still top sergeant! So he orders his company to march on, and with a steady *Tramp! Tramp!* they disappear in the distance. The music provided by the composer for this song is inimitable. Before words or melody have been indicated, the swing of the marching troops is clearly suggested by the sonorous chordal accompaniment. At the close, when melody and words have ceased, the rhythmic swing of the chords is the last sound heard.

A song must have personality to live. Ravishing melody, appropriate accompaniment, colorful modulations, inspired rhythms, are all but a symbol of intensified speech; and fortunate is the composer who finds a poem worthy of all these things!

* See *Martha* and the Richmond ("Mop") Fair, page 312.

FROM GREEK DRAMA TO
RADIO OPERA

MANY centuries ago it was the custom for the Greeks to amuse themselves by gathering in the market-square to listen to alluring tales of adventure told and enacted by strolling story-tellers, who, very often, embellished their tales by improvising songs which they accompanied by plucking sweet chords from the strings of the lyres they carried with them.

Many of the tales related by these wandering story-tellers were the beloved myths of Greece, and told of the miraculous achievements of the Greek gods and goddesses. In the larger cities annual festivals were held in open-air theaters, and here longer stories were acted and sung, and much beautiful music made upon lyres and flutes. Before the beginning of each tragedy—as these Greek dramas were called—an actor known as the *prologue* would come before the audience to announce and explain the drama about to be given, and to tell his sentiments concerning it.

In the rural parts of Greece, and presently, in rural Italy across the Ionian and Adriatic Seas, strolling stages, or play-carts, provided popular entertainment by carrying the drama from place to place. In Italy, through the efforts, mainly, of a good man named Filippo Neri, who thought more beautiful stories might be presented, there began a telling of stories from the Bible, with action, from the steps of the churches, and to these were often added the singing and playing of beautiful music. This led the strolling players, especially, to build carts three stories high, so that, in their dramas with music they might show what was supposed to be going on at the same time in Heaven, on Earth, and in Hell.

It was the charm and popularity of such efforts as these, in which drama and music, and sometimes dancing, were combined, that led the music lovers of Florence, toward the end of the sixteenth century, to attempt the reconstruction of the early Greek tragedies, with their formality and dignity. The first stories set to music by the Florentine musicians were therefore those handed down from Greek mythology. Not until later did the Italian composers use the more realistic stories of their own times and people.

Such were some of the beginnings of opera. The first of the operas thus given in Florence was the work of a group of men who called themselves the *Camerati* (Comrades) and who met frequently at the home of a Count Bardi, who was himself a poet. The little opera they assembled (*Dafne*) was finally given at the palatial home of Jacopo Corsi, in 1594.

There is no record of another opera being given in Florence until the year 1600, at the time of the great political marriage of King Henry IV of France to the beautiful Marie de' Medici of Florence, when, among all of the many dazzling events planned to honor the occasion, the most striking was the performance of what is known, historically, as "the first opera." This too told a Grecian myth, the story of *Eurydice,* and contained among its parts solos (arias), *recitative* or spoken song, choruses, dance, and an instrumental accompaniment. The instruments used included a harpsichord, triple flute, large lutes, and large viols. The poem upon which the music was based was by Rinuccini. Peri and Caccini had each, independently, written a musical setting of it, and so the performance included the most beautiful parts of each work.

Seven years later Monteverde, a musician in the service of the Duke of Mantua, presented at Venice a still more elaborate opera (*Orfeo*), and the following years saw a tremendous development of this attractive new art.

At first the people exclaimed against the "unnaturalness," as they called it, of performers who sang their conversations instead of speaking them, and called the composers of the opera "the Greeks." It was soon proven, however, that musical declamation might appeal to the emotions and imagination as spoken lines could not do, and within four or five years opera had become a favorite diversion of the Italian public, which has been warmly devoted to it until the present day.

Italian opera gradually developed into an art form in which special attention was paid to lovely melody and to vocal display, rather than to the plot itself. Modern Italian operas, while still beautifully melodic, are more realistic in style, presenting the story, through the music, as it might actually happen.

Opera spread rapidly to other countries, in some of which styles peculiarly national have been developed. *Grand opera* came to mean opera in which all the conversation was sung. *Opéra comique,* essentially French, required that the dialogue must be spoken.

In Germany much use has been made of German legend as the basis for the book, or *libretto,* and in that country melodic beauty has been enhanced by the addition of fluent and scholarly and often dramatic orchestral accompaniment. England, more truly the land of the oratorio than of opera, is known for its successful development of light opera, such as the Savoy Operas by Gilbert and Sullivan.* Russia has contributed to the world a richly colored national opera built upon the immense resources of national folk music and legend.

In America, where but few native operas have yet been written and produced,† there is a growing appreciation of this form of musical art. Many of the millions of people who live in the United States have never seen an opera, living, as they do, so far from the few large cities where opera is usually given. Many will never see one, but now, thanks to the magic of the radio, and to the meticulous care given to operatic broadcasts by the great broadcasting companies, all may now *hear* it frequently, sung by the finest artists in the world.

This was possible in Great Britain before it was in the United States, for, since the earliest days of its existence, the British Broadcasting Company made a practice of broadcasting operatic performances, both

---

* See under Sullivan, page 393.

† See the operatic works of Cadman, Rossetter G. Cole, Walter Damrosch, Victor Herbert, Reginald De Koven, Horatio Parker, Charles S. Skilton, and Deems Taylor in "Biographical Sketches."

of the "International" summer seasons held at the Opera House, Covent Garden (London), and the performances of the British National Opera Company, in the provinces and elsewhere. These transmissions were further supplemented by studio broadcasts of opera.

In America, studio broadcasts—tabloid arrangements of popular operas, or programs of "favorite" operatic arias and concerted numbers— were the beginnings from which has come about a wonderful expansion. On Christmas Day, 1931, the first complete broadcast from the Metropolitan Opera House of New York City went on the air over the networks of the National Broadcasting Company, and appropriately for the day this first broadcast from America's leading opera house was the perennial favorite, *Hansel and Gretel* by Humperdinck.*

It would be impossible to estimate the number of listeners that day, probably several million, but it is certain that a still larger number has heard each succeeding Metropolitan broadcast, as the response from the first was one that stirred both the Metropolitan management and the broadcasting company which is said to have paid many thousands of dollars for the privilege of offering this unusual entertainment.

From being an occasional and experimental feature, sponsored, it was said, with some trepidation, these operatic broadcasts are now an established part of the air program; and because of the beauty of the music and the vivid appeal to the imagination—the privilege, too, of hearing the most famous "stars"—are a constant source of pleasure.

The only difficulty now encountered was the length of an opera, and the exigencies of modern radio which often prevent use of enough time to broadcast a complete work. Thus it is interesting to note that the first complete opera written expressly for radio production, *The Willow Tree* (first performance on October 3, 1932), was done by an American, Charles Wakefield Cadman, acting on a commission from the National Broadcasting Company. In *The Willow Tree,* Mr. Cadman has, in a twenty-three minute opera, covered the round of emotions usually included in a whole evening's entertainment. To accomplish this he and his librettist, Mrs. Nelle Richmond Eberhart, had to forgo a plot

* See p. 337.

and present, instead, a dramatic situation. The result is typically American in its directness, and is, as well, replete with beautiful melody and skilled workmanship. The opera begins with a brief overture, and ends, true to form, in the death of the hero. In it Mr. Cadman has followed the accepted form, with arias, duets, ensembles (all in miniature), the scale being commensurate with the limitations of time, and a colorful accompaniment for small orchestra.

Broadcasting is therefore the latest, and the greatest, ally that opera has had. It is the final step in the making possible for all of an artistic pleasure that had its beginnings in the sweet singing of a strolling bard on some open square in Greece, many centuries ago.

BEHIND THE SCENES AT
THE OPERA

WITH LAWRENCE TIBBETT, *American Baritone,*
Metropolitan Opera

IT is evening in the great opera house and a gala atmosphere pre-
vails. The orchestra, all timed and ready, awaits only the lifting of
the conductor's baton. The Prologue begins . . . through the great
golden curtain Tonio thrusts his head and asks, "Si puo?" ("A word?")
then steps through and before the curtain and begins the famous aria
of *Pagliacci* which ends so brilliantly with the words, "Come then, ring
up the curtain!" Another opera at the Metropolitan has begun! What
other phase of the art of music has so varied and glamorous an allure
as opera—the stage settings, the lighting, the principal artists, the chorus
which acts as vocal background for the principals and sometimes assumes
a supreme importance of its own, the ballet, the orchestra, and that
very important feature not listed on the program—the audience? Opera,
with its many great and perfect moments, is one of the most marvelous
creations of man's imagination!

There is just one thing that the listener to opera should not do. That
is to decide, once for all, that *this* opera is good and *that* one is bad.
There is so much beauty in it all that it is worth while sitting through
a few disappointing moments for the sake of the many great ones that
are always there. Maybe the listener just doesn't understand the message
of the opera he thinks "so bad." When I first heard Wagner's *Tristan
and Isolde* I was still quite unfamiliar with German and so sat coldly.
Bit by bit the powerful allure of the music took possession of me and
when the opera ended I found myself weeping. I feel that there is no
comparison between two beautiful or thrilling things. Why compare

Debussy with Wagner? Or Wagner with Verdi? Why try to decide who is the greatest composer?

A lot of people apologize for having a "popular" taste. They think that anything hard to understand is "classical," and anything easy to understand is "low-brow." That is no sign that it is bad. We can understand a sunset with one glance and yet we know that it is beautiful! To be sure, there is much modern opera which may lack the sweet and simple melodies which characterize the older "school," but each opera offers something for someone. There is *La Bohême* by Puccini—the ideal opera; and *Die Meistersinger* by Wagner—my favorite opera. Consider its purity, mellowness, and the supreme beauty of this masterpiece. Consider Hans Sachs, noble-spirited cobbler-mastersinger, one of the finest creations in all opera, a man old enough to look on life with mellow understanding, and young enough to respond to youth and nature with warmth and affection. Here was a man with the height of tenderness and self-comprehension. Such characters are dreams to the actor-singer.

Then there is *Simone Boccanegra* by Verdi, the story of the fourteenth-century corsair who became a Doge of Venice. *Boccanegra* happens to be a good opera, very often a genuinely beautiful and touching opera. What makes it so strange is that it belongs pretty much to the baritone who sings its title rôle and who is neither young nor handsome. But Boccanegra's love for his daughter dominates the piece and was so fine that it moved Verdi to write some of his finest and most nobly expressive music for it. An interesting thing about it is that it is an opera saved by Verdi himself from the limbo of his early years. A quarter of a century after its composition—when it was not much of a success— it recurred to the composer's mind. He took it out and rewrote it; and while smiling at the flamboyant style of performance in which opera had its beginning one is captivated by its new growth in power and imagination, and by the aptness with which the renewed music characterizes the scenes, and at the same time, Boccanegra and his daughter Maria. Boccanegra is shown to have emotional depths of tenderness, and of tragic pathos, great nobility of spirit, magnanimity, majesty of anger, and majesty of grief. His really royal attributes, in the hands of an able singing-actor, may turn a rather banal operatic death into a dénouement of tragic and searching beauty, unforgettable for its poignancy and sincerity. . . . Yes, surely there is enough in opera to satisfy all tastes. I place a lot of emphasis on acting, and sometimes, to act a part convincingly, must use a vocal tone not lovely, but positively—for the moment—ugly. That is truth in delineation, as I see it, for so the speaking voice responds to great emotion.

But the general public, a part of it sitting in the shadow of the "Diamond Horseshoe," and a part made up of those smaller audiences of one, two, three, or more, who sit in the easy chairs at home before the radio, seldom realize how much in preparation goes to the making of a single evening's offering of opera, or the triumphs of stage mechanism which cause the fascinating stage pictures to move as scenes from life.

First there is a management willing and anxious to provide the audience with the finest art that can be produced, and the artists with every chance for progress. Neither may one forget those unseen "artists" in basement, sub-basement, and scene-loft who furnish the intricate shifting and arrangement of scenic effects, the visual allure and illusion which are the foundation for so many operatic successes.

For every opera, there is unlimited rehearsal, a new opera, or revival, taking many weeks to bring about the flawless perfection demanded. Of course the conductor chosen for the particular opera to be given is in charge of it all. Under and with him work all others connected with the production—the assistant conductors, chorus master, ballet mistress, as well as all singers and players, each of whom makes an intensive study of the score and libretto. The players of the orchestra have intensive rehearsals, being drilled to a perfection of performance almost unthinkable.

Meanwhile, the stage manager is busy planning effects, with painters, costumers, and electricians all contributing to the whole. Away up near the roof of the opera house, in a bare and mirror-lined studio, the ballet goes through arduous and protracted hours of work in synchronizing of rhythm of music and action. The "stars," too, are hard at work with their coaches, for only such unceasing effort will bring about the desired relaxation and naturalness when the time of performance comes. My coach, Mr. Frank LaForge, with whom I have worked for more than ten years, leaves nothing to chance; memorizing of the words to be sung, for instance, being attacked in many different ways, one of which is that the artist shall be able to write from memory, ten times, every "line" he will have to sing, and its cue or reply. His own lines he writes with blue pencil, those of his colleagues, with red; all this so that the voice shall not be worn by needless repetition, and that when the real singing begins, there shall be no physical nor nervous strain brought about by attempt to recall the text. Musically, the same care is taken, and the singer may work for many hours on a single phrase or a single word.

Presently the whole cast is assembled, the prompter takes up his place, and there is a general rehearsal minus costume and other visual effects, and usually with piano rather than orchestra. Then other rehearsals, with the orchestra, the chorus—and sometimes small choruses, bands, or orchestra back-stage, these kept in uniformity with the conductor by the aid of skilled assistants, who relay his beat. There are even lighting rehearsals, when the elusive color effects, which play such an important part in some scenes, are tried out; and the many curious mechanical aids to dramatic exposition are put through their paces. The colorful waves of sea-green water, which surge (via magic lantern) in certain operas, are liberated. If the *Ring* is in rehearsal, the noble Valkyries ride their hobby horses heavenward, and the Rhine Maidens swim about in their apparatus. Even the steam that conceals Alberich in his startling disappearances, in *Rheingold,* practices. All the time, artists and chorus are trying to act naturally and sing beautifully at the same time.

New trends in opera are already distinguishable. Music often tends to retard drama, yet when one remembers *Pelléas and Mélisande,* with the mysterious music of Debussy, its wondrous color and light, one seems to hear the outcry of human passions from the other side of

ERNESTINE SCHUMANN-HEINK

JOHN McCORMACK

TITO SCHIPA   LAWRENCE TIBBETT

JOHN FINLEY WILLIAMSON

LUCREZIA BORI

ROSA PONSELLE JOHN CHARLES THOMAS

life. And so it is with Gruenberg's music for *Emperor Jones,* where singing is deftly interwoven with the music to create a conglomeration of emotional effects. At one moment, when Emperor Jones has seemingly reached the apex of his terror, he breaks forth in a singing prayer. Gruenberg, so it is said, studied for two years over spirituals of the Negro, worked with this one, and that, and finally, after trying out a dozen or more, chose the familiar and absolutely appropriate "Standin' in de Need of Prayer," which is so superbly and theatrically magnificent.

For *Emperor Jones,* the stage of the Metropolitan was made to seem smaller by the addition of two panels on each side. On the upper halves of these were painted crude figures of half-naked Indian gods, while the lower halves were made into gratings, conventionalized designs of tropical branches or rushes. Back of these were seen the figures of the living members of the Negro chorus, which assisted the regular opera house chorus, here used as scenic accessories. Their yells and chants in conflicting rhythms and keys were magnificently effective and always hurled forward the action of the opera.

The libretto used by Mr. Gruenberg he himself prepared, and when he sent it to O'Neill for approval, the playwright is said to have replied that the adaptation had been admirably prepared, and that all the dramatic quality and flavor of the work had been preserved. Gruenberg has written the opera in two acts. He has, naturally, made use of the monotonous beat of the tom-tom which pursues Jones through the drama. This primitive drum-beat, which gradually accelerates as the action goes on, ceases only in certain brief scenes. These are during the vision and hallucinations which haunt Jones as he flees through the forest.

This work calls for unique arrangement of stage. The chorus of pursuing Negroes is grouped out of sight of the audience, below and in front of the stage flooring. At first only the crossing of hands and arms thrown about by the unseen pursuers are seen above it. Then as the pursuit draws nearer to its quarry, the bodies of the pursuers gradually emerge into view, as yells of hate and triumph gather in volume. The hallucinations of Jones—of the murdered crap player, of the sheriff whom he has killed, and of the auction block—are shown on a small raised stage, to indicate that they are figments of the poor man's imagination. Finally Jones is seen, a nearly naked savage, seated on the ground, swaying in terror as the medicine man leaps upon the stage and indicates him as the tribe's victim. At the end, the body of the fugitive, who, in the opera, shoots himself with his precious silver bullet, is carried off by the tribesmen into the forest amid a chorus of shouts of savage exultation which are soon heard dying away in the distance. . . . To all this drama Gruenberg has written what appears to be swift and pungent music. The principal moment of lyrical expression is Jones's prayer for the Lord's aid in his plight, which is made in the general character of the exquisite old Negro spiritual. This moment in the opera seems always to make an exceedingly strong emotional appeal, and the reasons for it I cannot doubt, as I was myself utterly touched and unable to speak for a moment after my first experience in hearing a group of devout Negroes in their utterance of this song.

The score is also reflective of every passing incident and gesture on the stage. Each of the scenes of the tragedy has its own musical counterpoint. Toward the close, there is an immense *crescendo* and acceleration, as several pairs of drums unite to create the intensely stirring finale. The opera takes about an hour for performance, and throughout this time there is not one single moment when the element of suspense is absent. Although there may not be—as some critics have suggested—tunes in *Emperor Jones* that the audience may whistle as it leaves the opera house (an acid test of the worth of any piece of music in the minds of some people), there is, for once, plenty of impression for it to carry away, and this is, also for once, just as important as a tonal commentary.

Opera may be the foundation of our musical art. But, should one listener prefer the primitive appeal of *Emperor Jones,* or the modern viewpoint of some other opera, he should also remember that there is no such thing as old-fashioned opera! Each opera is just a slice of life, and singing in it is just about the best fun anyone can have.

"FAVORITE" CHORUSES FROM OPERA

WHILE the opera-going public will always be particularly attracted to the scores of dramatic and melodically intriguing arias for which opera is noted, it is true that many of the most spectacular climaxes, much of the intensity of tragic moments and of the poetic appeal to the emotions is created, in opera, by its vocal ensemble. By this is meant any combination of voices between the forms of duet and operatic chorus, and includes such effective groups as trio, quartet, and sextet, celebrated examples of which, notable for special melodic or rhythmic charm, are popular with all music lovers, and interesting whether thought of as separate and independent choral numbers or in their appropriate settings in an opera.

The Verdi operas offer many captivating and expressive illustrations of these vocal ensemble forms. "Home to Our Mountains" from *Il Trovatore* is a favorite operatic duet. It occurs in the Finale of the last act, and is sung by Azucena (the old gypsy) and Manrico, who has always considered himself her son but who is, in reality, the brother of Count di Luna who was abducted in childhood as a revenge for the killing of the gypsy's mother. Both are prisoners in the tower, held there by the Count who is Manrico's rival for the hand of Leonora. Azucena has been telling of her mother's death at the stake and, comforted by the faithful Manrico, begins to sing the tender melody.

In the same opera (founded upon a historic tale of Spanish border life in the fifteenth century) are several stirring choruses, including the brilliant "Anvil Chorus" for male voices, and the mournful "Miserere." The "Anvil Chorus" has a simple melody which is enhanced by a colorful orchestral accompaniment in which are frequent trills and turns, forceful rhythmic patterns, and a constant use of per-

49

cussion instruments including the anvils upon which the men of the chorus beat out the accents. The "Miserere" or "death chant" never fails of its poignant appeal. It is sung by an invisible male chorus within the walls. The prisoners are about to be put to death, and prayers are being said for them. Eloquent interpolations are the tolling bell, Leonora's terrified lament and questionings, and Manrico's meditation from the tower above her.

Verdi's ability to produce choral effects of stupendous force is evident also in *Aida*, written in 1870 for the opening of the new Grand Opera House of Cairo, Egypt. Its music is colored by modal and Oriental characteristics. Great numbers of people are used to represent the life of ancient Europe and the magnificent pageantry of the stage scenes and romantic quality of the choral numbers make the opera a landmark in the history of music. "Return Victorious" is the vivid song of Aida and the multitude as they cheer Rhadames, their hero, as he departs to conquer the invading Ethiopians. In the gorgeous "Triumphal March" which serves as a Finale to Scene I and Act II, the melody increases in vigor and pompousness with each repetition, the first three of which are identical, and the fourth—after an abrupt modulation—sung in a higher and more brilliant key. See also page 400.

Moussorgsky's *Boris Godunov*, based upon actual scenes from Russian history (see page 21), is rather a series of closely connected historical scenes than a unified and artificial dramatic plot. Here the people assume the important position usually given to a romantic hero, and the opera is notable for realistic and colorful choruses. For the opening scene, following a very brief orchestral prelude, the crowd is seen kneeling on the open square in front of an old convent in Moscow. Boris, a traitor to the Tsar while living, has, at his death, caused the heir to be assassinated. Pretending that he does not wish the throne for himself, he secretly orders his officers to summon the people to the square for the purpose of urging him (Boris) to accept it. The sun is setting, and, as from a distance, there is heard the music of a band of chanting pilgrims. The music increases impressively as the pilgrims approach and cross the square on their way, their song being a hymn of rare exaltation, "Great is Thy Glory, Lord!" Equally realistic are the choruses from the Coronation scene * in Act III.

Deeply contrasting, in its simplicity and naturalness is a choral ensemble from the second act of *La Juive* (The Jewess) by Halévy, a choral prayer, "O God of Our Fathers," sung by a group of faithful Jews during a religious ceremony of the Passover. This pitiful story of Eleazar and his devoted foster daughter Rachel, who are finally sacrificed by being plunged into a cauldron of boiling oil when they refuse to renounce their faith, is so pathetic and touching that no display of vocal arabesque or theatrical stage setting is necessary to increase its sensational success.

Some operatic choruses are as devout in their atmosphere when taken alone, as any chorus from an oratorio. Of such is the Easter music, "Let Us Sing Our Lord's Wondrous Story," from the early scene in Mascagni's melodious *Cavalleria Rusticana.* Here again a scene representing an open square before a house of worship is the stage setting, and the music of the choir within the cathedral is supplemented by the singing of the kneeling villagers as they join in the joyous "Resurrection Hymn."

Characterized by rhythmic vitality are the lilting "Spinning Chorus" from Wagner's *Flying Dutchman,* in which Senta and a group of her girl friends sing as they while away the hours of waiting the return of her father from the sea by spinning; and the sturdy "Soldiers' Chorus" from Gounod's tragic opera *Faust.*

In these, and in many other of the so-called "favorite" choruses, their dramatic greatness and vitality will be found to have arisen from the composer's use of simple naturalness, or because of a wonderful charm of melody or rhythm.

* A Russian folk air employed by Moussorgsky in this music was used by Beethoven in the finale of his *Quartet in E Minor,* Opus 59, No. 2.

RICHARD WAGNER AND THE
MUSIC DRAMA

FOR many years composers of opera, especially those of the Italian "school," wrote much of their music for the purpose of exploiting the vocal abilities of the singers rather than to portray through the music the happenings and moods of the opera's story. Later operatic history tells of the efforts of certain composers to unite dramatic incident and appropriate music. Such a composer was Richard Wagner who, through early association with Ludwig Geyer, his stepfather (an actor) learned many essentials of dramatic success.

As a youth Wagner was a pupil in the Thomasschule in Leipzig, in which Bach had been a teacher, many years before. Here he learned the technique of writing music. His natural preference for tragedy led him, when only fourteen years old, to write a drama which was so lurid that by the end of the fourth act all the characters in it had been killed. The composer had therefore to bring them all back as ghosts so that he could finish the play.

Wagner's first operatic writing consisted of just two musical numbers for what he had planned to call *The Wedding*—a chorus with a short orchestral introduction, and a septet. His first complete opera, *The Fairies,* was written when he was twenty, and is based on a Scottish legend. The music was not especially original but contained reminders of Weber, Marschner, Beethoven, and others. The opera was never played until after Wagner's death, when it became popular enough to have seventy performances in Munich alone. The principal importance of these early works is that they show the same love of tragedy and interest in mythology and legend which are the foundation of all his later music-dramas.

Wagner felt that the mere display of beautiful singing was not enough reason for the composition of an opera, and based his own work on the idea that equal prominence should be given to the text and the music, and that no single note should be included which did not have a definite part in the expression of the plot. Because of this balance which he thought desirable he called his own works *music dramas*. In them soloists are not often given many "set pieces" (separate arias) to sing, although such "popular" numbers as "O Thou Sublime Sweet Evening Star" from *Tannhäuser,* or the "Prize Song" from *Die Meistersinger* prove Wagner's ability to write fascinating melodies. There is a frequent use of a combination of singing and speech which is called recitative.

Wagner also developed the idea of *Leitmotif,* by which is meant the idea of identifying certain objects or characters by the playing of definite combinations of tones each time the object or character is seen or mentioned. He also arranged great pageant-like processions which were accompanied with elaborate choruses, such as the "Pilgrims' Chorus" in *Tannhäuser* or the "Procession of the Knights" in *Parsifal.*

As a stage manager Wagner was able, before the advent of electricity, to devise stage settings of a mechanical nature which were unknown to his time. He placed the orchestra, which he increased in size and to which he added new instruments, so that it should be invisible to the audience.

The subjects of many of the Wagner music dramas are taken from Northern mythology, or from the historical lore of the Teutonic nations. And there are always, in each of his works, many delightful original characters which rank with the greatest characters in literature.

Tristan and Isolde, for example, is a setting of an ancient Irish legend. Cornwall had paid tribute to Ireland until King Mark revolted, and the adventures of Tristan, the king's messenger, constitute the basis for the tragedy. *Flying Dutchman* is based upon a variant of the old legend of the "Wandering Jew"; *Tannhäuser* (see page 403), upon historical facts; *Parsifal,* upon ancient lore of the Holy Grail, including an Irish story of a "magic goblet" and a "bleeding lance"; *Meistersinger,* upon the history of the old "free city" of Nuremberg, to which the drama stands as an imperishable monument. (There is also much shrewd symbolism in this work. Walter, of the "Prize Song," represents Wagner "bringing something new into music"; and Beckmesser, the disagreeable critic and noisy singer, is a sly reference to Hanslick, a contemporary critic whose writings had offended Wagner.) The *Ring,* with its four units, is a massive setting of material taken from the German epic, the *Nibelungenlied* (including bits of the old Icelandic sagas), a popular poem in Europe during the Middle Ages, recited for centuries by wandering minstrels.

National interest was increased by the fact that many of the scenes of the dramas were placed along the River Rhine. Siegfried, the hero of the *Ring,* is supposed to have been born at Xanten on the Rhine. The waters of the Rhine, near the foot of the Lorelei Rock, are supposed to have hidden the golden treasure which symbolizes an insane desire for power. Drachenfels, the ruins of which may still be seen on the Rhine bank, recalls many a miraculous tale of the dragon which is one of the important characters in the *Ring.*

Wagner for long wished for an ideal theater in which his works might be given exactly as he planned them, and finally selected Bayreuth on the River Main, already familiar to him as the town of Jean Paul Richter, the famous writer, as the appropriate site for his *Festspielhaus,* the foundation stone of which was laid in May 1872. Four years later the first Bayreuth Festival took place, when the entire *Ring* was performed under Wagner's direction, for the first time. Wagner died in Venice in 1883, and his body was brought back to Bayreuth, where it lies in a private plot just back of Villa Wahnfried, his palatial home.

The four dramas—*Rheingold, Valkyrie, Siegfried,* and *Twilight of the Gods*—which together constitute the *Ring,* were written by Wagner over a period of twenty-eight years. He had thought, at first, to tell the whole story in one drama, and the reason why he did not is given in a letter which he wrote to a friend:

"When I tried to dramatize the most important of the myths of the Nibelungen in *Siegfried's Death* [the fourth of the dramas, now known as *Twilight of the Gods*] I found it necessary to indicate a vast number of antecedent facts so as to put these main incidents in the proper light. . . . So I came to write *Siegfried*. Here again the same difficulty troubled me. Finally I wrote the *Valkyrie,* and then *Rheingold,* and thus contrived at last to incorporate all that was needful to make the action tell its own tale."

Although Wagner's expressed desire was that, in his dramas, music should never overshadow the text which it helps to interpret, he displayed such remarkable command of purely orchestral writing (as in the "Prelude" to *Rheingold,* or the Finale of the *Ring*) that it is not surprising that a famous contemporary critic prophesied that Wagner may, in time, be remembered not so much as a reformer and master of opera, as an orchestral composer of transcendental skill.

CHORAL MUSIC, SACRÉD AND SECULAR

BY DR. JOHN FINLEY WILLIAMSON, *President of Westminster Choir School, and Conductor, Westminster Choir, Princeton, New Jersey*

SINCE the days spoken of in the Bible, when the people of Israel, after their safe deliverance from the heavy years of bondage in Egypt, offered to the Lord dramatic songs of praise and thanksgiving, the world has been singing. In that exciting story of the passage through the Red Sea, we are told that "then sang Moses and the children of Israel this song unto the Lord." Seventeen verses later, in the same chapter, the story is told of the joyous reply of the Hebrew women, led by Miriam, the prophetess, who "took a timbrel in her hand; and all the women went out after her with timbrels and with dances. And Miriam answered them, 'Sing ye to the Lord for he hath triumphed gloriously.'"

In even earlier days than these, among the most primitive people, the chants of the multitudes were wonderfully inspiring, more than the songs of any soloist. Great composers have always realized this, and from the efforts of the earliest musicians until the time of Giovanni Pierluigi da Palestrina (1525–1594), a human choir was thought to be the most powerful of musical instruments. Palestrina's music is considered the culmination of all religious music written for chorus, and was the model by which that of other composers was judged, for many years. Then, for a while, though still admired, it ceased to be sung generally. Now it is again heard, not only as a part of church services, but on programs in concert or over the air.

Because of the very elaborate and complex way in which much of Palestrina's music, and that of other medieval composers, was written, it is, at first, difficult to understand, particularly if one listens for an out-and-out *tune*. The melody is always there, but is often veiled by the many other melodic lines that are interwoven with it, as this is polyphonic choral music, by which is meant that type of composition in which two or more independent melodies are combined harmoniously. Polyphony may be illustrated by so simple a bit of song as an old round in which the same melody is sung over and over, round and round, the combinations of its various sections interweaving and making simple harmonies.

Divisions into which medieval choral music may be divided include the *motet*, the *madrigal*, the *canon*, and the *Mass*.

The motet was, from the fifteenth century, a dignified musical setting of a text of Biblical character, made in a rather elaborate and many-voiced manner, usually for from three to eight voices, and unaccompanied. Later, in the eighteenth century, the style of the motet became more free, and the name came to be used, in general, with the same meaning as the English "anthem."

The madrigal was the secular counterpart of the sacred motet, and both are spoken of in the list of choral music as features in the general growth and popularity of *a cappella,* or unaccompanied vocal music, Madrigals are most charming when sung by small companies of singers, while the sacred music of Palestrina and other composers of his time is highly effective when sung by large choral groups. Madrigals might also be both sung and played (one or two voices and the rest of the parts taken by instruments). Important English writers of the madrigal include William Byrde and Thomas Morley.

The word *canon,* when used in its strict sense in connection with music, means exactly the same as the term *round* and comes from a Latin word meaning "exact law or rule." This style of writing was used by Palestrina in much of his music, as, for example, in his choral work, *Exultate Deo,* in which the melody is sung first by the soprano, then taken up in turn by the first alto, the tenor, the bass, and second alto, going on with the same melodic figure until a brilliant climax is reached and the entire first section of the music completed. It would be very helpful when listening to such a work, if possible, for the listener to learn this thread of a melody (which is known as the *cantus firmus*) before he listens to the complete piece. He would then be able to follow the progress of the melody as it is carried through the seeming labyrinth of sound. *Cantus firmus* was a name given in the Middle Ages to a thread of melody, or theme, about which other melodies were woven, making it, therefore, the foundation of the whole work.

Antonio Lotti, another medieval composer, who lived some years after Palestrina (1667–1740) and who was a choirmaster at St. Mark's in Venice, also wrote great choral music which is being enjoyed by singers and listeners today. His religious compositions were so admired throughout Europe in his own day that he was called to many of the larger cities on the continent to conduct his own works, among them a deeply expressive motet, *Crucifixus* (Crucifixion). In this work parts are written for eight voices, and in it Lotti took the single word "Crucifixus," with its melody as sung at first by a single voice, and constructed a whole section of his marvelous composition by adding voice after voice in repetitions of it in the style of a canon. After the climax has been reached the music dies away in volume, gradually, as though to suggest deep humility. This is done, not by diminishing of power by all of the singers taking part, but by the withdrawal of some of the voices as the music is going on. The effect of great stress was produced by many composers of the early days either by gradual addition or withdrawal of voices rather than by the present customary plan of singing more loudly or softly, and came to be known, presently as the "Rossinian crescendo" after its frequent use by Rossini, a nineteenth-century opera composer of Italy. (The same effect is used with instruments by Percy Grainger in his "wedding music." See page 323.)

In the second part of this same great sacred work, the composer changes the mood of the music by livening the tempo, and by adding other words and harmony. The third section, which tells of the sufferings and burial of Christ, follows the sentiment of its text closely.

It is interesting to contrast this setting of the Crucifixion text with one made by Johann Sebastian Bach, only a few years later, as a part of his *Mass in B Minor*. Bach uses a short musical phrase which is played by the basses of the accompanying orchestra, and repeated by them without change thirteen times in succession.

Bach's choral music, a model by which other music of the eighteenth century was judged, makes its deep appeal by means of its rare simplicity, and its deep spiritual sincerity. Bach's "Passion" music, sung so seldom in its entirety except at festival seasons (although parts of it are frequently heard) is so called because of its being a musical setting of the story of Christ's last week on earth, as told in one or the other of the four Gospels. There is therefore the *Passion According to St. Matthew,* and the *Passion According to St. John.* Bach is said to have written five works of this character, but the other three have been either lost, or their scores so scattered that there is no certainty that they are really Bach compositions.

Into each of the two authentic *Passions* Bach has interwoven many fine old chorales, the hymn which takes the place in the Lutheran ritual (for which Bach wrote much of his music) of the Gregorian chant or plain-song in the ritual of the Roman Church. These chorales are interspersed between groups of solos and ensemble or group numbers written to be sung by special choirs or soloists. The chorales are sung by the audience as well, which thus participates in the musical service. Bach frequently used a favorite chorale melody many times within a single large work, as he did with the tender melody of "O Sacred Head, Now Wounded," which he causes to be sung five times during the course of the *St. Matthew Passion,* and which is therefore known as the "Passion Chorale." Each time that the melody is repeated Bach has provided a new harmonic accompaniment in which he seeks to reflect the sentiment of the changing words of the text.

The great size of many festival choruses of the present day is a distinct contrast to the simple church choir of about twenty-four singers for whom Bach wrote much of his greatest music. Additions might be made to this group on special occasions, when added "spectacle" and volume were desired, even to the point of two choirs which might sing antiphonally. The Bach choir was always a male choir, the parts written for (and now often sung by) first sopranos being then sung by the little boys, while the low second bass parts were sung by the older boys of possibly eighteen years.

Many more modern writers have also been successful in composition of choral music. Brahms, in his motet "Grant Unto Me the Joy of Thy Salvation," Opus 29, No. 3, has come more nearly to the perfect expression of religious joy than any other modern composer. Vaughn Williams, the eminent British composer, in his *Holy City*, in form an abbreviated oratorio, has employed unusual musical groupings to secure many of his effects. These include a full choir, a half choir made up of soloists, a "distance" choir of boys, a full orchestra, and a "distance" band of trumpeters.

The chorus in certain operas, both on secular or semi-religious subjects, is equally necessary for dramatic effect, and there it often expresses vividly the sentiments of an entire multitude. This is illustrated in *Samson and Delilah* (Saint-Säens), *Parsifal* (Wagner), or even in such a very modern work as Honegger's *Judith*.

Elgar, of England, displays a splendid feeling for the voice in all his choral works. His secular *Go, Song of Mine* is a spirited number, and *Snow*, which he has written for ladies' voices, with accompaniment for two violins, is particularly pleasing. Choral music of exotic charm comes from the Russians who have produced such popular songs as *O Praise Ye* (Nikolsky), *Laud Ye the Name of the Lord* (Rachmaninov), and *Salvation is Created* (Tschesnokov). The American composer may also be depended upon for inspirational partsongs, such as the exquisite *Shepherd's Story* (Clarence Dickinson), *Children, Come on Home* (Noble Cain), *Hosanna* (F. Melius Christiansen), *Oxen* (Alma Stedman), and the marvelously lovely folk-settings by Howard Brockway.

No instrument so nearly approaches the human voice in quality, intonation, and temperament as does the violin, and stringed instruments are the most fitting instruments for use in accompaniment of vocal music, suggesting the teachings of Richard Wagner that the performance of even the most brilliant virtuoso must return in the end to the standard of the human voice.

MEDIEVAL CHURCH MUSIC

BY ROSSETTER GLEASON COLE, *American Composer and Teacher*

SPECIAL features of international broadcasts in recent years have been the concerts of church music given in European music centers, especially at festival seasons of the year. Much of this music has been founded upon the plain-song of the Middle Ages which served as a basis for much later art music, both sacred and secular.

The term "Gregorian chant" (also known as plain-song, Gregorian melody, or chorale) applies to that particular type of music which came into being in connection with the growth of the liturgy of the Church, which has always been a musical liturgy. The name "Gregorian" is derived from Gregory the Great (590–604) who, until near the end of the nineteenth century, was believed to have been largely instrumental in establishing the system of plain-song on which the whole medieval music down to about the year 1600 was built. It is now well established that, however much he may have accomplished in fixing methods of permanency and universality in the ritual music, the processes of selection, addition, and assimilation went on until the eighth century.

At the foundation of this ritual music (and later of the secular music influenced by it) are the eight Gregorian "tones" or modes (also called Church modes) that date from the time of Gregory. Two other modes were later added. Each mode consisted of the eight tones within the compass of an octave, corresponding in pitch to the tones along the white keys of the piano. For example, a melody or chant in the Dorian mode consisted of the tones within the octave from *D* to *D* along the white keys of the piano (*DEFGABCD*). The Phrygian mode consisted of the tones from *E* to *E* along the white keys of the piano. The Lydian mode was the same as from *F* to *F*. These three are mentioned here as they are the modes whose influence is most frequently apparent in the instrumental and other non-liturgical music of Scandinavia, Russia, Bohemia, and some recent French and Italian music.* The influence which the ecclesiastical modal music exerted on secular art music was almost negligible until near the middle of the nineteenth century and in Russia and Scandinavia this influence came, not directly, but indirectly through the folk song, which in these countries, as in others, had taken melodic and harmonic color and character from the modal music that the people heard in the church.

Until the tenth century this ritual music was sung entirely in unison, the emphasis and rhythm of the melodies being governed wholly by the emphasis and rhythm of the text (words), rather than by measured tone-values. After the tenth century free parts (called *descant*) were gradually added to the chant melody, or *cantus firmus,* and out of this practice grew the science of counterpoint. Until the thirteenth century the intervals most used in the old styles of part-writing were fourths, fifths, octaves, and unisons. Combinations of tones a third apart, or a sixth apart, were sometimes permitted, but were regarded as dissonant until the period (about the year 1500) when the combination of *three* tones (the triad) became a conscious feature of musical thought.

The basis of all the art music of the Middle Ages was the chant melody and the science of music concerned itself wholly with the addition of more or less free and independent parts to it. Musical invention, until probably the fourteenth century, or even later, was limited entirely to these accompanying parts. Since music in the Church was never considered apart from the liturgy to which it was wedded, not only did the melodic form of the chants themselves follow closely the words of the liturgy, but for several centuries after the principle of polyphony was thoroughly recognized, the most intricate church compositions,

* Examples may be found in some of the *Lyrical Pieces* by Grieg; the "Ballade," "Danse," and "Reverie" from the *Album for Piano* by Debussy; *Church Windows* for orchestra, the piano *Concerto* (Mixolydian Mode), and the "Catacombs" episode in the *Pines of Rome* by Respighi; both of the Borodin Symphonies; and much of the music of Béla Bartók, particularly in his early works.

such as masses and motets, were constructed by using chants as themes and adding free parts to them.*

Until about 1550 nearly all art music in Western Europe was choral music. Though the first important steps in the development of music were taken in Italy, devotion to the principles of *unison* Gregorian chant kept the polyphonic (many voiced) idea from gaining a foothold there until the fourteenth century. Vocal polyphony (or counterpoint) was brought to its perfected and most complex form under the care and guidance of Northern musicians (the Paris school during the twelfth and thirteenth centuries, and the Gallo-Belgic school, 1360–1460). After these "apprentices" had prepared the crude tools of composition, real master composers appeared, the Netherlanders who, between 1400 to 1550, worked to convert the elaborate technical forms and devices of writing into music which should express deep feeling and religious devotion. They succeeded so well that for two centuries all of Western Europe considered the Low Countries the musical headquarters of Europe.

The Netherland period was one of astonishing activity, the names of nearly four hundred composers being recorded, whose output, both in quality and quantity, measures not at all unworthily with that of the other arts of this period. The masses and motets of the period reflect all the changing phases of the gradually advancing musical art; and the madrigals and chansons—written in the composer's lighter moments of relaxation—were composed mostly for the entertainment of wealthy and noble patrons. Composers of this period include Antoine

---

* The word *mass* has been used from the early centuries of church history to designate certain constant portions of the liturgy to which unusually solemn and impressive music has been set. These are the *Kyrie, Gloria, Credo, Sanctus* (and *Benedictus*), and the *Agnus Dei*, and with slight variations form the essential parts of the musical mass whether written for church or concert performance. The *motet* is of great antiquity, having been mentioned by Franco of Cologne (who died about 1200) as one of the three kinds of choral composition of his time. The words are selected from the Bible or office-books, and in the church service is sung in the place of the *offertorium* of the day. Beginning probably in France it was cultivated by the Netherlanders, brought to perfection by Palestrina, adopted by both the Lutheran and Anglican branches of the Protestant Church, superseded in England by the "full anthem," and brought to its culmination in Germany in Bach's time.

Busnois (1440–1492), whose *Ecce Ancilla* is considered one of the "most important musical historical monuments up to 1475," and Josquin des Prés (c.1450–1521), one of the greatest geniuses of the time.

In the motet (its richest period was from 1500 to 1600) the composers strove to portray the meaning of the words rather than to work out contrapuntal devices. Many of the older works still seem of impressive beauty, such as Arcadelt's *Ave Maria,* which is probably the best known of sixteenth-century motets, and which sounds wonderfully modern with its compact chords, sweet tunefulness, and simple pathos.

After Des Prés the greatest and last great Netherlander was Orlandus Lassus (1532–1594), who spent the larger part of his best years in Munich in the service of the art-loving Dukes of Bavaria, Albert V and his son William. Next to Palestrina the greatest genius of the sixteenth century, he left a deep impress on the development of Germanic art. The most celebrated of his nearly 2500 separate compositions are his *Penitential Psalms,* which though written comparatively early in his career (before 1565, published in 1584) possess in a marked degree qualities of strength, dignity, and repose. Lassus had also an open heart for secular inspiration and no composer of his century was so prolific in humorous works.

Palestrina (so called from the name of his birth-place, a small town southeast of Rome) completed the magnificent structure of polyphonic ecclesiastical music founded and developed by the Netherlanders, and in his music summed up all the best qualities of his predecessors. In his music each voice-part is equal in independence and importance with every other; the voices begin, intertwine, and drop out with absolute freedom of movement; one key is maintained throughout the entire composition with no modulations in the modern sense; the beginnings and endings of the melodic phrases usually occur at different points in the different voices, thus producing a constant shifting in the rhythmical flow of the music that creates a feeling of vagueness and indefiniteness of design. The changes in dynamics and in speed are never startling or abrupt. Palestrina's masses number ninety-three, the most important being the *Missa Papae Marcelli,* chosen by the Council of Trent as the model in style and structure of what all future ritual music should be. (Palestrina also published between twenty and twenty-five madrigals under the pen-name of Gianetto.)

The second half of the sixteenth century has been called the "Golden Age" of ecclesiastical music. After Palestrina further progress was impossible, yet his style was imitated for a half century at least. The triumphant progress of secular music, instrumental as well as operatic, soon broke down the opposition of the "purists" and after Allegri, remembered for his celebrated *Miserere,* the Palestrina style practically disappeared.

Instruments and the Music They Make

THE ORCHESTRA AND ITS INSTRUMENTS

THE word *orchestra* comes from the Greek, in which it meant the open space in the great outdoor theaters between the seats of the audience and the stage. It was a curved enclosure set apart for the chorus. Later, in Roman theaters, seats for the use of Roman senators were placed in this space, but the name remained, and now "the orchestra" is always the section of a theater in which the audience sits on a level with, or slightly below, the stage. In *a strictly musical sense,* the word now means a body of instrumental players and their instruments, and also implies that the players are, in the main, seated.

The written history of the orchestra before A.D. 1100 is rather meager, but it is certain from such records as are available, that the earliest civilizations favored music played by groups of instrumentalists. An early Egyptian record speaks of "six hundred players of lyres, harps, lutes, flutes, and rattles."

The modern symphony orchestra owes much to the development of the instruments themselves and to the growing importance, in early days, of musical accompaniment to dramatic works. In connection with the earliest Florentine operas of 1600,* an orchestra, large for its time, was used. But we are also told by historians that not all of the players were heard at one time. Instead, certain instruments accompanied scenes to which their voices were thought appropriate. These instruments were all hidden from view of the audience, as are the players in the orchestra of today at the Wagner *Festspielhaus* at Bayreuth in Bavaria.

The development of the orchestra as a unit in itself, instead of being merely an accompanying body, was naturally slow. As late as 1800 it

* See "From Greek Drama to Radio Opera," page 38.

was still the custom for the conductor to lead his players from his seat at the harpsichord or piano. A baton was seldom employed.

Joseph Haydn (1732–1809) was the first composer and conductor to make full use of the individual possibilities of each instrument and to divide the instruments into the four choirs or groups with which they have, ever since, been associated. Although even Haydn had only a small group of players in his orchestra, as compared with a modern symphony orchestra, he brought about many remarkable developments through his thirty years of experimentation while chapel-master to Prince Esterhazy in the famous Esterhazy Castle near Vienna.

The four choirs of the modern orchestra are the strings, the wood-winds, the brasses, and the percussion instruments.

The *strings* include violins, violas, 'cellos, and double-basses.

The *wood-winds* are the flute, piccolo, oboe, English horn, clarinet, bass clarinet, bassoon, and contra-bassoon.

The *brasses* are the French horn, the trumpet, the trombone, and the tuba.

The *percussion* instruments include bells, glockenspiel, celesta, kettle-drums, xylophone, drums, tambourine, triangle, cymbals, and various other instruments having a special effect, such as castanets and rattles.

A symphony may also employ harps, the pipe-organ, and the piano.

Of all these the strings are most important and form the foundation about which the rest of the orchestra is built. Interest in orchestral music is increased with knowledge of each instrument by sight, sound, and name, and with as much acquaintance as is possible with its individual personality. It is also of advantage to learn the customary seating of these various instruments in a symphony orchestra.

Each great orchestra differs from all others in size and arrangements, but for the sake of comparison it is interesting to enumerate the instrumentation of the New York Philharmonic-Symphony Orchestra for 1933: first violins, 18; second violins, 17; violas, 14; 'cellos, 12; double-basses, 10; flutes, 4; piccolo, 1; oboes, 4; English horn, 1; clarinets, 4; bass clarinet, 1; E-flat clarinet, 1; bassoons, 4; contra-bassoon, 1; French horns, 6; trumpets, 4; bass trumpet, 1; trombones, 4; tuba, 1; tenor horn, 1; timpani, 2; percussion, 5; harps, 2; piano and celeste, 2; organ, 1. One may also notice that piccolo, English horn, bass and E-flat clarinets, and contra-bassoon, as well as the tenor horn, are instruments not used constantly, and so are played by performers of standard instruments in a like group.

A brief introduction to the individual instruments is here given in the order in which they are presented to the conductor on each page of his score, where the strings (fundamental instruments) are placed at the bottom:

Flute. Notable for its ease, agility, and bird-like quality in the higher registers, in which its voice is comparable to a human voice, and has also a luscious and mellow quality in the lower range. Is now frequently made of silver, but is still known as a wood-wind instrument. It holds a supreme importance in the history of primitive music, and was a favorite among ancient Greeks and Romans. Its forerunners include grasses, reeds, bamboo and bone whistles, pipes of bone and clay, and pipes o' Pan (made from reeds of graduated lengths and pitches).

Piccolo. A small-sized flute, less than one-half the length of the regular instrument. Takes its name from the Italian abbreviation *flauto piccolo* (little flute). It sounds one octave (eight tones) higher than the written music, and lends to a performance, as the composer may desire and indicate, a military atmosphere, or special effects of brilliancy, shrillness, or decoration, through use of scales, trills, or other embellishments.

Oboe. A double-reed instrument having a long and distinguished history. Is mentioned in the Psalms and in the earliest history of primitive people. The oboe has a fixed pitch and other instruments of the orchestra are tuned from it. It has a penetrating and slightly nasal tone quality and is appropriate for pastoral effects.

English horn (*cor anglais*). This is neither a horn, nor is it English, but is, indeed, an alto oboe. Its upper metal end which holds the reed is bent and its lower end is bell-shaped. Its voice is well-fitted to music of a sad or meditative character.

Clarinet. A single-reed instrument invented in Nuremberg by J. C. Denner, about 1700. Its use was not common for seventy-five years, but it is now the "prima donna" of the military band, holding the same important place in it that the violin does in the orchestra. Mozart was the first composer to realize its importance for the orchestra. The bass clarinet is of the same general construction but speaks an octave lower.

Bassoon (fagott). Resembles somewhat a bundle of sticks, hence its Italian name. This appearance is caused by the folding of the instrument so that its nine feet of tube are reduced to the length of about four feet. The instrument has two distinct personalities. In its lower register it produces a very sweet tone rivaling the 'cello in mellowness. In the higher registers it is capable of humorous effects. The contra-bassoon speaks an octave lower.

Trumpet. This instrument, familiar since the dawn of history, is capable of a stirring blast of sound, but of rich and velvety tonal effects. In smaller orchestras it is sometimes replaced by the cornet.

French horn. A descendant of the old-time hunting horn, noted for the purity of its tone. Though a brass instrument, it is sometimes included in the wood-wind choir because of its tone quality.

Trombone. Often spoken of as the "slide" trombone because of the telescopic slide used to produce change of length in the tube, and therefore varied pitch. It is really a big trumpet, capable of producing imposing effects.

Tuba. Commonly used to supply the deeper bass and foundational parts in orchestral music.

The percussion choir includes those instruments which must usually be struck to produce a sound. Many are used to accent rhythms or to create desired atmosphere and unique effect. They are of two classes, (a) those which produce noise but have no definite pitch, and (b) those of definite pitch. The first division includes drums, tambourine, triangle, cymbals, castanets. The second includes bells, glockenspiel, celesta, kettle-drums (timpani), and xylophone.

Harp. Constructed in primitive days from strung hunting bows, and a favorite with bards and minstrels, it is mentioned in the history of all European and Asiatic countries. In its modern perfected form it is the product of Sebastian Érard, a celebrated European piano-maker.

Violin. Gaspar de Salo is credited with being the inventor of the four-stringed violin, and to have perfected his instruments between 1550 and 1610. Stradivari of Cremona brought the instrument (during the early part of the eighteenth century) to a state of perfection never since surpassed. The violin is capable of producing any desired effect. It may be played with a bow, plucked with the fingers (*pizzicato*), muted, or may produce harmonics. Divided in the orchestra or string quartet into first and second violins, the instrument is the same, the parts written being comparable to first and second soprano parts. Normally tuned to *G, D, A,* and *E.*

Viola. Larger than the violin and tuned to *C, G, D,* and *A* (a fifth lower than the violin), and often spoken of as the tenor of the string choir.

Violoncello. Commonly called the 'cello, in pitch an octave lower than the viola, it plays the bass in the string quartet. One of the loveliest of solo instruments, it is a descendant of the viola da gamba, Amati—one of the famous violin-makers of Cremona—being one of the first to convert the gamba into a 'cello.

Double-bass. The largest of stringed instruments to be played with a bow, and one of the foundation instruments of the orchestra. Of deep and powerful tone, it is especially valuable in harmonic or obbligato passages.

BANDS AND BAND MUSIC

BY HARWOOD SIMMONS, *Associate in Music, Columbia University, and Conductor, Columbia University Band*

THE most democratic musical ensemble is probably the wind-band. Although it accompanies kings at coronations and all officialdom marches to its measures, the band is most at home as the bright spot on the musical horizon of bourgeois culture. The plebeian feels somehow that bands—brass bands, he calls them—belong to him. They are within his ken, he thinks; and rightly so, because did not Uncle George play in the village band and is not Dick learning the trombone at school? The member of an average band is generally not a musician in the strict use of that term. The word artist is seldom attributed to him because he is first Mr. Average Citizen and next a musically inclined performer upon an instrument. This is not to belittle his musical preference; rather it is to recognize perhaps the most significant medium through which refined ensemble music is to reach the masses.

Just as other art media lack uniformity, especially in their less developed stages, so does the band. There are many kinds of bands even when the definition is narrowed to include only ensembles of wind and percussion instruments, ignoring the great variety of so-called dance bands which are really orchestras. In any case there is no set rule as to instrumentation. Contemporary bands are more or less balanced groups of wind instruments arranged in choirs very much as are human voices in choral singing, with the addition of percussion instruments. There is a brass choir of soprano, alto, tenor, baritone, and bass; and a wood-wind choir built upon the same pattern. Except for a few important exceptions the band is little more than an overgrown wind section of the symphony orchestra. Or, to put it another way, the sym-

74

phony orchestra is a band plus a large choir of stringed instruments.

Before the middle of the eighteenth century, ensembles known as orchestras were, in our terms, more properly bands. Members of the oboe family constituted the real nucleus of the orchestra rather than strings, and often no strings at all were present. In fact, whatever can be said of the early history of the orchestra applies equally to the band. It was only after the eighteenth century that they were in any way differentiated, and none but the most modern vocabulary designates the windband as something different from the orchestra. In point of lineage, therefore, the band is as well born as its more distinguished relative. Why the orchestra is more distinguished is obvious. It is vastly more versatile and is capable of expressing the composer's ideas, much more readily, due to the addition of strings, with all their warmth and brilliance of color. But this does not say that the band lacks virility or robustness, or a subtlety all its own. Within its limitations the band has survived and developed remarkably and is at present on the verge of a renaissance promising to rival that which saw the birth of the symphony orchestra itself.

The ideal band is coming to be known in America as the symphonic band. The average band, however, is far less pretentious. In the vast majority of cases the term band generally means a brass band of about twenty-five pieces, an organization which is the chief criterion of musical art to the inhabitants of thousands of communities. Splendid work is now being done by the larger school systems and the American Bandmaster's Association, under the guidance of such eminent musicians as Edwin Franko Goldman, in insisting upon balanced instrumentation and good editions of better music and in teaching correct methods of technique upon instruments of high quality.

The instrumentation outlined in the chart below, if completely represented, would approach that of the symphonic band, but the average band generally lacks many of these, being something like this: 1 solo cornet, often played by the conductor as was the harpsichord by the early orchestral conductor; 2 first cornets (trumpets); 2 second cornets (trumpets); 2 third cornets (trumpets); 2 alto horns; 1 baritone horn;

BAND INSTRUMENTATION

VOICE	BRASS CHOIR	WOOD-WIND AND REED CHOIR
soprano	solo cornet (or trumpet); 2 players	(*coloratura*) piccolo, flute, E-flat clarinet; 1 or 2 players each flute, upper registers of B-flat clarinets, soprano saxophone; 1 or more players
mezzo-soprano	1st cornet (or trumpet); 1 to 3 players	oboe, 2nd clarinets; 1 or more players
contralto	2nd and 3rd cornets (or trumpets); 2 to 4 players	2nd and 3rd clarinets, alto saxophone, alto clarinet; 1 or more players
tenor (divided harmony)	French horns (altos or melophones), 3 or 4 players; 1st trombone, tenor horns, 1 to 3 players	alto clarinet, lower register of B-flat clarinets, tenor saxophone; 1 or more players each
baritone	euphonium (baritone horn), trombones; 1 to 3 players each	bassoon, baritone saxophone, bass clarinet; 1 or more players each
bass	tuba, (sousaphone), bass trombone; 1 to 4 players	bassoon, bass clarinet, bass saxophone; 1 or more players each

PERCUSSION

Same as for the full orchestra.

3 trombones; 2 sousaphones or tubas; 1 piccolo; 2 first B-flat clarinets, 2 second B-flat clarinets; 1 third B-flat clarinet; 2 alto saxophones; 2 drums. Clearly the effect is predominantly brassy and of a rather strident character. With the addition of a fife or bugle and drum corps, this instrumentation is fairly representative of the military band heard in army, navy, and police units.

Some may consider it presumptuous to employ the word "symphonic" in connection with a band, when at present that term is dignified by its application to great orchestras. "Symphony" means "harmony" but from about the fourth to the sixteenth century the word applied also to musical instruments as such, these varying from drums to crude horns. If we look, therefore, to antiquity for authority, the wind-band has even more right to the word than the orchestra as we know it.

The term helps to distinguish between the brass band and the larger, fully instrumented ensembles specializing in concert and program music. While military marches and music of dance rhythms characterize the former, the latter has successfully invaded orchestral, piano, organ, chamber music, and operatic literature, for the symphonic band finds itself with almost no literature of its own.

The brass band is largely an outdoor affair, while the symphonic band is adapted to both indoor and outdoor playing. It is two or three times the size of the usual military band, with the wood-wind instruments as its central feature. The military band is present within the symphonic band but is emphasized as such only for special effects. The symphonic band has developed possibilities for the composer not to be found in any other medium. Tone colors impossible in the orchestra or organ can be produced with tremendous effect, and the greater versatility in dynamics and scale range is an asset not yet adequately explored.

The clarinets take, in a general way, the place of the strings in the orchestra, but in the symphonic band, strings are not wholly wanting. Double-basses are now a regular component, together with harps, and occasionally 'cellos and piano.

On the next page is an outline of the ideal representative instrumentation of a symphonic band, based upon a group of one hundred and sixteen players.

It will be noticed that the large majority of symphonic band instruments is also to be found in the orchestra, in some cases in exactly the same proportion. Others, such as the clarinet, vary; the symphony orchestra having, at most, five, while the band has thirty-nine. The largest group of instruments unique to the band is the saxophone family, and even they are sometimes heard in modern orchestral works. (Bizet's *L'Arlésienne Suite* uses the alto saxophone for a beautiful solo passage.) Saxophones are among the latest arrivals in the family of reed instruments, having been invented about 1840 by Adolphe Sax, the tone being one that blends admirably with either wind or stringed instruments. When well played, saxophones possess a charm and

VOICE *	WOOD-WIND AND REED	BRASS
coloratura-soprano	piccolos 2, flutes 6, E-flat clarinets 2	E-flat cornet (F trumpet)
soprano	B-flat clarinets 16, soprano saxophone 1	solo cornets 2
mezzo-soprano	2nd B-flat clarinets 8, oboes 2	first cornets 4
contralto	3rd B-flat clarinets 8, alto clarinets 2, alto saxophones 2, English horn 1	2nd and 3rd cornets 6 flüglehorn 2
tenor	4th clarinets (third divided), tenor saxophone 1	French horn 8 (divided harmony), 1st trombones 3
baritone	bassoons 6, baritone saxophone 1, bass clarinets 2, hecklephon 1	euphoniums 2, 2nd trombones 3
bass	contra-bassoon 1, contra-bass clarinet 1, bass saxophone 1	tuba 6, bass trombones 3, string basses 4

Percussion—1 timpani, and four miscellaneous players

1 harp, 1 piano

piquancy placing them far above the level of the jazz orchestra with which they have been identified in spite of the fact that Sax invented and first employed them for the military band. They are named soprano, alto, tenor, baritone, and bass, the most popular and versatile being the alto.

Other especially important instruments are:

Euphonium (baritone horn) is one of the few not known to the classic orchestra, and may be described as a small tuba. It substitutes admirably for the 'cello in transcriptions from orchestral music, having a beautiful high tenor quality in addition to its full rich baritone in the middle and low registers.

E-flat clarinet. This instrument has a shrill, unpleasant high register and a thin, hollow middle register, and its low tones are beautiful though not often used to advantage.

Alto clarinet is the modern equivalent of the basset horn of Men-

* It must be understood that abundant overlappings in voice range occur. Several instruments possess as many as three voice registers.

JOHN PHILIP SOUSA

EDWIN FRANKO
GOLDMAN

HARWOOD SIMMONS

SYMPHONIC BAND OF COLUMBIA UNIVERSITY

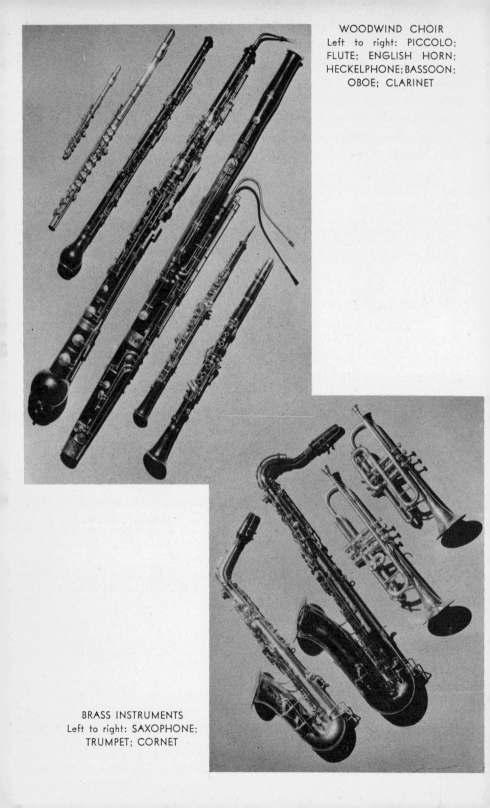

WOODWIND CHOIR
Left to right: PICCOLO;
FLUTE; ENGLISH HORN;
HECKELPHONE; BASSOON;
OBOE; CLARINET

BRASS INSTRUMENTS
Left to right: SAXOPHONE;
TRUMPET; CORNET

delssohn's time. It is a fifth lower than the *B*-flat clarinet. Although valuable in its low register its weaker high tones restrict its use somewhat.

(Brief descriptions of all the remaining instruments will be found in the chapter "The Orchestra and Its Instruments.")

PATTERNS AND STYLES—
A CHAPTER ON FORMS

EVERYONE enjoys best the music he can recall. To make this possible the music should be written with regard to a definite form so that its melodies, the parts of a masterpiece which make the first appeal, are easily recognized.

As plot is to a story, so form is to music; it is the pattern upon which the composition is built. Pattern is based almost entirely upon repetition of certain bits of music, these being made more interesting by the use in the same composition, of contrasting phrases. Repetition in musical sound, as in common rhymes, also helps to make the phrase groupings of the notes and rests felt. Some repetitions are exact and others are merely suggested.

Different pieces of music have their repetitions arranged in different ways. The old round "Three Blind Mice," for instance, is made up of just two two-measure phrases, the one on which the opening words ("Three blind mice") are sung, and that used later in the little tune for the first time on the words "they all run after the farmer's wife." By using these little phrases, or motifs, in this order—1,1,1,1, 2,2,2,1—the piece will be found to be complete in the form in which it has been sung for ages.

Repetition of very brief bits of melody (motifs) is heard in, for example, the old Christmas song "Silent Night, Holy Night," by Franz Gruber.

"Träumerei" by Robert Schumann—one of the ten "favorite" melodies, is made from a single theme repeated several times, in varying pitches. So, also, is the same composer's "Wild Horseman," in which the simple melody is changed from major to minor, and from soprano to bass. A pattern thus made from a single theme is said to be in *unary form.*

In two-part (*binary*) form, two different themes, each complete in itself, are contrasted. An illustration of this is found in the familiar "Sicilian Hymn," sometimes also known as "O Du Heilige." Here the first half of the song melody is contrasted by an entirely different second half.

Three-part (*ternary*) form is one of the most important of all forms, and one used in the writing of a large number of the world's master-pieces, such as sonatas, symphonies, and overtures. Such longer pieces may have many subdivisions, but they will usually be found to be written in three large parts. This form may be recognized by the similarity of the first and third parts, although the third part, in its repetition of the first, may be varied, or considerably shortened. This form is illustrated in "Old Folks at Home," the first part ending with the words, "that's where the old folks stay." The second part—shorter than the first—begins with the melodic phrase which accompanied the words "all my heart is sad and weary, everywhere I roam," after which (with the words, "there's where my heart is turning") there is a return to the expressive melody of the opening measures.

Many simple folk airs are in this three-part form, as will be seen by singing the melodies of such familiar songs as "All Thro' the Night," or other old favorites.

A piece may have three or more themes, or separate tunes, arranged in such an order that the first one not only begins the piece, but alternates with each new theme and closes the composition. If one should indicate each theme by a letter, the pattern of such a form, which is known as *rondo form* is as follows: *A B A C A.* This form had its beginnings in the ancient round dances, or singing games, in which the refrain was sung first and last, and contrasted with a solo response from one of the dancers, as in the storied "On the Bridge of Avignon."

The *sonata form,* so often mentioned in concert program notes and in oral interpretations given over the air, refers only to (usually) the *first* movement of a sonata, a symphony, or a concerto. This is written with regard to three-part form, having three large parts, known as the statement of the themes (or exposition), development section, and recapitulation. Each of these, in turn, has its divisions. The exposition presents the themes, of which there are at least two, which are in contrasting style and keys. In the course of the development section these themes, or fragments of them are repeated in new keys, and in as many different ways as the taste and ingenuity will permit. The recapitulation —like the return of *A* in the simple three-part form—brings a return of all the themes, all of which are now in the main key of the composition. To all of this the composer may, if he wishes, add an introduction and a coda, or end-piece, but the addition of these is entirely optional.

The *sonatina*—a small sonata, is similar in form except that it has no development section.

Some compositions make use of a simple, small, but easily recognizable, bit of music, known as a motif, through the entire piece, its use giving unity to the work as a whole. This is illustrated by the "Fate" theme which Beethoven used throughout his *Fifth Symphony*.

There is also the *fugue*. This form, in its usual acceptance, is built about a single theme, which is given out first by a single voice, then answered in turn by each of the other voices.

Lyric music owes its name to the ancient lyre, and to the fact that the Greeks were accustomed to classify as lyric any poem which was not narrative or story-telling in its character, and which was sung to the accompaniment of that historic instrument.

Many pieces known by such names as *serenade, romance, barcarolle, reverie,* or *meditation,* are frequently spoken of as being lyric forms. It would be more accurate to speak of their lyric style, for each expresses its own type of emotion. It is the *character* of such music, rather than its formal design which gives it its name. A number of the more familiar lyric "forms," and of the old dance forms so frequently a part of the suite, with brief notes about each, are listed:

Allemande, in the classic suite usually following the prelude, is of German origin, and in four-beat measure. (The general order of movements in a classic suite is, prelude, allemande, courante, sarabande;

then optional movements, such as minuet, bourrée, gavotte, and musette; and usually ending with a gigue.)

Barcarolle. The name given, in early days, to the gondolier songs of Venice. It now suggests any boat song and is characterized by a gentle swaying rhythm.

Bolero. A Spanish dance of decided rhythm and lively tempo.

Bourrée. A dance from either Biscay (in Spain) or from southern France, cheery in mood, and of lively tempo. It begins on the last beat of a measure, and in its rhythm two short notes are followed by a long one.

Chaconne. A type of theme with variations. See page 124.

Courante. A gay and quickly moving dance, often embellished by the addition of doubles (elaborate variations).

Czardas. A Hungarian dance taking its name from the word meaning "country inn," where it was first performed.

Fandango. A Spanish dance similar to the seguidilla and the bolero.

Farandole. The name of a procession of festal character often seen on fête days in Provençe.

Gavotte. An old French peasant dance taking its name from the section in which it originated. Begins on the up-beat of the measure.

Gigue (*giga, jig*). Usually in six-eight measure, a lively dance of southern Italy.

Habañera. A languorous dance common to Spanish or Cuban music.

March. A form of regular rhythm (2–2, 4–4, or 6–8) having many divisions as to style, such as funeral, military, wedding, or as used for processions.

Mazurka. A folk dance of Poland taking its name from the duchy of Mazovia. Its rhythm is a slow triple.

Meditation. A lyric style the name of which suggests thoughtful contemplation of some specific idea.

Minuet. A dance in three-beat measure which originated in the French province of Poitou. It became a court dance and was later brought to America by migrating colonists.

Musette. A simple dance in duple measure, beginning on the last half of the measure, and taking its name from an old-time instrument which gave out a drone bass.

Nocturne. A lyric piece the name of which suggests night music, the form said to have been invented by John Field.

Passepied. An old-time Breton dance of lively rhythm.

Polka. A Bohemian dance invented about 1830.

Polonaise. A processional dance or march originating in the parade of returning soldiers before the king of Poland.

Reverie. This general title leaves the interpretation to the individual whims of the listener. A piece of retrospective music.

Romance. A lyric piece suggesting a tender or fanciful mood.

Serenade. A lyric piece taking its name from the Spanish *sera,* meaning "evening," and of romantic history, having originated with the troubadours of Provençe.

Siciliana. A rhythmic piece from Sicily where it is always sung as it is danced, and which in its atmosphere suggests a shepherd's pastoral. An instrumental *siciliana* is characterized by a drone bass, suggesting the primitive bagpipe.

Tarantella. A furious folk dance of Italy, taking its name from Taranto.

Waltz (valse). A dance in triple meter, derived from the country dances of Germany.

STORIES IN SOUND—
DESCRIPTIVE MUSIC

SINCE the beginning of time people have told stories. Many of the oldest of these—myths, fables, legends, and folktales—handed down for centuries by word of mouth, have become a precious heritage reflecting the thought and actual history of the past. Some have been preserved by means of highly colored pictures and carving found buried under the dry sands of Egypt and the Orient. In the ancient days, in Greece, Arabia, and Persia, many men became professional story-tellers, traveling through the country from market-place to market-place, reciting tales of valor and adventure. Traveling story-tellers are still seen and heard in Arabia.

As poets have told stories in words, and artists in carvings and color, musicians have told them in sound, and this type of music is known as program music, in contrast to absolute music, which makes no effort to suggest or imitate any special object or story, but merely to be lovely in a formal way. (An illustration of absolute music is the elegant orchestral overture to the *Magic Flute* in which the graceful theme is developed in fugal manner.)

Program music may be divided into realistic, narrative, and impressionistic types.

The realistic piece tries, through clever imitation—such as the cracking thunder in the *William Tell Overture* by Rossini, or the hissing steam and rumbling wheels in *Pacific 231* by Honegger—to bring real objects instantly to mind.

Narrative music is less definite in its imitation, but seeks to describe some event by means of association, as is done by Ernest Schelling in his *Victory Ball* for orchestra. Here the listener knows, quite certainly, when the ghosts of the Scottish highlanders have entered the ballroom, and that they are ghosts instead of living soldiers, because of the trumpet call "To Arms," the spirited playing of the bagpipes which accompany the marchers, and the strains of the *Dies Irae* (Hymn of Death) which follow.

Impressionistic music merely suggests a mood, story, or idea, leaving the details to the imagination of the listener. By many this is thought to be the finest type of program music. The greatest master of this type was Debussy, whose elusive effects were often produced through the use of old church modes, the whole-tone scale, unusual harmonies, and an equally unusual manner in the use of them. This is illustrated in his fantasy, *Afternoon of a Faun*.

A very simple piece of program music, in which certain instruments become symbolic of the characters in the story, is MacDowell's *Of a Tailor and a Bear,* one of the *Marionettes* which he wrote under the nom de plume of Edgar Thorne. It is based on a fairytale by Hans Christian Andersen and tells of a tailor who was so fond of music that he always kept a fiddle near him under his bench so that he could play on it when not busy. One day there was a great commotion in the street, and in through the doorway walked a huge bear. The tailor was badly frightened but, remembering that bears are supposed to like music, pulled his violin out and began to play. The bear began to dance, for, after all, it was a tame dancing bear that had broken away from its master. Soon the owner came in and claimed it, to its evident displeasure, and its discontented growls, as it is led away, furnish one of the most delightful moments in the music. The tailor is deftly characterized in this music by the tuning of the violin, and the jolly dance tune that is played. These, with the deep "growls" from the basses, which herald the bear's arrival and departure, make of this a splendid example of realistic imitation.

Another is the episode "Puss in Boots" from Tschaikowsky's ballet of the *Sleeping Beauty,* in which the white cat (through clever orchestral imitation) miaows and spits in cat fashion with superlative drollery.

Less obvious is the orchestral suite *Caucasian Sketches* by Ippolitov-Ivanov, four musical pictures of elemental scenes in the life of a mountain settlement in the Caucasian Mountains, written after the composer has spent some years in Tiflis as a teacher in the music school maintained there by the old Russian Empire. Many of the people of the region are nomad shepherds, and the folk music of the settlements—sung at night or played upon primitive shepherd pipes, about the glowing camp fires or within the shelter of the black tents—is of a wild and barbaric nature.

The first number, "In a Mountain Pass," opens with a persistent horn-call which is echoed and repeated as though reverberating through the deep gorges and difficult mountain trails. The second, "In the Village," suggests a street scene in one of the mountain settlements. The cadenzas for English horn and solo violin (muted) suggest the rhapsodical improvisation of the folk musicians. Soft beating upon the tambour, or Oriental drum, introduces the dance in the village street. "In the Mosque," which follows, is a brief and solemn episode, suggesting a religious service of the East. "March of the Sirdar" (March of the Caucasian Chief) needs no interpretation, as its vivid rhythms and melodies, accentuated by the high shrill tones of the wind instruments, depict a war-like procession against an enemy.

No discussion of "stories in sound" would be complete without reference to the *Scheherazade* suite of Rimsky-Korsakov. Scheherazade, that "Queen of Story-Tellers" of the *Arabian Nights,* is doomed to die the morning after her marriage, but that night she spins a fascinating tale and her life is spared, day by day, so that she may finish it. When the story has continued for a thousand and one nights, the Sultan, in admiration of her courage and resourcefulness, pardons her completely. Each of the pieces of the suite is like a chapter from a book, a complete incident in itself. A special feature of the music is Scheherazade's own theme, a delicate air played by the violin at some time during the progress of each of the stories she tells, and again at the very close of the suite, as though to reassure the listener that she is still alive, like the "signing off" of a radio announcer. Of almost equal interest is the deep-toned melody which suggests the Sultan's voice.

The first sketch, "The Sea and Sindbad's Ship," depicts the restless undulations of the sea, upon which Sindbad has gone adventuring. The

"Tale of the Kalendar Prince" tells the story of the three Kalendars (wandering dervishes) who appear disguised as princes. Scheherazade is heard first (her violin solo accompanied by the harp), after which the bassoon, typifying the Kalendar, is heard, to the accompaniment of a drone from the basses suggesting Oriental bagpipes. Scheherazade's sweet melody concludes the tale. "The Young Prince and the Young Princess" tells a picturesque tale of Oriental courtship, and is accompanied in truly Eastern manner by triangle, tambourines, cymbals, and drums. The suite closes with "Festival at Bagdad," a gorgeously brilliant review of an Oriental fête. The foreboding motif of the sea and the song of the heroine preface the riotous music of the bazaars in which blatant and boisterous noises of old Bagdad are heard to the full.

One need not look for a "story" in all music, but if the composer has given a title or motto, or if the music has a legitimate historical or literary background, it will aid the development of the composer's plan and increase the listener's enjoyment to learn and think about it.

FOLK DANCE AND THE BALLET

RHYTHM is the oldest element of music and before there were other musical instruments men beat upon crude hand-made drums, either to send messages through the air by means of prearranged signals (as is still done in Africa), or as accompaniment to the dance. Folk dancing has always been a popular form of entertainment and the dances of the various nations differ greatly in character, rhythms, and rates of speed. Such folk dancing is a forerunner of the more modern ballet, by which is meant a kind of pantomime opera in which a complete story is told through gesture and dance, aided by costume and scenery, and rhythmic accompaniment of vocal or instrumental music, without a single word being sung or spoken. Some of the most interesting music in the world has been written for the ballet and much of this has also been arranged as concert material for the orchestra.

Other forerunners of the ballet include the ancient Greek choruses which assisted in the presentation of the classic Greek dramas. Records of their art are still to be seen in the frieze on the Parthenon at Athens, in which the dancers are seen in action. Later, when the art of the Greek theater was carried to Rome, an adaptation of the dancers' art was made by the Romans and called pantomime. Musicians were retained to chant the text while a single actor on the stage performed all the gestures and steps expressive of the story.

Then came the "fa-la" dances, so called because of the custom, in the sixteenth century, for composers to write gay dance tunes, to the choruses of which were sung light-hearted refrains on the syllables *fa-la, fa-la,* as in *Now is the Time of Maying.*

With the coming of opera, classic dance numbers, patterned after those of the Greeks, were inserted between the acts. This practice has been continued ever since and not only has the dance itself come to be known as the ballet (from the Italian *ballare,* meaning "to dance") but the special group of people who do the dancing. The dance may tell part of the opera's story, or may be merely a beautiful spectacle.

In certain European countries classic ballet came to mean more than a mere addition to opera, and became a separate art. In Russia schools for the training of ballet dancers were formerly under the direct patronage of the Tsar. Much of the Russian love of color has come to be associated with the music, decorations, and costuming of the ballet, and many composers write especially for it. Anna Pavlowa was the most famous of the many celebrated Russian dancers.

Délibes, a French composer of the past century, devoted his best efforts to the art, and no ballet is more charming or graceful than his musical story of Coppelia, the wonderful mechanical doll, so life-like that she is thought to be alive, both by the village swains and her chagrined rival, Swanilda. (This story is also the basis of an act in Offenbach's opera, *Tales of Hoffmann*.)

Many ballets are based upon familiar subjects, such as the *Mother Goose* by Ravel (written originally as a piano duet, then arranged as a stage ballet, and as an orchestral suite); or on legends handed down from pagan days, such as the famous Russian legend of the "Fire Bird" upon which Igor Stravinsky wrote his celebrated ballet of the same name.

Another ballet by this composer is *The Rite of Spring* (*Le Sacre du Printemps*), a highly dramatic work, primitive in its elemental appeal to the emotions, and modern in its tremendous use of percussion instruments and its harmonic structure. *The Rite of Spring* refers to a pagan custom of the worship of the forces of Nature by means of sacrifice. The first part tells of the adoration of the earth; the second of the sacrifice of the chosen victim, who is the loveliest maiden in the village. Much of the music is in the style of ancient Russian folk song. The climax is a terrific frenzy of rhythm as the maiden dances herself to death. The composer has said that in the music he tried to create a picture of pagan Russia in which the peasants were dancing in the springtime, accompanying the rhythms by their gestures and their feet.

Another modern ballet, but one characteristically American, is *Sky-*

scrapers, written by John Alden Carpenter of Chicago in response to an invitation from Sergei Diaghilev, director of the Russian Ballet, to send him a work that "should embody the bustle and racket of American life, expressed in the prevalent American musical vernacular of jazz." It had its first performance at the Metropolitan Opera House in New York in 1926. *Skyscrapers* reflects the many rhythms and sounds of American life without having any definite story, and shows the American's violent alternation between work and play. It develops in a series of brief sketches. Scene one shows traffic signals at work; scene two shows a skyscraper upon which men in overalls are at work; scene four shows "any Coney Island." The sixth and last scene shows the skyscraper again in relief, and the whole work is a use, on a symphonic scale, of the exhilarating features of jazz. Into the music are also interwoven versions of several American melodies, such as Negro spirituals, "Massa's in de Cold, Cold Ground," and "Yankee Doodle."

A contemporary ballet of unusual romantic charm is *The Jar,* a story of rural life in Sicily, by Alfredo Casella. The plot is from a burlesque tale of Luigi Pirandello, and tells of Don Lollo Zirafe, a rich and miserly farmer who owns a huge oil jar of which he is very proud. An awkward peasant overturns the jar accidentally and breaks a piece from its side. The Don is furious, and calls an old hunchback from the village to mend the damage. That he may do so better, he enters the jar, and when the work is finished finds himself unable to get out. Don Lollo refuses to have the jar broken again, and the hunchback faces a long imprisonment. But he accepts it cheerfully, and as night falls and the moon appears the curls of smoke from his pipe are seen pouring upward from the mouth of the jar. A distant singer begins the air of a popular Sicilian air, *Chiovu,* and the farmer's daughter comes from the house and begins to dance about the jar. Peasant neighbors gather and sing to their imprisoned friend, dance, and make so much noise that the Don cannot sleep. He rushes angrily from the house and in the excitement the jar is sent rolling to the foot of the hill where it strikes an olive tree-trunk and breaks again. The hunchback is then picked up by his friends and carried from the scene on their shoulders in noisy triumph.

HAYDN, MOZART, BEETHOVEN, AND THE CLASSIC SYMPHONY *

THE CASUAL listener to a concert being played by a standard symphony orchestra, conducted, perhaps, by the celebrated Arturo Toscanini, or to one sent over the air from a spacious theater-like studio in Radio City, is apt to take the orchestra for granted and to forget its long years of development which began centuries ago in the incidental grouping together of musical instruments, possibly for the accompanying group for folk dancing or singing.

Then came the matching of similar instruments, as in the "string bands" of twenty-four which were the pleasure of many noble patrons during earlier years. There were also groups of wind and stringed instruments as assembled by Lully, favorite of Louis XIV of France. Special groups sprang into prominence, such as Henry VIII's famous band of sackbuts of the sixteenth century; and the Austrian and German town bands like those in which so many members of the Bach family played that, in certain neighborhoods, all town pipers came to be spoken of as "the Bachs." The size and grouping of an orchestra was then dependent upon the pleasure or purse of its patron, and this explains the seeming oddities in composition of those composers who wrote for instruments before standardization of the orchestra took place.

The formation of the orchestra was also influenced by its use as accompaniment to dramatic action. In 1600, when *Eurydice* (the "first opera") had its first performance, an added "feature" was the playing of three flutes behind the scenes to furnish the music simulated by the shepherd Tirsi who, on the stage, held a triple-flute in his hands and pretended to play.

* See "The Orchestra and Its Instruments" and "From Greek Drama to Radio Opera," pages 69 and 38.

Later in the century Alessandro Scarlatti (1659-1725), the famed virtuoso, showed a preference for bowed instruments. Handel and Bach, both born a few years later, in 1685, and only thirty miles apart, each used the orchestra in an individually expressive way. Meanwhile, the instruments themselves were being developed.

A detailed study of the Bach orchestras would repay any music lover. It was in 1714, when he was less than thirty years old, that Bach entered ducal service at Weimar where one of his duties was the direction of the court orchestra. His was a very small organization, the records still extant showing that there were, altogether, twelve players, of whom three played the violin; one, the viola; one, bassoon; six, the trumpet; and one, the drum.

At Anhalt-Cöthen, to which Bach went as chapel-master three years later, his orchestra was made up chiefly of stringed instruments. There were only eight regular players. Four extra players were available for special occasions, in addition to which there was a corps of three trumpeters who also played the drum when needed. But the Prince and his friends also owned instruments and frequently played with the musicians. For them Bach wrote much of his finest chamber music, including the four *Overture* suites * in which the flute (the Prince's favorite instrument) played a prominent part.

In Leipzig, where Bach spent the last twenty-seven years of his life, his orchestra regularly numbered from eighteen to twenty, and their unusual seating arrangement is shown in prints, made at the time, showing Bach and his musicians in the church choir-loft. In their use as accompaniment to his church and secular cantatas, Bach often used the instruments in an almost naïve manner, that they might stress the meaning of the text. He wrote no violin music he could not play himself, this fact proving his unusual ability as a performer. Handel also used the instruments in special settings.

The middle of the eighteenth century saw further improvement of the flute and oboe and a quite widespread use of the clarinet.

The years in which Haydn and Mozart wrote their first master-

* For analysis of *Overture* No. 2, see page 260.

pieces were those which saw the culmination of the so-called "classical" period. Haydn was encouraged in all his experiments toward standardization of the orchestra by his royal patron, Prince Esterhazy. He had, at first, only a tiny group of players—six first violins and other strings in proportion; one flute, two oboes, two bassoons, two horns, two trumpets, and drums. The harpsichord, which had served as a foundation for the orchestra for so long—even by the famous Mannheim "school" under Johann Stamitz (1717-1757)—was now found to be unnecessary. Haydn assembled the instruments into definite choirs (wind, brass, string, and percussion). Mozart added the clarinet and trombone. Beethoven added more clarinets and extra horns and so employed the entire group that each instrument became an individual, contributing its own peculiar personality to the ensemble.

Twenty-three years passed between the performance of Beethoven's first symphony (C Major, 1800) and his ninth, the wonderful *Choral Symphony*. No more effective illustration of both the charms and the limitations of the "classical symphony" could be made than in both seeing and hearing its reproduction as done so faithfully by Toscanini in the "Beethoven Cycle" given by the Philharmonic Symphony Society of New York under his direction during the season of 1932-1933. At that time the Symphony reproduced the exact size and instrumentation of the organization for which Beethoven scored his first symphony (two flutes, two oboes, two clarinets, two bassoons, two horns, two trumpets, timpani, and strings).

Later composers molded the orchestra to their own needs and ideas. Weber, Mendelssohn, and Berlioz either introduced new instruments into the different choirs, or multiplied the numbers of those already present. Wagner regrouped the wind instruments and divided the strings, using various instruments so as to produce remarkable and unique effects. Modern composers have added many devices, particularly among the percussion choir, but these are not the fundamentals which will, doubtless, remain for many years what they were in the days of Haydn, Mozart, and Beethoven, the three great masters of form.

THE "ROMANTIC" IDEA IN MUSIC—SCHUBERT, CHOPIN, AND SCHUMANN

THE MIDDLE of the nineteenth century is known as the "Romantic" period in music history, and those composers who wrote between about 1875 and 1900 are grouped in a general way as post-romantic.

The musical meaning of the word *classic* is a reverence for formal beauty. That of *romantic* is that the emphasis is given to the meaning of the music—what it *says* to the listener. In vocal music one may contrast a formal composition of Palestrina with the choral accompaniment to the ballet in *Prince Igor* by Borodin; in instrumental music one may contrast a *Pastorale* of Corelli with *Russian Easter* by Rimsky-Korsakov.

In romantic music the subject chosen as the title is usually fanciful and the treatment of it is unconventional and exciting, representing the personality and mood of the composer. Great masters of the period include Chopin, Schubert, Schumann, Robert Franz, and Mendelssohn; with Beethoven, whose most classic works are pervaded with romantic feeling acting as a link to earlier periods; and Johannes Brahms as its climax.

Further contrasts of "classic" and "romantic" compositions may include the formally beautiful *Surprise Symphony in G* by Haydn, with the "March to the Scaffold" from the *Symphonie Fantastique* by Berlioz. Both are orchestral works. The earlier work is classic in its use, for instance, in the familiar second movement (with the drum Bang! from which the symphony takes its name) of one of the oldest musical forms, the theme with variations. The little theme is as simple as a folk song, and is followed by four brilliant variations and a tiny coda.

Or one may compare a formal sonata for harpsichord with a piano composition by Robert Schumann, such as his delightful "Scenes from Childhood." These are thirteen very short pieces each of which is a poetic reflection upon the joys of childhood, the seventh of them being the delicate "Träumerei." The suite closes, after "The Child Falls Asleep," with a musical retrospect, "The Poet Speaks."

In his "Papillons" Schumann follows the same general plan. Each of the sketches is short, and they are nameless. The set closes with a reference to an old folk air and custom, the "Grandfather's Dance," toward the end of which the bell in the church tower is heard striking the hour as the dancers stroll homeward.

In his brilliant and extremely difficult "Davidsbündler" (David's Band Dances) Schumann refers to the Biblical story of the Philistines and their warfare against the followers of David. The reference is symbolic and suggests two rival "schools" of musicians—the classic and the more modern. He also gives expression to the two natures within each person, allowing the title Eusebius to represent the tender, gentler nature, and Florestan, the more vivid and sensational mood.

Schumann's "Carnaval," one of the most favored program numbers of all concert pianists, is equally romantic.

Mendelssohn's graceful "Songs Without Words" (including the favorite "Spring Song," "Spinning Song," and "Hunting Song") as well as the utterly charming *Midsummer Night's Dream Overture* with its open references to the magic realm of Fairyland, awaken the imagination of the hearer in a manner which is one of the aims of the "romantic" composers.

The romantic period also owes much to the beauties of the music of the gifted Schubert, or to the supreme art of Chopin as expressed in his poetic piano works.

Brahms, whose mastery of the technique of composition and love of formal beauty for its own sake is shown by the classic charm of his four symphonies and his "Haydn" (and other) variations, also wrote expressive romantic works of which his early "Ballade" for piano, founded on the Scotch ballad of "Edward," is an example.

The truest test of the value of any Romantic piece of music is not to be found in its general popularity, however great or small that may be, but in its subtle but sure power to carry the listener unconsciously past the commonplace or trivial, into the imaginative realm of the ideal.

BRAHMS AND "ABSOLUTE" MUSIC

"ABSOLUTE" music may be defined as music written for beauty's sake and without any thought of expressing, in it, a definite mood or story.

Some music may be considered as either absolute or program music, depending on the listener's point of view and his information concerning it. An illustration of this is Beethoven's Sonata, Opus 27, No. 2, sometimes known as the "Moonlight Sonata." The listener who is unfamiliar with this music and hears it mentioned or sees it listed on a program by its opus number only, will expect to find the music formally proportioned, and beautiful for that reason. Should he, however, know the legend of Beethoven's visit to the blind girl, whose playing he is said to have overheard while passing her home, and his improvisation at her piano, later written out and used as the first movement of this sonata, he is apt to hear in the music a suggestion of the romantic story. And the fact that this first movement does not happen to be written in true formal design, but as a fantasy, will help him to interpret it in that way.

Some pieces really belong to both divisions, as the Beethoven *Pastoral Symphony,* which has both form and story.

Of those great composers whose instrumental music needs no story (program) to add to its popularity is Johannes Brahms, whose works—such as the four symphonies, and the *"Tragic"* and *"Academic Festival" Overtures,* or the twenty-four larger pieces of chamber music—are celebrated for devotion to simple classic beauty. A knowledge of Brahms's life-history adds to the enjoyment of the music.

Brahms was born on May 7, 1833, in Hamburg, the son of one of the best double-bass players in the city. The father, a member of one of the early "little German bands," was the boy's first teacher, but took him, at the age of ten, to Otto Cossel, assuring that teacher that "Johannes is to learn just as much as you know, no more." Later Cossel took the youth to Edward Marxsen, his own teacher, to whose careful instruction Brahms paid tribute all his life.

When just a small boy Brahms wanted to write music and confided to a friend that his "best tunes" always came to him as he blacked the family boots in the early morning. He was thoroughly acquainted with several instruments, thanks to his father's insistence that he should be able to play at cafés and dances, and to take his part in arranging music for and playing in the little bands.

Brahms was deeply fond of folk songs, and in his later years made collections of them which earned him the gratitude of all music lovers. He was also fond of the way of writing music known as variation form, in which a chosen melody is repeated several times, but always in a different way, the change being made through alteration of key, from major to minor or minor to major, of tempo, of rhythm, of accompaniment, of melodic embellishment, or in still other ways which the art and imagination of the composer may devise. His first known composition was in this variation form, his début program as a pianist, at the age of fourteen, including variations on a folk tune. Among his most scholarly and brilliant compositions in later life are the celebrated "Paganini" and "Handel" variations for piano (on themes by those masters); two sets written on themes by Robert Schumann; the variations which form the final movement of the *Fourth Symphony;* and the remarkable "Haydn" variations for orchestra, so called because their theme is one used, years before, by Haydn, in his *Divertimenti.* He frequently used folk songs as variation themes, as in his Sonata in C, Opus 1.

When he was sixteen, Brahms met Edward Remenyi, the Hungarian violinist, and, through him, Joachim, the eminent violinist whose friendship was to influence the rest of his life. Through Remenyi, whom Brahms accompanied on a concert tour, he became acquainted with

Hungarian folk song and its rare charm, and his first work to gain world fame was a set of dances based upon Hungarian airs.

In the fall of 1853 Brahms met Robert and Clara Schumann and this was the turning point in his career, for Schumann wrote the celebrated article entitled "New Paths" in which he hailed Brahms as the "coming Messiah" of modern music. So that he might be more fitted for his life work, Brahms went to the small town of Detmold, where he held a small musical post. Here he worked for several years making a serious study of all the great classic music of earlier composers, and at a self-drill in writing counterpoint which included a regular exchange of contrapuntal exercises between him and Joachim. It was his complete mastery of contrapuntal writing, and consequent ability to develop a theme in a rich and complex manner, which impart to the four symphonies (discussed in greater detail on pages 281–3) their varied and bewildering beauty.

Critics of Brahms were at first apt to say that his music was dry and pedantic, because of its formal perfection. Now some of them say that it is too melodious, this because of the composer's lifelong attachment to folk song and his attempts to reflect its artful simplicity in his own work. In any case Brahms's music speaks for itself and he is recognized as one of the most scholarly and also popular of composers.

ORCHESTRAL SUITES, CLASSIC
AND MODERN

NO PART of an orchestral concert program is more certain of a general popularity than the suite which is so often included in it. There are several reasons for this. One is that the suite is usually made up of fairly short pieces, each of which is quite easy of comprehension and interpretation. Many suites make an especial use of certain instrumental effects not so frequently heard in longer works, where they might become tiresome. Also, a suite, whether it be of classic or modern style, is always unified by some central idea. In the classic suite (which may be written in the present year, as well as in the far-off past), the central idea is usually a certain key, or tonality. All of the parts of the suite are written with regard to established form (the so-called suite-form being a two-part form). The modern suite is usually a story-telling piece of music in which each separate part is like the chapter of a book which is complete within itself and yet contributes to the dramatic effect of the whole.

The history of the suite leads to the Orient where the Arab singers of the great deserts were accustomed, even in early centuries, to making arrangements of little sets of short barbaric folk songs in which each little song formed a contrast in mood or style to the one which had just been sung.*

Many of the oldest written suites were simply collections of pretty folk airs, or of quaint court dances such as the minuet or the gavotte. The music of these, planned at first only as an accompaniment to dancing, became pieces for performance. Many of them were first arranged for the early keyboard instruments and the ever-popular lute.

* A modern vocal suite is the set of "Children's Songs" by Moussorgsky. See page 229.

For many years all music copying had to be done by hand, but as the art of printing developed, composers were able to publish longer pieces. One of the oldest suites written for the harpsichord, and yet still heard on concert programs, is the very unusual "Bible" sonata called "David and Goliath" written by Johann Kuhnau in 1700. In the different sections of this suite the composer tells, in very thrilling manner, the episodes in the lives of these Old Testament heroes.

Josef Haydn also wrote a suite of seven orchestral pieces to illustrate a Biblical text. It is a setting of the "Seven Last Words of Christ" and was composed for the use of the Cathedral at Cadiz in Spain. An eighth piece which he called "The Earthquake" forms an end-piece to the suite.

Some of the instruments played in the early centuries were mechanical and might be tuned at will, but to a single key. The lute is an example of this. The player had then only to follow the tablature (the early music notation which indicated the fingers to be used, rather than the pitch of the notes) and so, naturally, groups of pieces played one after the other were put into one key so that the instrument need not be tuned again. The variety and contrast was secured mainly through changes in rhythm or rate of speed. This, in part, explains why the classic suite usually is written in a single key.

These sets of pieces were known by different names in different countries—*suites,* in England; *partitas,* in Germany; and *sonata da camera,* in Italy. Some were also known as sonatas, or as overtures, though written in genuine suite form.

The term *suite* was never used by Bach, who wrote four important works of this character for the pleasure of the Prince Leopold of Anhalt-Cöthen, calling them *overtures.* (I, C Major; II, B Minor; III and IV, D Major.) Their original parts may now be seen in the Royal Library of Berlin.

The typical pattern of a classic suite is illustrated by the second Bach Suite, written in seven parts, all of which are in the same general key and which are introduced by an overture in French style, as follows:

1. "Overture," a quaint old-style movement in three-part form, acting

as a prelude to the dance movements. 2. "Rondeau," * in the manner of the old-time circle dance. Here the main air is heard three times, contrasted with other themes. 3. "Sarabande" (in the related key of D Major), is in the style of an Oriental type of folk dance common to Spanish life in the sixteenth century. The principal melody is introduced by flute and violin. 4. "Bourrée." This movement is in two parts, each of which might easily be played as a separate piece. 5. "Polonaise," in the Trio section of which the flute introduces an ornate obbligato to the main melody. 6. "Minuet," in the manner of a lively court dance. 7. "Badinerie," the name of which comes from the old Provençal word which meant "a sprightly jest." The main air of this gay number is played by the flute.

Many of the charming old-time dances might not be heard at all today were it not for the artistic transcriptions † made of them by contemporary composers. This is illustrated by the suite, *Old Dances and Airs for the Lute* assembled and freely transcribed by Ottorino Respighi for the modern symphonic orchestra. This faithfully preserves the spirit and style of the original pieces which are: 1. "Balleto detto Il Conte Orlando" by Molinaro (born, 1599, in Genoa, and *maestro di cappella* at the cathedral in Genoa. A famous lutenist). 2. "Gagliardi" by Vincenzo Galilei, father of the celebrated astronomer. The *galliard* was an old dance of extremely lively character in 3-2 meter. 3. "Villanella," composer unknown. (This was a title formerly used with an otherwise unaccompanied rustic dance.) 4. "Posso mezzo e mascheradi," composer unknown. (This is of the type of the old-time Italian dance known as a *Pavan.* When less stately in character it is called *mascherade,* a dance for masked revelers at a fête.)

Respighi has also transcribed, as a suite for small orchestra, a number of graceful harpsichord works of the seventeenth and eighteenth centuries, under the general title of *The Birds,* a typical selection being Rameau's "The Hen." Not only is this Italian composer interested in the

---

* An example of the rondo, in prose, may be seen in Psalm CXXXVI, in which, throughout twenty-seven verses, the refrain is constant, "For His mercy endureth forever."
† See "The Art of Transcription," page 121.

old-time music, but he has written an original suite, *Four Symphonic Impressions (Church Windows)*, each "impression" taking for its subject the figures seen on a stained-glass window in a Roman church. The four suite movements are 1. "The Flight into Egypt"; 2. "St. Michael Archangelo"; 3. "The Matins of Santa Chiara"; and 4. "St. Gregorio Magno." Into these Respighi has interwoven appropriate suggestion of old church modes.

In sharp contrast to the more austere suites of older writers is the vague and impressionistic music of Debussy who, in his suite, *Nocturnes,* for orchestra, has suggested the ethereal and transient appearances of the clouds, their intangible texture, and their constantly changing coloring and rhythm. In this suite of three pieces Debussy has outlined his own ideas but left it to each listener to fill in his own imaginative interpretation. The first movement, "Nuages" (Clouds), is a slow and delicate prelude, mystical in its suggestion of the passage of clouds across the heavens. The second, "Fêtes" (Festivals), suggests the restless motion of a fantastic procession. The suite closes with "Sirènes," a glamorous picture of the sea, its undulating motion, its colors, and its fantastic tales of sirens and mermaids. At one place the composer uses women's voices as though they were instruments to suggest the gay laughter and song of the sirens.

Many other gifted composers have contributed to the rich store of popular suite literature, among whom are such notable Americans as Edward MacDowell (*Indian Suite*), Edgar Stillman Kelley (*Alice in Wonderland*), and Douglas Stuart Moore (*Pageant of P. T. Barnum*).

One of the most impressive of modern symphonic suites is Gustav Holst's set of pieces which he calls *The Planets*. In this he gives to each of the planets a musical picturing of its mythological character. The son of a British musician, and educated at the Royal College of Music where he specialized in the study of the trombone, Holst has given much prominence to the wind and brass instruments. "Mars," god of war, is symbolized by music of wild and barbaric style. The use of irregular 5-4 meter, an incessantly repeated rhythmic figure, and much dissonance help to create the effect. "Venus" is a delicate bit of music, charmingly scored. "Mercury" is a modern scherzo in which much humor is created through clever use of the harp, piano, and percussion instruments. "Jupiter," "bringer of jollity," develops into a typically British march. "Saturn," "bringer of old age," is a magnificent episode. It opens with a relentless *ostinato* (set figure), and in the middle section is a sinister passage suggesting the constant ticking of the clock of time. "Uranus" is followed by "Neptune," with which the suite closes, and here the human voice is again used as an orchestral instrument, singing its part on the syllable *ah*.

FAMOUS OVERTURES

THE principal purpose of an overture, according to the older meaning of the word, is to act as a starting piece or introduction to a larger piece of music, such as an opera, oratorio, or suite. The words prelude, præludium, préambule, and prologue have the same general meaning. As the individual instruments became more perfect, and the organization of the orchestra became more definite, there appeared new and attractive incentives to composers to write other instrumental concert works than symphonies. So it came about that the concert overture came into being, and many of the most popular works written for orchestra are these independent compositions.

When used to introduce an opera or ballet the overture usually suggests, through its use of musical themes, the principal characters or events in the opera; or else, through its general atmosphere, "sets the scene." A charming illustration of this is heard in Humperdinck's *Hansel and Gretel*. Here the opening notes of the Overture are those of the simple little "prayer theme" heard at some time during each act of the opera to reassure the listener that the children have not come to harm. There then follow, in quick succession, the "disenchantment" theme, a bit of the Dew Fairy's graceful song, and a repetition of the prayer song, so that, by the time the action of the opera begins, the audience is already familiar with several of its most alluring melodies.

In some other operas, however, the overture has little to do with the atmosphere or action of the drama that follows, serving only as an elegant and dignified opening piece, a composition beautiful and complete in itself. This is illustrated by the brilliant overture to Mozart's *Magic Flute*.

Wagner gave a "program" character to many of the overtures that he wrote as introductions to his music-dramas. The overture to *Die Meistersinger* includes the sturdy melody later associated in the drama with the mastersingers' guild, a reference to the love-duet of Eva and Walter, the "marching theme" of the singers (heard in the main body of the opera during the second scene of Act III), and a fervent presentation of the air later used by the victorious Walter in his "Prize Song."

In the overture to *Parsifal*, Wagner's last opera, to which he added the sub-title "A Sacred Festival Drama," he created music of an exquisitely devotional character partly by means of a constantly repeated and upward-moving progression of sixths taken from the celebrated *Amen* of the Saxon liturgy, known familiarly as the "Dresden" *Amen* from the fact that it was used at the court church at Dresden. This drama is based upon the medieval legend of the Grail, the cup supposedly used by Jesus at the Last Supper, and by Joseph of Arimathea at the Crucifixion. It is therefore appropriate that the musical theme afterwards identified with the Grail is also introduced into the overture.

The overture is also an important feature of the suite, whether it be written in classic or modern style. No more attractive example of a miniature "opening piece" can be cited than the dainty overture which introduces the action in Tschaikowsky's ballet (and orchestral suite) on the tale of the *Nutcracker*. This music, in the ballet, accompanies the procession of the dolls and other toys as they march about the Christmas tree. It is written in classic sonatina form.

Modern composers have devoted their finest efforts, in many cases, to writing concert overtures which do not depend upon any further story for interpretation. Brahms, in his *Academic Festival Overture* (See page 279), has made development of themes in classic manner, rather than story-telling, the basis of his work, although local color is introduced by his use of familiar student songs which he had once heard at Göttingen while a guest of Joachim.

Rimsky-Korsakov, on the other hand, has used all the instrumental devices of the orchestra to depict the romantic program of his *Russian Easter Overture* (*La Grande Pâque Russe*), in which he also included themes of a national character. This music aims to picture the mood and almost pagan merry-making of the "Bright Holiday," as the Easter celebration of the Greek Orthodox Church of Russia was often called. To his music the composer prefixed a selection of appropriate Biblical texts which include passages from the Psalms and the story of the resurrection as told in the Gospel of St. Mark. In the music he reproduced many of the sounds he had heard as a boy when he lived near the Tikhvin Monastery. The early part of the overture suggests the plain-song chant of old Greek liturgy. A later section gives prominence to startling percussion effects, and recalls in realistic manner the rhythmic chiming of the bells in old-time Russia.

THE SYMPHONIC POEM

S TORY-TELLING music, discussed in earlier chapters, is written in many ways. Story-telling (or "program") music for orchestra is found in many famous symphonies (as in the "Village Festival" movement of Beethoven's *Pastoral Symphony*), in such popular overtures as Rossini's *William Tell,* and in such colorful orchestral suites as the *Scheherazade* music by Rimsky-Korsakov. Another way in which writers of orchestral music have created story-telling pieces is in a form known as the *symphonic poem,* so called because of its symphonic proportions and use of all the resources of the modern orchestra while remaining freer in form than the strict symphony. No two symphonic poems are ever alike in their form for no two stories are ever alike, and the pattern followed by the symphonic poem and its use of certain instruments or instrumental combinations is dictated entirely by the story or "program" which is being followed.

One of the first composers to make extended use of the form was Franz Liszt, the spectacular Hungarian pianist, and the fact that most symphonic poems are inspired by legend, history, or literature is illustrated by Liszt's choice of subjects. One of his most familiar symphonic poems is *Les Préludes,* a connected series of thirteen emotional impressions based upon the *Méditations Poétique* by Alphonse Lamartine, an extract from which Liszt prefixed to his music: "What is our life but a series of preludes to that unknown song, the first solemn note of which is sounded by death?"

Another of the Liszt symphonic poems is his popular *Mazeppa,* in which is given, through music, a stirring account of the historic ride of that Cossack chief of the seventeenth century. Mazeppa was a page at the court of the King of Poland. As punishment for misbehavior, he was corded to the back of a wild horse. After a terrible ride he gained his freedom and in later years became an Ukrainian prince. Local color is brought into Liszt's realistic music through his use of barbaric rhythms of Eastern song, the melody of a Cossack march, and martial trumpet calls.

Another user of this form is the French composer Saint-Saëns, whose *Danse Macabre* (Dance of Death) and *Le Rouet d'Omphale* (Omphale's Spinning Wheel)—two of a series of four symphonic poems— are extremely popular. The first follows a medieval legend in which, on Hallowe'en, all the skeletons emerge from their graves to dance. In it the striking of the midnight hour is heard, Death is heard tuning his fiddle, and the dance proceeds, continuing until the crowing of the cock announces the approaching dawn. The other poem follows a story of Hercules at the court of Omphale, where, as a punishment for having killed Iphitus he is forced to spin with the Queen's maidens.

A more modern composer whose works in this form are widely known is Friedrich Smetana, a pupil of Liszt. After his student days Smetana set himself a task of glorifying Bohemia, his native land, in music. This patriotic devotion was expressed by the writing of an elaborate cycle of six symphonic poems to which he gave the general title of *My Fatherland,* and of which the most picturesque is the highly descriptive "Moldau." This music contains several parts which, taken together, describe this Bohemian river from its source in a tiny brook (impersonated by a single violin), through its union with other brooks (other instruments are added, one at a time), to its impressive and triumphant passage through the old city of Prague. The varied beauties which the music suggests include the forest, the wide meadows, and the historic ruins and historic buildings past which it flows. In the section called "Hunt in the Forest," the sound of a hunter's horn is heard; the rhythms of a polka, the national dance of Bohemia, are heard in section three, "Peasant Wedding"; and the climax, "Vyšehrad," referring to historic ruins, is of a dignified and hymn-like style. At the close the theme which represented the river at the beginning is again heard,

ARTURO TOSCANINI

IGOR STRAVINSKY

LEOPOLD
STOKOWSKI

SERGEI KOUSSEVITZKY

BRASS INSTRUMENTS
Left to right: TUBA; TROM-
BONE; FRENCH HORN

PERCUSSION INSTRUMENTS
Left to right: GONG; CAS-
TANET; TAMBOURINE; TRI-
ANGLE; CYMBALS

decreasing in volume as the waters of the stream flow along on their way to other scenes.

Many contemporary writers have delighted in using this free and flexible form in their composition and its constantly growing popularity is one of the greatest possible evidences of its intrinsic value.

CHAMBER MUSIC, PAST AND PRESENT

I N THE British Museum there hangs an interesting picture of Handel and a group of musicians. It is a chamber orchestra and some of the music is being made by the players and some by singers. The players are divided into three groups. The first, at Handel's right, is made up of two violins, a 'cello, and two flutes. This group of soloists is called the *concertino*. Next there is a group of accompanying players (the *concerto grosso,* or large ensemble). Last of all are the supplementary musicians, known in those days as the *ripienists,* who strengthen the parts of the larger group as needed. In the center, seated at the clavier, the lid of which is raised, sits Handel, directing the whole group in their music-making by means of directions and glances.

Other pictures of the period illustrate the manner of performance and the constant depiction of instrumentalists and vocalists together explain the old description of chamber music—"apt for voyces and viols." Chamber music is generally understood, today, to be exclusively instrumental music suitable for performance in a small or private room, when it really refers to both vocal and instrumental music. The Germans use the word *Hausmusik* to designate it, but the more common name comes from the Italian *musica da camera,* meaning "room" music.

One of the loveliest features about chamber music is that so much of it may be played by the amateur, by which is meant that musician who sings or plays because he likes music so much and not because he is seeking a career or gain from its performance.

The origin of chamber music may be traced back to the Middle Ages. All music was then performed by one person, or else, as in the case of the church chants, in unison. Even there one found no great mass singing. Although the troubadours and similar types of singers may often have sung together it was not until about the sixteenth century that there was mass feeling for music. Chamber music was then just a part of every-day life and one reads of the "dinner music" of those early folk who, seated about a table, sang familiar and popular airs of their day to the accompaniment of their quaint instruments. It was a usual thing for any cultured person to be able to read his part in the music, and the chief accompanying instrument was the lute which had a special form of notation known as tablature. Examples of the music thus used include the lovely madrigals of William Byrde, John Dunhill, and Thomas Morley of England, whose "Plaine and Easie Introduction to Practicall Musicke" was the popular instruction book of the age.

Up to about 1650 the music was comparatively easy to perform, partly because of tablature and partly because of the instruments themselves. The viol which was commonly used was much simpler than the present-day violin, and a chest of viols (the term used for a complete set) was customary in every upper class home. Frequently the players had already sung the music, and so were familiar with its melodies and rhythms.

From the very beginning there was an interest in variations, known in England as "divisions," in which extra notes were added for ornamentation of the melody. The favorite instruments on which these "divisions" were played were the virginal, the gamba (ancestor of the 'cello), and the lute. Folk tunes were in constant use as themes. The composers soon began to write instrumental variations, taking for their models the improvisations of the amateur performers.

These were also the days of the chamber orchestra, which is again being revived for the delight of all classes of music lovers, as it can perform music of an orchestral character without requiring the huge apparatus of the modern symphony.

It was Haydn who took chamber music back to the contrapuntal perfection which vocal music had reached under Palestrina nearly two hundred years before. Haydn had sung the exquisitely fluent music of Palestrina as a choir boy in Vienna and set out to give purely instrumental music the same grace and elegance. At first he used the harpsichord to assist the strings in the same way that his forerunners among the composers had done when the old-time viols needed its support. As he came to a realization of the absolute perfection and balance of such a combination as that which is known as the string quartet—first and second violins, viola, and 'cello—he devoted all his finest efforts to writing music for that combination. This standardization of the string quartet is one of the several important steps for which his name is honored in the history of music.

Although stringed instruments became the leaders in the field of chamber music all others followed them, including such wind instruments as the flute, the oboe, and the bassoon. Wind instruments are given great prominence in the chamber music of today.

An unexpected aid to the growth of chamber music was the *collegium musicum,* the name taken by groups of students in various university towns who gathered at their university or in the open square for the performance of music at definite occasions or festivals. These societies became the life of their communities and to their activities is due the inspiration of some of the finest instrumental "serenade" suites written, such as Mozart's *Kleine Nachtmusik* (Night Music).

Although there is much chamber music written for every conceivable combination of instruments, the string quartet remains the finest and most beautiful combination of all. Next in beauty may be the string quintet, the classic "favorite" among quintets being the celebrated *Minuet* by Boccherini. In these combinations an immense variety of tone color is possible, each instrument sounding as an individual voice with its unique personality. During the last century technical ability in performance increased and with it a different and more professional attitude toward playing, and the formation of such remarkable chamber music groups as the Flonzaley, Kneisel, Lenz, Roth, Pro Arte, and Gordon String Quartets.

At the opening of the century Debussy was the central figure in impressionism with its vague and subtle appeal to the imagination. He wrote for such unusual combinations as the saxophone, flute, harp, and viola. Some still more modern composers, desiring realistic effects, as opposed to impressionism, have written highly imitative chamber music. There is now, however, a tendency toward the composition of music beautiful not only in form but for what it "says," and toward the use of folk melodies as thematic material, so charmingly illustrated by Haydn, by Percy Grainger, and, in America, by such an appealing and inspired composition as the beautiful quartet based on Negro melodies by Daniel Gregory Mason.

CHAMBER MUSIC AND
ELIZABETH SPRAGUE COOLIDGE *

BY CARL ENGEL, *Chief, Music Division, Library of Congress* †

THOUGH the Muses are trying to forget their Olympian descent and the liberal arts would pass for plebeian, chamber music, if anything, throws back its head more proudly. Born and reared at court, it never feels quite at home in humbler surroundings. Hailed and seized upon as *Hausmusik,* it suffers the enthusiasm of scratching and squeaking amateurs, but surrenders not a particle of its perogatives. Familiarly dubbed "room-music," it ignores the slur and remains as distant as ever.

Chamber music is essentially an aristocratic art. It needs the support of the discriminating and the rich. It must lean upon such patronage all the more in a day that exalts the massive effects and Brobdingnagian proportions of symphonies "of the thousands" and "bowl" audiences of ten thousand.

No doubt, true chamber music is an anachronism, yet it flourishes at present with the vigor of a strong, fresh plant rather than with the

---

* William Cobbett of London has said, "Mrs. Coolidge is the 'Lady Bountiful' of chamber music. Her benefactions are on a scale so generous as to transcend the bounds of what any lover of the art could in his most sanguine moments have expected from a single individual."

† New ideas in art usually have a "rocky road" to travel, and the offer of a helping hand and comprehending mind may be of incalculable value in the development of young creators. Mr. Engel draws a parallel between Elizabeth Sprague Coolidge, of our times, and de la Pouplinière of the eighteenth century—two people separated by hundreds of years, but each maintaining, in his or her generation, the same unswerving standards of discrimination, intelligent generosity, and hospitality to new ideas. The salon of de la Pouplinière constituted, in his day, "a musical laboratory for an art in the stage of transition"; similarly, Mrs. Coolidge's activities in founding the Berkshire Festivals of Chamber Music, and endowing the Library of Congress that it may present concerts of finely prepared compositions.

tenacity of a surviving old tree. One reason is that the composers of the experimental school, like the innovators of an earlier age, have found concerted music of smaller dimensions best adapted to their tentative methods. But chiefly responsible for the revival of a patrician and more or less cerebral form of art, in the midst of shallow "popularization," are the gallant efforts of a few intelligent and munificent fanatics who have had the good sense to make chamber music once more fashionable.

It is not too extravagant to compare our day with the heyday of chamber music: we have first-rate composers and players of it in abundance and certainly we can match an Alexandre Jean Joseph Le Riche de la Pouplinière * with an Elizabeth Sprague Coolidge. A number of resemblances between the two come instantly to mind. Thrice blest, she has the knowledge, the taste, and the means, which enable her to do whatever she does on a large, on a princely scale. And these virtues are capped with her kindness, her golden heart, which makes her the fairy-godmother of music and musicians. She is not "one of the world's richest persons." But she accomplishes more with her generosity than people who command ten times her wealth.

When de la Pouplinière felt his end was near, he wrote his testament. It began: "Considering the way I have lived, probably no one will wonder at the little that I leave." His estate, though still far from that of a pauper, was decidedly shrunk. His yearly expenditures had amounted to the equivalent of twenty thousand pounds sterling and more. Music took up a large slice of this. For over twenty years he enjoyed the company of Rameau, and his services as conductor and

* De la Pouplinière was born at Chinon, France (the scene of Joan of Arc's historic meeting with the Dauphin of France), in 1693, the fifty-first year of the reign of Louis XIV, his family having been prominent since 1438. He was employed in the revenue department of the government, but, a lover of the best music of his time, became a patron of musicians. His wife was a pupil of Rameau and wrote an analysis of his "General Harmony," and for more than a score of years Rameau, a precocious clavier-player, celebrated French organist, writer on harmony, and composer whose prestige finally displaced that of Lully, the King's favorite, was a member of de la Pouplinière's household. From 1745 on, theatrical performances were held in his own house, including those given by the *Bouffons,* or Italian comedians. Many steps in the development of the modern symphony were taken in his salon in its use as a "musical laboratory." Rameau was for a time conductor there, also Stamitz, and Gossec.

organist. Then came misunderstandings and a parting. Johann Stamitz succeeded Rameau and acquainted Paris with the ways and arts of the Mannheim orchestra.

If de la Pouplinière supported an orchestra of fair size—at his death in 1762, when Gossec was the conductor, it numbered about twenty— he did so not because of a desire for ostentation, but because he prized good music. He loved splendor and enjoyed the good things of this world, having the instinct of excellence. If his patronage of music has left an indelible mark on some pages of musical history, it is chiefly due to the fact that the salon of de la Pouplinière was not the rendez-vous of the great and the smart, but the "musical laboratory" for an art in the stage of transition.

Some day the story of Elizabeth Sprague Coolidge will be written and in many ways it is likely to resemble that of de la Pouplinière. He had the advantage of an insatiable artistic curiosity. He revered Rameau, but he was above all things *"le protecteur des jeunes, des débutants, des étrangers."*

Just so Mrs. Coolidge joins to the cult of the old masters the love and encouragement of the new. She has imported to America many European composers and performers. She has introduced to Europe many works written especially for her. Their list by now is a long one. It betokens a catholic choice that includes Malipiero, Loeffler, Bloch, Schoenberg, Ravel, Frank Bridge, Goossens, Arthur Bliss, Pizzetti, Casella, Respighi, and many more. There is a slight preponderance of British and Italian composers, possibly in keeping with a predeliction for London, Venice, and Rome. Also the young and the venturesome are conspicuous. Mrs. Coolidge is ever eager to discover new beauties, new talents. And her joy of discovery is surpassed only by her satisfaction in letting others share her joy. The charity that is applied to the crea-tion of a "thing of beauty" has lasting ends in view.

Out of a chance suggestion made to her by her old and devoted friend, Frederick Stock, were born the Berkshire Festivals of Chamber Music at Pittsfield, in the autumn of 1918. A "house-quartet," with Hugo Kortschak as leader, formed the nucleus. It was engaged origi-

THE GORDON STRING QUARTET

JOHN ALDEN CARPENTER

A. WALTER KRAMER

FRANK LaFORGE   SIDNEY HOMER

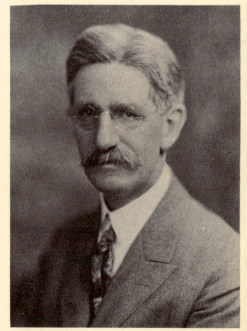

nally to help while away days over which sickness and death, grief and loneliness, had cast their shadows. The pastime became a vocation. Since then Mrs. Coolidge has grown into a national and international figure in music. She has been decorated with the Royal Order of Leopold by the King of Belgium, and with the cross of the Legion of Honor by the French Republic. In 1926 the "Worshipful Company of Musicians" presented her with the "Cobbett Medal." The Czechoslovak Government, the city of Frankfort, and other cities and countries of Europe, have taken official cognizance of what Mrs. Coolidge has done for chamber music.

Out of another chance suggestion Mrs. Coolidge, in 1924, formed the idea of endowing the Music Division in the Library of Congress, placing in the hands of the United States Government the means to perpetuate in Washington, and in other cities, what she had so auspiciously begun in Pittsfield. It was her boldest stroke and it succeeded beyond expectation. It inaugurated a new era for America's national library; it engaged the Federal Government, at last, directly and definitely in the affairs of music and musicology.

In the past thirty years the government has built up one of the largest and most comprehensive collections of music. Now, through the "Elizabeth Sprague Coolidge Foundation," it is enabled to perform music in the chamber music auditorium of the library of Congress— another gift that Mrs. Coolidge has made to the nation. Further and wider musical activities, the offer of prizes and commissions for new works, are provided for under the broad terms of the deeds of trust.

Her main purpose is best expressed in Mrs. Coolidge's own words: "I have wished to make possible, through the Library of Congress, the composition and performance of music in ways which might otherwise be considered too unique or too expensive to be ordinarily undertaken. Not this alone, of course, nor with a view to extravagance for its own sake; but as an occasional possibility of giving precedence to considerations of quality over those of quantity, to artistic rather than to economic values, and to opportunity rather than to expediency."

A whole creed is embodied in these terse, clear sentences.

Ancelet, in 1757, published his *Observations sur la Musique, les musiciens et les instruments*. In it we find this significant passage about de la Pouplinière: "Musicians in general should be filled with gratitude toward Monsieur de la Pouplinière; he has always been the protector of the Arts, and the citizen best qualified to do the honors for France, in lending generous aid and protection, not only to Frenchmen, but to foreigners who have come with distinguished talents. If he himself has enjoyed the benefits he wrought, he has shared his pleasures with his friends, and with those who are able to listen, to compare, and to judge."

Every word of this tribute fits the case of Elizabeth Coolidge. And a great deal more will have to be said when the time comes to appraise the full contents and the yield of her days, the breadth of her mind, and the goodness of her heart.

THE ART OF TRANSCRIPTION *

BY A. WALTER KRAMER

THE ART of transcription, which had its real beginnings with Bach, in his adaptation of sixteen of the Vivaldi † violin concertos for clavier and organ, offers an opportunity for discussion of the many interesting questions which frequently arise, when a modern composer attempts to provide substitutes for obsolete instruments, orchestral

* A striking illustration of appropriate and artistic transcription is that done by Mr. Kramer himself in the Arensky-Kramer "Valse Pathétique," an explanatory footnote from which is here appended by permission of the publisher, M. Witmark & Sons.

"Anton Arensky (1861–1906) was one of the ablest of Russian composers of his time. Cut off in the midst of his promising career, his name is today remembered only for a half-dozen works which have won for themselves a place in the affections of music lovers in many lands.

"Of them none is more admired than this song, best known by its English title, 'But Lately in Dance I Embraced Her,' a song of wistful beauty. The subject matter of the poem, by A. Fet, I have rendered freely in English and have transcribed the song for three-part women's chorus, violin, violoncello, and piano. In the main, the voices sing a choral adaptation of the original voice part, but at times I have created for the choral voices matter that in the original song is only to be found in the piano part. The violin and violoncello parts are to be considered not as obbligato parts but as essential units in the performance of my version and are to be played richly, so that they blend with the choral tone.

"The main melody of the song, one of the most fetching waltzes I know, is not Arensky's own, as a footnote in the original edition states. It is a popular tune which he adopted as the melodic basis of his song, idealizing it, no doubt, in the process.

"There is in this song something that has won for Arensky a place in the literature of song alongside the best of his compatriots. It is with the intention of making familiar to others than those who sing or attend song recitals this exquisite composition, that I have made this choral adaptation, and in doing so I have introduced a violin and violoncello to play the waltz melody which recalls the occasion at which the beloved last danced, a melody which was certainly played by stringed instruments instead of on the piano, for which it is cast in Arensky's original version.

"If there is truth in the statement that there are composers who are great in small things, Arensky was surely one of these, and his right to a place among them is well set forth in his affecting song-drama in miniature. The title, 'Valse Pathétique,' is my own, based on the idea of the poem and music and one which, I hope, will seem as appropriate to others as it has seemed to me."

† Antonio Vivaldi (c. 1680–1743), director of a conservatory of music in Venice, and a member of the orchestra at St. Mark's, was a virtuoso violinist and composer, noted especially for his many brilliant concertos for violin.

parts for the music originally set down for organ, or harmonies from a figured bass. Many people, in discussing it, use the words arrangement and transcription as synonyms.

To be sure the principal difference may be said by some to be the same as that between boots and shoes. *Arrange* is a verb which is freely used for all sorts of versions of music, but to me its definite meaning is a distribution of parts. *Transcription,* such as the Bach and Liszt adaptations, means the transference or *translation* of a piece of music from the instrument for which it was written by the original composer to another instrument, as from violin or orchestra to organ, organ to orchestra, voice to violin or piano, and so forth. In this the voice is considered as an instrument.

Free transcription permits the transcriber to do a little composing of his own, but not in the usual meaning of that word. Instead, he is to reconsider, or view anew, the original composer's thought product, but always in *the light of the original piece.* A good transcription is one that absolutely, and without exception, gives the composition in the terms of the instrument (or instruments) for which transcribed, while at the same time preserving the *spirit* of the original, never adding, in the new medium or version, frills or furbelows for the purpose of displaying the possibilities of the instrument. The new viewpoint often greatly clarifies the music, as in the case of fugues from Bach's *Well-Tempered Clavichord* when transcribed for strings, as it is impossible for a single player, no matter how skilled, to bring out the three or four polyphonic voice lines he must handle as clearly as can four string players, each responsible for only one.

Care must be taken in each re-creation, as, for instance, in my own transcription for strings of a very ancient five-voice madrigal, *"Tu m'uccidi, o crudele"* by Gesualdo *—a lovely old work shown me by Malipiero when I was in Italy. I did not give these five-voice parts to the usual five strings, but to first and second violin, viola, and first and

---

* Carlo Gesualdo, Prince of Venosa, a member of one of the noblest families in Neapolitan history, was born about 1560 and died at Naples in 1614. He was, among the madrigalist before Monteverde, one of the most notable for imagination, boldness, and inspiration.

second 'cello, a very different transfer from 'cello and double-bass, as the bass, if duplicating this lower voice part, would be playing constantly in a very uncomfortable range. The "Cat's Fugue Sonata" by Scarlatti (originally for clavier), on the contrary, lends itself admirably to transcription to the first and second violin, viola, 'cello, and bass, the usual string orchestra.

In transcribing music taken from old lute tablature,* one has an entirely different proposition. Here the problem is to make the music readable. Some of the note values must be changed, a half or whole note in a lively tempo often being of the same *actual duration* as a sixteenth note in a tempo marked *lento grave*. It also *looks* easier, and I fully believe that the appearance of some of the ancient compositions keep them from being used.

Some people have the notion that it is a bad thing, musically, to use a transcription, but I hold that a transcription, like any other phase of music, has its own inherent values. If it is good, it is worthy to be played by any artist; if bad, no good at all! There are few artists among violinists and pianists who do not welcome a fine transcription, as it makes available to them many treasures of the past. Some organists, however, will not, and thus miss some of the finest music ever written.

For instance, no music lends itself better to the organ than does Wagner's—this because of the incomparable sustaining power of the organ. There are some marvelous organ transcriptions of Wagner.

It is possible to transcribe the music written for the harpsichord, or for the virginal of Elizabethan days, for the modern piano, without thickening it or sacrificing any of its graceful, unhurried, or refined texture.

In the Schubert "Ave Maria," it is both unnecessary and unworthy for a transcriber to add showy frills, reminding one of a synthetic harp, as Wilhelmj has done in his violin transcription of it.

---

* By *lute tablature* is meant the instrumental notation of early centuries, a staff of lines (the number differing slightly in different countries) each of which referred to a single string of the lute and indicated the fingers to be used on that string to produce certain tones. A colored line (red, in Spanish tablature) was often placed at the top, for use in indicating the melody to be sung by the voice. See also p. 250.

The element of tonality, the key in which a piece is written, has a vast importance in transcription. The exquisite "Bird as Prophet" by Robert Schumann, a popular number both with amateurs and artists, as well as with the general public, is an example in which tonality and style must be carefully considered. A transcriber who understood the violin would immediately see that the sixths in the middle section in G Major, were written for the piano exclusively, and that these sixths are not sixths for the violinist, as most violinists would play them with excessive vibrato, thereby destroying the purity of the original. However, if the violinist does wish to play the piece (and who can blame him?) he should put it into the key of D Minor, in which it lies and stands well. But I must say that the little piece is such a gem that one likes it *in spite* of a bad transcription.

No one has done better by Schubert in piano transcription than Franz Liszt, or worse by Bach. In the Schubert music, he has retained all of the supple and radiant spirit of the original; but in the Bach he has actually changed some of the harmonies, and added stuffed-out chords, quite unlike Bach.

The master transcriber of all time, to my mind, is Ferrucio Busoni, who, in his re-creations, presents not only the *actual notes* of the original, but also the possible ones inherent in the musical subject under discussion.

There is, for example, the "Chaconne" * of Bach, the final movement of the "Fourth Sonata" in D Minor, for violin alone, a dazzlingly brilliant and complex set of variations for unaccompanied violin, which calls for the fullest possible display of violin virtuosity.

Busoni's piano transcription of the same "Chaconne" is as magnificently worthy as the Bach original, for Busoni has translated into pianistic terms music which is practically impossible for any but the most remarkable violinists, and even then overloads the violin, as it is so excessively polyphonic. The original Bach "Chaconne," like many

---

* The chaconne is an old dance form in which a set of variations is written upon a rhythmic eight-measure theme in triple measure. The dance is of Spanish origin. Mr. Kramer has transcribed Bach's *Chaconne* for symphony orchestra.

other compositions, is superbly conceived by the greatest of contrapuntal masters, but, like many others, it looks better on paper than it sounds, *except* in the hands of a superbly trained artist.

Finally, the transcriber's name should certainly be included upon any program where his work is used, along with that of the original composer. If his music is worth playing, his name is worth mentioning.

But, speaking both truly and humorously, a hyphen used to designate the transcriber's name means little to some people. On one recent occasion a certain artist was playing a transcription over the air, and suggested that announcement of the piece—Schubert-Wilhelmj "Ave Maria"—would be enhanced if the announcer stated that the composition about to be played was the "Ave Maria" by Schubert, transcribed for violin by Wilhelmj. The announcer learned the lesson well—too well!—for on the following week he announced with clear and careful precision that the "next number" would be *Scheherazade* by Rimsky, transcribed for orchestra by Korsakov!

THE PIPE-ORGAN,
KING OF INSTRUMENTS:
THE CHORAL PRELUDE

THE pipe-organ is often called the "king of instruments" from the fact that it is at once the largest, the most complicated, and the most orchestral of all single instruments, and it is also one most often heard as it is played constantly in the church, the theater, and the concert hall, and is found in many homes. Each of the organ's stops represents an orchestral instrument and produces a tone which greatly resembles it in sound.

The organ has several keyboards (from two to five) including one of the large wooden keys to be played by the feet (known as the pedal keyboard). It may also have as many "attachments" or "special effects" as the taste and purse of the owner dictate.

This mighty instrument had its beginning, traditionally, in the little bunch of reeds known as the syrinx, supposed to have been first made by Pan, the shepherd's god.

One of the first uses to which the organ was put was in accompaniment to the plain-song of the church service, where it was so effective that small organs, so tiny that they might be carried about easily, were very popular during the Middle Ages. Some of these were called regals from the fact that they were so often played in castles and palaces of royalty and nobility. Others were called Bible regals because they were made so that they folded up like a book. Many of these little instruments were beautifully decorated with paintings, the keys tipped with gold or jewels. The bellows, if made in pairs, were kept full of air by a page who pressed down first one and then the other while the musician played. Others were made with a single bellows which the musician worked with one hand while he played with the other. Examples of both these types may be seen in the Metropolitan Museum in New York City.

The essential divisions of any modern organ are its wind supply, the pipes, and the action. Following the use of water as a power (See "The Story of the Pianoforte and Its Forerunners," page 129) bellows were constructed which might be kept filled with air by "treaders," men who applied their weight first to one bellows and then to the other. (The author has played on an organ so equipped in an old church finished in 1513, in Arnsdorf—fifteen miles north of Salzburg in Austria—and just a few feet distant from the schoolhouse in which Franz Gruber lived when he wrote "Silent Night.") More modern organs are thoroughly equipped with every electrical device to keep them supplied with even air pressure.

The presence of the organ in the early churches naturally influenced the kind of vocal music written for use there. This is illustrated by the story of music in St. Mark's Cathedral in Venice, to which, in 1527, Adrain Willaert came from the north to act as organist and choirmaster. Here Willaert found two organs, instead of the customary one, both of them, it is said, having been brought to the church from the East by marauding sailors. Because of the presence of the two organs, Willaert thought of the idea of writing music for two choirs, to be sung antiphonally (in the manner of a musical response) and with the accompaniment of the two organs. This was the first time this had been done and the idea was widely imitated and developed.

Organ making in the centuries that followed developed into a high art. Each country, such as Spain, France, and Italy, made contributions, until now the skilled organist has many advantages over a performer on any other one instrument. The capacities of the organ are well illustrated by the many kinds of music that are written for it. It is used as an instrument in the orchestra, as an important element in religious service, as a solo interpreter of much music of an extremely programmatic character, and as a concert instrument.

A type of organ music which reached its culmination in the art of Johann Sebastian Bach, although later composers—as Johannes Brahms,

and others—have also written in this form, is that of the *chorale prelude.*
The chorale here discussed refers to the chorale hymn which came into
being with the formation of the Lutheran Church. These chorales were
sung, at first, in unison, but parts were soon added for the choir of
trained singers while most of the members of the congregation continued to sing the air. As the organ music of the seventeenth century
developed in variety and beauty it became quite common for organists
to improvise or compose instrumental variations on the hymn tunes.
Then the writing of more formal chorale preludes was begun by the
finer composers.

Each of these preludes (whether of early or modern composition) is
based upon some favorite melody, and consists of artistic elaboration of
the melodic, harmonic, or rhythmic characteristics of that melody. The
melody may be repeated several times during the course of a single
prelude, each repetition or its accompaniment being altered so as to
interpret the words of the various verses of the hymn. Frequently
chosen by church organists for use as a part of a church service because of the appropriateness of the familiar words, they add greatly
to the devotional character of that service. Many of them are heard as
concert pieces in concert or on the air.

THE STORY OF THE PIANO
AND ITS FORERUNNERS

THE story of the pianoforte, one of the most popular musical instruments of the age, and the most frequently heard in concert or on the air, reaches, in its entirety, over a period of about two thousand years. There were, of course, no pianos in those early days, but the first keyboard was probably played upon before the beginning of the Christian era. The first of the story was not recorded in books as would be done today, but through pictures an artist carved upon stone walls near his dwelling in Egypt. There it remained for centuries, unseen and forgotten until the carvings were found by archeologists. Clay models of the keyboard were also found, and a part of the water-organ of which it was a part, near Carthage, in northern Africa, where it had lain for centuries.

This water-organ, a crude instrument used by both ancient Romans and Egyptians, had tiny pipes through which the air was pushed to make the sound, the power being furnished by stone buckets full of water hung at either side. The keyboard, a model upon which all later keyboards have been built, had only a few keys, all of them of about equal length and all of one color, and so large that the musician playing them had to use his fist or entire hand to push them down.

The piano of course, has no pipes, but strings, and the story of the first stringed instrument tells of one made—so long ago that the story is a mere legend—from the shell of a tortoise across which strings were tightly stretched.

Whether or not this is true no one can tell, but many ancient Greek lyres display tortoises in their decorations. Much precious musical history has been taken from pictures found in the temples and pyramids in which are pictured instruments in common use among the peoples of the day, including the lyre and the harp.

Other primitive stringed instruments include the lute, an instrument of Oriental origin which came to the general knowledge of the Western peoples at the time of the Crusades. There was also the psaltery—a box with strings stretched across it, each string being played by a quill —and the dulcimer, a somewhat larger instrument, the strings of which were played by being struck with a hammer, much in the manner in which the modern xylophone is played.

There were no keyboards attached to these early stringed instruments, the earliest to use it being the viol (a forerunner of the violin), to which someone presently attached a revolving wheel and rude keyboard, giving the name of hurdy-gurdy to the creation. This simple keyed instrument is the ancestor of the very jolly and often noisy mechanical instrument sometimes called a barrel-organ, which grinds out tunes on the streets of many large cities.

The zither (or clavicytherium, meaning keyed zither) came into being in the eleventh century, and its popularity and usefulness took it through many stages of development. In the fourteenth century a skilled workman living in or near the city of Venice perfected the clavichord, a musical instrument used by the most skilled and famous artists of the time. On it such a virtuoso as Johann Sebastian Bach produced charming and beautiful effects, and for it were written many of his greatest works.

During the latter part of the fifteenth century there were two main types of clavichords in general use—the spinet, in which the strings were plucked, and the other of a dulcimer type in which they were struck. The spinet took its name from its Venetian originator, Giovanni Spinnetti; while the virginal, as the same type of instrument was called in England, was so called in honor of Elizabeth, the Virgin Queen.

A charm of many of these earlier keyed instruments was that they were very light and small and could be carried easily from room to room. A story is told of Haydn, who when still a very young boy, and student, was encountered, one day, carrying his clavichord out through the hall into the garden. Asked why he was doing it, he replied that no one would let him alone and that he was going out into the garden where he could practice "in peace."

The makers of the early instruments decorated the sides and tops with exquisite paintings, and even the legs which were presently added so that the delicate instruments could stand alone instead of being laid on a table, were often covered with hand carvings and painting. The keyboards had now grown into works of rare beauty, the raised keys (often white instead of black) being often made of ivory inset with precious jewels and bits of gold.

All of this time the tone of the instruments had remained very sweet, rather than powerful. Makers, experimenting to secure more powerful tone, now perfected the harpsichord, often made with two keyboards, one above the other as in a modern pipe-organ, and several pedals, this making it possible for the player to produce several varieties of tone quality. This harpsichord was a very important part of the early orchestra and it was the custom for the conductor of the orchestra to sit before the keyboard, playing or directing his men as the need arose. Many of the finest harpsichords came from Antwerp and were made by Hans Ruckers, the most celebrated "maker" of his day. Handel's favorite instrument was a Ruckers and it is said that the great master was so incessant in his practice that every key was hollowed like the bowl of a spoon.

At last there came the first piano, invented in Italy by Bartolomeo Cristofori, a well-known instrument-maker of Padua who had gone to Florence where he had charge of the musical instruments owned by the Medici family. His first piano was made in 1708 or 1709 and it differed from any keyboard instruments in use in that its strings were sounded by a blow from the head of a small hammer. It was now possible to control the volume of tone more than with any earlier instrument, so the name given to the new instrument included the words *piano e forte* (soft and loud), and pianoforte has remained the correct name for the instrument until this day.

The first pianoforte made by Cristofori is no longer in existence. By 1720 and 1726 he had completed two more, and the first of these, the oldest piano in existence, may be seen in the Metropolitan Museum of New York City. It is a work of art, every detail of it, including the small wooden pegs which hold the pieces of wood together and the iron hinges of the lid, made by hand in the most careful manner.

In those early days the completion of a pianoforte called for a great ceremony. The maker had often been at work upon the instrument for many months, each part of it being constructed with the same loving care that is lavished upon a great painting or piece of sculpture. When it was finally finished, and ready to be delivered to its new home, a general celebration usually took place. The maker of the new instrument was the hero of the day and was honored in every possible way. A procession, led by the cart or wagon in which the new pianoforte reposed, traveled through the principal streets of the town or city; when the home was reached there were speeches by the mayor and other dignitaries; and clergy often attended to bless the instrument and the use to which it should be put. There was singing, and the usual feast was generally followed by an evening of dancing and gayety. This is very different from the present day, when instruments are made in vast factories and in huge quantities. However, the care bestowed upon those hand-made pianos is still evident in the work of the better piano-makers of today, many of whom employ great artists and skilled scientists who spend their entire time in experiments tending to better the mechanism and tone quality of the instruments constructed by their firms.

The first piano to come to America was a part of a rich cargo captured at sea by a privateer, and sold in Boston. This was a public sale, and the proceeds are said to have gone to the National Treasury.

It is not possible to give the exact date of the first piano made in America, but it is known that one made by John Behrend of Philadelphia about 1775 was one of the first, as was another built by Benjamin Crehore of Milton, Massachusetts, at about the same time. An old newspaper of 1791 relates that "there are twenty-seven pianos, all of English make, owned in Boston." In 1789, it is certain, there were two teachers of piano and harp in Boston, and a local newspaper of that date tells its readers that one of these could also "tune and repair the instrument if needed."

The first pianos copied the general shape of the harpsichords, and resembled the modern grand piano. Then came a development in which the piano was made to resemble the clavichord, this resulting in an oblong, like the old-fashioned "square grand." Still later, the modern and popular "upright" was devised.

All these improvements acted as a spur to the composers who vied with each other to create new music which should use the possibilities of the new instruments. Now the piano is—like the earlier harpsichord —frequently made a part of the orchestra, and whether for solo or ensemble use, there is scarcely any music so elaborate that it cannot be given adequate performance on the piano.

HUMOR IN MUSIC

"NOT ALL music is written with the intention that it shall be heard with a straight face," wrote a famous critic, in discussing Beethoven's *Pastoral Symphony,* into which the composer wrote more genuine, care-free fun than is found in the contents of many a comedy. Here the scherzo—or "Village Festival"—movement is a musical description of rural life and of a jolly country dance. The village band has a bassoon player who has only three notes that he can play on his battered old instrument, but these he plays, lustily and industriously, over and over, in and out of season, and without any worry about the harmonies or keys used by the other players. The effect is one of absolute hilarity.

Beethoven brought playfulness into another of his symphonies, the eighth, in the second movement of which he uses the air of a gay little song he had written some months earlier for the entertainment of a group of friends gathered at a farewell supper in honor of Mälzel, the inventor of the metronome, upon the latter's departure from Vienna. Mälzel had also made a fine ear-trumpet for Beethoven, who, filled with good spirits at being able to hear again, led the company in the singing of a clever original round, "Ta, ta, ta, lieber Mälzel." After the party Beethoven laid the little song away and later when he had adapted it to his needs in the symphony, in which the persistent "tick-tock" in sixteenth notes imitates the metronome, from beginning to end, he wrote to a friend: "I, too, am in the second movement. It was a right jolly evening when we sang the canon. Mälzel was the bass. At that time I sang the soprano."

Joseph Haydn created an equally humorous effect in his classic *Surprise Symphony,* in the second movement of which, after a graceful, charming melody, he introduces a sudden *Bang!* from full orchestra. This, it is said, was the composer's courteous, but effective, manner

THE
OLDEST PIANO
IN EXISTENCE,
MADE IN 1720
AT FLORENCE,
ITALY.
NOW IN THE
METROPOLITAN
MUSEUM,
NEW YORK

THE VIRGINAL,
FORERUNNER OF
THE PIANO

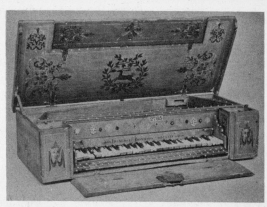

ANCIENT INSTRUMENTS

HARPSICHORD (FLEMISH, 17th CENTURY)

SERGEI RACHMANINOV

FRITZ KREISLER

IGNACE JAN PADEREWSKI

of reproving the Prince for his custom of sleeping through the daily concerts. At any rate—the story goes—it woke him so suddenly that he fell from his chair and never slept at concerts again.

One of the most delicious bits of humor in all operatic literature is the serenade of Beckmesser, in Act II of Wagner's *Meistersinger*. The meddlesome Beckmesser, determined to capture the fancy of Eva, comes boldly to her window after dusk to sing to her. He is not sure of the notes of his song, and his harsh and strident voice, combined with the ill-timed chords which he attempts to pluck from the mis-tuned lute which he carries on his romantic venture, awaken the neighborhood. Hans Sachs, the cobbler, whose shop is across the way, adds a disconcerting accompaniment by thumping with his hammer each time Beckmesser makes a mistake. The singer becomes more and more agitated, the thumpings grow more frequent, and louder, until the Town Clerk, angry at having his sleep disturbed, jumps from his window and gives the surprised serenader a sound beating. The humor of the situation is accentuated by its immediate contrast with the quaint archaic song of the night-watch, who is heard approaching, singing in a quavering voice:

"Hark to what I say, good people!
Eleven strikes from every steeple."

Many more instances of humor in music might be mentioned. There are the absurdities of the noisy acrobats of Satie's *Parade;* the stilted mock tears of the forgetful mourners in Gounod's *Funeral March of a Marionette;* the amusing distress of the lazy boy over the destructive activity of the hard-working broom (impersonated by the bassoon— clown of the orchestra) in the tale of magic told by Dukas in his *Sorcerer's Apprentice;* the droll scurryings of "Br'er Rabbit" in Mac-Dowell's *Fireside Tales* and the roguish wiles of the same composer's *Uncle Remus.*

An example of humor in "composed" song is Hugo Wolf's story of the Three Wise Men, "Epiphanias." In many so-called humorous songs, it is the message of the words which produce the effect desired, but in this song the accompaniment done by itself would create a droll result. In this song of Epiphany (written to celebrate the birthday of a friend,

Frau Melanie Kochert, and sung to her by her three children, in costume of the Wise Men, on Epiphany), each king recounts his own peculiar recommendations. They presently decide that they have come to the wrong place, in their search for the little Jesus, for "here there are only beautiful men and women, but no ox nor ass. So we are not at the right place, and must travel farther on our way." And, the composer adds in parenthesis, "They depart, each alone, after his own characteristic rhythm," the departure being depicted by the clever and varied pianistic coda, which grows ever weaker and weaker, as the travelers disappear in the distance. In this song, the composer has been able to suggest very vividly certain qualities of human nature, without being at all irreverent.

Most of all do even the most scholarly listeners occasionally enjoy a slyly humorous reference to their own foibles, or to some object with which they are thoroughly acquainted. Thus they are not only amused at the music, but are also momentarily pleased with themselves in having recognized the familiar object in the tale the composer has told. So, the city dweller laughs at the "Hurdy-Gurdy" by Goossens; the pianist, at the clever "Pianists," a parody on Carl Czerny's long-suffering five-finger exercises, which Saint-Saëns incorporated in his *Carnival of Animals;* and all genuine Americans, at the "Circus Parade" in Douglas Moore's diverting musical reminiscences of P. T. Barnum.

Many a person—including some celebrated virtuosos—has, in a light-hearted moment, played the childish piano-jingle known as "chopsticks." It caught the attention of even such renowned composers as Borodin, Rimsky-Korsakov, Cui, and Liadov, and filled their leisure moments for nearly a year, as they took it into their minds to write a joint series of elaborate variations upon the jolly old tune. These "Paraphrases," which the composers dedicated to "pianists capable of playing the theme with one finger of each hand," are in the form of a piano duet, the upper part of which is a series of unchanging repetitions of the familiar two-finger classic, which may be learned in a moment by anyone, whether he already knows a note of music or not. The other part, however, demands a skilled pianist for performance, for to this the several composers contributed variations which include a piquant mazurka, a cradle-song, a polonaise, an uncanny dirge, a waltz, marches, a requiem with vocal parts, a chaconne, a polka, a jig, a tarantella, a minuet, a gay carillon, grotesque fugal movements, and other alluring dances. Rimsky-Korsakov called it a "joint composition of peculiar nature." Liszt found the work so entertaining that he offered still other variations to it, and the whole composition is again popular and frequently heard.

American Music Makers

EARLY AMERICAN MUSIC

BY DR. FRANCES ELLIOTT CLARK, *Director of Educational Activities, RCA-Victor Talking Machine Company*

TO TRACE the beginnings of music in America, like the genealogy of an old family, is a difficult task. It leads us at once to the, as yet, undiscovered store of music lore possessed by the eastern Indians. Much valuable research work has been done in recent years in music among the western tribes, and many very beautiful melodies discovered as well as legends and uses of music in ceremonials, games, and dances.

It is quite certain that the eastern tribes, many of them now passed out of existence, had music as worth while and seemingly more melodious, but very little of it has been collected from the remnants of certain tribes still existent. One lovely melody, a lullaby of the Penobscots, was sung widely by Princess Watawasso of Maine, also a song of greeting used when one tribe visited another. A few others are now being salvaged from the Mohawks of northern New York by Oskenonton and others, also from the Menomonees, and the Winnebagos of the Great Lakes country.

Some day some ambitious musician will probe the possibilities of the few remaining Seminoles of Florida. The bayous and everglades may reveal a wealth of information, shedding light on the type of music heard by Cortez, De Soto, Ponce de Léon, and indeed may reflect that heard by Columbus himself. It is stated in historical documents that Columbus and his sailors chanted the *Te Deum* on his first landing in the New World. Palestrina had not yet lived, and theirs was the archaic song of the Middle Ages.

The French missionaries established churches in which there was much singing, along with the trading posts in Quebec (1608) and down the waterways to the mouth of the Mississippi. A wealth of French folk songs accompanied these pioneers and can still be heard among the descendants of the early settlers in Vincennes, Ohio, in the northern peninsula of Michigan, and in Nova Scotia. New Orleans has already yielded a rich store.

When the earliest permanent settlers came to Jamestown in 1607 they were a small group, but of good families of social position in the homeland. Secular song and the gay measures of the dance of both the folk and court types were more appealing than hymns of the church.

Our own early American folk dances are drawn from or inspired by those early importations. "Turkey in the Straw" is but a version of the old game "Jolly is the Miller." The Virginia reel is best danced to "Sir Roger de Coverley." "Money Musk" is an old Irish reel. "Old Dan Tucker," "Miss McCloud's Reel," "Old Zip Coon," "White Cockade," "Arkansaw Traveler," "Soldiers' Joy," and others are all imitations of older well-known tunes. These dances are still the basis of social diversion, as may be witnessed at the Folk Festivals of western Virginia, Tennessee, and North Carolina.

From the Virginias we have the greater body of the old English ballads and folk tunes, in their primitive form, from among the Appalachian mountain folk.* These fine old folk songs found in the eastern mountains were a gold mine to the late Cecil Sharp and other collectors, since many of them had become obsolete in England. They were the source and pattern of much of our earlier ballad writing. Stephen Foster, for example, gained much from certain of these old songs with which he came in contact in Kentucky. The song writers of the seventies and eighties had them in remembrance.

The Dutch settlement in New York (1613) brought much culture and implanted stolidly substantial manners and customs which are found among the old first families to this day; but it left comparatively little music.

The Pilgrim migration to Plymouth was a small but dynamic force. The little band sang their Psalms on board the *Mayflower,* and on their landing at Plymouth. Music was given scant attention, yet the seeds

* See "Virginia Finds Her Folk Music," page 167.

were sown in the rich soil of sturdy spiritual life for a new and higher order of hymn experience which has given us the foundation for our present phenomenal development.

The larger group of nearly a thousand souls who came to found Boston eight years later were Puritans, but not "Pilgrims," and had a more liberal code, many of them being highly educated people from "best" families. Their failure to use more music, as it was then known, is easily accounted for. They suffered too much from the tyranny of the court, of which music was a conspicuous part, and so music remained to them a symbol of the "evil life." We hear them often maligned, too, for not introducing the violin, the piano, the orchestra, and so on, forgetting that while the Amati family was struggling toward the development of the violin, the great Stradivarius who brought it to perfection was yet unborn. The little "French Fiddle" which Monteverde used in his so-called "orchestra for accompanying" his opera *Tancred* (1624) may have been known, but the Puritans were much too busy picking rocks out of their scanty gardens to trouble about a new fandangle which was bowed, and not plucked, as was their familiar lute.

Corelli, who established the first violin school in Rome, was born in 1653, when our doughty conquerors were fighting King Philip's War. (A distant relative of the writer has in his possession a fine old long drum played by our common ancestor in this war.)

The pianoforte as we know it was not developed by Cristofori for more than a hundred years after the settling of Jamestown. Broadwood and Erard contributed their improvements *after* the Revolutionary War, while Hawkins here in America made the first upright piano in 1800, after the death of Washington. It is difficult to imagine where the then rather new harpsichord (or "arpicordo") could have been stored in the *Mayflower,* or even a virginal, a spinet, or a cembalo.

Quite rightly these colonists left the bagpipes to their protesting Scottish brethren to bring over, a hundred years later. They too came singing their Psalms, but brought with them also the lovely old Scottish songs and ballads, and later the lyrics of Robert Burns. My old grandfather, of Scottish ancestry, used to walk along, leaning on his twisted cane, singing to himself "I'll take my petticoat under m'arm and over the river to Chairlie," "Wha'l be King but Chairlie," "Bonnie Dundee," and "Blue Bonnets over the Border."

It is an interesting study to trace many of the same old folk songs and singing games in New England as well as in Virginia. I had a singing uncle of pure New England ancestry who regaled the family at home in the evenings with a version of "The Frog in the Spring" (a more whimsical version than any of the printed ones I have seen), "That's the Time to Remember the Poor," "Billy Boy," an old melody sometimes called "Warranty Deed," "Frog Went A-Courting," and "Birds' Courting Song," one verse of which was

> "Hi!" said the blackbird to the crow.
> "If you ain't black then I don't know.
> Ever since old Adam was born
> You've been guilty of picking up the corn."
> *Chorus:* Tow-dy, ow-dy, dil-doldum,
>   Tow-dy, ow-dy, dil-do-day.

My father would contribute "Old Butter and Cheese," a version of the Old English "Poacher's Daughter"; and we children sang and played "King William was King James's Son," "The Needle's Eye," "Green Grow the Rushes, O," "London Bridge," "Jolly is the Miller," and "Here We Go Round the Mulberry Bush."

The singing of the Psalms furnished the emotional outlet of these devoted souls. While very few tunes were essayed, those were sung with true feeling. Rev. Cotton Mather said of John Eliot,* the "Apostle to the Indians," that his Indians sang "ravishingly." The first book published in America was the "Bay Psalm Book" (1640). This work was done by three ministers, Reverend Messrs. Welde, Eliot, and Mather.

If New England seemed slow in music development, she atoned by being the first in the New World to establish singing schools, music

---

* Mrs. Clark, the author of this chapter, is a direct descendant of John Eliot, "Apostle to the Indians."

in the public schools, to organize the first music school (1876); and her subsequent history sheds glory on the musical world.

The German settlements at Ephrata and Bethlehem have left a worthy legacy. These fine people brought instruments into their church services, particularly the trombone. The singing of the Bach chorales was made foundational. The great Bethlehem Bach Festival of the present day is an outgrowth.

One cannot speak of the early music without recognizing the contributions of the Negro. The date of the first importation of slaves is set down as 1619. This naturally most gifted race, musically, has been slow to show great development on modern music lines, but its type of chant, spiritual, mystery hymns, and the natural rhythmic energy, the sense of worship through singing, have permeated the music life of America. Special attention has been given to the music of the Negro in recent years, and it is certain that it has been a feature of the music of this country since an early day.

One of the great influences upon the development of music in this country in the early days was undoubtedly the old-fashioned singing-school, first established in New England in 1717. The first book on the subject was published by Rev. Thomas Walter in 1721. The first singing-school of the South was organized in 1730, by John Salter. In Philadelphia one Josiah Davenport announced a "summer season evening singing-school" in 1757, and the well-known James Lyon conducted such a school in 1760. In 1764 Francis Hopkinson (the first American composer) was conducting a singing-class in psalmody in Christ Church, while Andrew Adgate organized a continuing school, in 1785. The most famous of all these early choristers was William Billings, a tanner of Boston, who founded a class in 1774 at Stoughton, Massachusetts. Twelve years later the still flourishing Stoughton Musical Society was formed.

A curious renaissance of both the old English folk songs and the singing-school took place in the settlements of the Northwest Territory. The tide of migration streamed across from Connecticut, through New

York, into Ohio, and, in a generation, on to Indiana, Illinois, and Iowa. These, too, were pioneers in a wilderness, and thrown upon their own resources for entertainment. The "quilting-parties," "corn-huskings," "apple-paring bees," "barn-raisings," and the "play-party" all utilized the singing of the old songs, the playing of the old games, and, later, the type of the new singing-school. These often took the form of ending up with conventions or institutes of some three days, closing with a concert, at which several "glees" and "anthems" were sung by a selected group, and a few numbers offered by the conductor and perhaps some members of his family. Very primitive, yes, but also very full of the elements of growth which make this nation. If any there be who would criticize the early stages of our development, they should remember that at the time of the Revolution the population of the entire colonies was scarcely more than two millions, scattered all up and down the eastern seaboard.

Even so, musical life began to blossom. Johann Conrad Beissel, founder of Ephrata, who came to Germantown in 1742, was a well-trained violinist. An organ was ordered for the Brattle Square Church in Boston, but, being refused, it was sent to King's Chapel in 1710. The first pipe organ was owned by Christopher Witt and made by him in 1704. Johann Klein was the first builder of organs in Philadelphia, in 1736. The first American spinet is also claimed by Philadelphia, and was made by Hessilius in 1743. In Philadelphia, then the metropolis of the colonies, a school for teaching the harpsichord, guitar, and German flute was opened in 1763 by James Brenner (the teacher of Hopkinson). In Charleston, South Carolina, there were many concerts, at an early date, and in 1792 its St. Cecelia Society ordered from England "one grand piano-forte and twenty pounds' worth of the best modern concert music." In a festival of 1773, Charleston's orchestra of thirty pieces gave works by Haydn.

Immediately after the Revolution, concerts, opera, and orchestras became well-known in Baltimore and many other Southern cities; also in Philadelphia, Boston, and New York. And it is interesting to recall that at just this time Bach and Handel had just finished their work, Gluck was closing his reforms of opera, Haydn was at the height of his career, Mozart was just beginning to startle the world with his genius, Beethoven was only a babe in arms, and Schubert and Schumann yet unborn.

Considering the scattered population, and the exigencies of developing a new nation, music in the Colonies progressed with amazing force. The unparalleled growth of the past hundred and fifty years we leave to other chroniclers to establish.

MUSIC OF THE AMERICAN
INDIAN

BY DR. THURLOW LIEURANCE, *Director of Music, Municipal
University, Wichita, Kansas*

WE Americans, so proud of our nationality, love to talk much these days of the Americanization of art, but the fact remains that long before Christopher Columbus sighted our continent there had been established in America a "school" of music which had developed splendid artists among its pupils, and compositions which, in an unchanged form, have kept their vogue for many centuries. At present this music has met its crossroads, a period of transition in the life of the Indians. Civilization is placing its stamp on the new generation of Indians. The old-time Indian is now but a vestigial member of the social organism, and civilization is under perpetual obligations to those who preserve the arts of the past.

It was in 1903 that my attention was called to the songs of the Red Man when I was sent by the United States Government to the Crow reservation to secure records for the Smithsonian Institution. In gathering Indian songs, since that day, I have visited thirty-three tribes. It was impossible to learn all the many dialects, but I did learn the Indian sign language, which furnishes a common means of communication to all but a few tribes, so that an Indian from Canada can communicate with an Indian from Florida, although their speech differs widely.

I am convinced that the American Indian has a theme for every activity and characteristic of his life. His best songs are his spiritual songs, and his flute or flageolet is his only real musical instrument, although the tom-tom, the big drum, and the rattle are featured in many Indian ceremonies. The flutes of the Indians are constructed for different musical scales. In my collection of Indian flutes are a six-toned Hopi flageolet, a four-toned Hopi flageolet made from a hollow bone, a Kiowa and some Pueblo flutes; also a four-toned flute which shows marks of civilization, having been made by a Ute Indian from a piece of gas pipe. The tone was produced on it by blowing on the rim. Exquisitely beautiful flageolets are seen among the Southern Pueblo Indians. These Indians are splendid silversmiths, and I have one flute made by pounding silver dollars together, by hand. Still another interesting flute in the collection is of Cheyenne origin and is made to correspond with the ancient five-tone, or pentatonic scale, which is the Cheyenne scale.

The long-suspected relationships between American Indian tribal musical forms and those of the earliest Orientals have come to be more than tradition to me. Even today we may find writings on rocks in many states of this country—especially in Idaho—which show three distinct developments of the human race in this country. Near Boise there are rocks bearing carvings which have been there, with certainty, during the lifetime of the oldest citizens, and traditionally, as held by the resident Indians, for countless centuries. These carvings resemble somewhat the Chinese writing of today, and the oldest Indians of the region will occasionally relate—when they have decided to place faith in the person questioning them—the traditions and legends told them by their forefathers of a tribe of wandering, primitive people who came to this country from another land to the west, across the water (Bering Strait) in the Great North.

That these wanderers brought with them their primitive musical instruments is a certainty to me, and I have made a certified official report of findings along this subject for deposit with the Smithsonian. The ancient five-tone scale of the Chinese is absolutely the scale of the Cheyenne flute. In the Chinese scale the individual tones, named by the Chinese themselves, are known as Emperor, prime minister, subject people, state affairs, and picture of the universe. Then I have two ancient Chinese flutes which employ the whole-tone scale, and, of the twenty-five most typical examples of Indian flute-making in my collection, more than one-half employ this scale, familiar in the earliest known types of primitive music. Many skilled musicians and ethnologists who have examined the flutes will verify this statement.

I have made the following analysis of the natural scales used by Indian musicians of the various tribes when making their flutes. These are all from hand-made instruments presented to me by the Indians themselves as I visited them to record their tribal melodies and rituals, and I give the scales in ascending form:

Cheyenne: F-sharp, G-sharp, A, B, D, E, E-sharp, F-sharp

Omaha (alto): F, G, A, B-flat, C, D, E-natural, F, or F-sharp, G-sharp

Omaha (small flute): A, B, C-sharp, D, E, F-sharp, G, A

Winnebago: A-flat, B-flat, C, D-flat, E-flat, F, G-natural, A-flat

Kiowa (whole-tone flute): G-sharp, A-sharp, B-sharp, D-natural, E, F-sharp

Shoshone: A, B, C-sharp, D-sharp, F-natural, A

Chinese (whole-tone flute): A, B, C-sharp, D-sharp, E, F-sharp, G-sharp, A-sharp

Sioux (whole-tone flute): F-sharp, G-sharp, A-sharp, B-sharp, D-natural, E-natural, F-sharp

Ute (four-tone flute): C, G, B-flat, D

Hand-carved figures, often of animals, are added, many times being bound to the flute with thongs of sinew or skin, with the wish that they will bring the player "good medicine." Feathers attached to a flute are a further symbol of good luck, and are believed by the tribal musicians to ward off evil spirits.

Much account is taken by twentieth-century composers of the scales employed. They would find a unique effect created should they attempt artistic composition with the aid of any one of these authentic primitive scales, and one much more personal than is sometimes heard.

I am also finding daily that the tribal rituals and customs of our most primitive Indians correspond very closely, dovetail exactly, in fact, with those being brought to light by scientific delvers into the background of Oriental life, whether in China, Assyria, or India.

The flute is the dearest and most valued musical instrument of the

Indian. He will take a piece of red cedar, hollow it out, glue the two halves together with pitch-pine, and wrap the whole tight with sinew or cord. All Indian flutes are blown into the end like a flageolet, and are made to imitate the songs of different birds, even the cry of the night-owl, also to play melodies. Semi-tones are produced by cross-fingering. The tone produced by these primitive instruments is, in most cases, of an appealing quality, and is, in the case of each instrument, modified or individualized by the personality of the Indian who fashioned it.

It is a mistake to suppose that Indian music is all alike. There are almost as many "schools" of music as there are tribes. The Indian uses music as a ritual to illustrate a fixed purpose in life. For that reason he cannot exhibit the music of the tribe for the passing stranger. It would be sacrilege to him to sing such religious songs, for example, as the hymn to the sunset, out of their proper setting.

Words are seldom used except in the love songs and in the prayers or petitions to the deity. Other songs are sung to syllables, like vocalises. The syllables most frequently used are *hay-uh* and *high-uh*. Strange to say, tribes thousands of miles apart will use these same syllables. Indians sing with no visible movement of the lips or jaw. They rarely open their mouths in singing as a white man does—the opening of their lips will be just a little slip. Their voices, especially in the low registers, are marvelously resonant. Their singing endurance is beyond belief. For a singer to go on continuously for twenty-four hours is in no way extraordinary. The reason that this is possible is that the Indian sings only vowels. Each tribe sings the same vowel as all others, but with a different placement.

In the ritualistic activities of the Indians of the Chippewa Clan, or Society, music plays an important part. The initiation, which may last over a period of six weeks, is a pageant or dramatization of Chippewa ideas of the creation of the world, and contains two hundred songs.

Some of my choicest recordings of tribal music come from the Taos Pueblo Indians. At first I had great difficulty in securing the chieftain's permission to make them, as he told his braves to have nothing to do with the phonograph, for, he said, "You give away your spirit and get nothing in return. If you play for it you will become poisoned and die before sundown." However, some of the best singers (the ones who could sing the highest—the Indian standard of judgment) came to me outside of the pueblo and made about a hundred records. Then one night I gave a concert with these for the old chief which won him completely, and through his kindness I was able to secure many valuable records.

The pueblo village where this concert took place is built like two great apartment houses. No one knows when the two huge pyramidal piles of dwellings of mud, built story upon story, were made; they have certainly been a part of the desert for centuries. The little Pueblo River, crossed here and there by bridges built of hewn logs, runs between these houses. Near them are the corrals where the wheat is threshed by driving goats or burros over it, the adobe ovens where the women bake, and all the other features of the community's life, with its many ceremonies, each of which has its interpretation in song.

The music of the formal Indian ceremonial is at once forceful, graceful, and poetic. One ceremony may continue for days, and include from two to three hundred songs. Careful practice is given these songs during the weeks which immediately precede the festal occasion, as, once the ceremony has begun, there must be no deviation from the ritual or traditional version of any song. In case even one singer should so transgress, the rite would cease abruptly. In many of the songs, no words are sung to the simple, effective tribal melodies, but syllables only. These, through long and affectionate use, have come to exert a profound appeal upon those feelings which often elude definite expression in the use of words.

No more beautiful illustration of the union of tribal music, impressive ceremonial dramatization, and spectacular, colorful pageantry may be found in America, than that which occurs during the annual Pueblo Festival of San Geronimo at Taos.

This Indian village is situated in northern New Mexico, about thirty miles from a railroad that runs through the famous Santa Fe valley. In easy walking distance are the Taos Mountains, which tower above the town to a height of thirteen thousand feet. Here two community houses—one of two, the other of seven stories—built in adobe fashion more than a thousand years ago, still stand, each capable of sheltering about two hundred inhabitants. These houses—one of which stands on either side of the Taos River—were the homes of the Pueblo Indians centuries before the Spanish explorers came riding through the valley in 1540 in search of fabled treasure.

The Pueblo Indians were originally sun worshipers, and the San Geronimo Festival, given each year, on September 30th, is a curious mixture of old pagan rites and the religion brought to these Indians by the Spanish friars, who dedicated the village to St. Jerome (San Geronimo).

The festival really opens on the evening of the twenty-ninth, just as the setting sun begins to cast shadows upon the mesa. The festival is celebrated, in nearly every particular, as it has been celebrated for nearly two hundred years. After a service in the adobe chapel, during which boughs are blessed, the dance begins, accompanied by a weird monotonous chant in the minor mode. As the darkness deepens, the flaming torches, the occasional flash of gay colors in some lighted spot, the chilly air, the wide distances, and the wild fervor of the participants, create a scene of ghostly beauty.

The Pueblos start the festivities with chant and dance at sundown. Sung as it is by five hundred selected male voices, in perfect unison, the chant is impressive to the utmost degree. The warriors, attired in white blankets, form in two straight lines, then sing in unison and dance away from the pueblo, straight toward the setting sun, carrying with them boughs of the aspen tree. They continue dancing until the moment the sun drops behind the horizon, then fall to the ground and remain there in meditation all during the night, hoping, by this act of devotion, to get some word from San Geronimo. The meditation takes on almost the character of a séance, and some of the warriors presently feel that they have received a message from the absent saint.

In the morning, just as the sun appears again in the east, they dance back to the pueblo, waving red blankets in greeting to it, and bringing word to those at the pueblo that San Geronimo has sent them a message that he cannot come to them this year—but will at some later time— this and other messages for their comfort and advice. The sacrifice pole is usually set on the evening of the twenty-ninth, and topped with the sacrifice, so that it will be there to greet the god, should he come with the rising sun. After the dancers leave the pueblo, camp fires are lighted, and through the clear night air the visitor can sometimes hear, in addition to festival songs, the crooning of ancient Pueblo lullabies by the Indian mothers.

Early the next morning, the tops of the five- and seven-story cliff-like dwellings are crowded with a gorgeously brilliant throng of Indian spectators, watching with breathless interest the scenes at their feet, where the dancers are gathering. In the morning the procession takes place, with two daughters of the pueblo governors carrying the images of Christ and San Geronimo. These are placed in a chapel made of aspen boughs, where they may watch the ceremonies planned in their honor. A part of the festivities is the big race between members of the different clans. The afternoon dance is preceded by proclamations from the housetops. This dance is in the nature of a revel or carnival, when the Indians play native games and sing their picturesque *chiffonetta* or clown songs. More festive dancing follows the setting of the sun.

One of the quaint customs of the Pueblos is that of building *kivas* or underground rooms which are entered by a ladder reaching down into the ground. These *kivas* are sacred spots and are constantly guarded, and in them secret councils are held and treasured war songs are taught in secret to those who are to sing them. All war-dance songs and most love songs speak for themselves without words. The songs of each tribe have differentiating characteristics. The best love songs come from the Sioux; the best ceremonials from the Crow; the best sun dances from the Cheyennes.

When one reproduces Indian music one should, for the time, think with the Indian mind. Many of the songs are surrounded by beautiful legends. One of these is that of the "Weeping Waters," a Chippewa tribal song which a Chippewa squaw taught me at Old Red Lake in Minnesota. The Indian legend has it that in a fight between some Sioux and Chippewas, the Chippewa war party was slain at a spot just above some falls. As the blood poured over the falls the waters mourned, and they have been mourning ever since. All this is told in the pantomime which accompanies most Indian singing.

Several years ago I was in Taos near Christmas time and witnessed the fire dance ceremony to the sun god. Just at this time of the year the sun seems to hesitate on its way south. The Indians at Taos have been isolated from civilization and live the same lives now as their ancestors did centuries ago. The pueblos are seven stories high and during this ceremony the Indians kept fires burning on the tops of them. Watching these, they waved red blankets and three-hundred men singers sang in unison for hours while they waited for the sun god to come to them out of the sun. The sun priest kept intoning the hymn to the god.

Nothing more clearly indicates the devotion of the Indian parent to the Indian children than the tenderness of tribal lullabies, or "sleep songs," as they call them. These of course differ with different tribes, but some of the loveliest things I have captured with my "box that sings," as my phonograph was called, are these songs. As they are nature people, the words of many of their songs refer to the scenes and living objects they see about them. The beetles often encountered on the steep trails of the Hopi villages are blind, so many Hopi mothers tell their babies, as they lie awake on their cradle boards, to be "blind like beetles." In many of these songs the five-tone scale predominates, with an occasional minor seventh added. Some of the Yuma songs are actually modal in character, as are some of the dance melodies.

Tribal dances, which play so important a part in the tribal rituals, are handed down from one generation to another as are the songs. Many a baby has his first lesson in manipulation of the dance rattles and in keeping time to the intricate dance rhythms, at his father's knee. But so far as I have observed, there is very little systematic private instruction. During many of the dances, the children of the tribe are gathered in the middle of the group and in that way they hear the melodies so as never to forget them. Little children of six and seven years often catch them very easily. Some of the Indians' singing is done with surprising expression. In the "Eagle Dance," for example, the soaring of the eagle as he flies from rock to crag is illustrated by wonderful *pianissimos* rising to astonishing *fortes*.

Strangely, too, all Indian music begins high and ends low. The climax of the song comes first, then the tune trails off to the bottom of the scale. The choral songs start out crisply and with energy, and always on a high note. Indian songs are also always very brief, being the single expression of a single idea.

For his drums and his rattles, the Indian turns again to nature. Many of the finest drums, which have the same personal qualities of tone as do the flutes, are made from hollowed-out logs, over which a wet skin has been stretched. Should the head of the drum thus constructed become too tight, or loosen too much, the Indian player will wet it thoroughly again, then place red-hot stones underneath to dry it. Then the head and the stones will be watched carefully and adjusted frequently until just the desired pitch is achieved.

For a drum-stick, nothing is any better than the stalk of a yucca-tree or bush, so common to the desert. This the Indians bend and fold to the right length, and then bind with fiber from the plant itself, or with thongs of hand-cured leather.

For a rattle a marvelously decorated gourd is used. Or, the Indian musician may gather empty turtle shells and hoofs of sheep or mountain goats, and fasten these to his knees with thongs. Then, as he dances, they rattle together and make a dry clattering sound.

Many people have an incorrect idea about the Indian love song, thinking of it as a creation of poetic words, sung at night. Instead, most Indian love songs are wordless, are personally owned, and are usually very flowing and lovely flute melodies. While they are sometimes heard at night, as some lonely Indian thus whiles his lonely hours away, the real Indian serenade takes place in the early morning. In the early days, when the Indians still traveled over the prairies in bands, the camping place was always, if possible, by the side of clear running water. Then, at dawn, when the women of the camp went to the brook or spring for water, the Indian lover, concealed be-hind some sheltering stone or bush, began to play to the object of his devotion. The chosen maiden might pretend, for many mornings, not to hear the tender message; but it would be repeated patiently, until some response had been made to the plaintive and questioning phrases.

In sickness, the weird rhythmic songs of the Medicine Man are chanted as prayers for the return of health to the stricken one. In health, rhythmic song is employed as a message-bearer to the spirit land. In death, rhythmic song, as a distinct part of the burial ceremonies of many tribes, is said to help guide the departing spirit to its future home. Thus the mysterious force of rhythmic utterance may be said to be the constant companion of the primitive Indian from his cradle to his grave.

THE QUEST OF THE
"LONESOME TUNES"

BY HOWARD BROCKWAY, *American Composer; Professor of Composition, Juilliard School of Music*

EARLY in the spring of 1916 an expedition into the Cumberland Mountains in the southeastern corner of Kentucky was planned by Miss Loraine Wyman and myself. She had made the singing of folk songs her especial field, and I, as a composer, looked forward to the discovery of vastly interesting material. During April we busily prepared for our approaching trip, the object of which was to be the quest of the old "song ballets" of the mountain whites in the Appalachian region. These preparations took the form of riding lessons (on my part), of inoculation, of vaccination, and of the purchase of suitable equipment for outdoor life. Everything had been looked to, I thought, as the "Memphis Special" drew out of the Pennsylvania Station in New York that Saturday night. But—I had made one mistake of omission! I had not prepared myself for the astounding fact that I was to find myself transported back into the eighteenth century! Within forty-eight hours I became aware of the miracle that had taken place, and after a few days had adjusted my mental processes to the strange conditions. We stepped out of New York into the life of the frontier settler of Daniel Boone's time!

Here are people who know naught of the advance which has been made in the world outside of their mountains. It surpasses belief. Many of them neither read nor write, and their knowledge is summed up in the facts of their daily life. In woodlore they shine, in planting and cultivating their corn, raising "razor-back" hogs, carding, spinning, weaving, and the distilling of their white "moonshine." Their land is a land of tumbled foothills—Pine Mountain, the highest in the

Kentucky region, has an altitude of 3000 feet. It is a land of primeval forest, "creeks" which are the larger streams and "branches," their tributaries. There are no roads up in the hills, and no vehicle with wheels is seen except in the vicinity of a town. Trails lead down a creek, and at intervals actually descend into the bed of the stream; one jumps from stone to stone for a mile or two before regaining the solid ground of one side or the other. When a "tide" (freshet) comes, one remains at home, as all communication with one's neighbors is at an end. "Nagging" is the mode of transportation, that is, riding mule or horse. I did not call upon the skill acquired in one riding lesson, but welcomed the opportunity to walk through such beautiful country, rough as the going was. Miss Wyman soon forsook the horse and we tramped some three hundred miles during our six-weeks' stay.

Amongst these people the folk song exists today as it did in Great Britain centuries ago. Not as an accomplishment but as an ever-present mode of daily emotional expression. In the seventeenth century their ancestors brought the songs from England, Scotland, Ireland, and Wales, and they have been handed down orally from generation to generation. Songs that died out in the old country a century ago are still sung every day in our Appalachian region. The statement has been made that amongst these people one can find nearly all the folk songs ever sung in the British Isles, and perhaps the claim is not far wrong.

It was with a thrill that I heard my first "song ballet"! It was sung to me by a little girl of twelve who was too shy to sing alone. She engaged the services of three sisters, all younger than herself, and even then insisted upon withdrawing into the "dog-trot," which is a passage running through a log cabin, covered but doorless. After a few minutes of whispered instructions the quaint old melody with its Elizabethan text came quavering to my ear, and stanza by stanza the Choir Invisible grew more confident. The melody was perfect as to form, the intonation true, and the story unfolded itself verse after verse with but slight deviations from the ancient original ballad. I sat in the rough little room which had no window and was lit by the daylight that entered by way of the door, and back and forth underneath my chair there scuttled a tiny razor-back shoat. The mother of the choir sat on the opposite side of the open fire and spat tobacco juice into the flames with unerring aim and range. Strange setting for the performance of an Elizabethan ballad! But I could only think: from many a frontier cabin has this old "Pretty Polly" sounded out into the night, to echo and die away in the stillness of the virgin forest.

The next day a young matron, perhaps some twenty-five years old, sang for me the beautiful old ballad of "Sweet William and Lady Margery" the while she unconcernedly nursed a tiny babe. Here again both tune and intonation were perfect and the text but slightly altered. It is intensely interesting to hear these people sing of things that lie entirely out of their ken. Had they the power of reading, one could not wonder at anything, but to hear these mountain folk, born into the frontier life of the eighteenth century and spending their days among these isolated hills, sing of "ivory combs," of lords and ladies, of castles and moats, of steeds and knights, is an astonishing thing. It brings home to one the whole process of transmission, stretching back through the generations into the period when such things were of the Present. One old man had sung a ballad which contained the word "steed." He was asked what the word meant. He scratched his head for a moment and slowly replied, "Wall, I reckon hit is some sort o' hoss-animil." The context had assured him of that! We were told in answer to a similar query as to a certain word: "Shucks! Hit jus' comes that way."

These people are the real simon-pure Americans! They are the "mountain whites" and are not to be confounded with the "poor white trash" of the South! A sturdy race, with individual characteristics, isolated in a unique way from the rest of the great teeming land, which has been covered by a network of railways and telegraph and telephone wires. Perhaps nowhere in the United States can one find a community so absolutely innocent of any knowledge of the progress of the world at large. One hears of ranchers in our West who live in utter isolation, with rides of a hundred miles to reach the nearest flag-station on a railroad. One hears also that the man owns a phonograph and calls upon Harry Lauder, even perhaps Caruso and Farrar, to entertain him of an evening! But here in the Appalachian region it is not so. Here a man may live but twenty miles from the nearest railroad and close his eyes for his last sleep without their having once rested upon a locomotive or a car! Those twenty miles may contain six or eight mountain ridges to be surmounted, their flanks and summits clothed by a very jungle of undergrowth and laurel thickets, all but defying the passage of a man's body. A daughter will marry and move over a mountain, perhaps not more than ten miles from her parents, and not see her parents again for ten years!

Life is a simple matter in these mountain wilds. The daily functions are few but imperative. The great staple article of diet is corn. From this is made the "corn-pone" and "hoe-cake" which are regular features at each meal. Razor-back hogs, which run wild and are to be met constantly as one tramps over the mountains and through the woods, need little attention. The planting and cultivating of the corn crop, on the other hand, calls for energy and perseverance to an almost superhuman degree. Someone has told of the Appalachian mountaineer who slipped while working on his corn crop and fell out of his cornfield and broke several ribs! After a few days in the depths of Harlan County, I recalled the tale and acquitted it of any divergence from strictest truth. Corn is planted on mountain sides sometimes at an angle of fifty degrees, and the plow must find its way through such a maze of stones that one is appalled by the patience and physical endurance demanded on the part of the farmer. The women play their part in the work in the cornfield, and one sees frequently the entire family of father, mother, and an army of children of graduated sizes busy high up on the rugged flank of a mountain. They sing at their work with lusty lungs and the sense of limitless space about them. The songs they sing are the old "song ballets" which were the object of our search and many times during our tramps were we thrilled by the strange and haunting melodies which were borne to us from on high, sometimes across the intervening valley.

It was with a peculiar sense of the fitness of things, almost too good
to be true, that I found that the people themselves call these old songs
"Lonesome Tunes"! Never was more apt title bestowed! It sums up
the pathos and mournful quality of many of them perfectly. We found
that the songs are roughly divided into three classes. The old ballads
of a narrative and sad character are "Lonesome Tunes." Those which
deal with such a theme as the favorite one of a lover who departs, is
absent "seven years" and then returns to marry his lady, are called
"love songs." The third class contains all songs of a rollicking character
and these are known as "fast music."

Our experiences in collecting the songs were varied and interesting.
We were at first looked upon with undisguised suspicion. The presence
of a "furriner" (anyone who comes from outside the mountains) at first
makes the mountaineer suspect a government revenue spy in new guise.
The wilderness in which we were tramping is full of the "moonshine
stills," and our first endeavor was to free ourselves from this suspicion.

"Where do you come from? What are you a-doin' here?" These
queries were fired at us point-blank with no moment's hesitation. After
my invariable reply, "We are from the Pine Mountain Settlement
School and we are looking for the old song ballets," the air was instantly
cleared, and in spite of a wonderment which was all-consuming they
showed a spirit of hospitality and courtesy which no words could describe.

The poise and innate dignity of these mountain people made a deep
and increasing impression upon us, as the weeks of our stay among
them mounted up. They are illiterate but not uncultivated. Their
ignorance of the outer world is absolute, but, as the preservation of
the "song ballets" shows, they have a culture all their own. To one
old man I said, "We have come all the way from New York to get
these songs." I saw in his face no evidence of any sense of surprise at
the journey we had undertaken, and repeated, "New York, you know."
Again no answer. "You know where New York is?" To which he seriously replied, "No. I never heerd of hit." Another man told me he

knew where New York was, but "didn't know hit war nigh the water." These astonishing instances are the result of isolation, of lack of the power to read and thus keep in touch with the world outside; yet the conversation which I held with these very two men was significant proof to me of thinking minds and a philosophy of life both broad and trenchant.

Our regular process of accomplishing our purpose rarely failed, just on account of this very quality in the mental equipment of the mountaineers. They were interested in our quest as soon as they felt our serious point of view. This established, they entered into the matter with zest and enthusiasm, and often we spent many hours at a stretch, exchanging songs and recalling the stories of ballads which might frequently run into twenty-odd stanzas. The hunt for particular and rare old Elizabethan ballads was one which made us thrill oftentimes as the gold-seeker must thrill when he finds proof of the presence of the precious metal. Perhaps it might be some ballad the mother had sung years ago as she worked about the little log cabin, when the present singer was a tiny "bar-footed" child, "rocking" at an improvised target just outside the door with the ever-present stones. Verse by verse it would emerge from the "hinterland" of memory, and we would almost breathlessly await its reconstruction, afraid to suggest, for fear of breaking the thread which led away back into the Past. It seemed sometimes to me as though I were groping and feeling my way with the singer's mind through the generations back into the England of the seventeenth century from which his forefathers had journeyed forth into the fabulous New World! They brought with them these priceless old treasures and the vital quality of them has kept them alive through all the generations in spite of obstacles which would have killed any oral heirlooms of less significance.

These songs as I found them were simply melodies unaccompanied. The mountaineers have none of the instinct for part-singing which one finds so marked in the case of the Negro, for instance. I heard, at different times, singing by large groups of men, women, and children and they sang strictly in unison. Not even the familiar second part so customarily sung as the "alto" by impromptu choruses in our communities was ever essayed.

In gathering the songs, Miss Wyman and I made a division of the labor. She collected the text and I the melody. The patience of the singers was in almost all cases unbounded. They would sing an entire ballad with its well-nigh endless number of verses, and cheerfully go over it slowly, so that the words might be accurately transcribed. The writing of the melody was often an affair of puzzling difficulty. The melodic intervals were frequently of an unusual and curious character. To add to the difficulty, there was the fact that the voices, while excellent as natural voices, were untrained—and this made the question of intonation in the case of certain steps an important one.

In Knott County, for instance, we found a man who came from a neighborhood famous for singers. He was born on Carr Creek and that is always referred to as "Singin' Carr." Among the lovely melodies which he gave me, with a zest which I revered in him, there was one of such haunting and pathetic beauty that it seemed too good to be true. I wrote it down very carefully and the longer I considered it, the more worried I became lest my desire had lent cunning to my ear and had even led my pencil to write the intervals which I fain would have come true! I had been told beforehand that this man could also play on the fiddle. I bethought me that it would serve as a perfect test of the intervals if he were to play them as he sang them, and casually asked him if he played, too. He modestly said that he could play "tunes" and brought out the fiddle. It was a regularly strung violin and to my utter astonishment he played upon it left-handed!

I soon forgot the strangeness of his method of playing, however, for my heart leaped with joy as he reproduced the wonderful old melody and I realized that it had come true! The intervals were exactly as he had sung them, and in my music pad I had one of the most remarkable melodies I had ever encountered in the entire literature of music! I have shown this old tune to a number of my colleagues and all of them have agreed with my estimate.

Through the many generations of oral transmission changes have, of course, taken place, both in text and music. Astonishingly little change as to words, one must admit, when the process of transmission and the long period of years are considered. The melodies, on the other hand, have experienced a much greater metamorphosis, and in almost all cases the changes have added new beauty and poignancy. The old tune mentioned above is a remarkable example of this cumulative beauty, and as it stands today it defies any attempt to discover its origin. I feel the more confident in making this statement, because the greatest expert of the world on the subject of folk song said to me: "Mr. Brockway, I do not know where this wonderful old tune comes from"!

At rare intervals in our search we encountered a fiddle, used to service and evidently a member of the family, with all the distinguishing traits of rough appearance and dependable quality. More frequently we found the "dulcimore," which is the real indigenous Appalachian instrument. It is made in the mountains and fits its environment in quite a charming and piquant way. It seems most thoroughly a part of the spirit of the culture represented by the old songs. In shape, a pochette, the little instrument carried by dancing-masters in the olden days, although very much larger, of course. It is strung with three strings, either gut or wire. Two of these are tuned in unison while the third is tuned a fifth below. The outer one of the two in unison is the only fretted string, the other two supplying a drone bass, giving somewhat the effect of a bagpipe. The dulcimore (accent on the last syllable) is held on the knees and the strings are plucked with a piece of leather or a quill. The melody is played upon the fretted string, for which purpose a quill or small stick is employed. We found that the dulcimore players were very particular as to the media employed, and that the adherents of the different schools, divided by the use of quill or leather, were distinctly temperamental in their allegiance! I heard one man sing and accompany himself most skillfully, and the effect was extremely delightful and quaint. He was apparently a *virtuoso* and his performance will always remain in my memory as the unique one of my experiences in the Kentucky trip.

When we reached small towns which were in communication by stage with the nearest railroad we found banjos and guitars. The realization was soon forced upon us, however, that the "banjo-pickers" and "guitar-pickers" were never conversant with the real object of our quest. They played a type of song which had for us no interest whatever, with little or no relationship to the "song ballet."

This brought home to us the displeasing conviction that the great deposit of beautiful folk songs in the Appalachian region is bound to suffer contamination and to be utterly obliterated as the mining and lumber railroads gradually creep nearer and nearer to the heart of the mountains. It is indeed a sad and depressing thought. Once let such a community gain communication with the outer world, and amidst all the advantages which enter, there will also come the insidious appeal of the trivial and commonplace music of our musical comedies. The newer generations will wish to ape their fellows of the great world outside the mountains in playing and singing the popular song of the day, and the rich store of ancient folk song will go the way it has long since gone in Great Britain. Would that we might gather in the entire harvest before the killing blight falls upon it!

VIRGINIA FINDS HER FOLK MUSIC

BY JOHN POWELL, *American Composer*

FOR as long as I can remember I have been the voice of one crying in the wilderness. It began when I was a child and heard other people saying, with sad shaking of their heads, "No, we are not a musical people. Music seems to be left out of the Anglo-Saxon temperament."

Instinctively I knew that something was wrong about this. I myself felt decidedly musical. Quite naturally, I turned to my mother, who had sung to me as she held me on her knee almost every day of my seven or eight years. "Why," I asked her, "do people say we are not musical?" And I grew very angry. "It is not true," I asserted. "I know it is not true!" "Alas, my son," she answered and she, too, shook her head, "I am afraid it is true. I should like to think it is not, but wise people who know say that the best of a people's musical gift lies in their folk music. The beginning of all music comes from the folk, the simple people, not from the great composers. The little songs the people sing for themselves and the simple tunes they dance to are the origin of all the work of the great composers. And of all the peoples in the world, only the Anglo-Saxons have no folk music."

I still recall how triumphant I felt. "Oh! but we have folk songs," I proclaimed. "I know lots: 'Can She Make a Cherry Pie,' 'There Was an Old Man Came Over the Lea,' 'Good Morning, Neighbor Jones,' 'Frog Went A-Courting,' 'Lord Thomas and Fair Eleanor,' 'Hangman, Stay Thy Hand,' 'Lord Randakm,' 'Barbara Allen.'" But my mother continued to shake her head. "What are they?" I asked. I thought that for a moment she looked a little puzzled. "They are not folk songs,"

she answered slowly; "not in the way 'My Luv's Like a Red, Red Rose'
is a folk song or 'Annie Laurie.'" (In that she spoke more truly than
she knew.) "What are they, then?" I persisted. "Just old songs everybody knows and loves," was her final word. And since I was still un-
convinced and consequently disturbed, she lifted me—great boy that
I thought myself—to her lap and rocked me into comfort and peace,
singing balm into my unquiet mind to an air which she had learned
from her mother, who, as a little girl, had heard her grandmother
singing:

> " 'Twas in the lovely month of May,
>   When green buds all were swellin',
>   A young man on his death-bed lay
>   For the love of Barbara Allen."

As I grew older I continued to meet the same statement on every side.
During my school and university days, I was regarded as something of
an anomaly in that music was evidently to be my career. The general
attitude was that it was a misfortune for an American and an Anglo-
Saxon to spend his life working in music. And yet many of these very
people whose habit of thought produced this opinion would sit cheerfully for hours to hear me play.

Abroad, again, I found that Europeans felt the same way. People
who heard my music doubted the veracity of my statement that I was
a Virginian. They felt there must be some mistake. For Anglo-Saxons,
they all declared, were notoriously unmusical. And as proof they brought
forward the staggering argument that the Anglo-Saxon peoples have
no folk music.

And it was the Anglo-Saxon peoples themselves who were the worst
offenders in this respect. As I became intimate with life in England,
I found that the English regretted that they had no composers, that
they were dependent on the continent for the large part of their music.
Some attempts were being made to establish an English school. But
among Americans it had come to be a matter of pride. Actually, a few
years ago, an American woman, who made a point of her interest in

music, who loved to spend lavishly her great wealth on expensive imported musicians, would always sigh and remark with an air of pardon-
able pride, "No, we are not a musical people."

When, on one occasion, an American of great musical attainment
both here and abroad pointed out that Americans spent annually more
money on music than on motor cars, and that this fact would seem to
argue the contrary of her assertion, she stuck to her guns, finally bringing up as a crushing and unanswerable climax that the Anglo-Saxons
have no folk music. But this gentleman knew his folk music, knew
his history and regaled her with both fluently. As his facts piled up she
grew more and more angry until at last she cried in high indignation,
"I don't care what they say! I know we are unmusical!" as if that,
above every other ambition, were the apex of achievement.

The explanation of this widespread error, like that of Columbus's
famous egg trick, is simple once you know it. It is necessary merely
to turn back to the time of Queen Elizabeth, in which period lies the
key to many of our problems. In those days England was Merrie England. And it was so dubbed because the countryside rang with laughter
and music. Shakespeare's pages are filled with songs and dances; the
stage direction: "sennet," * "tucket," "hautboys," † and "musicke," occur again and again. The Queen herself is said to have been no mean
performer on the virginals. At Court the dance was of great importance.
And although the education of a gentleman required that he be able
to write little more than his name and spelling was entirely of the
impressionistic school, it was demanded of every well-bred person to
be able to "carry his part." During the past few years the delightful
concerts of the English Singers have made known to many people all
over the world the beauty of English vocal music, and the charm of
Elizabethan musical habits. After dinner the guests, still seated about
the table, joined in the singing of madrigals, many of which were very
complicated. A person of whichever sex who could not join the singing
would have been thought ill-bred and awkward. Probably he would

---

* "Sennet" and "tucket" refer to instrumental fanfares, or "flourishes."
† The "hautboy" is now spoken of as the oboe.

not have been asked again. The songs they sang and the music they played were the work of Englishmen. In this music, the English language, which has since that time come in for some harsh criticism as being "unsingable," proved to be, on the contrary, eminently fitted for singing, and this is of great importance in considering our English traditional songs. In that day no one dreamed of wondering that Anglo-Saxons should write or make music, nor could the boldest have stated that they were unmusical people, for then it was clear enough that they had a folk music.

Not that it was called folk music, for the term is a German one. But up and down the land and in the streets of London, the people went about their work and play with music in their heels and on their lips. Every country village had its "Morris Side," a group of dancers expert in the ritual and feat in the capering performance of the Morris dance. No Davis Cup team ever trained more rigorously or sought more zealously for laurels than these Morris men. Those who danced the sword dances were perhaps the most highly trained, and if you should visit England, you might, with luck, still see in the North a "side" of old men, all over seventy, grown gray but not stiff in the tradition, weaving the mysterious web of the sword dance. If you have a drop of English blood in your veins, it will give you a thrill nothing else can give: some deep racial memory will stir. The Sword and Morris dances require special skill and were danced only by men, but there was also in the villages the tradition of the Country (contra) dances. These were the social dances of the period. Women and men danced them together, and summer nights with their long twilights found the green gay with their frolicsome measures. The tunes were made by fiddles or pipe and tabor or perhaps were sung by the dancers themselves. For it is evident to a student that many of the dance tunes once had words.

In addition the country was alive with ballads and songs, which had been handed down like the dance tunes and dances from immemorial times. The ballad-monger was a familiar and popular figure, as witness Shakespeare's Autolycus. From top to bottom—it might be better to say, from the ground up—Merrie England was musical.

Then came the Revolution, the rise of the Puritans to political power. For a time the merriment was stripped from the land. Everything which savored in the least of beauty for beauty's sake and in most cases all decoration, however innocent, was obliterated. It is a commonplace that paintings and glass in churches were destroyed. But perhaps the greatest blow of all fell upon musical England's native music. Organs were taken from churches and burned. The magnificent church music, which had reached the very highest state of development, was proscribed. And if music were forbidden in the religious life of the people, how much more was it frowned upon in secular life! The songs and dances of the countryside were forbidden: there was even a time when to sing a folk song in England was a crime! And so it is as if one of the magic new silencers had been established everywhere, no longer did the village green ring with laughter and merriment, no Maypole could be set up with pagan rites, no Morris men win admiration and wonder in the public eye, no lads and lassies do their courting to the delicate strains of "Newcastle." To all intents and purposes England had become dumb and silent.

But the Puritan rule passed, and with the Restoration came a new demand for music. The Stuarts imported musicians from the continent. The new music became fashionable and the foreign musicians won popularity. It was a bonanza to them and their self-interest led them to look with scorn upon all the old native music, although it may well be said for them that they no doubt failed utterly to understand it. But the convention was soon established that these strangers had at last brought music to an unmusical people. With haughty condescension they consented to put their wares before the English public and the musical English, rusty from disuse, humble-minded because they felt certain and thirsty for a concord of sweet sounds, accepted the newcomers at their own valuation.

However, there were protests. The *Beggar's Opera* is today a living example of such remonstrance. This parody on the imported opera, filled with exquisite native and traditional airs, has sung its way down to us today, delighting untold thousands who, like my mother, were ignorant that they were listening to English folk tunes. It was one of sixty-odd which were popular in the eighteenth century.

And the simple people refused to forget their songs. Mothers still sang them as they rocked their children to sleep. Young men picked them up from their elders at work and in their 'turn handed them on to their children. And every now and then some person of perception made an effort to collect and preserve them. Bishop Percy was among the earliest with his *Reliques,* Child followed with *English and Scottish Popular Ballads,* while less widely circulated collections were frequent. The literature of the ballad became firmly established, for the tradition of English speech had not been harmed; but the musical tradition among educated people had been broken, and the tunes, when they were written down, were often recorded by people who—even when appreciating their beauty—were at a loss to know how to handle them, because they did not conform to the now firmly established continental pattern.

It remained for the last of these collectors, Cecil Sharp, to restore to us this musical tradition. In spite of his inestimable gift to England and to the world, I think English musicians have failed to give this great man his due. He went about among country people—who alone in England remembered the old songs—coaxed them to confide what had become a secret treasure, and wrote down with scholarly care for the forgotten modes which they employed, the precious tunes as well as the words.

When his collections in England had covered all possible territory, Cecil Sharp came to this country. He went for his hunting into the Appalachians, following the range. There he tapped a mine of musical wealth. Songs already discovered in England he found in abundance and variety, and also many which he had not collected in England were still going strong in these mountains. He wrote so well of his American adventures that he has made a cult of "Mountain Music." It is a rare person with any musical knowledge who is not aware that in the depths of the Appalachians live a people—chiefly illiterate—with a beautiful musical tradition. The work of Loraine Wyman and Howard

Brockway has been added to our knowledge of them. The hills of Vermont have contributed to the collection until the term "Mountain Music" came to mean a great deal to most Americans.

It is not true, however, in Virginia, that these tunes are limited to mountain retreats and fastnesses. Until the last year I have not realized how widely dispersed is the knowledge of the old music. Since it has become generally known that I am interested and since an exposition of just what the old music is and means has got abroad through the state, I stumble upon it everywhere. Not long ago, I took a manuscript to the drug store at the corner where there is a postal station. I asked the clerk to register the package. "A new piece of work?" he inquired with such a friendly interest that I told him it was and based on old Virginia tunes. He stood staring at me, motionless, for a moment and then, "I'm certainly glad," he said. "I've been wondering why no composers use our fine old tunes. Over the radio I am always hearing orchestras play symphonies made on Russian folk songs." A little later I was wiring a long message in which such surprising titles as "Jenny Put the Kettle On," "Walking in the Parlor," "Old Gray Mule," and "Cluck, Old Hen," appeared. At the end I paused to compliment the intelligent operator who had taken it all down over the telephone without a slip. "That's very kind of you, Mr. Powell," he responded, "but I used to play the fiddle myself." Again, breakfasting in the garden, I was suddenly aware that nearby someone was whistling "Old John Hardy." Leaving the coffee to get cold, I went in search of the folk musician who confessed that he knew many old tunes and who cheerfully promised to come and make my heart glad with them one day after union hours.

Moreover, this knowledge is not limited to any one class of society in Virginia. Our folk musicians are by no means illiterate people. Some few, no doubt, are. Among simpler people there are many who still get out fiddles and banjos to enliven the evenings and who have preserved the ballads. But one afternoon at a fashionable teaparty when the folk music was under discussion, a friend, whom the newspaper would be certain to call "a young society matron," suddenly asked, "Is this a folk song?" and sang an exquisite typical tune which I had never heard before. When I asked her where she had picked it up, she smiled. "I sing it to my children at bedtime," she said. "My mother used to sing it to me and she learned it from her mother."

It is to this wide dispersal and to the fact that educated people knew, loved, and sang these songs in Virginia that I attribute the unusual beauty and refinement of many of the tunes which are to be found there. Virginia was settled when the Elizabethan tradition was still a living thing. The songs escaped with the colonists and the very isolation of the pioneer life made them more precious. They were cherished by all classes. For this reason many have kept a purity of style that was lost in England where other musical influences were all about. This is especially true of the dance tunes. It is a pathetic fact that Cecil Sharp's collection of dance tunes is so small. The Morris tunes, since they were the accompaniment of ritualistic dances, had been fairly well preserved. But the country dances had made use of the popular music—music which was fashionable from time to time—and in many cases where the dances obviously had a long history, the tunes to which they were performed were practically worthless. Sharp was forced to turn to Playford's *English Dancing Master,* which, although of great interest, is not strictly of the folk by any means. In Virginia, on the other hand, the old fiddlers had kept the tunes alive where the dances had died out. And now, when they are learning that people are interested in hearing them, they are bringing them out by the score. In the mountains and remote villages these dance tunes and ballads and songs do exist, many of them beautiful and all of great interest. Two of the loveliest tunes I have collected came from a mountain district, but, of the others, I have found by far the most remarkable in those parts of the state which were centers of culture, where the high standard of taste either preserved the finer tunes or, as they passed from one individual to another, improved and polished them.

The history of ballad collection in Virginia has followed that of England. Just as Percy, Sir Walter Scott, and Child preserved the verses of traditional English and Scottish ballads and songs, so here in Virginia,

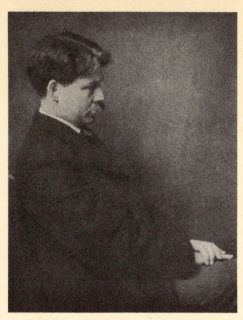

EDWARD MacDOWELL   LILY STRICKLAND

EDGAR STILLMAN KELLEY

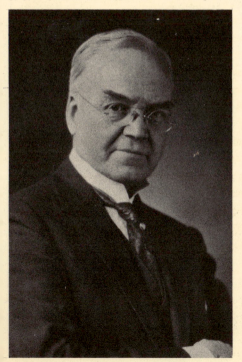

EDWARD MacDOWELL'S CABIN

JOHN POWELL

HOWARD BROCKWAY

PUEBLO INDIANS RECORDING TRIBAL MELODIES FOR THURLOW LIEURANCE

Dr. C. Alphonzo Smith, and Professor Arthur Kyle Davis, who completed and published the collection begun by Dr. Smith, have done yeomen's service: *Traditional Ballads of Virginia* is a magnificent piece of work; it contains fifty-one ballads with their variants, making several hundred in all, a veritable treasure house for the literary student. But, as was the case in England's early collections, the music is almost neglected. Only a few tunes are given at all, and many of these were collected by people who did not understand their peculiarities, and consequently they are inaccurate or distorted. The emphasis which has been put on the words is all the more remarkable to me in that the ballad poems, delightful, and even highly developed, as they are, are not to be compared as poetry with the tunes as music. For the tunes, unlike the great body of folk music, are not naïve, simple, and charming only. They are amazing as melody; the most highly trained musicians often gasp at their subtlety. I do not exaggerate when I say that many of them are not surpassed even by compositions by men of greatest genius. Their subtlety makes careful study imperative before it is possible properly to record them, and this in part accounts for the fact that so few have been put on paper. Sporadic individual attempts, which should be greatly commended, have been made. Alfreda Peel, of Sale, preached the doctrine of their value at a time when they were neglected by the generality. And Virginia is also indebted to Cecil Sharp.

The impression made by the folk musicians upon Sharp is doubly interesting since he was a complete stranger to them and their ways and since he had behind him the experience of similar collecting in England. He saw chiefly the people of the mountains, of whom he says in *English Folk Songs from the Southern Appalachians:* "That the illiterate may nevertheless reach a high level of culture will surprise only those who imagine that education and cultivation are convertible terms. The reason, I take it, why these mountain people, albeit unlettered, have acquired so many of the essentials of culture is partly to be attributed to the large amount of leisure they enjoy, without which, of course, no cultural development is possible, but chiefly to

the fact that they have one and all entered at birth into the full enjoyment of their racial heritage. Their language, wisdom, manners, and
the many graces of life that are theirs, are merely racial attributes which
have been gradually acquired and accumulated in past centuries and
handed down generation by generation, each generation adding its quo-
tum to that which it received."

In connection with this tribute, it is equally interesting to know
with what feelings the stranger from London was received by his
hosts. Maud Karpeles, who accompanied Mr. Sharp on his tour, taking
down the words of songs in shorthand, told me in London in 1928 that
one of these mountaineers paid Mr. Sharp a compliment which he
valued above any praise he had ever received. He was preparing to
take his leave after spending the night in a primitive farmhouse. His
host and hostess expressed the keenest regret that he could not linger
with them. "We all wish you would stay," declared the old man wist-
fully at parting. "You are so nice and common." And this was merely the
unlettered man's way of expressing what Mr. Sharp had felt of him and
his fellows: that they shared a racial heritage which gave them, more
than anything else could, a basis of understanding and mutual enjoyment.

The just use of the good old word, "common," as we know it in
the *Book of Common Prayer,* precisely suits the feeling which springs
up between those who share the love of this old music. Now that I am
familiar with this fact I have learned to obviate difficulties which collecting involves. In my early days I often made mistakes. My inquiries
for folk songs brought blank looks, as, when I consider it, was only
natural. "Ballets" these old songs are called in some places and in
others, "love songs." However, the demand for them by these names
rarely brought them forth. I learned to make the approach in a less
direct way: to mention casually some old song that I knew as a boy:
"Do you know an old song called 'Barbara Allen'?" In Virginia that will
usually turn the trick. Before I had made this valuable discovery I had
some amusing misadventures. On one occasion en route to a concert
engagement I was forced by lack of proper connection to spend the

night at a little village hotel and, getting into a chat with the proprietress, coaxed from her a promise to sing me some old songs after she had wiped the supper dishes. With keen anticipation, indeed, hardly able to wait, I sat down at the square piano in the parlor and turned my attention to a little practice to control my impatience. Soon I was engrossed. Some time after I became aware that I was not alone, and saw outside the windows, on the porch, a group of attentive listeners. I paused long enough to invite them in and returned to my work. At last, my program finished, I left the piano. A young woman with an eager face gravely approached me. (I discovered later that she was the school-teacher.) "Young man," she said, "what circuit are you on?" And would hardly credit my modest response that I was attached to none. "You should be," she assured me, "for I never heard such playing. Never fear, you'll soon be engaged." But my pleasure in this approbation was quite destroyed when the innkeeperess joined me, wiping her hands on her apron. "Now," I began enthusiastically, "for the old songs." She sternly shook her head. "If you had wanted me to sing to you," she announced severely, "you hadn't oughter played that pi-anna like you done." Nor could I soften her decision. I heard no old songs on that trip.

However, taught by such experiences, as I traveled all over the state year by year, I discovered here and there gems of great beauty, until I had proved to my own satisfaction what I had always known: that Virginia was filled with traditional songs and dances. And I became more and more eager to see established an agency for the preservation of the old music before it became crowded out and lost. I knew that every year old people were dying and carrying to their graves beauties which could never be replaced. The younger generation was not learning the tunes. The whole tendency to specialize in our modern life has been making us turn more and more to professional artists for our music, and, with the distribution of the work of great artists over the radio, I saw a future in which not even the most remote dwellers in the mountains would be dependent upon themselves for the delights of music. It became clearer every day that traditional music was doomed.

In 1930 a small music club in southwest Virginia invited me to address them. It is a beautiful country; great mountains tower up to five thousand feet and the fertile valleys are green with blue-grass pasture and ten-foot corn. The people are proud of their colonial history, of their rich land, and of their own energetic activities. I determined to rouse them to an enthusiasm for the music that I knew was lurking about them in the hills. And it is quite possible that this would have been merely another of my preachments which went in one ear and out the other of a polite audience, had it not been for the spontaneous—and I think rather mischievous—assistance of a prominent young business man whose wife was the president of the club and hostess for the evening. The club was puzzled how to entertain me, for although the members were all musicians, none would consent to make music for me. The young business man, therefore, thinking quite rightly that much unnecessary fuss was being made, offered to provide the program. "I'll engage the jug-band from the High School and send my fiddlers from the factory," he volunteered.

The fiddlers and the jug-band provided just the object lesson my lecture needed. In case you have never seen one, a jug-band is a string aggregation—violin, banjo, and guitar—with the addition of an ordinary stone jug such as usually holds molasses or vinegar. The performer blows into its mouth and varies the pitch with no little skill by the distance at which he holds it, producing a pleasant tone that sounds not unlike a grunting bassoon.

I called for old dances. "Turkey in the Straw," "Arkansaw Traveler," and "The Mississippi Sawyer" were promptly forthcoming with band and fiddlers united. Here was something which gave an edge to my talk. I actually had at hand folk musicians to emphasize my point that the woods and hills were full of them. Beginning with the question, "How many of you know what the Dorian mode is?" I startled the club members into real attention and made them listen while I told them that all about them were neighbors—many of whom were patronized as poor illiterate creatures—who could play or sing in that mode. My exhortation was so keen that the next day a lady who had not been present asked me, "Whatever did you say to those people last night? At least twenty women have been here today on fire to go out and save a folk song!"

Nor were the fiddlers and the band neglected. The former, Frank and Ed Blevins, told me that their father, too, had been a fiddler since his youth and knew many tunes which they had never learned. Their promise to amend the oversight they have faithfully kept. And in the band I found an instrument which to me was far more interesting than the jug: this was a banjo. It was not a modern four-stringed, but an old-fashioned five-stringed one, such as is rarely seen nowadays. "I can't play the fifth string," said Ellis Wohlford when I questioned him, "but my father can. It is his banjo."

The next morning, Ellis brought his father, Mr. Wohlford, with the banjo to see me. That day will always stand out in my mind, for not only was Mr. Wohlford the repository of a great banjo tradition but he was also a very great artist. As he warmed to his work, I realized that nowhere in the performance of any artist on any instrument had I met a finer sense of style. He modestly protested that he was not in practice, and I could easily believe his assertion that twenty years ago when he played for dances he could begin at seven in the evening and play until seven the next morning without repeating a tune. And it was comical—if a little pathetic, too—to observe the increasingly shame-faced look and attitude of his son as our enthusiasm grew and the father with a sidelong glance from time to time remarked: "Ellis says my tunes are 'fogy.'" In this connection I should like to add that Ellis is now one of the most eager students of his father's "fogy" tunes.

On that morning plans were made which have brought about a real musical revival in Virginia. Mrs. J. P. Buchanan (known to the musical world as a composer of songs) was quick to see a practical use which could be made of the accomplished musicians at her door: she adapted them to the needs of the Virginia State Choral Festival which was to be held at the University of Virginia in April. A Folk Program was planned for Children's Day, to be divided into three parts: traditional music played by native musicians, settings of traditional tunes, and, finally, compositions based upon the tunes. When April came this program was quite the most distinguished of an entire week of music.

The first Virginia State Choral Festival was held at the University of Virginia. It was directly the outcome of work done by the Virginia Federated Music Clubs in encouraging choral singing throughout the state, and its duration was that of the annual joint convention of the Federated Music Clubs and the State Teachers' Association. Nowhere could a more perfect setting have been found: The University of Virginia is the most perfect work of Thomas Jefferson's great architectural genius; it is surrounded by the distant shapes and green slopes of the Blue Ridge. The MacIntire Theater, with classic rows of seats and a green carpet of spring grass, held the large audiences comfortably under a shining sky and at the same time let no sound escape; for it is one of those rare outdoor theaters with well-nigh perfect acoustics.

Twelve hundred auditors gathered for the Folk Program and for over three hours sat spellbound or broke into all but riotous cheering. So many fine folk musicians had been brought to light that it was difficult to choose among them. Owing to the length of the program, encores were an impossibility. But when Jack Reedy, one of the ablest of the banjoists, finished "Cluck, Old Hen," the applause was deafening. As in other cases—for everybody wanted to hear each tune a second time—I was about to introduce the next performer when the ring of a deeply moved voice stopped me. "John," it called from the very back row, half a city block away. I looked, to see the Professor of French with big tears running down his cheeks. "John! make him play it again!" he begged. It was impossible to resist such a plea, and "Cluck, Old Hen" had the distinction of being heard twice.

An optional fourth part of the program had been added to include many delightful features which could not be squeezed into the program proper. This part was not reached until six o'clock. The audience, however, was undismayed by the lateness of the hour, and sat on to watch "square dances" deftly performed by dancers from a neighboring small town. Dancers and their accompanying string band, which was directed by J. B. Wells, had been transported en masse to dance as they are accustomed to do on Saturday evenings. The music was so enticing that folk musicians from all over the state could not keep from dancing and the afternoon closed with a general ensemble of all the performers. And practically every member of the company whether performer or listener was ready to agree with Mr. Wohlford, who said in bidding me good-by, "Never in all my life have I had such a good time."

It has been a surprise to me to find what interest has been roused by this program all over the country. But what was most vital in its effect was the fact that through the publicity connected with it, word was carried to the folk musicians of the state that what they have in their possession is something which many people are keen to hear. There has been a tuning of fiddles and banjos all over Virginia; many which were unstrung and dusty have come out of attics; and memories, also dusty, have been subjected to a freshening. The result has been a new activity in several localities, where the musicians have met in festive mood to exchange their tunes. The largest of these purely folk gatherings was carried out under the direction of Mrs. Buchanan. With John Blakemore she planned an all-day Folk Festival to be held on Whitetop, the second highest point in the state. The rich verdant valleys and the surrounding hills, made a magnificent amphitheater for the pageant. Under the shelter of a tent, contests were held all day long. Some three thousand people gathered before eleven o'clock in the morning in spite of the fact that the road up the mountain alone is several miles. People came on foot, on horses and mules, as well as in cars of ancient and the very latest patterns. The majority of the people were the natives of the neighborhood, but they came from three states, as it is on this mountain that Virginia, Tennessee, and North Carolina meet. The prize-winner on the guitar came from Delaware. When I asked him what he was doing here he replied, "I was passing through the country and I happened to hear some of their tunes. I simply couldn't leave until I had learned them all."

Certainly two hundred musicians took part in the contests—fiddlers, banjoists, guitarists, string bands, and performers on the dulcimer, a delicate little instrument which has been completely lost except in our hills. The dancing contests in the late afternoon brought a renewed vigor just at the close. But what made the day most memorable was the fact that folk singers actually made their appearance on the stage and sang folk songs to a large audience. The real folk singer is a shy creature. He—or she—usually makes no pretension to a voice and whatever voice is there, is untrained. As he sings without vocal props and without accompaniment, and as he is accustomed to a single listener or at most a very small group, it is difficult to persuade him to sing for strangers. An audience seems to demand a performance and this is just what your true folk singer does not give. He sings his song impersonally, in a quiet, almost secret voice, as if he tells his tale largely for his own enjoyment. And there would have been no folk singing at Whitetop, had not a young man—an able performer on the banjo and the conductor of a band and consequently accustomed to appearing in public, who was, in addition to all this, reared in the folk song tradition— taken pity upon our pleading. He finally agreed, like a good sport, to be the first to try. As Council Cruise stood there, telling the tale of "Pretty Polly" to breathless thousands, the chills which ran up and down my spine were only in part due to the thrill of the weirdly tragic tune: they were quite as much attributable to a feeling that his singing was a prophecy of the cultural future of Virginia. And the eager attention on every rapt face in the audience made me suddenly conscious that I was no longer a voice crying in the wilderness.

For we are, it seems after all, a musical people. The chorus of a thousand voices which sprang up spontaneously from every corner of the state, from places as far apart as London is from Edinburgh, and came together to sing the Schubert *Mass in E Flat* at the University of Virginia certainly indicated no lack of musical feeling. To be sure, the Federated Music Clubs could get blood out of a turnip. They had, too, called for the work of Virginia composers; but no amount of calling would have produced from ungifted people the programs which for two years have reflected great credit upon the musicians of the state.

In addition, many people are musical without knowing it, indeed, while disclaiming it. The young manufacturer, whose half humorous introduction of the jug-band and the Blevins boys has proved a valuable contribution to our musical life, is a case in point; for he gave those boys a job in his factory, actuated partly by kindliness, no doubt, but chiefly because he liked their tunes. His musical acumen was established in that moment. And it is to people who make no profession of musical education that the revival of folk music will mean much. All progress is from the simple to the complex. Musical response is easily led from a folk tune through suitable settings to the larger forms. It is literally possible to see within a minimum of time the development of musical appreciation, granted that the subject be sensitive and intelligent.

Not long ago I was giving a recital in a girls' school in a Virginia town. My wife found herself next to a woman in the audience, no longer in her first youth, whose whole appearance indicated that her life had been laborious. The fine character in her face made my wife wonder whether she was perhaps the grandmother of a student. During the early part of the program, she sat, her rough hands folded in her lap, politely and passively attentive. Then I began a group of dances of folk origin. The first, a vigorous *Contra Tanz* of Beethoven, did not stir her. The second was based on tunes which are a commonplace of the Virginia countryside, "Old John Hardy" and "The Mississippi Sawyer." As the first strains reached her neighbor, my wife felt her relax with a sigh and then, delighted, heard her remark in a tone audible through half the auditorium: "Well, thank the Lord!" As the music drew to a close, she turned to my wife and continued, "I say that because I am not literate in music. To play those other things to me is like reading Hamlet to a baby. The baby would not understand it." With this she turned animated attention to David Guion's "Turkey in the Straw," and expressed the keenest pleasure in the "Arkansaw Traveler" by the same composer. By this time she was utterly in a receptive mood, and when I returned to play the A-Flat "Polonaise" of Chopin, she continued to drink in every note eagerly, nor did her attention fall away when it was followed by the quiet "Nocturne" in D-flat. With perfect self-unconsciousness she turned to my wife, her voice no more than a whisper: "Oh! that was beautiful." Half an hour before, she could not have been coaxed to express an opinion of such a composition: it is doubtful whether she could have heard it properly. Without knowing it she had been educated in those few moments, her taste had been led from something which she understood and loved, which spoke to her in her own language, through the expression of the Polish folk feeling in the slightly foreign polonaise to what she no doubt would have called "a classical piece." Quite naturally and suddenly its mood and emotional message reached her.

With this sort of activity and education going on all over the state, it does not seem too much to hope that Virginians will gradually get rid of the notion that they are unmusical. To accomplish this end, many interested people are working to establish a department of Folk Music at the University, in order that the tunes which are in danger of being lost may be preserved, that they may be available for future study, that they may be analyzed and be kept as a permanent part of our cultural life. Nor is Virginia alone in her efforts. North Carolina has already begun the task of collecting her folk tunes, and the University of North Carolina has established, under the able and enthusiastic leadership of Lamar Stringfield, the Institute of Folk Music at Chapel Hill. The Institute is in its infancy, but like most infants is rapidly outgrowing one set of clothes after another. Folk musicians are being sought out, tunes are being collected, students are being given an opportunity for playing ensembles, laboratory concerts are given at intervals, young composers are having an opportunity to hear their works. The experiments of the first foundation of its kind are of tremendous importance to the musical life of the whole country and should be watched with sympathetic interest by all musicians.

Nor do I have the least hesitation about assuring everyone who asks my advice that the tunes of both songs and dances will fully repay any amount of study. I have put to the test the old rule and have proved to more than satisfaction that in their case familiarity does not breed contempt but leads to deeper admiration and keener delight. As I have been studying these tunes, I have also studied with growing reverence Beethoven's development of melody through years of thought as revealed in his notebooks. The wonder of that master's achievement has only served to increase my astonishment at the so-called simple folk melodies. Not only have we a folk music, but we have the finest in the world. These tunes have beauty of line and structure. They have sustained length of phrase with surprising punctuation by emphasis on unexpected degrees of the scale. They have cunning preparation of climax and its unfailing pointing. They have inexhaustible diversity, freshness, and vigor of rhythmic effects both in phrase and measure rhythms to keep the interest tense and alert. Most remarkable, however, is their structure. They are not pieced together, but grow into being like living entities. These melodies are organisms. That is why even the sauciest or most jolly give the impression of elegance, of a chaste and classic nobility. Judged by the most stringent standards, many of them are well-nigh flawless.

THE NEGRO AND HIS SONG

BY HARRY T. BURLEIGH, *American Composer*

THE story of the Negro is told in his music for, from its beginning to its end, his life is attuned to song.

The history of Negro song in America is comparatively short, no successful attempt having been made to collect it before 1830, from which time a few letters or articles describing it have been preserved. Best known to the world are the plantation songs known as Spirituals, which, on account of their great number, their lovely melodies, compelling rhythms, and deeply emotional content, are unique examples of folk song.

The origin of the Negro's song is problematic, and to attempt to trace its history is to venture upon controversial ground. I differ with some musicians who think it a form of the German chorale, and also with others who feel that the Spirituals are derived entirely from the hymns the Negro heard in the religious services of the white people. The songs are entities in themselves, influenced in some instances, no doubt, in their form and substance, by the songs which the colored people heard from itinerant missionaries; and if at all African, resemble more the exalted beauty of the songs of the Israelites than the barbaric yells and rhythms of the Negroes of Africa, the latter probably the result of structural peculiarities of African languages. Who can tell, a beautiful melody sung by the Hebrews in those far-off days recorded in the Old Testament may have come, by being overheard by African Negroes and carried through centuries of trials and countless mutations, to flower on American soil!

White critics, and some of the Negroes as well, classify the songs as Spirituals, "work" songs ("John Henry" songs), the "blues," and the social songs. As to the so-called "work" songs, they are a very small minority of the whole mass of Negro song, and I call them "dialect" songs. Very few white people have heard the Negro really singing at work, what songs they have heard have been, rather, rhythmic improvisations. The "blues" have a characteristic syncopation which, if not overdone, is very fascinating, but which, in its abuse, forms the dominating element of jazz.

The main feature of the most intimate and finest of the Negro's songs is its simplicity, for, like the colorful folk music of Russia, it is usually made up of just one idea repeated over and over in the stress of deep fervor in an effort to give some expression to an inner emotion. The Negro just takes a few simple words, and about their rhythm creates a beautiful musical picture. When given the right interpretation this reiteration does not produce monotony, but seems absolutely inspired, as illustrated in the appealing "De Blin' Man Stood on de Road an' Cried," where a simple phrase is repeated sixteen times.

The Spirituals are the spontaneous outbursts of intense, whiteheat, religious fervor, and had their origin chiefly in camp meetings, revivals, and other religious exercises. They were never "composed" but sprang into life, ready made, during some "protracted meeting," as the simple, ecstatic utterance of wholly untutored minds, and are practically the only music in America which meets the scientific definition of folk song.

Success in singing these folk songs is primarily dependent upon deep spiritual feeling. The voice is not nearly so important as the spirit; and then rhythm, for the Negro's soul is linked with rhythm, and it is an essential feature of most all Negro song.

It is a serious misconception of their meaning and value to treat them as "minstrel" songs, or to try to make them funny by a too literal attempt to imitate the manner of the Negro in singing them, by swaying the body, clapping the hands, or striving to make the peculiar inflections of voice that are natural with the colored people. Their worth is weakened unless they are done impressively, for through all these songs there breathes a hope, a faith in the ultimate justice and brotherhood of man, and that eventually every man will be free.

Many of the songs are in the five-toned (pentatonic) scale which has been used by all races who have been in bondage, including the Hebrews. It is so old that no one knows its origin. The Scotch use it in their folk songs, and it has always been heard in music of the Orient. If one sings the common major scale, omitting the fourth and seventh tones, he has the pentatonic scale.

There is also a fondness in Negro song for use of either the major or minor scale with a flat seventh tone. This gives a peculiarly poignant quality. Dvořák, in his *New World Symphony,* made great use of the flat seventh in the minor. This great master literally saturated himself with Negro song before he wrote the *New World,* and I myself, while never a student of Dvořák, not being far enough advanced at that time to be in his classes, was constantly associated with him during the two years that he taught in the National Conservatory in New York. I sang our Negro songs for him very often and, before he wrote his own themes, he filled himself with the spirit of the old Spirituals. I also helped to copy parts of the original score. A study of the musical material of which the *New World* is made will reveal the influence of Negro song upon it.

The introduction of the Symphony is pervaded with syncopation common to Negro song, and by a use of the flat seventh in the minor mode. This is suggestive of the strangeness of the new country. The syncopation is even more marked in the first theme of the opening movement which is followed by a four-measure subsidiary theme of real charm in which Dvořák employed the lowered, or flat, seventh. Then comes the second theme with its open reference to the beloved Spiritual "Swing Low, Sweet Chariot" of which Dvořák used the second and third measures almost note for note, as a comparison will show. The colorfulness of this entire movement, as well as that of the final movement, lies largely in the use of the flat seventh in the harmonization, this remark in no way belittling Dvořák's superb gift for instrumentation.

Negro Spirituals may be classified as narrative songs, songs of admonition, songs of inspiration, of tribulation, of death, and of play.

Of the latter none is so gay as "Lil 'Liza Jane," of the Mississippi levees. The tribulation songs, strangely, are not all melancholy. Many of the Negro's best songs vacillate oddly, sometimes within a single phrase, between major and minor. But even when entirely in the minor, they are not always sad: poignant and appealing, yes, but never melancholy.

No songs in the world have a greater or more deserved popularity than those Spirituals which tell of the universal striving and weariness of all men, not alone of the Negro race. There is the tender "Somebody's Knockin' at Yo' Door," and "I Bin in de Storm So Long," the imploring "I Want to Be Ready," and "Standin' in de Need of Prayer," this latter song being used, with modifications, by Louis Gruenberg, in his *Emperor Jones;* and the truly exquisite "Deep River."

In the narrative Spirituals, the Negro has translated the marvelous stories of the Old Testament into simple home language, each tale, in his telling, being colored by his own exaltation and understanding of the Scriptures. Here we find "De Gospel Train," "Didn't It Rain," "Who Built de Ark," and "Ezekiel Saw de Wheel."

Many modern composers see in the piquant rhythms of Negro song, and its simple but expressive melodies, material to use in a thematic way in the writing of great art works. The week that Dvořák sailed back to his Old World home, after two years spent as a teacher in New York, a prominent journal commented by saying that "no sum of money was large enough to keep Antonin Dvořák in the New World. He left us his *New World Symphony* and his *American Quartet,* but he took himself away."

But even if he did he left behind a richer appreciation of the beauties of Negro song, of its peculiar flavor, its sometimes mystical atmosphere, its whimsical piquancy, and its individual idiom, from all of which many other splendid artists have already drawn inspiration.

EDWARD MACDOWELL AND HIS MUSIC *

NOTHING could be more appropriate as an introduction to a study of Edward MacDowell and his music than the estimate of his importance as an international artist voiced by the distinguished founders of the MacDowell Association, in 1906. It said, in part:

"In Edward MacDowell America has found a new voice in music—noble and virile music, neither academic and imitative nor crude and barbarous, but full of that freedom which comes from true knowledge, and that mystical poetry which hides in the heart of a strong, resolute nature. Trained in the best schools of Europe, master of the Old World traditions, he came home to his native country in the flower of his youth, and for eighteen years devoted his genius and his vigor to the service of his great art, with the single purpose of doing work that should increase his country's joy and add to his country's glory. And he did much toward the accomplishment of his aim: sonatas, concertos, and idyls, symphonic compositions, songs, and studies, in which the old poetic traditions that belong to all humanity are treated with a new lyrical breadth and intensity of passion, and novel aboriginal themes are interwoven into forms of beautiful and coherent art. MacDowell's work in music, like Hawthorne's work in literature, is distinctly and unmistakably American. Yet it is also vitally related to the rest of the world's good work. It presupposes a long past, just as our civilization is the work of many centuries, while it develops in liberty toward a new future. It is an honor to a country to produce such an artist."

Edward MacDowell was born in New York City, on December 18, 1861, of Quaker descent, his father being a skilled draftsman, and his

---

* Discussion of individual compositions will be found in Part II of the book.

mother a talented and gracious gentlewoman, interested throughout her
life in the fine arts. From his Scotch-Irish ancestry, MacDowell inherited
an absorbing interest in legend and poetry which colored all his later
life. He went to school in New York. The boys and girls who played
with him and sat in his classes little dreamed that their young friend
and classmate, who liked, best of all, to read and to draw pictures on
the margins of his books' pages, would become one of the greatest of
all American composers and that one of his pieces—"To a Wild Rose"—
would presently be chosen as the outstanding favorite of any composition written by an American, and one of the ten greatest "favorites"
among all the music in the world.

Henry T. Finck, a distinguished American critic, wrote enthusiastically of MacDowell, at the time this choice was made, saying that there
were "enough diamonds and rubies and emeralds among the Mac-
Dowell writings to make a crown for him as king of contemporary
American musicians."

MacDowell began his study of the piano when very young, one of
his first teachers being Teresa Carreño, later celebrated as the greatest
woman pianist in the world.

Soon after he was ten years old, MacDowell was taken on a tour of
Europe by his mother, and delighted the party with which they traveled,
by the keenness of his observations. When he was fifteen, MacDowell
returned to Europe for the study of piano and composition, being for
a time at the Paris Conservatory, where he was a fellow pupil with
Claude Debussy. Later he went to Stuttgart and to Frankfurt, and was
so fortunate as to win the high regard of his teacher, Joachim Raff, who
brought his compositions to the attention of Franz Liszt, then the most
influential person in European musical life.

By the time he was eighteen MacDowell had acquired a mastery of
the technique of composition frequently reached by artists only toward
the close of their careers. This is illustrated by the fact of his composition of the *Concerto for Piano* in A minor, and its orchestral accompaniment, within the short period of three weeks, before he had reached his
eighteenth birthday. It was this dazzlingly brilliant work which the

young composer carried with him on the occasion of his memorable visit to Liszt.

At twenty, MacDowell was appointed head of the piano department at Frankfurt Conservatory, where one of his most talented students was Miss Marion Nevins of New London, Connecticut, who, in 1884, became his wife. In 1888, Mr. and Mrs. MacDowell returned to America, making their home in Boston until 1896, when he was called to Columbia University to establish a chair of music, which post he retained until his resignation, due to ill health, in 1904.

During the years which followed 1896, many of MacDowell's finest compositions were written at Peterborough, New Hampshire, where he and Mrs. MacDowell had purchased a farm homestead of the Revolutionary Period. The house, a sturdy dwelling put together in the olden style, with hand-made nails, and birch-bark lining the walls between the boards and shingles, was retained in its original form, the MacDowells merely remodeling it to suit their personal needs. The first addition was a music room, built on to the north of the house, but the following year Mrs. MacDowell surprised her husband by having erected, at what was then the edge of their property, the Log Cabin studio, the fame of which has encircled the world. MacDowell afterwards spent many hours each day in the restful and inspiring seclusion of his "House o' Dreams."

The years immediately following his resignation from Columbia were years of growing nervous strain, and in 1906 MacDowell suffered a severe breakdown from which he never recovered. He died in New York City, January 23, 1908. At the funeral service held in St. George's Church at Stuyvesant Square, tribute was paid by the greatest musicians and musical organizations of the nation. The Mendelssohn Glee Club, which MacDowell had once served as conductor, sang *Integer Vitae*. W. H. Humiston, at the organ, played the *Andante* from the composer's own *Sonata Tragica;* and the *Dirge* from his *Indian Suite* was performed under the direction of Sam Franko. The following day the composer was laid at rest on his own grounds in Peterborough. Just across the fields from the house, "Hillcrest," and not far distant from the Log Cabin, is the grave, guarded by the huge bowlder under which he was wont to rest after a game at the nearby golf course and which, marked by a bronze tablet placed there by the Boston MacDowell Club, now serves as a monument.

Such is, briefly, the history of MacDowell's life, but his name will be remembered so long as the art of music lives. His fame will rest not only upon the beauty of his larger works, the four sonatas for piano, two concertos, the *Indian Suite,* and others, but upon the magic charm of his many poetic and exquisite small classics, so popular with finely trained musicians and untrained music-lovers, alike.

Shortly after he had gone to Europe for study, and before his eighteenth birthday, MacDowell sent to Carreño, then in America, a roll of manuscript, accompanied by a letter in which he said, "You know I have always had absolute confidence in your judgment. Look these over, if you will. If there is anything there any good, I will try some more, but if you think they are of no value, throw them in the paper basket and tell me, and I'll never write another line." "So," said Mme. Carreño, "I sat down and played them. There were, in that bundle, the *First Suite,* the *Hexantanz, Erzählen, Barcarolle,* and *Étude de Concert!* I wrote to MacDowell, 'Throw nothing into the paper basket, and keep on!'"

Soon after this, Mme. Carreño was to give a recital in Chicago, and in this she included the *First Suite.* That was the first performance in the world, of music by Edward MacDowell. It was heard with great appreciation. Mme. Carreño recalled that W. Ș. B. Matthews came to her after the concert and said, "Who is that fellow MacDowell? Seems quite talented, that man!" Carreño replied that he should wait, that he would hear more of MacDowell, who would be famous after they had turned to dust.

In her reminiscence Mme. Carreño continued that even after Mac-Dowell began to be known he still remained very modest and retiring. She would ask him, "Have you written anything new?" to which he would reply, "Oh, some trifles." And Mme. Carreño would then command him to show her these "trifles," many of which she introduced to both American and European audiences, and played in concert until the time of her death.

The MacDowell music—more than one hundred and thirty pieces of music of highest quality—has been applauded by critics in both Europe and America. His greatest works are vivid with melody and spring from and are illumined by a personality strong and serious in character and of immense capacity for musical expression. MacDowell wrote clearly and compactly and his music displays a remarkable sense of organic unity and logical development of musical ideas. He possessed an enormous faculty for characterization and nature, and the subtler influences of the woods and fields appealed to him greatly. Because of his life-time devotion to folk lore and legend he found suggestion for composition in the tales of fairies, dryads, nymphs, and elves with which such lore abounds. He was also attracted by more human objects, and several of his finest works were stimulated by tales of knighthood and chivalry. In the case of his *Second (Indian) Suite,* and also in certain of the "Woodland Sketches," he made use of authentic Indian tribal airs, but these, he said, he did for the pure pleasure of using beautiful material, rather than with any thought at all of their use as a foundation for an "American school" of composition; and in them he wrote a message of universal emotion and sense of beauty. His infinitely pathetic "Deserted Farm" is filled with a loneliness, hopelessness, and feeling of the impossibility of the return of anything that is gone, strikingly symbolic of the physical state of man, illustrating MacDowell's oft-repeated statement that "the simplest things of life are often the greatest."

Illustrative of the shy and modest reserve of MacDowell is the story of the mythical "Edgar Thorne," who became a person of some consequence in New York City. Reference has frequently been made to MacDowell's use of this *nom de plume* in connection with the writing of his "Marionettes," the royalty of which was given over to a needy friend. But comparatively few people know of its first use, which was in connection with the Mendelssohn Glee Club. At the time of MacDowell's taking over the direction of the Club (1896) he found that the work with the singers offered to him a new avenue of musical expression and presented a desire to compose some music suitable for their use. But with his usual modesty he feared that if the men knew that the new songs he was presenting for their examination were of his own composition, they would feel under obligation to sing them. So one night he appeared at rehearsal with two new songs, under the name of "Edgar Thorne," and simply asked them to try them over, if they liked them to sing them, perhaps in concert. The songs proved very effective, won the instant approval of the club, and remained "favorite" numbers. MacDowell used the same acid test on his poems (many do not know that he possessed three gifts of expression: music, poetry, and art), often copying texts which he had written for his own songs on the board for the use of his classes in composition either anonymously or under the signature of "Edgar Thorne."

An intense shyness when among strangers and a desire to avoid miscellaneous crowds were characteristic of MacDowell and are illustrated by a story told of him by a close friend of the Boston years. "That's what I call playing!" he is said to have exclaimed to the friend, near whom he sat at a Paderewski recital; and then to have run all the way home across the Common to his own house after it was over, fearing to meet someone who might stop him "to talk" and thus break into his impression of the music.

MacDowell exercised a profound personal and musical influence upon his students at Columbia University, and his views, as recalled and related by some of them in later years, are of intense interest to those music lovers who had not that privilege of knowing him personally. Many of them illustrate the composer's warm humanity and wit, as well as the devoted care which he lavished upon his pupils, for whose welfare he was always planning. There he conducted one weekly students' class for the encouragement of composition, entirely free to those invited to join, and totally apart from the stipulated courses. Here, each week, the members of the class brought their compositions—whatever they had been working on the week previous—and played them over. MacDowell then offered valuable hints and suggestions, and not infrequently made little satirical remarks which were thoroughly enjoyed by all but the person at whom they were aimed.

One young lady, who later related the incident with deep appreciation, brought in a composition of doubtful tonality, and in criticizing it Mr. MacDowell said that it reminded him of a hedge with a hole in it through which an animal was looking out. "At first, seeing only the jaws," he went on, "you might say, 'It is a dog.' Then as more appeared, 'It is a fox,' and so on." Suddenly it occurred to MacDowell that perhaps he had said something very unkind, and he at once tried to apologize, saying that of course he did not mean that the music made him think of dogs and foxes; and, being oversensitive himself, was very much disturbed at the thought that what he had said might be misunderstood.

He often spoke of his own lectures as "mere music talks," but they displayed, through their numerous wide-flung references, an extremely broad view of various periods—especially the speculative periods—in music history. In connection with Egyptian music the students were asked to read Wilkinson, Petrie, and also Miss Edwards's *Thousand Miles up the Nile;* Ambros, on Chinese music; Da Vega, on Mexican music; Monros, on Greek music; and Westphal and Bellamore, on the same subject; also Plato, for the state of music in Pythagoras's time. In Homer they were asked to read of the first finding of the lyre. Gibbon's *Roman Empire* and the *Arabian Nights* were referred to as giving an idea of the magnificence and splendor of court life when Arabia was the center of civilization. Spencer was suggested as a reading on aroused emotion; Blaserna and Helmholtz, on vibration and sound; Hagen's great work on the Minnesingers; and articles in *Chambers's* and the *Encyclopædia Britannica* under "Troubadour" and "Poetry."

Of Richard Strauss's writings, then fairly new, MacDowell said, "This is not music; it is a new art." Again, "Harmony gives atmosphere to the melody; it is the tone background for melody; it enforces the melodic trend, but *the main trend is the melodic trend.*"—"The madrigals mark the first steps toward modern music; they attempted expression, to paint something."—"Bach spoke in close, scientific, contrapuntal language. He was as emotional and romantic as Chopin, Wagner, or Tschaikowsky; but his emotion was expressed in the language of his time. Some people who say they 'adore' Bach play him like a sum in mathematics. Beethoven is the first composer to build a poem and bring poetic thought to a logical conclusion. His music expresses *ideal* things, not actual things, as previous music had."—"It is not nationalism that makes Scotch music and melodies so poignant; they are simply good music. A good melody is always good. We find the Scotch 'snap' all over the world. Nationalism must be based upon the spirit of the people, not upon the clothes they wear. Music in America will rise after we get over our youthful money-making. Out of our idealism our music will grow."

Of the use of various instruments he said, "The violin is the 'queen' of them all. The bass drum is often used as an instrument of mystery, and in the picturing haunted woods or forests full of vague things; the faintest tap on the bass drum gives a marvelous effect. Certain uses of the cymbals are as picturesque as showers of silver. The tam-tam is at times quite terrifying and vulgar, and may be used for effects of horror; the tuba for effects of brutal strength." And, reluctantly, in a discussion of his own poetic works, "Music is not outside form, but rather a poignant expression of an idea."

Since the days when MacDowell used it, the Log Cabin has stood as one of the world's great shrines of music. It is all as Mr. MacDowell left it, pens on a tray on the corner shelf, a Moorish lamp still hanging from the ceiling, the old rush-bottomed chairs, the two ancient British fire-arms (one with a coat of arms)—relics of the Revolutionary War which MacDowell himself found under one of his own stone walls—crossed over the wide mantel, with a faded American flag above them; and the deep stone fireplace itself. On the cement floor of the hearth are the words, as they were written by Mr. MacDowell with the sharp end of his stick while the cement was still soft, "Edward and Miriam," a never-to-be-effaced reminder of the share Mrs. MacDowell had in all his thought and work and triumphs. On the porch, from which the crest of Mt. Monadnock is always visible, are chairs and a table, as he always had them, and down from its front door is the little path Mac-Dowell always took to and from "Hillcrest."

The Log Cabin is now surrounded by many added acres of wood-land, upon which, out of sight and sound of each other, have been built the nearly two dozen studios where, each summer, a goodly num-ber of creative workers in the fine arts—writers, painters, sculptors, and musicians—may work undisturbed, all this being the fulfillment of Edward MacDowell's dearest dream. This, the MacDowell Colony, is a *living memorial* to Edward MacDowell, made possible through the life-long devotion and effort of Mrs. MacDowell and a host of friends in a nation whose musical standard he raised and whose recognition in the world of music abroad he secured.

DVOŘÁK AND SPILLVILLE, FORTY
YEARS AFTER *

ON MAY 24, 1893, in the city of New York, Antonin Dvořák—
"Eminent Composer and Director of the National Conservatory
of Music of America," as he had been publicly heralded—signed his
name to the concluding page of his *New World Symphony,* which, together with his Quartet, Opus 96, called the *American Quartet,* and the
famous *Quintet* in E Flat, Opus 97, are the greatest fruits of his labors
on this continent. A few days later he and his family set out for the
Middle West, to spend the vacation months in little Spillville, a restful
inland village which lies along the banks of the Little Turkey River in
Winneshiek County, northeastern Iowa.

Some of the people who lived in Spillville then still live there, and
almost all the townspeople are descendants of the sturdy Bohemian
settlers who, as pioneers, first broke the sod on this reach of Iowa prairie.
Gentle in manner, devout and faithful in friendship and religion, they
recall with honest pride the visit of "the master" in their midst.

Visitors who travel to the village to see for themselves the spots associated with Dvořák, will find the home in which the composer and his
family lived still in use on the main street; and nearby, the church in
which Dvořák acted as organist during the summer. To reach Spillville they will probably drive along the Dvořák Highway—the only
public highway in the world, it is said, named for a musician—which
follows the course of the Turkey River from Calmar, a few miles to
the south, to Minnesota, about seventy-five miles north. This highway,
which combines scenic beauty with its particular interest to the world

* This story of Antonin Dvořák and Spillville, with its authenticated information concerning the sources of the *New World Symphony,* the *American Quartet,* the *Quintet* in
E-flat, and the "Humoresques," is reprinted, with permission, from the anniversary number (May 25, 1933) of *Musical America.* (For detailed thematic discussion, see pp. 307-9.)

of music, is marked for miles by hundreds of signs which bear a letter H inside of a larger letter D, and the name of whatever county in which they stand.

The highway will lead them past the delightfully rural Riverside Park in which there was dedicated, on September 28, 1925, a large rock memorial. On a bronze tablet set into the boulder are the words:

> In Commemoration of the Visit
> of
> Antonin Dvořák
> Renowned Composer
> to
> Spillville in 1893
> This Tablet Is Erected by
> His Friends
> and
> The Iowa Conservation Association

The chance that led Dvořák to Spillville, as recorded by the Iowa State Historical Society, is of interest: "That winter (in New York) was very trying for Dvořák. He was by nature a country gentleman, used to the serenity of rural life and accustomed to the solitary enjoyment of nature. In contrast to such an environment he was suddenly the center of great attention in New York. His social engagements were scarcely less numerous than his musical appointments. After meeting these private demands in addition to his duties as Director of the National Conservatory, he had little time left for composing. And when he did try to make a tune, it was invariably accompanied by the roar of elevated railway trains and the general clamor of traffic.

"As spring approached Dvořák wanted more than ever to escape from the noisy city. He was anxious to work on some new music that he had in mind. One day Josef Kovarik (son of the Spillville schoolmaster, and assistant and secretary to Dvořák) suggested that Dvořák accompany him on a visit to Iowa. Apparently his master did not hear, for he paid no attention to the remark and made no comment. A few days later, however, he quite unexpectedly asked Kovarik about Spillville. Kovarik explained that Spillville was a little Bohemian settlement, where his native language was spoken on the street; that it was peaceful and quiet, as well as beautiful; and most important of all, there were no railroads in Spillville. Several days passed. Then Dvořák asked his assistant to draw a map of Spillville, indicating every house, every street, every person who lived in each house, and what they did. That was all; Dvořák made no comments. But when some friends of his from South Carolina tried to persuade him to go there for his rest he said, 'No, I am going to Spillville.' So it was that a lovely day in June saw Antonin Dvořák, his wife, their six children, a sister, a maid, and his assistant, alight from the train at the little station of Calmar, eleven miles from Spillville. Kovarik sent the family on to the village while he remained to look after the baggage. Upon his arrival, he found Dvořák strolling around, smoking his pipe, quite at home, and apparently very much pleased with his surroundings."

The story of what happened in a musical way is best told by Prof. J. J. Kovarik, then schoolmaster, now living in New Prague, Minnesota, who, with a son and daughter, had the honor to join with Dvořák in the first playing through of the *American Quartet* when it was completed. Prof. Kovarik told the writer:

"It is erroneously believed by many that Dvořák composed the *New World Symphony* at Spillville, but this is not so. Dvořák had this symphony practically completed before he came to Spillville and it was only some minor details, namely the finishing of the trombone parts to the score of the Finale, that he did while at Spillville.

"One bright day, June 5, 1893, found the Dvořák ménage in the little town. Not only did the natural scenic beauty of the place appeal to the great composer, but also the fact that he was among his own countrymen reminded him of his mother country and he felt he was at home. But he barely got settled when his creative genius was at work, and on June 8th, three days after his arrival, he was at work on the first movement of his new composition, the *String Quartet* in F. He completed this movement in the early hours of the next morning and at once started the second movement, and even started the third in the evening of the same day. The next day he did the fourth movement so that by June 10th the entire quartet was completed. With a clear conscience and with much satisfaction he put a notation below the last line of the last movement: 'Thank God. I am satisfied. It went quickly.'

"He then went to work on the score, which he finished in a short time, writing each movement in about three days, so that the entire score was finished by June 23rd. Dvořák was so pleased that his new work was accomplished in so short a time that he felt a desire to hear it played, and so he formed a quartet of himself and members of my family, he playing first violin; myself, second violin; my daughter Cecelia, viola; and my son Joseph, 'cello.

"Immediately after finishing this score he commenced work on the *Quintet* in E Flat, Opus 97. This work took him longer, being started about June 26th and completed about August 1st.

"Dvořák was a very plain man and a great lover of nature. During this visit at Spillville a morning walk through the groves and along the banks of the river was on his daily program and he particularly enjoyed the warbling of the birds, in fact he admitted that the first day he was out for a walk, an odd-looking bird, red plumaged, only the wings black, attracted his attention and its warbling inspired the theme of the third movement of his string quartet.

"Neither I nor my son were pupils of Dvořák. When my son was at the Conservatory of Prague in the violin department, Dvořák was an instructor of composition there, and, when my son was returning to America, Dvořák also came to America. You ask whether I ever heard Dvořák talk of the source of the material he used in his *New World Symphony*. I must say that Dvořák was very reticent in regard to his compositions. He gave one the impression that he did not like to discuss them and I never gathered enough courage to ask him directly about them and cannot therefore make any authentic statement. I can say, however, that Dvořák was greatly interested in the Indians and one day while he was still at Spillville a band of Indians came to town selling medicinal herbs. We were told they were the 'Kickapoo' and belonged to the Iroquois tribe. Every evening they gave a little performance of their music and dancing and Dvořák was so interested that he made it a point always to be present.

"The 'Humoresque' was not composed at Spillville. This seventh of the 'Humoresques,' which has become so popular with the public at large, was composed on August 16, 1894, a year after Dvořák's visit to Spillville.

"Dvořák took great interest in the church music at Spillville. In fact, the first day he came there he visited the church just at the time the people were gathered at the morning mass and without hesitation he walked up the choir and commenced a prelude to the hymn, '*Boze Pred Tvou Velebnosti*' (O Lord Before Thy Majesty), so well-known to the Bohemian settlers, and it did not take long before the entire congregation joined in, and evidently Dvořák liked it because it reminded him of his congregational singing in his mother country. And after that, every morning found him at church playing for the service. His wife, Mrs. Anna Dvořák, had a fine contralto voice and she, too, contributed to the music at church on Sunday.

"I have a letter which Dvořák sent me just before he went back to Europe, the translation of which is about as follows:

New York, May 18, 1895

Dear Friend:

Tomorrow, Saturday, we are leaving for Europe and I am sending you a sincere farewell. Kovarik will remain here in the house and he will have plenty to do this summer as he got a job with Seidl, but I am sure that he will miss us. We are all looking forward to our old home but my joy will be somewhat marred because I will not see my dear old father any more. He died March 29th, being eighty years old. May the Lord give him eternal rest! I will be glad to see Vysokou [Dvořák's summer home in the old country] but I should again like to see Spillville, we all liked it there so well—let us hope we will meet again in the future. Write me at Vysokou. I will be glad to hear from you. My sincere regards to Rev. Bily at Spillville and to the Rev. Fathers at Protivin and Ft. Atkinson, and also give my regards to old grandma and grandpa Bily and to all yours. And tell them I will visit Vsetec and Sepekov and that I will be thinking of all of you. Good luck to you and may the Lord be with you until we meet again.

Affectionately yours,

ANT. DVOŘÁK.

"The Vsetec and Sepekov referred to are two villages in Bohemia, the first being my birthplace, and the latter the birthplace of Grandpa Bily to whom Dvořák refers and with whom he spent many and many a congenial hour. The other manuscript I have is on the front page of the score of *The American Flag,* the translation of which is:

New York, April 15, 1895

Dear Mr. Kovarik:

Kindly accept this remembrance. It is a composition which should have been performed at Carnegie Hall in New York the day of my first appearance in public in America, October 12, 1892. This composition I composed before my first visit to America and as I was not able to finish it in time I had to compose another, so I wrote the *Te Deum* which was actually produced for the first time on October 21, 1892, when I had the honor to present myself to the New York audience. This year upon the request of my wife I decided to have this composition published at the publishing firm Schirmer. When the *Te Deum* is published I will also send you a copy. I must wait until the publisher takes pity on the work and so please wait also. With friendly greetings,

Yours,

Anton Dvořák.

"While Dvořák was at Spillville a delegation came from Chicago to invite him to the World's Fair and Dvořák accepted. Later in the summer he went to Omaha to visit Mr. Rosewater (Editor of the *Omaha Bee*), who was born six miles from Dvořák's birthplace. On his return he stopped off at St. Paul and took in the sights, particularly the Minnehaha Falls in which he was greatly interested, having read Longfellow's *Hiawatha.*"

Other Spillville friends supplement this information with delightful anecdotes, as well as giving further information concerning the genesis of the perennial favorite, "Humoresque." It is of interest, too, to know that the little church of St. Wenceslaus in Spillville, in which Dvořák played, is one of the quaintest in America, modeled after St. Barbara in Kutna Hora in Bohemia, and built by the pioneer men and women there in Spillville, who gathered the stone and helped in the construction as was done by the devout in the Middle Ages.

The daily attendance of Dvořák at the Kickapoo Indian medicine shows—where, a neighbor told, Dvořák always sat in the front row—and the visit to Minnehaha Falls were occasioned by Dvořák's thought of writing an Indian ballet or opera. While at the Falls Dvořák asked for a piece of paper and a pencil, but as only the pencil was at hand, he scribbled some notes on the broad white cuff of his shirt, and later used these as the theme in the second movement of his *Sonatina* Opus 100, dedicated to his children, and still later rearranged by Fritz Kreisler for violin solo under the title of "Indian Lament." On his return to Spillville from this trip Dvořák did not really start another work, as he was leaving for New York so shortly, but he set himself to making notes and sketches of a work he intended to complete in New York during the season, and this was the set of "Humoresques."

Of the *Quintet,* the Spillville friends say that the theme and variation of the third movement are based upon an air written by Dvořák and first intended as a new "tune" for our "My Country, 'Tis of Thee," which he had thought to score thus for tenor solo, chorus, and full orchestra. But he changed his mind. The writing of the *Quintet* took so much longer than that of the *Quartet* because it was interrupted by preparation for the World's Fair visit where he conducted his *Symphony in G,* a group of *Slavic Dances,* and an Overture, *My Country.*

"Dr. Dvořák liked nothing better than to get a few of our Spillville 'old settlers' together every afternoon and listen to the narration of their struggles and experiences in the Middle West," says one of these friends. "They so allured him that he would ply the speaker with question after question. He, in turn, would tell stories of mutual friends in the Old World, or of the New Yorkers whom he could not entirely fathom. . . . At our house Mother was the first to rise. When, the morning following the Dvořák arrival, she saw the master strolling before the school building she thought something had gone wrong. When she ran out to ask what had happened, not knowing he was an early riser, he said, 'Why, nothing has happened. And yet—a great deal. I have been rambling in the wood, along the brook, and for the first time in eight months I hear the birds sing. But I must go home now to breakfast. Afterwards I shall come again.' "

In the front of the cottage to the north of the Dvořák house Frank Benda had the village shoe-repair shop and on his way home from his daily communion with nature, Dvořák never failed to stop in, after which composer and cobbler might talk for hours, discussing everything from world affairs to pigeons and cucumbers. The Spillville pigeons Dvořák once playfully called "down-and-out scrubs," yet when presented with a pair, he prized and cared for them as though they were pedigreed. Mrs. Benda had a garden patch of cucumbers parallel to the cottage. In Bohemia they water cucumbers at high noon but in Iowa the sun at this hour makes this impossible, and Dvořák knew this. Nevertheless, when he saw his neighbor near the noon hour he would always shout to her from street or upper window to "water her cucumbers."

On September 8, 1893, the village celebrated the composer's fifty-second birthday. First there was the church service, then a feast at which it delighted Dvořák to dispense cheer and mirth, as well as cigars, for which he had sent to New York.

The rest of the visit (except for the trips to Chicago and Omaha) was spent leisurely. Sometimes he would sit for hours at his second-story window as though again in an Old World village, gazing down silently at passers-by and listening to the sounds of nature. Sometimes, the neighbors say, he would sit that way all evening, then, late at night, they would hear him playing his violin, songs of the far-off homeland, or melodies which had come to him as he pondered.

And so the Spillville friends humbly and lovingly recall "neighbor Dvořák," and the vivid and extraordinary personality of "that modest artist" and "God-fearing gentleman."

RUDOLPH GANZ

PERCY GRAINGER

PHILIP JAMES   DOUGLAS STUART MOORE

HOWARD HANSON

CHARLES S. SKILTON

ROSSETTER GLEASON COLE   SETH BINGHAM

TENDENCIES IN AMERICAN MUSIC

DR. HOWARD HANSON, *Director, Eastman School of Music*

THE primary importance of the composer in the history of musical art is undebatable. Without the composer, music as a cultivated art would be nonexistent—indeed we may say that all music would be lacking, for the growth of the folk song is, after all, the product of the creative talent of many people.

Starting with the axiomatic truth, "Without the composer there can be no music," we may proceed to its first corollary. The corollary that must logically follow is the primary importance of the contemporary composer in the musical life of any period. In other words, if music is, as most of us believe, the expression of the subconscious emotional life of the age, it must necessarily follow that the most important musical figures of any period in history are those men who are creating the representative music of that period.

It is easy to establish the truth of such a corollary in terms of the past. With the perspective of time we can readily see that in the sixteenth century musical history revolved about the work of Palestrina, de Lasso, and their contemporaries. We can understand Monteverde as the embodiment of the experimentalism of 1600. We perceive in Johann Sebastian Bach the musical interpretation of the Reformation and in Beethoven the coming of a new philosophy.

When we come to our own age the problem is more difficult. Unaided by the perspective of time, we are caught in the maze of experiments, trends and counter-trends, national and racial expressions. It is an arduous task to analyze and evaluate contemporary movements and to attempt to understand their significance, but the cardinal truth remains. As in the past the composer stands out as the key-figure of each period, even so in the present time does the composer epitomize the character of his age. As in every other era in history the music lover may and should be loyal to the great creators of the past, but if he hopes to have any part in, or understanding of, contemporary music history, he must take an intelligent interest in the men who in various ways are interpreting through their creative genius contemporary civilization.

With the rise of nationalism still another factor enters. With the segregation of western civilization into highly nationalistic groups, there comes into being the development of group tendencies within the age. Whereas we see in Palestrina not so much an Italian composer as a composer of the Church, we observe with the formation of the Italian state the growth of a school of composition which may be truthfully referred to as Italian, a nationalistic development.

Now however much we may proclaim our loyalty to an international art we cannot blind ourselves to the fact that the present world is intensely nationalistic. It follows, therefore, that at least a fairly large part of contemporary music will develop within the bounds of nationalism, and that for some time to come it will be the duty and privilege of each national group to develop within itself its contribution to the music of the age.

This condition affects the creative musician in a very practical manner, for it means that each nation will be most interested in the development and propagation of its own music and each composer must look primarily to his own country for the stimulation and opportunities necessary for the practice of his art. This situation is already strikingly illustrated in several European countries, noticeably Germany, France, and Italy.

It means, in other words, that each country is to be held responsible for its contribution to contemporary music, and that those countries which refuse hospitality to their own creative sons will to a large extent stultify their possible contribution to the music of our time.

In the United States this condition has been especially serious. Our national consciousness has been slow in developing, due to the fact that we are a heterogeneous people. The large influx of foreign musicians during the latter part of the nineteenth and early twentieth centuries, though it taught us much in musical technique, hardly tended to develop a national musical consciousness.

The last fifteen years, however, tell a different story. With the rise of opportunities for music education in the United States we have become conscious of the vast amount of creative talent latent in our young people, and we have begun the work of developing that talent. The results have astonished even those of us who have had no doubts as to the musical powers of our people. Whereas fifty years ago there were few American composers and they for the most part were copies of German and French models, at the present time there are literally hundreds of American composers, of varying degrees of ability it is true, but each striving to make in his own way a contribution to musical literature.

Indeed many of these men have already gone far. They have made contributions not only to American musical development but their works have found their way to the concert halls of Europe where they have aroused interested attention. It is pertinent, therefore, to discuss prevailing tendencies in American music and especially to observe any characteristics which seem to be typically American.

The first thing that should be noted is that the prime requisite for musical expression is spontaneity. No mature composer who is worthy of our serious concern is moved by a consideration of what he "ought to write." All discussions of what American music "should be" are beside the point. No theory of Americanism in music can ever be effective. Each composer will write what seems good to him. He may be entirely uninfluenced by the American scene—though this is difficult to understand—and write music which is essentially international in character. Or again, if he represents perhaps the first generation of native-born Americans in his family, the influence of heredity may be so strong as to almost obliterate the effects of his environment.

What is most likely to happen, however, is that each composer influenced by his inheritance and by his own creative personality will be reinfluenced by those aspects of the American scene which appeal most to him. He will do this not consciously but rather subconsciously, and his music will bear the marks of these various influences. Anyone, therefore, who is looking for the growth of a standardized form of American music will, I believe, be doomed to disappointment—and fortunately so. For the development of a standardized expression is much less to be desired than the development of all of those rich heritages which constitute our enormous spiritual wealth.

I shall attempt to discuss a few of these American tendencies categorically. Outstanding, on account of its uniqueness, but, in my opinion, of least importance, is the theory of an American music based upon the native music of the Indians. This has always seemed to me to be highly artificial though it cannot be denied that some excellent technical work has been done in this field. There is no contradicting the wealth of material latent in Indian tribal songs and dances and it is quite possible that an American composer might be spontaneously influenced by this material, but any conscious attempt to found a school of music on the basis of a folk music that plays so little part in the every-day life of our people does not, in my estimation, seem promising.

When we turn to the field of Negro music the situation is very different. In the first place we are slowly developing a group of gifted Negro composers. Such men as William Grant Still, a composer of the highest sincerity, would naturally be moved by the songs of his people. This influence gives to his music not only an individuality which could be found only in America, but also a moving force resulting from the man's highly sensitive and powerfully emotional nature. This music can justly be called one branch of American music.

Nor is this influence confined only to the Negro. The music of that race has played an important part in the life of the white man as well. The musical influence of the Negro Spiritual is so wide-spread in our country that it may be said to have become a national as well as a racial inheritance. It is easily understandable that any American composer might be profoundly influenced by the emotional character of this folk music.

Another interesting phase of contemporary American music is the influence of popular music, especially the portion of it usually referred to as "jazz." As a matter of fact, jazz itself is an illustration of how a national form of popular music may grow spontaneously and naturally, and compounded of many subconscious influences. Many writers have attempted to trace its origin. It has been called Negro, Jewish, and urban. As a matter of fact it is all three and probably others! Certain of the almost Oriental qualities probably come from Jewish influence. Certain modal tendencies apparently derive from the Negro and the whole has been developed in terms of an orchestral palette that is typically American and has no counterpart in any other country.

The vitality of this music is enormous. In the best popular jazz there is added to this vitality a naïve emotional quality, a rhythmic diversity, and an ingenuity in harmonization and orchestration which raise such works to a high plane of popular music. Among academic musicians surprise has sometimes been expressed that such a frankly popular type of music should send its influence into the field of "serious" music. I cannot understand this attitude. To me the surprise would be much greater if such a vital form of music did *not* profoundly influence contemporary music. The active influence of jazz on symphonic music in America is one of the striking proofs of the spontaneity and genuineness of a large part of American symphonic expression.

The work of Robert Russell Bennett is a striking illustration. A man of unquestioned artistic integrity and at the same time a composer and orchestrator who has brought joy to the hearts of Broadway, he is thoroughly immersed in the popular music of the day. Possessed of an extraordinarily brilliant orchestral technique, it is only natural that his symphonic works borrow from his jazz technique in a way that is brilliantly American. In his *Sketches from an American Theater,* in the form of the old *Concerto Grosso,* the *concertanti* take the form of a dance orchestra accompanied by a symphony orchestra. The entire work, in its humor, its sentimentalism, its brilliance, and its energy, clearly reflects one aspect of the American scene.

And again it is not necessary that the jazz influence be so prominent as to be immediately discernible. In much contemporary American music there are illustrations of the influence of jazz technique, in many cases undoubtedly unconscious. This applies not only to orchestration but equally to harmony, melody, and rhythm. In such a work as Randall Thompson's *Second Symphony,* the subtle influence of jazz is discernible mingled with an influence of old American dance forms that is charming.

Which leads to the discussion of another important influence, the influence of the American folk song and folk dance. Countless numbers of these folk songs have existed for generations in our American life, preserved in more or less isolated rural communities and only "discovered" by musicians in recent years. Whether these songs come from the coast of Maine, the Kentucky hills, or the western prairies, they represent that most indigenous type of national music, folk music. John Powell, Leo Sowerby, and others have made settings of these delightful expressions of rural America, but the material is so rich in inspirational possibilities that the field may be said to be virtually untilled. It can hardly be doubted that some Americans will find themselves moved by these sources to write music that springs from the very soil of the country.

Another influence as subtle as it is powerful lies in the emotional character of our people. Perhaps the most outstanding trait in American character is a certain romanticism which pervades American life. This quality which permeates our popular songs, sentimental though it may be, is a warm and human expression of ourselves. No American composer who is keenly sensitive to life about him can escape its influence. And it is possible that from this sentimentalism will be distilled a new romanticism.

I have tried to point out a few of the many influences which are at work in the production of an American music. I do not mean to imply that the only worth-while music being written in America today is music which exhibits national characteristics. The composer must always remain untrammeled and unhindered by theories, nationalistic or otherwise, free to express himself according to the dictates of his own artistic conscience. There are American composers who are reflecting few, if any, of these tendencies, who are virtually untouched by their national environment and who are writing works exhibiting international rather than national tendencies. There are, too, the members of the experimental group who are stirring up in their harmonic test-tubes new sonorities or who are delving into new and abstract contrapuntal techniques. This is important because in every age music must move on to new forms of expression and experimentation remains as always a sign of vitality.

The significant thing is that there exists in these United States a large number of gifted creators of music, well-equipped technically and seeking to express through their art the life of our time and of our nation. What the American music of the next generation will be no one can prophesy, but that there will be a great American musical literature springing up from this rich and well-tilled soil no one can doubt.

FRENCH-CANADIAN MELODIES

ALL races have their characteristic national songs which they can at once recognize as their own, and this is especially true of those which had their beginnings in France. Many of these found their way, centuries ago, to the French settlements in the New World, and here in Canada they may still be heard daily in all their original grace, from the lips of homekeepers, farmers, hunters, tradesmen, voyageurs, and statesmen. They may be said to be true models of folk song for throughout the provinces they are graven upon the memory, have been learned by the folk without their knowing it, and the whole mass of the people love to repeat them.

A splendid tribute to any folk art lies in its appreciation by those who employ it and such tribute is not lacking for Canadian song in Canada, where several thousand of the melodies have already been collected and placed on file in museums and libraries of the Dominion and where annual festivals of folk song display its charms to the world at large.

In considering Canadian folk song it is not forgotten that sturdy Scottish patriots played an important part in the development of Canada. One of the most picturesque events in Canadian history was the landing of Scottish settlers from the wooden sailing vessel *Hector*, in 1773, when they waded ashore through the cold waters on the beach to the stirring skirl of the bagpipes. With the bagpipes came the endearing songs of the homeland, many of which are indebted to "Bobbie" Burns for their lyric texts. For many years no meeting of any kind, in Canada, attended by Scottish settlers, broke up without the singing of "Auld Lang Syne."

It was presently noticed, by both French and Scottish pioneers, that the melodies of many of their songs had much in common. This was credited to the real connection which existed between the French and

Scots in early days, when many families from Normandy settled in Scotland. Norman songs were well known at Scotland's court, and several popular Scottish airs—including that of "Ye Banks and Braes o' Bonnie Doon"—have recently been found recorded in treasured French manuscripts of the seventeenth century.

In 1832 the population of Lower Canada was approximately 500,000 of whom 425,000 were of French descent and spoke the French language. The general title, "French-Canadian Melodies," seems therefore appropriate, when reference is made to these valued folk songs, for comparatively few of those airs sung familiarly in Canada are truly native to the land.

The first recorded reference to music in Canada appears in a three-hundred-year-old account of Port Royal, written by Marc Lescarbot, a Paris advocate whose alluring story of life in New France of those early days describes the seventeenth century garrison which stood on the lonely shores of Nova Scotia. He mentions singing parties, and from his account we learn that the most popular of the songs sung there were those familiar at the court of Henry of Navarre, and sea chanteys and folk songs from the western provinces of France from which many of the men at the Port Royal garrison had come.

Not only these men but other settlers had migrated from Normandy and the Loire valley at a time when oral traditions were still thriving in France.

The new Canadian homes, established along the rivers and at the edge of the virgin forests, were so isolated from all turmoils and commotions of the Old World, and for so many years from the standardizing influences of the New World as later carried by new methods of transportation and communication, that they kept in constant use a tremendous hoard of songs and folk tales. Varied versions of these old songs may now be heard throughout the Montreal, Three Rivers, and Quebec districts, and while they may differ slightly, one from the other, the central elements are unchanged and are usually of an antique Old World flavor far different from the more universal character of other folk airs.

Some of the songs indeed feature distinctly modal or plain-song effects, or suggest historic melodies of the Troubadours of the twelfth and thirteenth centuries. Many a Canadian field is plowed today to the rhythm of a song which tells of knights and ladies, or of princes and palaces.

In 1608 Samuel de Champlain (whose native town was Saintouge, in the west of France) established an "Order of Good Time" (*L'Ordre de le Bon Temps*) to cheer the men in his Port Royal garrison, and favorite songs of the singing parties are still extremely popular in Canada—"*Gai, la, la, gail le rosier*" (*Gay is the Rose*) and "*A la claire fontaine.*"

Many of these airs have striking individuality, as illustrated by the odd three-measure phrases of the verse of "Gay is the Rose." The two phrases of the refrain, however, are of conventional four-measure length.

"*A la claire fontaine*" ("At the clear running fountain"), from Champlain's home town, tells of the gardens of Normandy, and of a lover who has lost the affection of his Dulcinea. She refuses his flowers. The song is still on all lips throughout the provinces, and was, for many years, considered the "national anthem" of Canada. Its personal note of grief was used to express a national lament when it was sung by the French-Canadians in 1759 after the capture of Quebec.

Another old song of French Canada is "*La Guignolée*," most frequently sung on the eve of special festival days and on New Year's Eve. At these times it is customary for groups of young people to go about the village or parish in search of families who may have "le guignon" (bad luck). To these they bring substantial relief, while at other homes they receive gifts of provisions or clothing to distribute. At each house visited during this "*courrir la guignolée*" they sing this song, which is so ancient that its words tell of the sacrifices of the Druids.

A dramatic native song, about two hundred years old, is "*Petit rocher de la haute montagne,*" which tells of Cadieux, a trapper, who, while bringing a party down the Ottawa River, learns upon reaching Calumet

Island that the Iroquois are waiting at the portage. By shooting off a gun he diverts attention to himself while his party shoots the rapids. The war party comes upon him and when rescuers return, his body is found in a shallow grave which he has evidently prepared for himself, and near by is a piece of birchbark upon which he has left a message traced in human blood.

The rivers of Canada have always been channels of song. Jacques Cartier's men sang *"Envoyons d'l'avant, nos gens"* as they paddled the St. Lawrence in 1534. The Canadian boatman always sings as he works and the work then "takes care of itself." Joliet, who discovered the Mississippi River, was a talented church organist, and utilized folk singing as a stimulant to unison labor among his oarsmen. Gaspé fishermen still accommodate many of their tasks to the rhythms of sea chanteys of the Old World. The *voyageur,* as the picturesque French-Canadian canoemen have been called for centuries, is often chosen for his ability to sing, and the sonorous—often weird—strains of melody which echo through the black forests which line many of the waterways, as the birchbark canoes are sent flying along to their rhythm, have inspired poets. The steersman is often the "solo," and he chooses the song and sets the pitch. Sometimes he sings the verse while the others join in the refrain. Many a lumber raft has come down the river to the tune of *"En roulant, ma boule"* ("Oh, roll on, my ball") which started its career as a fairy-tale song of France.

Other songs of labor dear to the heart of the French-Canadians include the *"Moulin Banal"* ("The Feudal Mill"). It was the custom of tenants, in the olden days, to grind their grain at Le Seigneur's mill. So in this song the story of the undertaking is retold, often accompanied by appropriate gesture and action.

Fun songs include the familiar *"Alouette, gentile Alouette."*

Tenderness is not a stranger to the French-Canadian song, as is illustrated by the lullaby *"Une pedriole"* ("The Opening Day of May"). In this unusual song, a present is promised for each new day of the month, and as the singer proceeds through the verses, the second word is changed from "opening" to "second," "third," "fourth," and on up to ten, it being evidently thought that ten verses should put the little one to sleep. As all the presents suggested are renamed with each verse, it is necessary for an extra measure to be added to each stanza of the song.

Lovely Christmas carols of great antiquity feature the holiday season, the melodies possibly varying slightly according to the districts in which they are sung.

Viewing the riches of the Canadian "treasure chest" of song, and its exuberant vitality, it is appropriate that Sir George Cartier, a distinguished son of the Dominion (a descendant of a nephew of Jacques Cartier, and writer of "O, Canada") should have exclaimed, in verse:

> *Le Canadien, comme ses péres,*
> *Aime à chanter a s'egayer.*
> *Doux, aisé, vif en ses manières,*
> *Poli, galant, hospitalier.*

In Our Own Time

MUSIC OF THE ORIENT

BY LILY STRICKLAND, *American Composer* *

IN India the sound of music is always in the air. In the Orient music has been found, through generations, to be the most effective method of expressing emotion. Many composers of Europe and America have tried to express, in their writings, the fascinating atmosphere of the East. The music of *Madame Butterfly* and *Turandot* has stood for the music of the Orient to many people. It is colored by the elusive and picturesque idiom of Eastern music, but no Occidental can truly duplicate that ancient lure, he can only suggest it.

The Russians, partly, no doubt, because of their Tatar origins, geographical location, and centuries of trade intercourse with the Orient, come nearer to succeeding than any others. *The Nightingale* (*Le Rossignol*), a fantastic opera-ballet by Igor Stravinsky, built upon a very old Chinese legend of the Emperor and the feathered songster whose golden tones restored him to health, is a charming example of this. So are parts of *Sadko* (the story of the poor boy who was called to the bottom of the sea to play his gousli for the King of the Waters), of *The Golden Cockerel* and *Prince Igor;* as well as short pieces by the Russian composers Cui, Rimsky-Korsakov, and Glazounov.

Some ultra-modern composers try to paint pagan tone-pictures by using much dissonance in their music, trying to imitate sounds from Oriental music which they do not understand; and so are not successful. There is no discord of the type they use in the colorful music of the Orient for the very good reason that the Oriental of aboriginal times used no harmony at all—the older the music, the simpler and more entirely melodic it is.

* Miss Strickland lived in the Orient for nearly ten years, so speaks with authority on this attractive subject.

The aboriginal tribes in India have been pushed back into the most remote parts of the country by civilization, and so remain uninfluenced in custom, costume, religion, and art, by the invaders and their manners. I have seen people in the mountains, deserts, and jungles of India living the simple pastoral life and using the same primitive utensils, weapons, and musical instruments as were used by their ancestors. They worship Nature as found in the trees, the rivers, and life itself. Their seasonal life is attractively marked by festivals which celebrate the planting of the seed, and the harvest, and in all these music plays a very important part. With these animists all religious ceremonies are punctuated by musical rites of great vitality.

All of this Oriental music has a mighty historic background. Each act of life has its song, a simple melody which cheers or comforts, and one of my most pleasing recollections of my visit to the Orient is of the quaint airs heard on every hand from flower-vendors, sweet-meat sellers, fishermen, shepherds, goat-herds, in fact every person encountered. Should one be going along a highway, it is unusual to have a single hour pass without some reference being made to the charms of music. One may suddenly hear the drums beating, a clashing of cymbals, tinkling of bells, and the eerie sound of a flute. A turn of the road will bring to view a native procession on its way to the river for a religious festival.

In studying Oriental music I have found that life in the East is closely interwoven with the symbolism of religion. Music is, to the Oriental, a sacred gift from the gods, and all Oriental music, except the folk music, is based largely upon a religious background, and is thought to be of divine origin. Many of the gods are given credit for the invention of the oldest scales, and of some of the most precious musical instruments, as, for example, Brahma is given credit for the invention of drum and flute. All scales evolve from a Mother Scale which is similar to our scale of C Major. The drum rhythms are many and fascinating, and the scale-modes, delightful and often weird, producing effects of shimmering elusiveness, emotion, or melancholy. Many of the scales seem to be minor; the five-tone scale is frequently used, and the whole-tone scale—so essential in much of the modern impressionistic music—is so familiar in the Orient that its beginnings are woven into the most ancient traditions of the land.

In the orchestra of India the drums have always the first place, a usual orchestra consisting probably of a drum corps, a few flutes, some cymbals, and bells. Drums are heard accompanying singing voices. One drum, beaten with the palm of the player's hand, in slow and muffled manner, may join with another, played quickly and *staccato,* in accompanying the same tune. The effect is indescribable. War drums are made from sections of tree-trunks, nearly all instruments being made from wood. The wooden tambourine with its goat-skin head, and the picturesque flute with its highly individual scale, both lend color and glamour to the already picturesque song.

The drums also set the pace for all dances of the Orient, so vivid and so unique. I have, for instance, seen the Devil Dancers of Tibet in their New Year festivities, a stirring sight not equaled by any other barbaric ceremony. At the time set for the ceremony everyone gathers about the Temple, many of the native spectators being handsomely garbed in brocade and satins. Then the drums begin to beat. On comes the procession, emerging slowly from the doors of the Temple. The huge horns and the gongs begin to sound, and immediately the air is filled with a swirl of sound. Out dash the Devils—dancers masked so hideously, and gowned so fantastically as to—it is hoped—drive away the evil spirits. All the time the frenzied beating of the drums stimulates the singers and dancers to wild and continued action.

More exquisite in their effect are the native flutes, most of which are made of the native bamboo. Their gentle, modulated tone pervades the air with sweetest melody, often embellished with improvised ornaments to suit the fancy of the player.

There are, besides, the *theku,* or Jew's Harp, and the *ubo,* a kind of stringed instrument with body made from half a gourd to which is attached a long narrow stem on which is placed one cotton or wire string. All the music played is memorized and handed down from generation to generation, all of it characterized by the simplicity of age.

The traditional music of Japan is a different language, molded into its present form by history, religious custom, and environment. The Japanese folk song is very simple, given without harmony, and with little embroidery or embellishment. The Japanese combinations of musical instruments produce many elaborate and strange effects, truly atonal effects being not at all uncommon. Thus does the contemporary composer find himself duplicating an effect as old as a nation. The Japanese ideal in music is rather that they shall create tone pictures of impressionism, rather than that they shall produce music made up of carefully related tones. Again there is the belief that music is of divine origin, the flute being thought to be a bird come down from Heaven.

The frequent mention of "temple bells" in travel stories of the Orient is not overdrawn, for one of the most alluring sounds of Japan is that made by the thousands of wind bells hung at the edge of temple roofs. This constant use of bells has influenced the character of the Japanese music, which is usually of a delicacy quite in keeping with the lore and art of the "Flowery Kingdom."

Of instruments familiarly used, the drums are prominent, and used on almost all occasions, even to accompanying, softly, the baby's lullabies. These are of all sizes and shapes, a common one being barrel-shaped, and played with the palm of the hand rather than with a stick. There is great similarity between many of the instruments used in Japan, China, and Korea, for Japan has drawn freely upon the culture of China, and many Japanese youths have had part of their education in Korea.

The *koto* is one of the favored musical instruments, a development of the Chinese *kin*. It carries thirteen strings made of waxed silk, these being pressed upon by the one hand of the player while with the other he plucks them with a bit of ivory. The *samisen* has an immense popularity, its three strings being played in much the same way as those of the *koto*. Both instruments rest upon the floor while being played. The *samisen* music is sometimes called by the natives their "looking-glass music," as they say it both hums and tinkles. The plectrum touching the string first starts it to tinkling, then the parchment commences to hum, and the result is a sound of ineffable charm.

The Chinese fiddle, used in both countries, is set on the floor when played, and, because of the clumsiness of its large horse-hair bow, is seldom used for solo playing, but rather as an accompaniment to *koto* and *samisen*. The Japanese flute, with its six holes and its mellow tones, and the Japanese syrinx (*shonefuyé*), with its twenty-two pipes bound together, are subjects frequently met with in fairy lore of the land.

Caravans carried much of the musical lore of the East into Arabia and Persia at an early day, and so we find the music of those lands a mixed art, colored freely by elements of the older culture. One can only say that to the individual and poetic beauties of the music of the entire Orient—including that of Java, Siam, Burma, Ceylon, and Malay— there is no end. It is the expression of a people so ancient in their written and traditional history that the beginnings are lost in mystery.

MUSIC OF THE TWENTIETH
CENTURY OUTSIDE OF AMERICA

ONE of the most astonishing developments of the decades that have passed since this century opened is that of music, and a question often asked by the music lover and concert-goer is "why is modern music modern?" New musical idioms, new influences and tendencies have been heard with increasing frequency. In many cases final judgments as to the permanent value of this new music are to be shunned, but temporary ones are desirable, and at all times the listener should follow the wise advice of Lawrence Gilman when he says, "Allow modern music to come into your ears." No real musical growth and development is possible unless the contemporary composer (of any date) is given a hearing.

The listener may also well recall that there always have been "revolutions" going on in music, in which old ways of writing have been subjected to new stimuli or new musical vocabularies added to those of other generations. This was true even in the Middle Ages through the years when church music was taking shape, and when new musical forms, such as the opera, oratorio, suite, and symphony, were being established, and when the instruments themselves were being perfected.

Peri, Caccini, and Monteverde, to whom must be credited the inauguration of opera and its characteristic musical features, in and near the year 1600, were the "futurists" of their day; as, later, were Gluck, in his reformation of eighteenth-century opera, Robert Schumann, Franz Liszt, and others.

The twentieth-century revolution is probably the most violent in the history of music. What are its causes and results? What are the meanings of the new musical terms that have come into use, such as neo-classical, tone-cluster, polytonality, and atonality?

Reasons sometimes given for these abrupt changes in music include the exploitation of mechanical instruments, the realistic influences of the World War, the tremendous spread of music through recordings, radio, printing, and mass production, a general growth of scientific investigation in all subjects, and extreme nationalism. These have led music into such innovations as use of very unusual subjects, such as in *Pacific 231,* the musical story of a locomotive, by Honegger; an effort to repress rather than express emotion; experimentation with new forms, or else no form at all; irregular use of rhythm, or else a tyranny of rhythm caused by a persistent use of the same little figure over and over again; increased use of dissonance or actual discord; and a conscious return in many cases to use of old Greek modes instead of familiar scales.* There are also being used combinations of many keys (tonalities) at one time, or else utter disregard of any fundamental key at all. This latter manner produces what is known as atonality (no tonality). Modern composers also often use the human voice as an orchestral instrument by writing parts for it which are either hummed or only sung in syllables. Recent music also makes more than accustomed use of wind and percussion instruments.

As the composers of different nations have reacted in differing ways to modern influences, each of the more important countries is now taken separately and a short summary given of the character of its composed music at the opening of the century and the growth of its national tendencies since that time.

FRANCE

As a preparation for a modern "revival" the French are indebted to several masters, some of whom lived in both nineteenth and twentieth centuries. These include Saint-Saëns, and his pupil Gabriel Fauré, who

* See "Medieval Church Music," page 62.

was director of the Paris Conservatoire for thirty years. Fauré's pupils included Ravel, Florent Schmitt, Enesco, and Ducassé. There are also Alexis Emmanuel Chabrier, Vincent d'Indy, Eric Satie, and Claude Debussy. César Franck also wielded a great influence on French music, both through his own music and his pupils.

Debussy is often spoken of as the climax of impressionism, by which is meant a style of composition similar to a certain type of painting (such as that of Claude Monet) in which effects are merely suggested, to stir and rouse the imagination.

Humor was carried into French music through the works of Satie, who seemed so anxious to mock his listeners through use of musical satire and such absurd titles as "Limp Preludes," or "Three Pieces in the Shape of a Pear," that the public refused to take him seriously. His music greatly influenced Ravel, one of the best known of the modern French musicians.

Ravel was born in southern France near the border of Spain, this fact explaining the presence of many Spanish elements in his music, as, for example, the Spanish dance rhythm in the celebrated *Bolero*. (See page 10.) Some of his pieces are clever imitations of unusual subjects, such as "Dream of a Naughty Boy," in which are heard vivid description of the results of the bad boy's behavior; and a humorous version of *Beauty and the Beast*.

D'Indy, a pupil of Franck, followed classic form but emphasized such modern characteristics as use of folk song (as in his *Mountain Symphony*), old modes, irregular rhythms, ostinato figures, and cleverly combined rhythms.

Of the younger French composers one must mention a group who banded themselves together in 1918 as "The Six," for purposes of propaganda. They have, in the main, elevated novelty in music, rather than beauty. Honegger, one of these composers, is widely known for his atonality, and for his clever workmanship. "King David" (for voice), "Pacific 231," and "Rugby" are his best-known works. Darius Milhaud of "The Six" has written many fluent orchestral works and has made some use of the elements of jazz.

(See "National Characteristics in Russian Art Music," page 19).

Music of the Russian Empire has long been influenced by the colorful song and savage rhythms of its Oriental and Asiatic neighbors, and by the character of the old church modes. Glinka and the famous "Five" (Borodin, Cui, Moussorgsky, Rimsky-Korsakov, and Balakirev) exploited these features. Of them all Moussorgsky was the fairest prophet of the new-century music, as shown in his humorous "Children's Songs." This utter freshness is nowhere more apparent than in his song in which the small boy says his evening prayer. "God bless,"—and here he mentions all the names he can recall, then asks the nurse if he has left out anyone. "Yes," she tells him, "ask God to make you a good boy." Where the music has been of hurried, irreverent character in keeping with the generality of the early prayer, it now assumes a beatific quality as the prayer is finished according to direction. Such informality was unknown in much earlier music.

Tschaikowsky, whose life span touched this century, used national song in many cases (*Marche Slav, Overture 1812,* and *Fifth Symphony*). Twentieth-century Russian composers include Gliere, Rachmaninov, Scriabine, Prokofiev, and Miaskovsky. Scriabine was known as a "revolutionary" in music, partly because of his use of dissonance, unusual chords, and composition of music for the human voice in which only syllables are sung. Miaskovsky's music is largely atonal. Prokofiev, son of a wealthy family of the old régime, writes music of great charm and interest, all of it made individual by his own colorful personality. (See "Love of Three Oranges," page 371.) Stravinsky, most spectacular of the younger Russians, owes much of his success to a combination of brilliant technique of writing and dramatic suggestion, as in ballet. He gained fame just before the opening of the World War by his two ballets, *Fire Bird* (1910) and *Sacre du Printemps* (1913). The latter caused a near-riot in Paris at its first performance by its savage rhythms and primitive dissonances, but today they are accepted without thought, so quickly has a violent "revolution" become an accepted idiom.

At about the close of the World War, the four great modern names in German music were Richard Strauss, Max Reger, Mahler, and Schoenberg. Strauss, as in *Till Eulenspiegel,* used many devices featured by modern music, such as a profound sense of comic humor, unusual harmonies, much use of chromatic scale, seemingly careless and wide skips which leave the melodic line harsh in outline, and odd uses of orchestral instruments.

The music of Arnold Schoenberg was at first either the object of passionate eulogy or bitter invective. Its audacious atonality shocked the more staid listeners but at the same time made a great appeal to the war mentality of Europe. Since that day different aspects of his music have come into prominence, one of his ventures into the bypaths of a modern type of melody is the *Gurrelieder,* a series of dramatic and connected songs written at a comparatively early date and later brought to public hearing. Another is his *Pierrot Lunaire,* a vocal setting of over twenty pieces connected by short orchestral interludes. In this last-mentioned work Schoenberg creates a new type of vocal expression, the speaking voice, or *Sprechstimme.*

A famous pupil of Schoenberg is Alban Berg in whose opera *Wozzeck* (1920) the singing voice is practically abolished, the real musical texture of the music being supplied by the orchestra.

Another prominent young German composer is Paul Hindemith, a gifted and musical artist who has shown ability to write dramatic melodies of distinction, and ensemble music of sure craftsmanship, and a warm and individual personality.

Here must also be mentioned the work of Bartók, and of Weinberger, Hungarian composers of the day, both of whom have been strongly influenced by the joyous charms of strong old peasant music of their native land.

The elder group of Italians whose works carried over into the present century—including Sgambati, Busoni, and Sinegaglia—were all, more or less, under the influence of German forms. The younger Italian composers set out to free Italy of this foreign influence, first, by the establishment of Italian orchestral and choral societies. Before the War was ended there were over fifty of these, including the Augusteo Orchestra in Rome, one of the finest in Europe. In 1914 a group of young Italian composers banded themselves together for a concert of their works in Paris. These, with a few of their pupils and disciples, form the bulwark of contemporary music in Italy.

Malipiero (1882–   ) whose *Stornelli e Ballata* took the Coolidge Prize, has made contributions to modern thought through such works as his *Variations Without a Theme* for orchestra, and his *Seven Canzoni,* a modern substitute for opera, really seven episodes for theater (vocal solo, chorus, and orchestral preludes and interludes). Riccardo Pick-Mangiagalli (1882–   ) exhibits a real sense of humor in his music, as illustrated by his *Musical Fables* for the theater, mimetic dances of a comic nature which might be used by a modern-tempo world as a substitute for the older and more conventional ballet.

Alfredo Casella (1883–   ), an international figure of strong personality, is the leader of the Italian nationalists. He uses such modern ideas as combination of major and minor chords, as in *Notte di Maggio;* *Puppazetti* (five pieces for marionettes) for piano, four hands, in which much piquant humor is displayed; and his *Sonatina* for piano, in classic form, but made into a caricature through the false proportions of the three rates of speed used and atonality.

Other Italian leaders are Tomassini, Pizetti, and Castelnuovo-

Tedesco, Respighi, and Vittorio Rieti whose *Noah's Ark* was first heard at the Prague Festival.

SPAIN

Principal among the modern Spanish writers of music is Manuel de Falla, who has followed in the steps of Albeniz and Granados. Much of his best writing is associated with ballet, in which he displays true Spanish atmosphere combined with French verve and style.

FINLAND

Jean Sibelius (1865–   ) stands as an example of Northern feeling and as a sincere expression of an international attitude toward life and music. His most popular works include *Finlandia, Tapiola,* and *Fifth Symphony.*

ENGLAND

In England the way of the younger composers was prepared by such essentially British composers as Elgar, Bantock, Stanford, Parry, and Delius, all of whom were knighted for their scholarly achievements in music. Later composers are making good use of England's beautiful folk song, and the strong Celtic feeling so prevalent. Delius, one of the older composers, was the first to directly use the folk tunes and rhythms, as heard in his delightful *Dance Rhapsodies* and *Brigg Fair*. Vaughn Williams is one of the most important composers to continue this use of national song. His *London Symphony* vividly recalls to mind many phases of contemporary life in that city and his *Norfolk Symphony* is based on English melodies.

Gustav Holst, a British artist tremendously interested in the literature and music of the Far East, has written several attractive suites based on jolly British airs for band instruments, and his *Planets* for orchestra which reflect mystical characteristics of India. (See page 104.)

AS THE COMPOSERS SEE IT

No statement concerning any art is so interesting as that made by the one who creates it. In the next pages, Music of the Twentieth Century is briefly characterized by a group of eminent contemporary composers.

MODERN TRENDS IN MUSIC

BY PERCY GRAINGER, *Composer and Concert Artist*

T O me there is an unbroken thread of continuity throughout all music. All music is, to me, equally perfect, complete, and complicated in its own way. This music or that—whether modern or "classic"—is not better nor worse than another type, such as the folk song; but each has its own individuality. The listener makes his choice.

Music, from primitive times until the present day reflects the use of varied types of scales. The primitive scale of 1, 5, 8 (or C, G, C) was prevalent in the earliest composed music. Therefore the use of widespread intervals, or combinations of sounds, was the custom. In the music of the future, intervals will not have any part, in my opinion.

The English folk-song scale (1, 3, 5, flat–7, 8) contains a third which is variable—either major or minor. A great many folk songs emphasize the notes of the harmonic series. Some sound pentatonic. The relation of the primitive scale of 1, 5, 8 to music is very simple. It has perhaps given the drone of the bagpipe music, and the uses of 1, 5, 1 in the drumbeats of primitive music.

Music at various periods of history expresses the life of the people at that point to some extent. A modern composer lives in the age of science, while Bach lived in an age of religion, and the primitive in an age of superstition. None of us quite escape science, which has, paradoxically, brought us to listen to the sounds of nature.

A great deal of modern music reflects the sounds of nature, as heard in the gliding nature of many modern melodies, such as those of the American composer, Arthur Fickenscher, and in their oscillation (resembling light on water) about a single tone. Therefore, to me, outstanding features of the music of the future, as contrasted with the music of the past, will be greater use of irregular rhythms, greater freedom of form, irregular measure formations, smaller intervals, gliding melodies, fewer harmonies (consonants), and more discords (dissonants).

THIS NEW MUSIC

BY DOUGLAS STUART MOORE, *Associate Professor of Music on the Joline Foundation, Columbia University*

THE young composer of today is challenged by a situation of great opportunity. He has advantages of education which were unknown to his predecessors; he has at hand a musical idiom which has been enormously expanded by the great masters of the twentieth century, Debussy, Stravinsky, and Schoenberg. If he can refrain from placing too great dependence upon modern methods at the expense of all that the past centuries have taught, and can, at the same time, keep himself from prejudice against the apparently revolutionary quality of the new music, he will be rich in resource.

It is dangerous to revolt so enthusiastically against the preceding age that one is intolerant of its beauties. It is equally unwise to insist upon the perpetuation of an outmoded technique. We can still learn much from Beethoven and Wagner as well as Schoenberg and Stravinsky, but no successful music will be composed by imitating any of them. I am confident that the future of music will center about the United States and that the great composer of this age, who is yet to appear, will be an American.

THE LISTENER'S OBLIGATION TOWARD
MODERN MUSIC

BY RUDOLPH GANZ, *Director, Chicago Musical College*

JUST as it is well-nigh impossible for the authors of text-books on harmony and counterpoint to keep pace with the daring but so welcome pathfinders in new musical expression, so it would be useless to claim to write studies for the modern listener that would include all the latest "discoveries of tonal combinations, such as poly-melody, poly-harmony, sound-against-sound, color-against-color, imitations of all kinds of noises, and impressionistic descriptions of life in nature." The listener must just recall that he has not only a great future *behind* him —the study of the classics—but also one *before* him, a future which he must approach with the same reverence that no doubt he feels toward the former.

There are masters in every generation, as well in ours as in those gone by. The older recognized ones were also young once. Practically without exception they were not believed in nor trusted, not recognized, not accepted, either by the public, the press, or other musicians. Why did a very clever woman write in 1853: "How is it that people over forty take unwillingly to Chopin?" We can readily understand it. Think of the jump from Beethoven to Chopin. And yet the Polish master was seventeen years old when Beethoven died at the comparatively early age of fifty-six. And this same woman looked into the future (in 1853!) and said that human ears would not be satisfied with half-tones and predicted quarter and eighth tones within "another fifty or a hundred years."

Only *one* of the eminent Parisian critics heard the new message of chaste simplicity and delicate sensitiveness when Debussy's *Pelléas and Mélisande* was performed for the first time. Seven years later they all had their ears "adjusted." To be sure, no one can fully realize the importance and value of a masterpiece at its first hearing. You may feel its greatness, its elemental message, subconsciously; but why *should* anyone be able to understand at a single hearing what was written in many months, or years, and with the life-blood and unshaken faith of genius?

Absolute music is no doubt the highest form of musical conception, because in its expression it stands solely on its own medium, its own merits. But that does not mean that all of the devices of so-called program music should be belittled. Modern music is not here to replace the classic repertory. It simply adds a new style of expression paralleling the old ones. Nowhere can we find the delicate or plain humor of Debussy except in the masters among the French clavecinists. Couperin, Rameau, Daquin, and their contemporaries were no champions of absolute music. They gave their pieces titles that justified the descriptive music they were trying to express. So it is with a good many moderns.

Not that we should bow to everything new *because it is new;* not in the least. But we must approach it with an open heart and an open mind. The gospel of beauty never changes with the times; it is always: THE SAME OLD TRUTH IN A NEW EXPRESSION. Be enthusiastic!

ON THE SUBJECT OF MODERNISM

BY PHILIP JAMES, *Dean, School of Fine Arts, New York University*

WHAT can one say of modern music and who knows its trend? Like everything else in art matters that amounts to anything, so-called modern music is born largely of controversy. The great and sincere composer tries to convince the world of his new experience in the tone realm, to accustom the world to his new expression and a new craftsmanship.

He is not troubled to any extent with modernism or any other "ism." He can stand alone. But in spite of that he is, consciously or unconsciously, influenced by the mass of smaller men, the imitators, who are the controversialists—either sincere or insincere—and who originate pseudo theories. The inspired individual artist rises above this seething mass of "isms" and "alities" and through his personal contribution brings about a new day in the composing of music, the evolution of which has been logical and inevitable, adapting itself perfectly to the course of our intellectual life.

MUSIC THE GREATEST JOY

BY LOUIS GRUENBERG, *American Composer*

THE question as to whether or not Indian or Negroid music should be used in musical art forms is much discussed. The answer must be left to the discretion of the individual composer. It is unimportant whether themes are this or that, but it is vitally important whether themes are *good,* and what you do with them.

Shakespeare actually achieved originality, although using foreign material, through the extraordinary genius of being able to use other men's ideas with individuality. It is, and has always been, a question of application or inspiration. Application, most of us can furnish, inspiration comes alone from Heaven above. That is the difference between a Beethoven and a Raff.

Music is such a miracle yet to me that I know I shall never under-it. I only know it is my greatest joy on earth, my greatest solace in trouble.

GEORGE GERSHWIN   HARRY T. BURLEIGH

DEEMS TAYLOR   LOUIS GRUENBERG

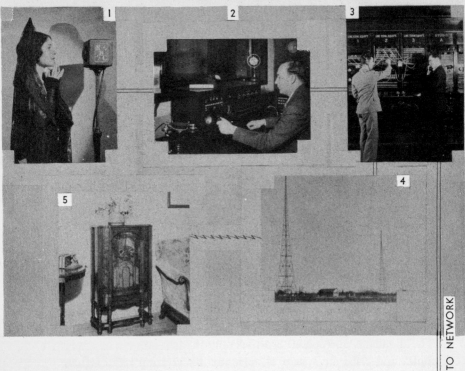

TO NETWORK

FROM MICROPHONE TO LOUDSPEAKER

1. MICROPHONE   2. CONTROL BOOTH   3. MAIN CONTROL BOARD
4. RADIO TRANSMITTER   5. LOUDSPEAKER
(Double lines—wire transmission. Zigzag line—radio transmission.)

FROM MICROPHONE TO LOUDSPEAKER

BY O. B. HANSON, *Manager of Technical Operation and Engineering, National Broadcasting Company*

TO THE average layman there is but one really important and essential piece of technical apparatus involved in a broadcast program. This is the microphone. He has seen it in pictures. He has seen it placed before the artists if he has visited the studios and witnessed a radio broadcast. If he has any conception at all of the equipment interposed between the microphone and his own receiving set at home it is usually extremely vague and indefinite.

The all-famous microphone is actually but the first element of a very complex and elaborate system of apparatus for creating radio signals to which broadcast receivers over a wide area may be tuned.

It is not necessary to describe in detail all the equipment used in a radio broadcast. What is attempted here is to present in its broadest aspect and the simplest possible phraseology the process by which a sound is transmitted from the broadcasting studio to the ear of the listener. (See page 3.)

Let us assume that a singer stands before a microphone in one of the New York studios of the National Broadcasting Company. The announcer has rung the chime signal, which is, so to speak, an assembly call to the network stations; he has announced the call letters of his own station and has signified to the orchestra conductor that the studio is "on the air." The poised baton of the conductor falls. A few measures of introduction are played. Then the singer begins. Her first tone is, let us say, an A. Let us see what happens to this tone before it reaches the ear of a listener fifty miles away.

To begin with, it should be borne in mind that sound as we perceive

239

it is a sensation produced in the organs of the ear by vibrations—that is, a series of variations of pressure—in the air. In the present case, these air vibrations have been created by corresponding vibrations of the singer's vocal chords, which, in turn, have been set in motion by the passage through them of the singer's breath. These sound waves, traveling in all directions away from the point of origin, are intercepted by the microphone. This instrument contains an extremely delicate and sensitive metallic membrane which vibrates in sympathy with the sound wave and sets up a series of feeble electrical impulses. A *microphone amplifier* builds up the strength of these impulses before they are sent through a cable which connects the microphone to the adjacent *control-booth*. The impulses are now sufficiently strong to be detected with earphones if these were attached to the cable.

Entering the control-booth, which is separated from the studio by two or three thicknesses of heavy plate glass, the electrical equivalent of the original sound enters the *mixer* and *volume control*. Here a studio engineer by skillful manipulation of the controls adjusts the intensity to the proper value. This is necessary to prevent overloading and distortion in the equipment through which our tone has yet to pass.

Leaving the control-booth, the as yet minute electric pulsations, now called "the program," go to the main control or apparatus room where they are amplified approximately one thousand times by the *studio amplifier*. At this point the now full-fledged program does several things.

First, it operates a loudspeaker in the control-booth so that the studio engineer can hear what is happening in the studio. Next, it causes a *volume indicator* to function so that the studio engineer can see by means of the pointer on a meter whether the program is of the correct electrical strength. A second volume indicator is made to operate before the master control supervisor, thus giving a double check. The program also enters several *distributing* or *line amplifiers* having an amplification of only three or four times. These feed the program to the various special outgoing *wire lines*. Network stations connect to certain of these lines and the local station, WEAF in this case, connects to another.

Following the program on its route to WEAF we travel twenty-five miles out on Long Island from New York City, to Bellmore. It is not difficult to find the station, since the three-hundred foot antenna towers serve as guide posts for miles around. Our program enters the low brick building in which the radio transmitters are located through an underground lead-sheathed cable which connects to an amplifier in the station control-room. This amplifier restores the program to the strength at which it entered the wire line going to the radio station.

From this amplifier the program goes to the *radio transmitter* proper. To describe in complete detail all the stages and electrical processes through which the program will pass in being converted into fifty thousand watts of radio energy, would be unnecessarily complicated. It will perhaps suffice to say that electrical energy known as the *carrier* (heard in old-time sets as a squeal) is generated. The program is then super-imposed or *modulated* on to this carrier energy and the resulting energy stepped up by giant vacuum tubes to fifty kilowatts of radio power. This power is sent through two heavy copper conductors to the small *antenna tuning house* centered between the towers and thence into the *antenna* leading directly upwards from the tuning house.

The next step in the progress of our program to the home of the listener is perhaps best explained by an analogy.

If a small stone is dropped into a pool of water, waves will be created which radiate uniformly from the point at which the stone fell. If a small piece of wood is floating on the water the series of waves will cause the piece of wood to move in accordance with the passing waves. In the case of the radio program the energy put into the antenna by the radio transmitter represents the dropping of the stone. The visible waves on the surface of the water are analogous to the radio waves in the so-called ether. The motion of the block of wood represents the small amount of electrical energy set up by the radio waves in the receiving antenna at the listener's home.

In this manner the power radiated from the antenna at the radio broadcasting station creates in the distant antenna attached to the listener's receiver a minute voltage. This *potential* is the same in every respect as that at the antenna of the broadcasting station except that it is greatly (several million times) reduced in strength. The receiving set when properly tuned to the incoming potential from the antenna amplifies the energy to a point where the original program can be separated or *demodulated* from the carrier. The program now in its original form is again amplified and sent into the loudspeaker which is usually built into the radio set. The program energy, by the same principles of magnetism which cause electric motors to rotate and electric bells to ring, then sets the diaphragm of the loudspeaker in vibration. This vibration, an exact equivalent of the electric energy which was in turn an equivalent of the artist's voice, now re-creates variations in air pressure which the ear recognizes as sound.

We thus have the voice of the artist in the studio reproduced in the home of a listener after having passed through apparatus of almost unbelievable complexity. Each piece of equipment—the microphone, the volume control, the amplifier, the special wire line, the radio transmitter—form an indispensable link in an electrical chain which provides radio programs to many thousands of listeners.

PART TWO

THE STORY OF MUSIC IN OUTLINE
FORM (to 1900)

FROM 3000 B.C. TO THE CHRISTIAN ERA

The Music of Ancient Peoples
  I. Primitive dances and songs of many peoples
 II. Music of the *Assyrians,* a war-like race
    (a) Much use of percussion instruments
    (b) Songs of a shrill and harsh quality
III. *Egyptian Music* of 3000 B.C. and earlier
    Records of the earliest instruments preserved by means of carvings and paintings found on the walls of tombs and pyramids and on ancient coins, and by the finding of actual instruments in burial vaults.
    From instruments extant it is inferred that scales in use were mostly diatonic; that there was some harmony is suggested by depiction of groups of musicians acting in concert, and from the size of the larger harps and lyres. From these same sources it is seen that dancing was accompanied by hand-clapping. Musical instruments were many and varied—harps with seven strings, lyres, lutes, flutes, bell-rattles, trumpets, and tambourines.
    300 B.C., invention of the water-organ by Ktesibius, an Alexandrian artisan.
 IV. *Music of the Hebrews*
    Data for Hebrew music found in the Old Testament taken from writings compiled about 800 B.C. (Chronicles about 300 B.C.)
    Early mention of music is of that made by a "band of prophets" organized by Samuel as a means of inducing religious ecstasy. (See also Gen. iv. 21.)
    Instruments commonly played include timbrel (small tambourine), trumpets of silver, shofar, psaltery, taboret, pipe, harp, small hand-kettledrums, lyre, and cymbals.
    (See Exod. xv. 20; Num. x. 2-10; Sam. vi. 5.)
    Music takes an important place in the service of the Temple, with solo singing, huge choruses, and antiphonal singing (Psalms of David).

Israelitic Folk Songs are mentioned in the Bible (see Num. xxl. 17–18; Deut. xxv. 4; Isa. lxv. 8—"Destroy it not"). Many folk songs are taken over for use in the Temple (see Psalms LVII, LVIII, LIX, LXXXV. In the original directions were given that each of these Psalms were to be sung to the tune of "Al-tash hîth," which means "Destroy it not").

V. *Music of the Greeks*

1100 B.C., the age of mythical stories of the power of music and of legendary heroes, as Pan (Pan's pipes, or syrinx), Apollo, Orpheus, and Hermes.

950 B.C., Homeric Age, epic songs of Homer and contests of rhapsodists.

776 B.C. Grecian game festivals, establishment of Olympic games, which included competitions in song and the playing of instruments.

c. 675 B.C., Terpander of Sparta (called "Father of Greek Music") enlarged the lyre from four to seven strings, and so completed what is known as the seven-tone scale; establishment of musical contests at Sparta.

600 B.C. Greek celebrations of spring with festivals to the gods, in which singing and dancing took prominent part.

Popularity of itinerant bards.

Pythagoras (584–504 B.C.) credited with invention of the monochord and scientific division of the scale into tones and half-tones. Greek modes and scales (see p. 38). He laid the foundation of the eight-tone scale (octave) by adding eighth string to the lyre.

The liturgies, special taxes, five in number, paid by the Greeks for the support of their Tragedies and Chorus. Greek Chorus—group of masked actors who appeared between acts and chanted the meaning of the play, or danced.

550 B.C. At the eighth of the Pythian Games were established contests for solo playing on kithara and aulos.

Plato (429–347 B.C.) made many allusions to music in his *Republic*.

Aristotle (384–322 B.C.), pupil of Plato, wrote many concise answers to specific musical problems of the day.

"Hymn to Apollo," composed 279 B.C. by an Athenian for a part of the celebration of repulse of the Goths (discovered at Delphi, 1893).

Greek instruments included drums, cymbals, harps, tambouras, and flutes. Records of instrumental playing found on Greek vases, bas reliefs, frescoes, and pictures, as found in excavations.

VI. *Music of the Northern Countries*

The beginnings of ballads, long epic songs.

1000 B.C. or earlier, ancient Britain, then ruled by Druids, encouraged and welcomed the singing of the bards, poets, and other musicians who traveled over the land singing the history and news of the day, praises of the gods, and legends of adventure. Their principal instrument was the crwth (primitive Welsh harp, ancestor of lyre and viols. See Eisteddfod, Welsh history).

In lands of the Norsemen and Vikings, bards known as Skalds or Sagamen perpetuated legend and history which gave rise to the Nibelungenlied, from which Richard Wagner drew material for many of his music dramas.

FROM BEGINNING OF CHRISTIAN ERA TO A.D. 1600

First Century

First Christian songs, a continuance of synagogue customs. "Composition" of new hymns (for singing of Psalms) called *rhapsodies.*

Paul's "Epistles to the Corinthians" written, in which are repeated exhortations to song.

Legend of St. Ignatius (49–107), who, in a vision, heard heavenly choirs singing antiphonally, and so originated, in the church at Antioch, two choirs which answered each other.

Nero (reigning 58–68) said to have played a primitive stringed instrument as Rome burned. (The fiddle, instrument popularly included in the story, not yet invented.)

Second Century

A.D. 110 or 112, Pliny the Younger, writing from Bithynia, describes the Christians as singing psalms and hymns antiphonally, a similar practice having existed in the church at Antioch, this custom of alternate singing having been carried from Syria to Milan and Rome.

A.D. 177, St. Cecelia, a patron saint of music, is put to death as a Christian martyr during the reign of Marcus Aurelius.

Establishment of the New Testament.

No instruments were used in early Christian services.

Third Century

First complete hymn written by Clement of Alexandria.

Odin, Saxon prince who came to be considered as Norse god, aided revival of Norse mythology and minstrelsy.

First use of the organ in public worship; the compass of the first organs very small, often only one octave.

The most ancient piece of Christian music now in existence—"Hymn to the Trinity"—dates from the end of the third century. This is the "Oxyrhynchite Papyrus." It was found written upon the back of a bit of papyrus upon which had been recorded a column of agricultural accounts of the early part of the century. (Purchased by H. Stuart Jones in Egypt in 1919, and put by him into modern notation; see Oxford "Proceedings," edited by Grenfell and Hunt, 1922; also S. Reinach *Revue Musicale,* July 1922.)

Fourth Century

Decline of Rome and Migration of the Nations (fourth to sixth centuries).

Constantine (272–337), first Christian Emperor, erected large churches in which the new methods of chanting the Psalms were introduced. In A.D. 325 he made Christianity the national religion of Rome.

At the beginning of the fourth century Pope Sylvester founded a school for singers at Rome.

A.D. 355–395, production of original hymns.

St. Ambrose (333–397) organized existing chants; established definite (authentic) modes, known as the Ambrosian modes; established antiphonal singing at Milan (as described by St. Augustine).

Definite separation in church service of the clergy and the laity.

All singing done in unison or octave, the principal melody—the one sung by most of the singers—called the *tenor* (from *teneo,* to hold, or carry).

Fifth Century

Pope Celestine (reigned 422–432) introduces antiphonal psalmody into Rome.

The organ now commonly in use in churches, especially in Spain.

Sixth Century

Pope Gregory the Great (reigned 590–604) reconstructed church service into a harmonious whole. He added new modes (termed *plagal*). In his Gregorian Chorale (called *cantus planus,* or plain-song, because of the manner of movement of the melody, its lack of fixed rhythm and of harmony) he laid the foundation of a free art. Founded the Schola Cantorum (School of Song) to prepare singers for religious duties.

Seventh Century

Missions, including trained singers of the plain-song, sent by Rome to England (604), to St. Gall (612), to Ireland (c. 620), and to Brittany (660). Irish psalmody and hymnody were distinctly Celtic by the end of the first half of the century. Minstrels and harpists were accorded many honors in Ireland, where there was already an acquaintance with harmony, also descant and the principles of counterpoint. It is of interest to note that Pope Gregory is said to have been a direct descendant of Cairbre Musc, son of Conaire, Head King of Ireland from A.D. 212 to 220.

Eighth Century

Missions, including singers, sent by Rome to the Franks (758) and to Fulda (744).

Charlemagne the Great (742–814) was active in the cause of music, establishing singing schools in many parts of France.

Rise in popularity of ballad singing in England and Denmark. The ability to play a harp and improvise now a necessary part of a gentleman's education.

Ninth Century

Hucbald (840–932) was the first to write a definite second part for a second singer or group of singers, this being always placed a fourth distant from the *tenor,* or principal melody (the Latin name of which is *cantus firmus*). He was the first to use two parallel lines indicating tonal relationships and thus simplifying the reading and learning of music. These lines were the forerunners of the present staff. Their parallel motion was known as *organum* or *diaphony*.

St. Odo of Cluny (879–942) suggested the use of the seven letters of the alphabet to indicate scale degrees.

Popularity of the harp and its music continued in England. Story of King Alfred who (878) disguised himself as a bard and carried his harp into the camps of the enemy that he might learn their secrets.

Tenth Century

As first two lines used by Hucbald were colored (one, red, indicating F, tone on the fourth line of what is now the bass staff; the second, indicating C, yellow); neumes were placed in relative positions. By this time all organ-keys were lettered. The round b was used for B-flat, and the square b (♮) for B-natural. This later became the familiar natural sign.

Eleventh Century

Guido of Arezzo (d. 1050?) is one of the most famous personages in the whole period. He is thought to have been born near Paris and have migrated to Italy. To him is attributed the development of the four-line staff; and the origin of use of syllables, now known as solfeggio, to indicate notes. The first six syllables—*ut* (later changed to *do,* for ease in singing), *re, mi, fa, sol, la*—being the opening syllables of the six lines of the Hymn to St. John the Baptist; the seventh tone of the scale (*si*) named from the initials of Sancte Johannes, as Saint John is called in the Latin.

Battle of St. Cast, story of common song. Battle of Hastings, attack of the Normans led singing into battle by Taillefer. *Chanson de Roland,* famous example of French chansons.

First of great Crusades (1095–1271) brought soldiers of Europe into touch with the general culture and music of the Orient. Types of singing and instruments new to Europe were carried back by returning Crusaders.

Decline of Gregorian chorale (plain-song) and rise of polyphony (many-voiced music).

Twelfth Century

Development of descant, introduction of new intervals, melodies subject to rules of mensurable music. One of the earliest inspirations to descant recorded is written in French—"Quicouques veut dechanter" (whoever wishes to may descant)—the extra voice part being not written out, but improvised, and being higher than the given melody, or *cantus firmus*. Of great significance in descant is the fact that contrary motion between the two voices here replaced the principle of parallel motion employed in organum.

Rise of the troubadours (Provence, now southeastern France) soon after 1100. Among their numbers were William of Poitiers (d. 1127); Richard the Lion-Hearted (d. 1199); Thibaut IV of Navarre (d. 1253); Alphonse II of Aragon (d. 1196); and Adam de la Hale (1240–1287). The troubadours combined the art of chivalrous poetry with that of song. Sense of definite tonality, use of four-line staff and square notes, regularity of rhythm, use of small portable instruments, and themes which exalted love were features of troubadour song as composed by men of noble or royal birth, and sung by them or by the *jongleurs* (professional musicians of the day). The name *troubadour* comes from the Spanish *trobar* or French *trouver,* meaning "to invent." Through the singing of troubadour songs in public squares and in general festival gatherings of the people by the jongleurs, many of these songs became part of the body of exquisite French folk song admired and sung to this day. Troubadour song continued until about the middle of the fourteenth century.

The *trouvères,* from the north of France, were singers who, though influenced by the melodies of the south, composed in a style more similar to the austere modes of early church music. Their *ballada* or *balerie* (from which comes the present meaning of *ballet*) were combinations of song, instrumental preludes and interludes, and dance accompaniment.

Beginnings of the rounde, ballata, serenade, and pastorale. Early rondo form, in which the same melody constantly appears in repetition by different groups of singers or instrumentalists.

Franco (from city of Cologne on the River Rhine) invented the signatures and also, to an extent, perfected four kinds of notes which should indicate time values, these being the *maxima* (▬), which developed into the whole note (𝐎); the *longa* (▬), which became the half-note (𝅗𝅥); the brevis (▪) becoming the quarter-note (♩); and the semi-brevis (♦), which later became the eighth-note (♪). Three-beat or triple time was considered "perfect time" and was marked with a circle (𝐎).

Thirteenth Century

Adam de la Hale (b. Arras, 1240, and often called the "Hunchback of Arras") wrote a song-play, *Robin et Marion* (first performance at the Court of Naples, 1285), often called the first comic opera.

"Sumer Is Icumen In," the oldest recorded round or canon, is thought to have been the first song of this type written in the language of the people of England. Dates of its composition vary from 1240 to much later in the century. It is known to have been mentioned by Johannes de Garlandia (the younger), who lived about 1300, in his *Optima introductio in contra-punctum.* The song is often held by the British to prove their claim that harmony was used in England long before it became common on the conti-nent. It was written at the Abbey of Reading, and the original manuscript is now preserved in the British Museum.

The *Minnesingers of Germany,* singers of noble birth (whose aristocratic movements culminated in notable song-contests such as those held in the Wartburg fortress in Thuringia, 1207, and celebrated centuries later by Richard Wagner in his opera *Tannhäuser*).

The *Meistersingers* (founded during the thirteenth century) came from the folk, often tradesmen and merchants. Formation of music guilds. Com-plicated rules were often substituted for musical inspiration in creation of song (as celebrated in Wagner's *Die Meistersinger*). The movement car-ried music into the homes, affected Germany's music and that of surround-ing countries until into the sixteenth century. Hans Sachs (1494–1576) was the most famous of the meistersingers.

Notre Dame "school" flourishes; Leoninus (from the twelfth century) and Perotinus, chief exponents of the *ars antiqua;* development of *conductus* (in which an absolutely free voice is combined with and above a sustained voice), and early *motets* (in which two or three free voices moved above a very sustained melodic line).

Fourteenth Century

At about 1300, the older type of organum and polyphony changed into the freely invented parts of the *Ars Nova,* a Florentine "school," whose masters (including Landino, c. 1325–1397, a blind organist of noble birth) supplied original themes for use in composition rather than continuing use of plain-song as *cantus firmus;* developed complexity in rhythms used; and brought about secularization of music. An important exponent and theoreti-cian was Philippe de Vitry (whose tract, written about 1321, *Ars Nova,* gave its name to the movement). An important composer was Machault, who stressed the use of duple rhythm in addition to triple rhythm, already in constant use.

The first motets, written in contrapuntal style, often contained combina-tions of airs from popular songs and Gregorian plain chant.

Beginnings of *madrigal* writing, originating from the *trope,* but thought of mainly as secular lyric forms of from three to six parts, some of which might be taken by the voice and others by instruments.

Growth of small vocal forms, such as the *lais* or *lay;* and small dance forms, such as *ductia* (wordless), *stantipes, rotunda,* and *strombotta.* It is thought to be impossible to tell whether these were sung or played, or both; it may have happened, as it does in the Orient at the present day, when a piece of music may first be played, and sung, then the instrument laid down and the dance commenced.

Guillaume Machault (d. 1374) wrote his secular music in the *ars nova* style, but his church music often reverts to the methods of the *ars antiqua,* using awkward progressions such as parallel fourths and fifths.

Fifteenth Century

Dunstable introduced the *ars nova* into England; through his influence upon the earliest of the Franco-Flemish, the general doctrine spread over into the Netherlands. The first Flemish school included Nicholas Grenon (1425–1427), Binchois (1400–1460), and Dufay (1400–1474).

The second Franco-Flemish school included Jean de Okeghem (1430–1495), Obrecht (1430–1505), Antoine Busnois (d. 1492 c.), and Josquin des Près (1450–1521), a pupil of Okeghem.

Sixteenth Century

The first music printed (1501) in Venice, by Ottavino dei Petrucci.

Jean Tinctoris (1446–1511) founded the first school of music at Naples, and wrote the first published dictionary of musical terms.

Martin Luther (1483–1546) brought about the Reformation. Rise of Protestant chorale and congregational singing.

A.D. 1558. Forerunners of the first oratorio were brought into being through daily religious services in which music was given great prominence, under the direction of Filippo Neri, Florence.

Development of masques and religious pageantry on the continent and in England.

Adrian Willaert (c. 1490–1562) was for 35 years choirmaster at St. Mark's Church, Venice. He founded the "Venetian school" of music, his outstanding advances including double-choir effects and related developments in choral singing. He trained a long list of brilliant pupils who carried his ideas over Europe.

Andrea and Giovanni Gabrieli (uncle and nephew), organists, composers, and teachers of Venice (also connected with St. Mark's); originated new ideas in organ writing and instrumental ensemble (advance toward fugal form).

Giovanni Pierluigi da Palestrina (1526–1594), composer to the Papal

Choir, Rome; his works represent the climax of fluency and ideality in contrapuntal vocal writing.

Council of Trent (1545–1563), an ecclesiastical council convened for the purpose of purifying the Church, and incidentally its music.

Evolution of the violin, said to have been invented by Gasparo da Salo (c. 1542–1609). Other artists in its construction included Andrea Amati (c. 1520–1611) and other members of the family, continuing even into the eighteenth century.

Interest in dramatic music; formation of Florentine group which developed the "first opera" (Giovanni Bardi, Jacopo Corsi, Guilio Caccini, Jacopo Peri, Vincenzo Galilei, Cavalieri, and others).

Forerunners of the first opera: Poloziano's *Orfeo,* written and set to music the latter half of the century; *Il Satiro,* and *La Disperazione di Fileno* by Cavalieri, 1590; and *Il Giuoco della Cieca* by the same, 1595. *Dafne* (Rinuccini), set by Peri and Caccini, 1594. Vecchi's *Amfiparnasso* produced at Modena, 1594, a comedy in madrigal style (no overture, no instrumental accompaniment, polyphonic style, sung by five voices).

Early use of the word *symphonia; Symphonie Sacrae* for voices and instruments by Giovanni Gabrieli, 1597; by this name Monteverde called the piece which preceded the first vocal numbers of dramatic works.

Development of early instrumental forms: *ricercari* (from motet); *canzoni* (from madrigals); *ritornelli* (short instrumental pieces introduced between arias); the *suite;* and others.

Thomas Tallis (c. 1510–1585), master of St. Paul's School, and organist under four reigns in England; first composer of important keyboard music in England. *Mulliner's Book,* in which are the first English keyboard pieces, compiled c. 1500; now in the manuscript collection in the British Museum.

William Byrde (c. 1543–1623), organist and singer, Royal Chapel, London; pupil of, and joint publisher with Tallis; famed as a writer of clavier music.

Dr. John Bull (1563–1628), organist at Hereford Cathedral; Bachelor and Doctor of Music from Oxford University; virtuoso and composer. The works of Tallis, Byrde, and Bull form an important part of the background of the history of modern pianoforte music.

Thomas Morley (1557–c. 1602), pupil and successor of Byrd; writer of madrigals, ballets, and "ayres." His *Plaine and Easie Introduction to Musick* was written in 1597.

1600 to 1900

Seventeenth Century

Further development of the violin, important names connected with its perfecting being Maggini (1581–1628); the Guarnieri family, including Andreas (c. 1626–1698), Pietro Giovanni (1655– ?), Joseph, son of

Andreas (1666–c. 1739), Peter of Venice, son of Joseph, (1695– ?), and Joseph del Gesu (the letters *I H S* are placed in his finest instruments). Also Kaspar Diefenpruggiar (or Tieffenbrücker), from the late fifteenth century; and finally Antonio Stradavari (1644–1737).

A.D. 1600, about ten months before the performance of *Euridici*, there was given the first oratorio, *Rappresentazione di Anima e di Corpo,* by Cavalieri, Rome.

A.D. 1600, a setting of Rinuccini's *Euridici* by Peri (including some numbers from a simultaneous setting by Caccini); the first performance of this, the first opera, took place at the marriage festivities of Henry IV of France and Marie de' Medici.

A.D. 1600, the first "string band," assembled to accompany the singers in *Euridici.*

A.D. 1607, music drama or opera, *Orfeo* by Claudio Monteverde (1567–1643) at Venice; great advance in the art of writing for solo voice. *Arianne* by Monteverde, 1608.

A.D. 1607, composition of *Sinfonie* for instruments without voices, by Adriano Banchieri.

A.D. 1637, the first Venetian opera-house, making opera, for the first time, a public amusement instead of the possession solely of noble and wealthy patrons; *L'Incoronazione di Poppea* composed by Monteverde for the occasion.

A.D. 1637–1640, rise of operatic writing, more than 700 works being produced and large increase in number of public opera-houses; the term *opera* figures first in the title of such a work in 1696.

Giacomo Carissimi (1605–1676), developer of the *cantata* (dramatic form for single voice and small groups), in which the aria and recitative were utilized, and writer in oratorio form.

Jean Baptiste Lully (1633–1687), born at Florence; became court musician, and later director of music for Louis XIV of France.

Arcangelo Corelli (1653–1713), the first of the great violinists; one of the first to write in the *concerto-grosso* form; renowned as teacher, composer, and performer.

Henry Purcell (1658–1695), brilliant English writer of opera, church music, and chamber music.

Johann Kuhnau (1660–1722), organist of St. Thomas Church at Leipzig, wrote "Bible" Sonatas, early examples of program music.

A.D. 1685, year of birth of Johann Sebastian Bach, Eisenach; Georg Friedrich Handel, Halle; Domenico Scarlatti, Naples; Gay (writer of the *Beggar's Opera*).

The clavichord displaced the lute and opened a new field for composition. Expansion of opera in France.

Development of *concerto grosso;* first, two antiphonal vocal groups (as at

St. Mark's in Venice); second, groups of voices and instruments; third, division of instruments into *tutti* and *soli*.

Alessandro Scarlatti (1659–1725), pupil of Carissimi; master of early Italian opera; composer of opera, masses, and oratorio; molded the aria into more symmetrical form.

General acceptance of a modern idea of tonality, and of interdependence of melody and form.

Eighteenth Century

A.D. 1708, Bartolomeo Cristofori built the first piano at Florence.

The arts of organ-playing and composition for organ came into prominence in church worship.

Development of the *fugue,* and other large forms, including the *suite,* the *variation* form, and the *sonata.*

A large amount of literature is written about music, and there is an increased standardization of theoretical material.

Chamber music made a great advance, stimulated by improvements in the instruments themselves.

Activities in composition drifted toward formalism.

Bach's writings include the *Well-Tempered Clavichord,* a set of 48 *preludes* and *fugues,* written to prove the usefulness of tempered tuning.

Establishment of what was called a "classical" form of composition by a group of writers of whom Mozart and Haydn were typical examples.

Josef Haydn (1732–1809) defined sonata form; perfected the balance of the symphony, and divided it into four main choirs.

Wolfgang Amadeus Mozart (1756–1791), virtuoso and genius, wrote more than 1000 works which embrace almost every artistic form.

Advent of the *Singspiel* (a play made up of spoken dialogue interspersed with solos, duets, and part-songs) in Germany.

Christoph Willibald Gluck (1714–1787), famous as "reformer" of opera.

Handel and Bach devote themselves to organ composition and oratorio, making tremendous contributions to both types of music.

A.D. 1727, composition of *The Beggar's Opera* by John Gay, with first performance in January 1728.

Jean Philippe Rameau (1683–1764), a distinguished French organist, theorist, and composer.

K. P. E. Bach (1714–1788), developed many extended forms, and instrumental technique.

Nineteenth Century

(The better-known works of nearly all composers here mentioned are discussed in some detail in Part II of the Book. See also Chapters 4, 10, 18, 19, 20, 23, 27, and 30, in Part I.)

Luigi Cherubini (1760–1842), influential as church composer, writer of opera, and as teacher and director of Paris Conservatoire.

Ludwig van Beethoven (1770–1827) created, in his later works, what are regarded as the greatest models of instrumental form.

The rise of *Romanticism*. Schubert (1797–1828), Schumann (1810–1856), Chopin (1809–1849), von Weber (1786–1826), Hector Berlioz (1803–1869), Mendelssohn (1809–1847), Meyerbeer (1791–1864), and others. Development of new art forms.

Birth and development of the art song.

Rise of *Romantic* opera in Italy. Donizetti (1797–1848), Verdi (1813–1901), Rossini (1792–1868), and Bellini (1802–1835). Later Italian opera introduced such composers as Puccini, Leoncavallo, and Mascagni.

Opera in France gave prominence to Gounod, Bizet, Massenet, Charpentier, d'Indy, Ambroise Thomas, and Halévy.

Muzio Clementi (1752–1832) developed instrumental forms upon which Beethoven and later artists founded their works.

Karl Czerny (1791–1857) brought technical proficiency to a high art.

Beginnings of the Russian "School," with Michael Glinka (1804–1857) as its founder.

Rise of virtuosity and of increased artistry in instrument making. Great artists before the public included such pianists as Franz Liszt (1811–1886), Anton Rubinstein (1830–1894), Hans von Bülow (1830–1894) and Clara Schumann (1819–1896); and such violinists as de Beriot (1802–1870), Ludwig Spohr (1784–1859), and Nicolo Paganini (1782–1840).

Establishment of the *Symphonic Poem* as a form (See Franz Liszt and Camille Saint-Saëns).

Growth of the *Music Drama* (See Richard Wagner).

Work of the *Late-Romanticists* (See Johannes Brahms).

Rise of *Light Opera* and *Opéra Comique*.

The Modern School in Germany and Austria (Reger, Mahler, Wolf, Richard Strauss, Engelbert Humperdinck, Max Bruch).

Piano literature comes into a full development.

The "school" of *Impressionism* comes to full flower toward the end of the century with such composers as Claude Debussy.

In America, pioneers include Lowell Mason (1792–1872), a remarkable leader, authority on congregational singing and music education, and composer of hymns and music for juveniles. He was founder of music education as conducted in the schools of the United States. Later artists and educators include Dr. William Mason, Dudley Buck, J. K. Paine; and Dr. Leopold Damrosch, who organized in 1873 the first oratorio society of New York, and in 1881, the first choral festival (in which there participated a chorus of 1200 and an orchestra of 250 persons).

BIOGRAPHICAL SKETCHES OF COMPOSERS AND INTERPRETATIONS OF THEIR PRINCIPAL WORKS

ABT, FRANZ (1819–1885). Trained in Leipzig, and for many years theater and chorus conductor in Zurich, where he had some connection with the activities of Richard Wagner. He wrote more than 3000 songs and part-songs, including "When the Swallows Homeward Fly."

ADAM, ADOLPHE CHARLES (1803–1856). Born in Paris. Elected at the age of 33 to membership in the Légion d'Honneur, and, not long afterward, to the Académie. Taught composition at the Paris Conservatoire. Chief among his operatic works is the comic opera *Postilion of Longjumeau*. "O, Holy Night," one of Adam's less pretentious compositions, has won for itself the compliment of being thought a folk air.

ALBENIZ, ISAAC (1861–1909). Albeniz is an important name in the history of Spanish music, having been borne by at least three distinguished composers and performers. Isaac Albeniz was the creator of a real Spanish "school" of music.

"*Caprice Espagnole*" (Spanish Caprice). A characteristic triplet figure and a syncopated Spanish rhythm suggest the clicking of wooden castanets.

Iberia. A suite of twelve descriptive pieces for piano, the whole given the ancient name for Spain, and several of the pieces being named for towns in Spain. Number three is called "Fête-Dieu à Seville" (Religious Festival in Seville). "Triana," number four, is named for a town in which the *gitanos* (gypsies) are said to abound. "Malagueña," most familiar in Fritz Kreisler's arrangement for violin is an idealized folk song from Malaga often heard as an "echo song," always in a plaintive minor.

ARNE, THOMAS AUGUSTINE (1710–1778). A British composer of much importance. He was the first to use women's voices for the upper parts in a performance of his oratorio *Judith,* 1773. His songs include "Lass with the Delicate Air" and "Rule, Britannia!"

AUBER, DANIEL FRANÇOIS ESPRIT (1782–1871). A teacher at the Paris

Conservatoire, succeeding his teacher Cherubini in 1842. Imperial choirmaster to Napoleon III, and a brilliant writer of opéra comique.

Fra Diavolo. First performance Paris, 1830. Based on the life of a bandit from Calabria named Michele Pezza, better known as Fra Diavolo, who, pardoned for his marauding, became an officer in the Neapolitan army, was captured by the French in the Napoleonic wars, and hanged. The Overture, in sonata style, is a popular concert-piece for orchestra.

BACH, JOHANN SEBASTIAN (1685–1750). Born in Eisenach, Germany, Bach had over 40 professional or semiprofessional musicians among his immediate ancestors or relatives. His father was his first teacher. Left an orphan at the age of ten, he went to Ohrdurf to live with his brother Johann Christoph, who had just returned from Erfurt where he had been a student with Pachelbel. (It was Pachelbel's "From Heaven High" that Bach copied by moonlight, giving rise to a popular anecdote.)

Bach's compositions include choral works for the church, music for organ, clavichord (now played on the piano), the voice, for orchestra, and for various groups of orchestral instruments.

"Air for G-String" (Bach-Wilhelmj). Originally the second of the five short movements of the third *Suite in D Major* (composed while Bach was serving as chapelmaster to Prince Leopold of Cöthen), a collection of melodies written in the same key, the "Air" being written for strings only. As a violin solo (in the Wilhelmj arrangement) it is transposed to the key of C that it may all be played upon the sonorous G-string of the violin. There are but 18 measures in the entire composition, the first six being repeated, and the last 12.

"Ave Maria." Setting of a devotional text taken from the Latin ritual of the Roman Church. Gounod wrote the air sung by the voice, but used for its basis the principal chordal notes of the "Prelude No. 1, in C Major," from Bach's *Well-Tempered Clavichord;* and for the accompaniment, the Prelude itself. (Also often heard in transcription for organ, violin, and other instruments.)

"Capriccio." A piano piece written as a farewell tribute to his favorite brother about to enter the service of Charles XII of Sweden as an oboe player in his orchestra. The first theme, the symbol of the traveler's friends, speaks in almost wheedling fashion to dissuade him from the trip. The second movement is humorous and, through the use of fugal style, first one, then another, voice enters and describes the dangers that lie ahead of him. At the close of this section chords depict the friends as all talking at once. The postilion's horn announces the departure of the coach, and in a fugue based on the postilion's air, the capricious story comes to a close.

"Brandenburg" Concertos. A group of works completed in 1721 for small orchestra, commissioned by the Margrave of Brandenburg. The concerto of that day differed consid-

erably from the now accepted concerto form, which is that of a sonata or symphony.

"Chaconne." (See p. 124.)

Christmas Oratorio. Written for his own choir at the St. Thomas Church in Leipzig, it is, in reality, a series of six cantatas, one to be performed on Christmas Day, one for each of the two days following, one each for New Year's Day, for the first Sunday in the year, and for the first Sunday in Epiphany. It tells the story of the birth of Christ as related in the New Testament by Matthew and Luke. Outstanding among the instrumental portions is the famous "Pastoral Prelude" which precedes Part II of the oratorio, and the melody of which he places later in the oratorio in the bass and in interludes of one of the chorales (*Wir singen dir in deinem Heer*), as sung by the shepherds who join with the angels in making glad music together.

Concerto in D for Two Violins. This composition, written in the style of the old-time *concerto grossi* for two solo violins, accompanied by string quartet (or arrangement for piano), is in three distinct parts, or movements. The first is like a fugue; the second is song-like; and the third, or Finale, is of a brilliant style.

"My Heart Ever Faithful." This sacred aria from the *68th Cantata* is one of the most familiar of all the Bach solos for the voice. He wrote more than 300 sacred cantatas because of his duties in the court-chapel at Cöthen, and in later years, in Leipzig, where he is said to have written a new cantata for every Sunday's service at the St. Thomas Church. Many of these works were sung the one time for which they were written, then laid aside, and the cantata *"God So Loved the World,"* of which this aria is a conspicuous part, was not published for many scores of years after it was written. In many of the phrases of the song the first half is sung by the voice, while the instrumental accompaniment completes it by finishing the strain.

St. Matthew Passion. The Passion music interprets the story of the last days of Christ, and his death, as related in the four Gospels. Bach is said to have written a complete Passion oratorio according to the text of each Apostle, and of these the *St. Matthew Passion* is considered the greatest. In it Bach used the Biblical text without change, distributing the speeches between two choirs, each of which had its own organ and orchestral accompaniment. He separated the words of Christ, in effect, from the rest of the narrative, by giving it a different accompaniment, that of a string quartet; except in the last cry of Christ upon the Cross, where still further isolation is suggested by the majestic accompaniment of the organ alone. A choral prelude, or prologue, announces the Passion. The atmosphere for each event is created in dramatic recitative sung by the tenor, the necessary dialogue being supplied by appropriate principal voices. The disciples, the soldiers, and the mob are sung by the chorus.

The oratorio is written in two sections, which, in Bach's day, were separated by a sermon. The audience was brought into further sympathy with the message of the work by being given opportunity to join in the singing of the old chorales with which the choruses and arias are interspersed. Bach did not hesitate to use naïve tonal symbolizations, such as a quaint four-note figure on the words "cock-crow" as the story of Peter's denial is sung: and of using appealing melodies, whatever their source, such as the melody of the choral "Sacred Head, Now Wounded," which he uses five times in the *St. Matthew Passion* (and not only here but also in his *Christmas Oratorio* and in four of his church cantatas), and of which the original tune was that of an old German love song by Johann Hassler. The *St. Matthew Passion* was written for and first sung at the Good Friday service in St. Thomas Church, Leipzig, April 15, 1729. It was revived in Berlin by Felix Mendelssohn in March 1829, and again in St. Thomas Church on Palm Sunday, 1841. The first performance in America is credited to Dr. Walter Damrosch, in March 1880.

Suite No. 2, in B Minor. There are three distinct periods in the history of Bach's professional life: first, the years between 1708 and 1717, spent at Weimar, where were written his chief compositions for organ; second, from 1717 to 1723, at Cöthen, where his services to the Prince called forth scores of works for clavier, chamber music, and for the orchestra of his time (chiefly reed and stringed instruments); and third, in Leipzig, where he lived from 1723, and where the finest of his choral music was written. While in Cöthen, Bach wrote

four classic suites (called *overtures* by the composer) for the court orchestra, and in each he gave an outstanding part to some solo instrument. In *Suite No. 2* (for flute, strings, and harpsichord) the prominence was given to the flute, an instrument for which Bach had a great affection. The suite is composed of an overture or prelude, and a series of six dance tunes.

Well-Tempered Clavichord. The famous series of 48 Preludes and Fugues which Bach wrote for the clavichord, not only as works of art, but also to prove that, according to the theory of "tempered" tuning which he advocated and developed, one might play on a keyed instrument with equal ease, in all keys, whether major or minor. Until his time this had not been possible— one could play in only about 15 keys. The *Well-Tempered Clavichord* contains a Prelude and Fugue in each of the 24 major, and each of the 24 minor keys. These Preludes and Fugues are the especial property of the pianist, but they are also played by other instruments, or combination of instruments, for which arrangements have been made. Bach worked on these numbers for over twenty years before he considered them finished. (See also "Ave Maria.")

BALFE, MICHAEL WILLIAM (1808–1870). Born in Dublin, Balfe brought to his music the romantic tendencies of the true Celt. Studied under some of the finest masters of London, in Italy, and in Paris. Was the recipient of extraordinary honors, including the French decoration of Chevalier of the Legion of Honor. Wrote many stage works, the greatest of which is the *Bohemian Girl*.

The Bohemian Girl. First performance at Drury Lane Theatre, London, November 27, 1843. The action is placed in Pressburg, Hungary, during the eighteenth century. The story is of Thaddeus, an exile from Poland, who has joined a band of gypsies, and of Arline, daughter of the Governor of Pressburg, who, while her father befriends them, is stolen by the gypsies. Twelve years pass. Arline, now a beautiful young woman, is telling Thaddeus of her strange dream in the aria, "I Dreamt That I Dwelt in Marble Halls." The Gypsy Queen unites them in marriage. Being herself in love with Thaddeus, she contrives to have Arline arrested for theft. Arline is brought before the Count, who is magistrate of the district, for trial. Just before her appearance he sings, as he recalls his long-lost daughter, "The Heart Bow'd Down by Weight of Woe." During the trial the Count recognizes Arline and identifies her by an old scar on her arm. Restored to her rightful stations, Arline pines for Thaddeus, whom she thinks of as a gypsy. Their joy at his sudden visit is expressed in the aria, "Then You'll Remember Me," which he sings upon greeting her. The Queen discloses his presence in the castle to the Count, but after a series of dramatic episodes the opera closes amid a scene of great rejoicing as the lovers are at last united.

BARTÓK, BÉLA (born in Hungary, March 25, 1881). Studied with his mother in Pressburg, and at the Budapest Royal Conservatory. First important composition was a Rhapsody for piano and orchestra. In 1904 Bartók began his study of Hungarian national music, which has since so markedly influenced his composition. In 1905, he associated himself with Zoltan Kodaly in these studies, at the same time extending his research to Rumanian and Slovak national music. In 1913 an extensive trip was made to Africa to study the national element in the music of the Biskri, an Arabian tribe living near Biskra in Algiers.

The governing feature of Bartók's composition has been his endeavor to infuse new life into music by adding elements notable in strong old peasant music. Bartók also gradually abandoned the customary system of major and minor keys, reverting to tonal systems of ancient church compositions. His collection of *350 Rumanian National Melodies* is published by the Rumanian Academy of Sciences of Bucharest. In 1907 Bartók was appointed Professor of the Royal Conservatory of Bucharest. Important compositions of Bartók in addition to songs and *a cappella* choruses, include four string quartets (1908 and 1917); *Two Images,* Opus 10 (for orchestra); *First Sonata for Violin and Piano;* a one-act opera, *Duke Bluebeard's Castle* (with two characters) 1911; a dance play *The Wooden Prince* (1916); four orchestral suites, a piano concerto, and a piano sonata; and a pantomime, *The Wondrous Mandarin,* written to celebrate his fiftieth birthday.

BAUER, Marion Eugenie (1887–
). Born in Walla Walla, Washington. For many years a resident of New York City, where she is assistant Professor of Music at New York University, and where she acts as New York editor for the *Musical Leader* of Chicago. Miss Bauer is a member of the League of Composer's Executive Board, of the United States section of the International Society for Contemporary Musicians, and of the American Music Guild. She does much lecturing on modern music. Her compositions include "Here at High Morning" (*a cappella* men's chorus), "Lay of the Four Winds" (male chorus and piano), "Three Noëls" (*a cappella* women's chorus), *Orientale* for orchestra, and many other chamber and choral works.

BAX, Arnold (1883–   ). Born in London, of Irish ancestry. Illustrates in his writings the Celtic influence now so surely being felt by much of British music. For example his song, "I Heard a Piper Piping," is a melody in the old Dorian mode. His orchestral *Garden of Faud* is based on a legend similar to that of Debussy's *Submerged Cathedral,* except that Bax follows the version which places the sunken city off the Irish coast. He has written much choral music, chamber music, many songs, and has supplied several charming art works for solo viola.

BEACH, Mrs. H. H. A. (1867–
). Composer and pianist, born at Henniker, N. H. Taught by her mother, later studied in Boston. Mrs. Beach carried on her studies in counterpoint, composition, and orchestration for many years by herself from text-books, and scores. Has played with almost all of the major orchestras, and her works have been accorded enthusiastic reception in all the great music centers of America and Europe. At the age of 7, made several public appearances, playing selections from Beethoven and Chopin, and some of her own waltzes. At 16, made her début as pianist at the Boston Music Hall with the Moscheles *G-Minor Concerto,* and at 17 was soloist with the Boston and Thomas orchestras. She was commissioned to write the official hymn for the Panama-Pacific Exposition of 1915, the "Song of Welcome" for the dedication exercises of the Omaha Exposition, and the "Festival Jubilate" for the Chicago Exposition of 1893. Published works include the *Gaelic Symphony,* Op. 32; Concerto for piano and orchestra, Op. 45; Sonata for piano and violin, Op. 34; *Mass in E-Flat; The Minstrel and the King,* for male chorus and orchestra; and many other cantatas, orchestral works, songs, and piano pieces. Mrs. Beach is acknowledged as America's greatest woman composer.

"*Ah, Love but a Day.*" From the Opus 44, a group of Browning songs, one of the most brilliant as well as popular songs by any American composer.

"*Chambered Nautilus*" (cantata for women's voices). An outstanding setting of the poem by Oliver Wendell Holmes.

"*Christ in the Universe.*" A choral setting of a poem by Alice Meynell, had its first performance in 1932 at St. Bartholomew's Church, New York, the work being dedicated to the organist and choir of that church.

"Ecstasy" (Exaltation). A song from Opus 19 (a favorite number with the late Mme. Nordica), is a setting of a poem by Victor Hugo.

"From Blackbird Hills." A spirited *scherzo* for piano solo (dedicated to Hazel Gertrude Kinscella who supplied the composer with the leading theme), is built upon an old tribal song of the Omaha Indians.

Gaelic Symphony in E Minor. Said to be the first symphony ever written and brought to performance by a woman, had its first performance, from the manuscript, by the Boston Symphony under Emil Pauer. Mrs. Beach says: "I can ascribe no particular reason for my choice of Gaelic subjects for my first symphony other than having been attracted by some of the wonderful old tunes in a collection of Gaelic folk music which came under my observation. These tunes, of course, are of unknown origin and age and, like the folk music of every race, sprang from the common joys, sorrows, adventures, and struggles of a primitive people. Their simple, rugged, and unpretentious beauty led me to try their development in symphonic form. Most of the themes are actual quotations from this collection of folk music and those which are original I have tried to keep in the same idiom and form.

"The *codetta* theme, which occurs twice in the first movement, is used in canon form between the oboe and the flute. This is one of the old tunes from the Gaelic collection and forms the chief subject of the first movement. Two other themes are used, which are original with me, but are employed with the constant idea of carrying out the Gaelic character of the music.

"The second movement, *alla Siciliana,* is based upon another folk tune, introduced, after a prelude by horns and strings, in the first oboe.

"The subsidiary themes of the second movement are merely developed portions of the same tune, thus used in order to give unity to this rather short movement.

"The first and second themes of the third movement, *lento con molto espressione,* are genuine folk songs, the first one sung by the 'cello and oboe and the second by the full orchestra *fortissimo,* to be repeated, very softly, by the entire string orchestra in contrast. This movement voices the laments of a primitive people, their romance and their dreams.

"The last movement, *allegro di molto,* contains only themes of my own devising, though there are interruptive entrances now and then of a suggestion of the closing measures of the opening theme of the first movement. The finale tries to express the rough, primitive character of the Celtic people, their sturdy daily life, their passions and battles."

Mass in E-Flat. Mrs. Beach's first work in large form, took three years in the writing. It had its first performance by the Boston Handel and Haydn Society under Carl Zerrahn. It is notable for its beauty, dignity, symmetry, and scholarly mastery of musical form and technique of expression.

Sonata in A Minor, Opus. 34, for Violin and Piano. A favorite with the finest artists, both in Europe and America. The first movement is intensely melodic; the slow and deeply felt *Largo* forms an admirable contrast to the vivacious *Scherzo*—with its impressive trio—that precedes it; the Finale is in fugal form.

Summer Dreams. A series of six short piano duets in art form. Includes such suggestive titles as "Robin Redbreast," "Tarantelle," and "Good Night," and is one of the few American sets of art duets which such composers as Brahms and Dvořák loved to write.

"The Year's at the Spring." Mrs. Beach's best-loved Browning setting, written to the text of "Pippa's Song of Happiness" from *Pippa Passes.* Written expressly for the Browning Club of Boston.

BEETHOVEN, Ludwig van (1770–1827). Born in Bonn, Germany, where he spent his early years. Following a course of study under Neefe, the court organist, he had a long course of lessons in Vienna under Haydn. Among his own famous pupils was Carl Czerny. The force of his great genius led to the development of a highly original type of musical expression which, at last, brought about a new epoch in the history of music. (See "Haydn, Mozart, Beethoven, and the Classic Symphony," page 92.)

Coriolanus Overture. A tonal portrait. Coriolanus, an early Roman, is said to have received this surname from the valor he displayed in the capture of the Volscian town of Corioli. His arrogant attitude toward the plebeians aroused their hatred, and (in 491 B.C.) he was condemned to exile. Taking refuge among the Volscians, he promised to help them against his own people, and was appointed general of their army. Encamped, later, near Rome, he was approached by various embassies which sought to dissuade him of his object. None could succeed until his mother and his wife, with his two children, visited him. Their reproaches and tears succeeded, and Coriolanus led the troops back and remained in exile until his death. Legend says that he killed himself, and another tradition tells that the Volscians put him to death. Beethoven's music is like a musical accompaniment to a pantomime, so closely does it seem to follow the main events and mood of the old historic tale.

Concerto for Piano, Violin, and 'Cello, with Accompaniment for Orchestra (or Piano), Opus 56. In August 1804, Beethoven wrote a letter to the publishing firm of Breitkopf & Härtel in Vienna, in which he said, in part: "I have just now several works, and because I think of giving them to you, my wish to see them published will perhaps be satisfied all the sooner. I therefore tell you straight off what I can give you; my Oratorio [*The Mount of Olives*], a new Grand Symphony [the Third Symphony, the *Eroica*], a Concertante for violin, 'cello, and pianoforte with full orchestra; three new solo sonatas. . . . Now if you are willing to take these things, you must kindly tell me exactly the time at which you would be able to release them. . . . A concertante with three such concerting parts is indeed something new. If, as I expect, you agree to the conditions stated for these works as regards their publication, I would give them to you for a fee of 2000 fl. I assure you, on my honor, that, with regard to certain works—such as, for instance, sonatas, I am a loser, since I get almost 60 ducats for a single solo sonata. Pray do not think that I boast—far be it from me to do anything of the sort—but in order the quicker to arrange for an edition of my works, I am ready to be a loser to some extent."

The *Concertante* was among the more prominent musical works published in 1807, and was performed at a summer concert in Vienna, that year, after which it was not again played during Beethoven's lifetime.

The work is a nineteenth-century version of the older form of the *concerto grosso.* (See p. 112.) The first movement has a double statement of the themes, first by the orchestra, and then by the solo instruments. The first theme, in C Major, is given out by the 'cellos and basses alone, and the second, in G, by the first violins against a triplet figure for violas and 'cellos. In the solo statement, the main subject is given to the 'cello. The development section of this movement is extended, and there is also a long *coda.* The second, slow movement is a Largo, and leads, without pause, into the Finale, a *Rondo alla Polacca,* in which are fascinating effects of contrast between orchestra and the solo group.

Bagatelles, Opus 119. Four series of short piano pieces reflect the whimsy and delicacy suggested by the general title. Some of the brief works suggest the rhythms of the old classic dances, while others are merely suggestions of changing moods.

Egmont Overture, Opus 84. This, another work in heroic vein, follows somewhat closely the mood and historical sequence of the story of Egmont as written by Goethe. The story dates from the time of the revolt of the Netherlands against the Spanish rule. The Overture is one of ten pieces of incidental music which Beethoven wrote to accompany the Goethe drama (the Overture, two songs, four entr'actes, and three pieces of incidental music). In it he foreshadows the events which are to follow. His thematic material is of a two-fold character, seeming to be typical of Egmont as a hero and also as a lover of the heroine, Clara. The opening chords of the Overture typify the despair of the people. Then the two themes are unfolded and developed, in free fantasia form. This is followed by a brilliant recapitulation, and *coda.*

"Emperor" Concerto for Piano and Orchestra, E-Flat Major, Opus 73. One of a series of magnificent concertos for piano. It was written in Vienna, in 1809, during the months in which that city was held by the French. Beethoven's home was much exposed to the firing, the noise of which disturbed him greatly, and on several occasions the composer took refuge in the cellar of

his brother's house to escape it. Although there is, in the music, not even a hint of distress or hardship, it may be that the bravery which Beethoven saw displayed daily, and the anxiety of the people, had much to do with the heroic atmosphere which the music suggests. Following the noble opening pages, there is an inspired *Adagio* movement; and a captivating *Rondo,* at the end of which Beethoven has written an exquisite *coda.*

Fidelio. An opera in two acts, the music of which was written in 1805, Beethoven's only work in this form. It is a story of the wifely faithfulness and self-sacrifice of Leonore, who, coming in male attire as Fidelio, seeks to share the sufferings of her imprisoned husband, Florestan, a Spanish nobleman who has incurred the enmity of Don Pizzaro, the Governor of the State Prison. Disguised as a servant, she wins the love of the jailer's daughter and the hatred of the turnkey, Jacquino, who was the favorite in earlier days. The Governor decides to have Florestan killed. Leonore (Fidelio) overhears the plotters, and, as they leave, comes from her hiding place, exclaiming, in a highly dramatic recitative (one of the most famous arias in the opera), against the perfidy of the Governor. She then sings the famous "Abscheulicher, wo eilst du hin?" known as "Leonore's Aria," in which she affirms her faith that she will be able to save her husband's life. Leonore is called to help prepare the grave in the dungeon, and as, shortly, Pizarro comes to kill his victim, she thrusts herself between her loved one and the sword. Pushed aside, she again interposes, and at this dramatic moment a trumpet call announces the arrival of the Minister of the Interior, who has come to inspect the prisons. The cruel Governor is punished and Leonore and Florestan restored to liberty and happiness.

The story of the four overtures which Beethoven wrote for this opera is not always known. Three of these he entitled "Leonore"—the name by which he had wished the opera to be known. These writings have come to be incorrectly numbered. No. 2 is the one which was played at the opera's first performance. The greatest, No. 3, as it is called—and the one so popular as a separate concert piece for orchestra—was next composed. That known as No. 1 was written for an intended performance at Prague which never took place. The fourth is simply labeled "Fidelio." This is now usually played at the opening of the opera, and "Leonore" No. 3 (really a résumé of the entire drama) before the final scene. This latter work is very programmatic, the opening descending scale passage being thought by many to suggest the descent into the dungeon; the two main themes to be symbols of the two main characters; the sound of the trumpet call to be the same that plays so important a part in the drama; and the gay and lively *coda* to symbolize the triumph of justice.

"Gavotte in F Major." Takes its name, as do many of its predecessors, from the native dance of the dwellers in the district of Pays de Gap, in southeastern France.

Leonore Overture. (See the story of *Fidelio*.)

"Marcia alla Turca" from the *Ruins of Athens*. Had its origin in a brilliant set of Variations which Beethoven wrote at the time of the fighting of Napoleon's troops, near Vienna. As he wrote, Beethoven could hear the roar and booming of the cannons, not many miles away, and the sound, and the emotions which it stirred in him were both so impressive, that the composer at once wrote a march-like melody which he put into the music he was writing. Years later he was asked to write incidental music for a drama called *The Ruin of Athens*. This told of the war between Greece and Turkey, 1821 to 1829, during which the city of Athens was captured by the Turks. Beethoven took out the march-tune, rewrote it slightly, and included it in his score. Whether played in its orchestral version, or in the familiar Rubinstein transcription for the piano, the piece—also known as "Turkish March"—is a spirited work. It begins softly, as though at a distance, the roll of the drums of the marching troops being easily discernible. The music grows steadily louder as the troops approach, is very full and firm as they march past the onlooker, then dies away as the marchers fade from sight in the distance.

"Minuet in G." (See "Everybody's Music," p. 7.) This is one of a set of six minuets which Beethoven wrote for orchestra during the year 1796, a happy year for Beethoven, for during it he composed a large number of attractive small pieces, and made a successful concert tour of the Continent. This minuet is most familiar as a piano or violin solo, but it has been arranged for almost every solo instrument, and for every possible combination of instruments.

"Moonlight" Sonata, Opus 27, No. 2. (See "Everybody's Music," (p. 7.) This familiar and well-loved work for piano is surrounded by a halo of romance because of its association with the legend of Beethoven playing for the blind girl, and because of its dedication to the Countess Giulietta Guicciardi, with whom Beethoven was once in love. The first movement is in a free fantasia form. The second movement (*Allegretto*) is in happy, joyful mood. The Finale, a brilliant movement, builds up to a noble climax.

Quartet for Strings, A Major, Opus 18, No. 5. This, one of the six string quartets which Beethoven grouped under the heading of Opus 18, were all written about 1800, when the composer was only 30 years of age. Many of them result from sketches made much earlier. This Quartet in A, the fifth of the series, is one of the most charming and technically perfect of all the works.

Quartet for Strings, E-Flat Major, Opus 127. One of the finest of the later Beethoven quartets, is of a contemplative nature. The first movement, written in the classic sonata form, is built, almost entirely, upon a small but beautiful melodic figure. The second movement is a series of variations upon a gentle theme, half of which is stated by the violin, then answered by the 'cello. Variation I displays ornamentation in the parts written for each instrument, that of the first violin being of extreme delicacy. Variation II features a decorative motif in the violins, as contrasted with the more somber color of tone from the other instruments. Variation III shows Beethoven's superb ability to simplify a theme. Variation IV makes much use of repeated notes. An interpolated passage which furnishes a graceful contrast carries the music on into the Variation V. An exquisite *coda* brings this movement to a close. The variations are played without pause.

Romance in F. Originally composed for violin with orchestra accompaniment, this is a simple and romantic work, intended to express no set program but only a poetic mood.

Sonata, C Minor, Opus 111. The last sonata for piano written by Beethoven. Of unusual interest is the remarkable set of variations which forms one of the movements.

Symphony No. 1. Beethoven wrote, in all, nine symphonies, the keys of which and their dates of first performance, are as follows: No. 1, C Major, 1800; No. 2, D Major, 1803; No. 3, E-Flat Major (*Eroica*), 1805; No. 4, B-Flat Major, 1807; No. 5, C Minor, 1808; No. 6, F Major (*Pastoral*), 1808; No. 7, A Major, 1813; No. 8, F Major, 1814; No. 9, D Minor (*Choral*), 1824.

The First Symphony, given its first performance at a Beethoven "benefit" concert in Vienna, had its beginnings in sketches which Beethoven made in 1795 while a student with Albrechtsberger. In it are many things considered "very audacious" in its day, such as an introduction in a key other than that in which the main body of the work is written. The second movement displays Beethoven's sense of humor, and here he gives unusual prominence to the timpani, foreshadowing his later very individual use of drums. The third movement, a Minuet with trio, is a forerunner of the Beethoven Scherzo, often spoken of as the Beethoven "invention." The main theme moves scale-wise, and is built upon just two notes which are repeated in ascending pairs at the first statement, and in inverted form later on. (For size of organization which played these first works, see pp. 70 and 94.) The Finale reflects the style of Haydn, and suggests, in its thematic material, the scale-like passages of the movement which directly precedes it. It begins with a scale-wise figure of three notes, to which another note is added with each repetition, until the scale is at last complete, when it hurries off into the theme proper. This adds a note of youthful gayety to the music and caused so much amusement at the time of its first performances that the director of the Musical Society at Halle used to omit it on the ground that it would make his audiences laugh.

Symphony No. 2, D Major, Opus 36. This symphony is bolder, more vivid, and more varied than the first. The greater part of it was composed at Heiligenstadt, near Vienna. The first movement opens with an introduction (*adagio molto*), which leads to the statement of the first theme, characterized by a rhythmic group of notes heard in various shapes and combinations throughout the entire movement. The second theme is a stirring bit of rhythmically arranged arpeggio. The second movement (*Larghetto*) is of extremely lyric character. The third movement is here given the title of *Scherzo*. To accomplish its gay mood Beethoven makes use of many long skips, of frequent and unexpected modulations, and, in a few places, of cleverly shifted accents. The Finale is sometimes called a "second scherzo," and in some of its musical figures vividly recalls the trill-embellished figures of the opening introduction to the complete work.

Symphony No. 3, E-Flat Major (*"Eroica"*), Opus 55. Called the Heroic Symphony, and the dedication reads: "Composed to celebrate the memory of a great man." It had been Beethoven's intention to dedicate the music to Napoleon, but when, in 1804, Beethoven heard that Napoleon had declared himself Emperor, he was so angered that he tore up the original inscription. When, in 1821, he was told of Napoleon's death on St. Helena, Beethoven remarked, "I composed the music suitable for this event seventeen years ago."

The contrast between this symphony and the two which precede it is without a parallel in the history of music. Instrumentally this is due to Beethoven's use of certain voices of the orchestra, such as the clarinet, 'cello, and horns. His use of three horns, which gives the work a characteristic heroic color, was a distinct innovation. He also changed the horn used, within a movement— something never done before.

The brief two-measure introduction is a sort of condensation of the longer and broader introductions of the earlier *concerto grosso*. (See p. 112.) In the statement of his first theme, Beethoven follows the strictly classic idea, in which form is so important, by first giving it out, and then going back to pick it to pieces and develop it. This first theme is said to have been inspired by a very similar melody from one of the youthful operettas of Mozart, *Bastien et Bastienne,* written in Vienna in 1768.

The slow movement (a Funeral March) with its mature and slowly moving beauty, and the vivacious *Scherzo,* prepare the way for the remarkable Finale, in which, as a main theme, Beethoven uses a melody for which he must have had a great fondness, so often does he employ it. He uses it first through its bass, which is given a *fugato* treatment, and then in variation form.

Symphony No. 4, B-Flat Major, Opus 60. It is of interest to note the very strong influence which Haydn unconsciously exerted upon the writing of this symphony. Haydn had written a symphony in the same key, and one can see the logical manner in which both composers develop their musical material, the same spirit in the main themes both employ, the same use of deceptive cadences, and even the same use of instruments, especially the bassoon.

Symphony No. 5, C Minor, Opus 67. This received its first performance in the same concert which introduced the *Pastoral Symphony* (No. 6). Sketched and written during the same period as the *Pastoral,* it is contrasted greatly in mood and general character. This magnificent work owes its perfection of form to the composer's untiring efforts with his thematic material, as is proved by reference to the sketch books still in existence. In the case of the first movement, the entire *allegro* (and the introduction, as well) may be said to grow out of the one basic idea expressed in a figure of just two notes, arranged in striking rhythmic order. This "Fate" figure, with its frequent and insistent repetitions, in different voices, with differing harmonies, and sometimes as only a rhythmic suggestion, fuse the whole first movement into a firmly organized and inspired whole.

The second movement, *Andante con moto* (See "Everybody's Music," p. 7), is built upon two themes of quiet and pastoral character. The *Scherzo* differs greatly from the more headlong *Scherzo* of the third symphony. The Finale, in sonata form, opens with a splendid march theme in the wind instruments. Toward the close, the "Fate" subject is again heard, first in the violins, then from each group of the orchestra.

Symphony No. 6, F Major ("Pastoral"), Opus 68. In the various movements of this work, to which Beethoven himself gave the titles, he combined great formal beauty and a piquant bit of "program." He describes familiar country scenes and incidents that happen in them. Incidentally, he displays a rare sense of humor. (See "Humor in Music," p. 134.) It is claimed that in the opening movement Beethoven employed parts of two Slavonic folk airs (the

first measure of the violin part, the opening theme, bears a striking resemblance to a melody included in Kuhac's collection of folk songs published at Agram in 1878–81). The symphony has five movements. In the first—"Awakening of Joyful Feelings on Arrival in the Country" —the whole movement may be said to be constructed upon some variant of a melody. At times Beethoven has used the tune itself, and at others its rhythm, as, for instance, a little phrase, which, in one spot in the music, is repeated 20 times in succession, thus suggesting the constancy of the sounds of Nature. The mood is one of quiet joy. The second theme is played, in turn, by each member of the string choir. There is an extended development section, a recapitulation, and a brilliant *coda*.

In "By the Brook," the second movement, Beethoven used a little theme which he had set down in his sketch book fully five years before, labeling it, at that time, "murmuring of brooks," and adding, "the more water, the deeper the tone." This murmuring "brook music" is placed at the very beginning of the movement, where it is repeated constantly throughout the movement. The second theme, also introduced by the strings, is of lyric charm. Following an elaborate development of these two airs is that famous passage in which Beethoven imitated the singing of the birds near the brook, and which he so carefully labeled, that none should miss it. For the nightingale he used the high-voiced flute; for the quail, the oboe; and for the cuckoo, the clarinets.

LUDWIG VAN BEETHOVEN

FRANZ SCHUBERT

ORGAN IN THE ST. REMIGUNS CHURCH AT BONN, IN
WHICH BEETHOVEN OFTEN PLAYED

ROBERT SCHUMANN

FREDERIC CHOPIN

FELIX MENDELSSOHN

BACH'S BIRTHPLACE

JOHANN SEBASTIAN BACH

JOSEPH
HAYDN

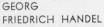

GEORG
FRIEDRICH HANDEL

ESTERHAZY CASTLE
WHERE MANY GREAT HAYDN
SYMPHONIES WERE WRITTEN

THE HOUSE IN WHICH MOZART
COMPOSED THE MAGIC FLUTE

WOLFGANG AMADEUS MOZART

"Village Festival," the third movement, is a rollicking musical picture of a gay holiday gathering in the country. It begins with the strings. After the strings have finished, the air is taken up by flutes, bassoons, and oboes, and finally by all the instruments. The real dance then begins, accompanied by a continuation of the little chords, from the violins, and the celebrated bassoon solo, in which the rural musician, who has but three tones that he can play, repeats them over and over. The trio (in two-beat measure), is notable for another dance melody.

"The Storm," the fourth movement, is vividly imitative, the wind, lightning, and downpourings of rain being depicted by easily recognized means, basses and kettledrums suggesting the distant thunder. The agitation reaches a sudden climax, followed by an abrupt lull, during which a soft descending passage in chromatics suggests the decreasing violence of the elements. A solo oboe and a gently played ascending scale figure, from the flutes introduce the "Shepherd's Song," the fifth section of the symphony, in which there is heard the alluring call of a shepherd's pipe, as he plays out his thanksgiving for deliverance from the storm. This air prepares the way for the final section of the music, "Gladsome and Thankful Feeling," which is a rich development of this simple melody. At the close the shepherd's song takes on the character of a hymn.

Symphony No. 7. Finished in 1812, four years after the completion of the *Pastoral.* This symphony had its first performance at a benefit concert given for soldiers wounded in the Battle of Hanau. The music is in four movements: (1) *Poco sostenuto; vivace;* (2) *Allegretto;* (3) *Presto; assai meno presto;* (4) *Finale: Allegro con brio.* Special attention may be called to the fact that Beethoven has used the same rhythm throughout the symphony. The lively opening movement, and the march-like *Allegretto,* prepare the way for the celebrated *Scherzo.* The melody of the scherzo trio was known for many years, in Lower Austria, as "Abbe Stadtler's Pilgrim Hymn." In the Finale, which is, at times, almost boisterous, there is heard the melody of an old Irish folk song, "Norah Creina."

Symphony No. 8, F Major, Opus 93. Completed by Beethoven in Linz. It has been spoken of by Sir George Grove, as the "Humorous" Symphony. (See "Humor in Music," p. 134.) Beethoven was himself very fond of this work, and often spoke of it as his "little" symphony. In its genial second movement Beethoven utilized the melody of a little song in canon form which he had written, some time before, to imitate the tick-tock of a metronome.

Symphony No. 9. Known as the *Choral Symphony,* it was written eleven years after the completion of the *Eighth.* Its beginnings, found in the sketch books, prove that the work was the product of a long and careful consideration on Beethoven's part. The original manuscript of the symphony is in the Royal Library at Berlin. Only the fourth movement employs the chorus.

The first movement (*Allegro ma non troppo, un poco maestoso*) opens with a prologue, which introduces the principal theme. In the second movement (*Molto vivace*), following an eight-measure introduction, the first main theme, in octave figure, makes its appearance in the strings. The subordinate theme is similar in style, featuring the downward skip of an octave. In the third movement (*Adagio*), the principal theme is given out by the strings alone, then echoed by the wind instruments. The lyric mood of this first theme is complemented by an expressive second subject in D Major, first played by the second violins and violas. The Finale employs a vocal quartet and a chorus, and is, in itself, a kind of cantata, with 13 episodes. The text of the choral passages is taken from Schiller's "Ode to Joy." (See "Patterns and Styles," p. 80.)

BELLINI, VINCENZO (1801–1835). A famous Sicilian composer trained at the Naples Conservatory, whose most familiar work is the opera *Norma*.

Norma. Founded upon a tragedy by Soumet, this opera had its first production in Milan, Italy, in 1831, and its first performance in the United States ten years later. The scene is in Gaul, about the year 30 B.C. Norma, the High Priestess of the Druids, has broken her vows because of her love for Pollione, the Roman proconsul. She learns that he no longer cares for her, and that Adalgisa, another priestess, is her rival. Desiring Pollione's happiness more than her own, she decides to murder her two children and then seek her own death. The innocence of the children, however, is so appealing that she entrusts them to her rival and goes to her own funeral pyre. Here Pollione comes to realize her worth and the power of his love for her, and perishes with her in the flames.

BERG, ALBAN (1885–   ). A pupil of Arnold Schoenberg. Music from his opera *Wozzeck* had its first hearing (in fragmentary form) at a Prague festival in May 1925, under the auspices of the International Society of Contemporary Music.

Wozzeck. A combination of drama and absolute music. It is largely atonal. Unusual features of the work are the facts that each scene is an entity, and that each is written in identical form. The whole work is said by the composer to be "in large *A B A* form." The music for the singers, as in Act II, is written in strict pattern, employing the sonata, fantasy, fugue, and passacaglia forms. The time of the action is the early part of the nineteenth century; the scene, a military barrack. In the work are employed three kinds of singing: truly vocal, *Sprechstimme* (speaking voice), and rhythmic declamation. Short orchestral interludes connect the scenes.

BERLIOZ, HECTOR (1803–1869). Born, La Côte-St. André, near Grenoble in southeastern France. After years spent in medical study, Berlioz found music the irresistible force of his life, and in 1830 he won the

Prix de Rome. Before his death, he had a series of triumphs in England, Germany, Austria, Italy, Russia, and France. He was recognized as a master of instrumentation and a brilliant pioneer in many important musical movements. Among these was his introduction of the *Leitmotif* (characteristic guiding theme) which was later a prominent feature of the Wagner writings; he was the first to write dramatic tone poems for orchestra in which form was subjugated to content—a form which Liszt developed in his symphonic poems; and he paved the way for new and audacious orchestral effects. His music owed much to the friendly exploitation of Franz Liszt.

"Carneval Romain" Overture. This music is from Berlioz's opera *Benvenuto Cellini,* which was produced at the Paris Opera in 1838. In the Overture is incorporated much material from the opera. The principal subject of the first section is from the carnival scene which closes Act II. The principal subject of the *Allegro* is from the carnival scene also, the air that of "Venez, venez, peuple de Rome."

Marche Hongroise-Rakoczy ("Rakoczy March"). A spirited transcription for orchestra of a national air of Hungary, so named because of its association with Prince Rakoczy, a prominent leader of early Hungarian history. The melody is supposed to have been composed by the Prince's court musician, a gypsy named Michael Barna. Berlioz is said to have first heard the stirring air on a visit to Budapest, and to have later found it written

out in a volume of historic songs. He at once wrote an orchestral composition about it.

Later, when assembling his material for the opera *The Damnation of Faust,* he caused his hero to be seen wandering on the plains of Hungary, where he is fascinated by a group of soldiers parading by in time to the famous march, which Berlioz here interpolated. When the opera was given its first production (Paris, 1846) the patriotic ardor of the audience was roused to a high pitch by the compelling rhythms and melody of the unexpected song. This theme was also used by Franz Liszt in his fifteenth rhapsody for piano.

BINGHAM, Seth (1882–   ). Born in Bloomfield, N. J. A graduate of Yale University (1904), pupil of Harry Jepson; and in Europe, following the completion of his collegiate work, of Guilmant, Widor, and d'Indy. Bachelor of Music, Yale (1908), and there won the Steinert Prize by his *Pièce Gothique* for organ and orchestra. He is also the composer of the famous Yale song, "Mother of Men." From 1909 to 1919, instructor in organ at Yale, and since 1913, the organist of the Madison Avenue Presbyterian Church of New York City. He is professor of theory and composition at Columbia University.

Chorale Prelude on the Tune "St. Flavian." The second of a group of compositions for pipe organ which, though not a suite, are grouped under one general heading. The first number, "Prelude and Fugue," (dedicated to the celebrated French organist, Charles Marie Widor) has been played by concert organists the world over, and in 1933 was selected as the test piece for the Fellowship Examination of the American Guild of Organists. "Roulade," the third of the group features a colorful chromatic melody. This, together with such flourishes as the title suggests, produces an exceedingly brilliant effect. "Adoration" (dedicated to Arthur Hyde) is deeply spiritual in character. "Aria" is in graceful, flowing style. "Counter-Theme," with which the suite closes, owes its unusual title to the fact that in it, presently, the second or "counter-theme" —which is of joyous carillon type, over a drone pedal-point—predominates over the first and so-called main theme. The two melodies are later used in counterpoint to each other.

Come Thou Almighty King. A choral work for mixed voices, *a cappella,* is an effective setting of the familiar words, and one pervaded by deep religious feeling.

Cowboy Songs. Five settings (for solo voice, male chorus, or mixed chorus *a cappella*) of ballads of the Western cowboy, frequently spoken of as "dogie songs." Mr. Bingham's collection, for which he has provided stirring piano accompaniments, includes the doleful "Dying Cowboy" ("O Bury Me Not on the Lone Prairie"), "Root Hog or Die," the melodramatic "Fuller and Warren" with its partly modal tune, and "Days of '49," which tells of the miners and the cowboy.

English Love Lyrics. For women's chorus, *a cappella,* these are settings of poems of the Elizabethan period.

Each song (some in 3, others in 4 parts) is short and melodic, the music reflecting the rather archaic style of the text.

Harmonies of Florence. An effective and pictorial concert suite for organ, including "Florentine Chimes," "Primavera," "Savonarola," "Twilight at Fiesole," and "March of the Medici," short numbers each of which has its own rhythmic and melodic character.

Pioneer America. A second suite for organ (also written for orchestra) is a series of tone poems, each of which portrays a striking phase of American Life. "Red Skin Rhapsody" presents authentic Indian characteristics. "Sailing over Jordan" features a Negro spiritual. "Along the Frontier" is a potpourri of Canadian and cowboy melodies, including "Isabeau si promène" (Canadian boat song), "Sur le pont de Nantes," and "En roulant ma boule." "Puritan Procession" features "York Tune," so dear to the hearts of those pioneers.

Memories of France. For orchestra, this was chosen from among 75 entrants in a recent contest, as one of five American works to be played at the North Shore Festival. It also was performed by the Cleveland Orchestra at the American Guild of Organists' Convention in 1933. The suite is descriptive of pre-war France. "Carillon de Château-Thierry" is built on the actual tones of three bells in the Church of St. Crepin. "Love in the Fields," is a pastoral in which English horn and oboe, are given prominence. And in "Mid-Lent in Paris" there is used much pre-war music, including fragments of old-time popular tunes.

The Strife is O'er. A motet for mixed voices, *a cappella,* unusual not only for its great beauty and highly devotional character, but for the cleverness with which the composer has divided the work into three distinct movements which have a community of text but no musical connection—"The Strife is O'er," "Weep No More," and "Forever with the Lord."

Suite for Wind Instruments. Written for and dedicated to the Barrère Ensemble and played by them extensively, consists of five movements: Prelude, Pastorale, Gavotte, Nocturne, and Jig. The "Prelude" is constructed on formal classic lines. The "Pastorale" features a flute solo of delicate charm. The third movement is a simple and dainty Gavotte written in the old form of dance, trio, dance. "Nocturne" features the clarinet and is more modern in its harmonies. The finale is the customary "Jig," and here Mr. Bingham has treated a theme from the opening Prelude, fugally.

Tame Animal Tunes. For chamber orchestra, has been played by the Little Symphony under George Barrère. These brief pieces, "New Kittens," "Love-Sick Rooster," "Pig in Slumber," "Rabbit Frolic," "Duck a la Barcarole," "Caper, the Billy Goat," "Dignified Rumination of a Cow," "Puppy Song," "Variations on a Turkey (interlarded with Goose-Step)," have been spoken of as an achievement in American musical humor. In them the composer has skillfully used all the extreme notes, squawks, and whines of the different instruments.

Wilderness Stone. This monumental choral work (for narrator, solo, chorus, and orchestra) on a text by Stephen Vincent Benét, was written in Europe in 1932. It tells a connected story, part of the narration being spoken and part sung. Principal solos are given to tenor and soprano (symbolizing the two principal characters). The chorus offers much incidental comment in the manner of the old Greek chorus; there is much *a cappella* singing; solo voices are frequently given choral accompaniment; and orchestral passages are often episodical in character.

Suite No. 1 for Organ, Opus 25. Dedicated to Lynwood Farnam. It consists of four separate numbers: "Cathedral Strains," in which the clangor of the bells mingles with the melody; "Rhythm of Easter," a joyous bit of music, in which delicate rhythmic pattern of notes is skillfully developed by means of imitation; "Intercession," of chorale-like dignity; and a brilliant "Toccata."

BISHOP, SIR HENRY (1786–1855). Professor of Music first in Edinburgh and then at Oxford, received his knighthood in 1842 as an appreciation of his great musical abilities. He wrote fluently for the voice, and produced many operettas and other stage pieces.

"Home, Sweet Home." The original manuscript of "Home, Sweet Home" is in the Sibley Library of the Eastman School of Music, Rochester,

N. Y. The words of this immortal song are by John Howard Payne. "Lo, Here the Gentle Lark." A setting made by Bishop of *Venus and Adonis,* a poem in six-lined stanzas said to have been Shakespeare's first published work. In the song, Bishop has written a delicate flute obbligato, intended to suggest the clear voice of the soaring lark.

BIZET, GEORGES (1838–1875). A student at the Conservatory of Paris, and winner of the Prix de Rome at the age of 19. His acknowledged masterpiece is the opera *Carmen,* although his *L'Arlésienne Suite* is almost as well known.

Carmen. An opera in four acts, founded upon a novel by Prosper Mérimée. First performance, Opéra Comique, Paris, 1875; first American performance, Academy of Music, New York, 1879.

The characters are: Don José, a sergeant (tenor); Escamillo, a toreador (baritone); Zuniga, a captain; Morales, a sergeant; Dancairo and Remendado, smugglers; Carmen, a gypsy cigarette girl (contralto); Frasquita and Mercedes, gypsies; and Michaela, a peasant girl (soprano). The action takes place in Seville in about 1820.

In the Prelude are heard suggestions of airs from the "March of the Toreadors" and of the "Toreador Song," prominent later in the opera, and also the ominous "Fate" theme, played by the brasses against a tremolo accompaniment from the strings, just before the curtain rises. This theme is taken by Bizet from the so-called "Devil's Strain," an ancient folk song of legendary origin in Spain, where it is sung only in whispers. It is said that the Devil, cast out of Heaven, could remember only one bit of the celestial music, which he henceforth sang, and that this is it.

Act I. It is noon, and groups of girls who work in a cigarette factory emerge upon an open square. It is also the time for the changing of the guards at the nearby guard-house. Michaela has brought a message and present of money to Don José, from his mother. Carmen seeks to attract the attention of Don José by singing and dancing the "Habañera." A moment later she stabs another girl in a petty quarrel, and Don José is detailed to guard her and take her to prison. On the way he allows her to escape. Outstanding musical numbers of the act are the ever-popular "Habañera," the duet of Michaela and Don José ("My home, my mother, again I'll see"), and the seductive air of the "Seguidilla" which Carmen sings as Don José guards her. The exotic melodies of both the Carmen arias were taken by Bizet from old Spanish folk songs.

Act. II. A group of smugglers from the mountains are eating dinner at a tavern. Carmen sings of the gay life of the gypsies and dances for them. Escamillo, the famous bullfighter of the moment, enters and sings boastfully of his own valor and prowess. Most of the company leave before the arrival of Don José, who has been in prison for allowing Carmen to escape. She now urges him to desert the army and join the smugglers. They all flee to the mountains. The very popular musical numbers from this are the tuneful "Toreador Song" with its bold refrain, and the tender "Flower Song" in which Don José sings of his love for Carmen.

Act III. A beautiful spot in the heart of the mountains, in which the smugglers have gathered. Here is enacted the celebrated card scene in which Carmen learns of her impending death. The "Fate" theme is heard with sinister suggestiveness. Escamillo visits the camp, is attacked by Don José, and saved by Carmen's intervention. Don José leaves for his home with Michaela, who comes to tell him that his mother is dying, calling back a threat to Carmen that they will meet again. The aria of Michaela, who is the personification of gentleness and purity—"I try not to own that I tremble," is one of the most beautiful of the entire opera.

Act IV. A brilliant crowd is entering the bull-ring. Escamillo appears with Carmen, whose friends warn her that Don José, now desperate, is approaching. She waits fearlessly outside the gate for him. They talk, Don José pleading, and Carmen defiant. In a fury of jealousy he plunges his knife into her breast just as Escamillo emerges at the head of a triumphant procession whose cheers end abruptly at the sight which meets their eyes.

L'Arlésienne Suite, No. 1. The Arlésienne Suites, two in number, are made up of excerpts from the 27 bits of incidental music written by Bizet in 1873 to accompany the performance of Daudet's drama of the same name. The story of *L'Arlésienne* (The Woman of Arles) contrasts the tragic love of the youthful Frédéric and Vivette, and the serene, faithful love of Old Balthazar, the shepherd of Provence, for aged Mère Renaud. The scene takes place near the old Provençal city of Arles in southern France, on Christmas Eve. For this reason Bizet used as his thematic material many of the early Provençal troubadours' songs, and other French folk songs. Especially prominent is the ancient "March of Three Kings," a French Christmas carol of great antiquity used as a marching song by the Crusaders of the twelfth century.

1. The *Prelude* (or Overture) is, in part, a set of unique variations on the air of this old French carol. Two other short themes are used for contrast. 2. The *Menuetto* is notable for its decorative arabesques, the bagpipe drone in the bass of the trio section, its delicate flute solo in double notes, and for its artistic ending, in which the instruments, one after the other, are hushed, until at the very close there are heard a group of extremely delicate and elusive chords. 3. *Adagietto.* The tender melody of this brief number was played, during the course of the drama, as an accompaniment to the meeting of Balthazar and Mère Renaud. 4. *Carillon.* A carillon is a set of bells so tuned that melodies may be played upon it. The suggested scene is a castle courtyard, gay with decorations. A happy song is being sung, and, as a background and accompaniment to it, is heard the triumphant pealing of the bells high overhead. The unusual carillon effect is produced by a simple but persistent three-note figure which is repeated

for 56 measures in succession. A short but more plaintive middle section closes with a return to the first melody, and the joyous chiming of the bells.

L'Arlésienne Suite, No. 2. This includes another minuet characterized by a dainty rhythmic harp accompaniment and a lilting melody. The Second Suite was assembled by Ernest Guiraud, after Bizet's death. This particular minuet was a favorite with the composer, who also used it as an entr'acte in his *Fair Maid of Perth.* The *Farandole* in this suite suggests a folk dance of ancient origin played for centuries in French villages on fête days. Here the main melody ("March of the Three Kings") is heard first in unison, and then as a round or canon for the orchestral instruments. Immediately after this there follows a tiny rhythmic interlude suggesting the dull beating of the tambourine and the patter of dancing sabot-shod feet. At the fourth repetition there is introduced the melody of another quaint old dance air of Provençe, said to have been brought there from Greece by the Crusaders. In the conclusion, the folk airs are combined contrapuntally.

BOCCHERINI, Luigi (1743–1805). A noted Italian musician, who was aided by the royal families of Italy, Spain, and Prussia. He wrote fluently and is said to have created a new style in chamber music. Among his most popular works are many more than 100 string quintets, and nearly 90 string quartets. (See "Chamber Music, Past and Present," p. 112.)

BOISDEFFRE, Charles Henri René de (1838–1906). A gifted French composer, winner in 1883 of the Prix Chartier for chamber music, who left many orchestral and chamber works of great charm. None of his smaller pieces is so graceful as "At the Brook," played as violin solo, and by many combinations of instruments.

BORODIN, Alexander (1834–1887). One of a group of Russian musicians known as "The Five." Borodin's chief activity was in his laboratory and in giving lectures on science, music being a well-loved pastime to which he was never able to give the desired amount of time. For this reason many of his finest works were unfinished at his death, and were completed from pencil sketches by musical friends with whom he had discussed and played them.

In the Steppes of Central Asia. A symphonic sketch written in 1880 for performance at an exhibition of tableaux illustrating episodes in Russian history at a celebration of the twenty-fifth anniversary of the reign of the Tsar Alexander III. On the original score the following program was given: "In the silence of arid steppes of Central Asia is heard a refrain of Russian song. One hears, too, the melancholy sound of Oriental music and the approaching steps of horses and camels. A caravan escorted by Russian soldiers crosses the immense desert . . . moves steadily onward, and songs of Russians and native Asiatics mingle harmoniously—the refrains die away in the distance."

The monotony of the wide prairie is suggested by a persistent violin tone throughout the first 53 measures. Presently a clarinet, then a horn, sing a Russian air beneath the prolonged violin tone. From an English horn comes the sound of Oriental music. Later in the work there mingle the Russian air (oboe) and the Oriental melody (first and second violins in unison).

Prince Igor. (See "National Characteristics in Russian Art Music." p. 19.)

"Nocturne" from *Second Quartet (A Major).* From a work dedicated by Borodin to his wife. It is unsurpassed for poetic beauty, and for its effective use of such Oriental characteristics as syncopated rhythms and copious embellishment.

BRAHMS, JOHANNES (1833–1897). (For biography, See "Brahms, and 'Absolute' Music," p. 98.)

"Academic Festival" Overture. Written in recognition of the conferring of the degree of Doctor of Philosophy upon Brahms by the University of Cambridge and Beslau (1877 and 1881). Student songs heard by Brahms during the course of a two months' visit with Joachim, many years previous, serve largely as its thematic basis. The opening theme was original with Brahms, and composed in the general style of the jolly student songs. This is followed by the gay tunes of *"Wir hatten gebauet*

ein stattliches Haus," "*Der Landes Vater,"* and the humorous *"Fuchslied,"* each verse of which opens with an ingenuous questioning after each member of the family (*"Was macht Papa?" "Was macht Mama?" "Was macht Schwester?"* and so on). The work had its first performance on January 4, 1881, in Breslau.

"Cradle Song," Opus 49, No. 4. This familiar and well-loved "lullaby, and good night" is another illustration of Brahms's delicate and lovely treatment of a simple subject.

Concerto for Violin. Written for and dedicated to Joseph Joachim, and first performed by him at a concert of the Gewandhaus Orchestra, January 1879. The solo instrument and the orchestra are here of equal importance. In the music provided for the soloist Brahms sought to avoid mere display. It is, however, extremely difficult and brilliantly effective. The first and third movements make great use of double-stopping; in the second movement, a *romanza ,* a colorful contrast is made between the tonal characteristics of the accompanying instruments and the solo violin.

Clarinet and Piano Sonata in E-Flat Major. One of the four chamber music works which Brahms was inspired to write through his friendship with Richard Mühlfeld, clarinet in the orchestra of the Duke of Meiningen. The work is in three movements, the first, *amabile;* the second *appassionata* in character; and the last in variation form. The graceful theme upon which Brahms has written his five variations is notable for its simplicity. Variation I is contrapuntal in its treatment; Variation II gives the melody to the clarinet, while the piano embellishes it with arpeggio figures; Variation III is lovely in its dovetailing of the melodic phrases in their give and take between the two instruments, and its delicate filagree work; Variation IV is an interesting illustration of the simplified variation, in which harmonic, rather than melodic features are stressed; and Variation V is a brilliant climax.

Clarinet Quintet. Also inspired by the art of Richard Mühlfeld. It is built upon simple material, the first theme from the opening movement permeating the whole work. The second (*Adagio*) movement is notable for its Hungarian type of phrases, and is built in three-part form, the first part based upon a simple three-note figure. The second part, in which the clarinet is particularly prominent, stresses these three notes, building about each a graceful and florid ornamental design. Finally, the *coda* suggests the opening section. In the third movement a song-like section is contrasted with a *presto* section in which thematic elements of the first are developed. The thematic material of the two sections is here contrasted. The fourth movement of the work is a series of variations. It comes back, at the close, to the first theme of the opening movement.

Hungarian Dances. These colorful *csardas* Brahms based upon authentic folk airs learned from the Hungarian violinist Remenyi. The national *csardas* of Hungary is usually of two parts—the first, a melancholy air; and the second, fiery and excitable, reflecting the variable gypsy temperament. Brahms first wrote his idealizations for piano, four hands; but the compositions owe their greater popularity to the arrangements made of them for piano and violin by Joachim. Still later Brahms scored the *Dances* for full orchestra.

Liebeslieder. A set of choral waltzes based upon little folk songs sung by the peasantry as improvised accompaniment to their national dances. They are varied in mood, from boisterous to plaintively primitive. The piano accompaniment is for four hands, one piano.

"Little Dustman." This is one of a set of fourteen "Children's Folk Songs" written to traditional nursery verses, and dedicated to the children of Robert and Clara Schumann.

Requiem, Opus 45. Of Brahms's choral works, the *Requiem* is the one with which he first made a wide reputation. His "Song of Fate," also choral, is a smaller work. This sacred cantata has seven numbers (two baritone solos and chorus; soprano solo and chorus; and four separate choruses). It was begun at the time of his mother's death, in 1866. It is said that at the time Brahms had no money with which to buy music paper, and so had to write his music upon sheets of odd sizes. The words he chose entirely from the Bible. The first part of the *Requiem* was given on the first of December that same year. The work was given as complete (although the fifth part was added later), in Bremen, on Good Friday, April 1868. Among the notables present was Clara Schumann. *Symphony No. 1, C Minor,* Opus 68. First performance in the fall of 1876. The first drafts of the work were made as early as 1862. The work is in minor mode, and is cyclic in form (all the thematic material being closely related). A brief figure of three chromatically rising notes known as the *basic motif* underlies the whole first movement, all the themes being developed from it.

The movement opens with an introduction (*Un poco sostenuto,* C Minor, 6–8 meter), followed by two themes of almost equal importance. These are frequently used in counterpoint to each other. The first of them, built from an ascending arpeggio, is similar to that short but striking phrase often spoken of as Brahms's "motto," a sort of musical signature found, at some spot, in each of the symphonic works. There are the usual development, a recapitulation, and a *coda* which brings the movement to a close in the same general mood in which the introduction started. The second movement (*Andante sostenuto*) opens with a theme given out by the strings and the bassoons. The wood-winds introduce the second, and contrasting, theme. There is a short development section, followed by a partial return of the first material. The third movement (*allegro e grazioso*) takes the place of the traditional scherzo. The Finale (fourth movement) opens with an *adagio* introduction. The movement proper (*Allegro non troppo*) is an individual work. The main theme (violins) is given considerable development, after which the second

subject, for strings, enters, accompanied by a figure previously used in the introduction. This Finale is written in sonata form, the development section being followed by a recapitulation in which the first subject is briefly mentioned and the second given in its entirety. A brilliant *coda* brings the work to a close.

Symphony No. 2, D Major, Opus 73. As arranged for piano duet by the composer, the *Second Symphony* was played by Brahms and Ignaz Brüll before a group of invited guests at the piano house of Ehrbar in Vienna, a few days before its first public performance by orchestra in December 1877, when Hans Richter conducted it with the Vienna Philharmonic Orchestra.

A characteristic feature of the first movement is the four-note basic motif given out, without introduction, by 'cellos and basses. The first theme and this motif are closely associated throughout the movement. The second main theme is given by 'cello and viola. Three codettas, employing unusual rhythmic combinations, bring the main first section of the movement to a close. There is a free development, a recapitulation, and a *coda* in which great prominence is given the material of the basic motif heard in the opening measures.

The second movement (*Adagio non troppo*) introduces three melodies. They are given elaborate development and restatement, and movement closes with a suggestion of the opening theme.

The third movement (*Allegretto grazioso*) has two contrasting trios.

The first theme, played by the wind instruments, is given a bit of variation in the first trio (*presto*); is then repeated in modified form, and again given a variation; after which a third repetition ends the movement.

The Finale (*Allegro con spirito*) is, as are the first and second movements, in sonata form.

Symphony, No. 3, F Major, Opus 90. This opens with a short three-measure passage, in which is heard the famous Brahms "motto." The strongly rhythmic first theme is stated immediately, by strings, being characterized by a downward-moving arpeggiated figure. The second theme, more graceful in character, is first sung by clarinets and bassoons, and is later taken, in turn, by almost all groups of the orchestra. The bridge passage between the two themes is here of utmost importance, being developed prominently in other movements, its most characteristic feature being a rhythmic repetition of a single note.

The second movement is in three-part form with *coda*. It opens, without introduction, upon a choral-like theme, a peculiar feature of which is the ever-recurring echo in the cadence.

The third movement (*Poco allegretto*) presents a song-like first theme, in 'cellos (C Minor), the most important melody in this movement. The Finale is characterized by an agitated theme of heroic type given out in unison by all strings, with bassoons.

Symphony, No. 4, in E Minor. This had its beginnings in 1884, and its first public performance at Meiningen on October 25th, 1885. A short time before, Brahms had played it in a two-piano arrangement with Ignaz Brüll, for a group of friends.

The first theme is given out at once and without introduction, by the violins, with response from woodwinds, and an arpeggiated accompaniment from lower strings. The first section of the theme contrasts charmingly with the more flowing second section. The long bridge section, with its introductory "motto" of "horn call" character, and its more lyric second section attains great importance through the development and recapitulation sections. The real second theme, in B Major, is given out in part by the woodwinds, and in part by the upper strings.

The second movement (*Andante moderato*, E, 6–8) opens with a brief horn call, in which the other wind instruments soon join. This ushers in the principal theme (clarinet) in which, in two-bar phrases, Brahms sets forth the pastoral character of the music. The structure is very simple throughout, though the composer here makes frequent use of contrapuntal development.

The third movement (*Allegro giocoso*, C Major, 2–4) is a rondo-like intermezzo, suggestive of the folk spirit. The first theme has a suggestion of a "drone" at the close of the four bars of melody. The second theme is of a folk song type of melody.

The fourth movement (*Allegro energico e passionato*, E Minor, 3–4), outstanding in modern symphonic literature, is a gigantic set of variations in passacaglia form, built upon an eight-bar theme which is simply an E Minor scale rising to the fifth with an interrupted A-sharp and returning to the tonic by way of the dominant in the lower octave. This same melodic line forms the bass of a *ciacona* in Bach's "Cantata No. 150." There are 32 variations, the last one of which becomes a fanciful *coda* in which the original number of bars is abandoned.

Two Serenades, Op. 11 and 16. Composed during his residence at Detmold, and frequently spoken of as the "Detmold Serenades." The first, in D Major, was first written for string octet, but, by the advice of Joachim, was rescored for full orchestra. Its first movement is of fresh and joyous humor. The minuet has a theme of artful simplicity. The scherzo is notable for clever workmanship, and the adagio, for its meditative character.

The second, in A Major, is said to have been Brahms's favorite of all his works. In it he uses no violins, and gives prominence to the viola. The work has five movements, the first being of a sprightly rondo character. The scherzo is decidedly original in character; the minuet characterized by constantly broken rhythms; and the adagio, of delicate beauty. Brahms also arranged it as a piano duet.

The Violin Sonatas. (G Major, Op. 78; A Major, Op. 100; D Minor, Op. 108). The first of the three is sometimes called the *Rain Sonata* from the fact that in it Brahms utilized the melody from his *"Regen-lied"* (Rain Song) written about six years earlier. The most outstanding theme of its first movement is characterized by the repetition of the three D's, and the incessant running figure in the piano part. The second of the sonatas is characterized by unity of mood throughout, and a happy, intense contentment. The *Sonata in D Minor,* of more passionate mood, features a particularly delightful allegretto, which takes the place of the customary scherzo. The adagio which precedes it is of almost folk-like simplicity.

BROCKWAY, HOWARD (1870–). Born in Brooklyn, N. Y. Educated at the Brooklyn Polytechnic. His home influences were remarkable from the musical standpoint. His first teacher of piano was Miss Delia Scarborough, who lived with his mother, and who took him, in his fourth year, to the Theodore Thomas orchestral concerts, and to many string quartet concerts. At the age of 19, he went to Berlin, where he studied piano with Heinrich Barth and composition with O. B. Boise, remaining from 1890 to 1895; returning there also for nine months of study in 1897. With the exception of six years spent in Baltimore, where he was on the faculty of Peabody Institute, Mr. Brockway has made his home in New York, teaching and giving concerts as pianist, and gaining renown as a composer. His most important contribution to the music of his native land is the perpetuation of the "lonesome tunes" and Kentucky Mountain ballads through his exquisite settings of these archaic melodies gathered in the mountains of Harlan (and nearby) counties in Kentucky. (See "The Quest of the Lonesome Tunes," p. 158.) Mr. Brockway is a member of the faculty of the Institute of Musical Art of Juilliard School of Music of New York, succeeding Dr. Percy Goetschius, in 1925, as teacher of highest grades of composition and of orchestration; and is also on the faculty of the David Mannes School of New York, as teacher of piano.

Important performances of Mr. Brockway's music include: Concert of Berlin Philharmonic Orchestra, when an entire program consisted of his compositions; production of his *Sylvan Suite* by Boston Symphony under Wilhelm Gericke, of his *Symphony* under Wilhelm Gericke, and of his *Symphony in D Major* under Karl Muck; of *Ballade* for Orchestra, by Anton Seidl, with the Seidl Society Orchestra in seasons 1897 and 1898; repeated performances of choral works by the Mendelssohn Choir of Toronto under Dr. A. S. Vogt, in Toronto and New York, and on tour; choral works by the Schola Cantorum of New York, under Kurt Schindler; and the production, in October 1929 (in New York) by the English Singers, of four "Appalachian Songs." Mr. Brockway has toured with Mary Garden; was appointed Judge of the Earl Grey Trophy Competition in Canada (1911) by Earl Grey, at that time Governor of Canada. He has also written a *Suite* for 'cello and orchestra (or piano); *Sir Olaf,* for chorus and orchestra; *The Singer's Curse,* and eight-part *a cappella* chorus; *Sonata for Piano and Violin; Romanze* for Piano and Violin; *Symphony in G Major;* and many songs and piano pieces.

Lonesome Tunes. These settings had their first hearing at the Bar Harbor (Mt. Desert) home of Ernest Schelling, during the summer of 1916, with Mr. Brockway at the piano. More than a score of world-famous artists, including Ossip Gabrilowitsch and Fritz Kreisler, were present. The appearance of the tunes in print, soon afterward, brought the following remarkable and spontaneous letter of appreciation to the composer, whom he had never met, from Percy Grainger: "Having your lovable *Lonesome Tunes* now before me I am tempted to unbosom to you some of my gratitude to you for the unique joy they give me. It seems inconceivable to me that the setting of such tunes could be more deeply satisfyingly done than you have done them. I am sure that it is an immortal work that you have accomplished, certainly one that will never lose its fragrance for me, a sort of sweet morning fragrance so redolent of this touching land and race. It seems to me, who am neither American nor English, that you have captured the particular subtle essence of both this country and the old country, in your harmonic weavings, so sensitive, so subtle, so appealing from every musical standpoint."

Again, on July 14, 1918, Mr. Grainger wrote to Mr. Brockway: "Your enthralling *Lonesome Tunes* have been part of my artistic life; and I wish to take this opportunity to tell you again what a beautiful world of tender emotion and subtle artistic fragrance your book of settings has conjured up for me: to abide forever in the gallery of my truest admirations. . . . I am convinced that your *Lonesome Tunes* is a work as deathless as it is perfect, and I beg you not to stint in the providing of such fare, which is a very lovely part of the 'common meal, equally set' on which our Anglo-Saxon music shall nourish itself and grow strong."

The *Lonesome Tunes* (1916) were followed, in 1920, by *Twenty Kentucky Mountain Songs,* settings of that many more of the airs collected in Kentucky. Mr. Brockway's artistic achievement so impressed Cecil Sharp, the eminent British collector, that, on his last visit to New York, he offered to Mr. Brockway full and free permission to use any of the melodies he had collected in any way, a permission granted to only one other person in the world, Vaughn Williams. (Two copies of the complete Sharp collections have been placed in accessible spots for preservation and study; the original in the British Museum, and a copy in the Library of Harvard University.)

Each of the songs has been given its own individual and fitting piano accompaniment, and Mr. Brockway has taken care that these shall never bury the lovely melody under a sophisticated mantle. It would be impossible to point out the special features of all the songs. In "Barbara Allen," simplicity is stressed. An art accompaniment (new for each verse, rather than strophic) gives a varied background to the air, as, at the words "When she got in two miles of town," the chiming of bells are heard suggested, as though from the church tower. In "The Old Maid," open fifths in the piano bass suggest the quaint drone of the folk accompaniment as still played on the dulcimer in the mountains. When Mr. Brockway recorded the "Ground Hog" ("fast music"), the girl who sang it to him at the same time held a fiddle against her side and "sawed away" at the G- and D-strings. These dissonances Mr. Brockway has incorporated into his piano accompaniment. In "The Frog Went A-Courting" the old modal scale from G to G has been employed. A little rhythmic figure fits the rhythms of the nonsense syllables. "The Nightingale" has a particularly lovely accompaniment. "Pretty Polly," which Mr. Brockway considers to be one of the most extraordinary airs to be found in any folk music, has a moving melody, which in its primitive form has already worn itself into a perfection of phrasing. Here there is encountered that vacillation between major and minor, and use of both the lowered and the raised leading tone, which give such an archaic charm to much of the oldest folk song. "Charming Beauty Bright" was obtained from a woman so shy that she requested the visitors to sit out of sight in the house while she sang it, seated outside her door knitting and facing the serene open spaces of the valley. The English Singers have featured these works both in Queen's Hall, London, and in New York, and paid the composer the graceful compliment, on Christmas morning of 1932, of serenading him with his songs from the foyer of his New York home.

BRUCH, Max (1838–1920). An eminent German composer of the latter half of the nineteenth century, who came of a musically gifted family from the Lower Rhine. Known as a talented composer of choral music, with three symphonies, chamber music, and smaller violin pieces, he is best known by his *Kol Nidrei* variations, inspired by an original synagogue lament, and his *Concerto in G Minor* which is included in the repertoire of almost every famous violinist in the world.

BURLEIGH, Harry Thacker (1866–   ). Born and educated in Erie, Pa., where he served, in his youth, as chorister in St. Paul's Cathedral and as soloist in the Park and First Presbyterian Churches, and the Jewish Synagogue. Coming to New York City in 1892, he was the winner of a scholarship in the National Conservatory of Music. Here he assisted Mrs. Thomas MacDowell (mother of Edward MacDowell) who was the registrar; and studied voice with Christian Fritsch, harmony with Rubin Goldmark, and counterpoint with john White and Max Spicker. He played double-bass, and subsequently, timpani, in the conservatory orchestra under Frank Van der Stucken, Gustav Heinrichs, and Antonin Dvořák.

Antonin Dvořák, brought to America to teach at the National Conservatory, was deeply moved by Burleigh's singing of the Negro spirituals, and spent hours listening to

them, both before and during the time occupied by the composition of the *New World Symphony.*

Constantly associated with Dvořák, Mr. Burleigh copied many of the orchestral parts of the *New World* from the orchestral score, getting it ready for its first performance and for the publisher.

In 1894 the young Negro singer overcame the obstacles created by racial prejudice and, against 60 other applicants, won the post of baritone soloist at St. George's Church in New York, a position he has held for nearly 40 years. He also sang for 25 years in the choir of Temple Emanu-El, New York.

He has been, for many years, an editor for the New York branch of G. Ricordi & Co., the music publishing house. Howard University has conferred the degree of Doctor of Music upon him. His original songs and settings of the songs of the Negro are sung by the greatest artists, and have resulted in invitations to the composer to sing before King Edward VII of England and other crowned heads of Europe.

The list of his arrangements of spirituals for solo voices, for two- and three-part choruses, for men's, women's, and mixed voices, and of sacred anthems totals more than 100 items, including such numbers as "Deep River," "Nobody Knows de Trouble I've Seen," "De Gospel Train," "Go Down, Moses," "Swing Low, Sweet Chariot," "Were You There?" Very appropriately, the list begins with "Deep River," a song known and loved in all parts of the world. The composer has taken the rune-like two-line melody of this spiritual, and supplied it with a middle section, and otherwise built it into a compactly organized whole. The song has not been written with a special view toward carrying out the Negro elements of the "spiritual" melody, but rather that it shall convey a message of emotional intensity.

Ethiopia Saluting the Colors. A setting of words by Walt Whitman, of great dramatic appeal. The poem tells of Sherman's march to the sea, and of an old Negro woman who comes out from the doorway of her hovel to curtsy to the regiments. She understands nothing of the mighty drama that is being enacted for her sake, but the soldier who passes catches a glimpse of the epic in which he is an actor. The Burleigh music, distinctly martial in character, moves upon the discordant tread of the marching army. A bit of barbaric melody calls to mind the dark continent whence came the Negro. Now and then the opening phrase of "Marching through Georgia" is interwoven in the tonal picture. The whole scene, a moving tableau, is ably depicted.

Five Songs of Laurence Hope. Representative of Mr. Burleigh's finest writing; they have been sung repeatedly by John McCormack. The songs are notable for haunting melody, well-balanced accompaniments, and expressive effectiveness. "The Jungle Flower," second in the group, gains distinction from the exotic syncopation. "Pale Hands I Lov'd" is most effective of the whole group in its deep pathos. "Among the Fuchsias," exploits an alluring Oriental

charm. "Till I Wake," with which the cycle ends, is a distinguished lyric in which the opening theme is intoned as though by a brass choir, giving way presently, to a lyric passage of tender beauty. The songs are orchestrated for large symphony orchestra.

"The Gray Wolf." A somewhat lengthy declamatory scene of heroic mood to words by Arthur Symons. The accompaniment, with its constantly shifting harmonic scheme, is dramatically effective.

"I Remember All." An artistic song built on a four-note motif. It was introduced by Sophie Breslau.

"Little Mother of Mine." Text by Walter Brown; also frequently sung by John McCormack. An eloquently tender song which has remained a "favorite" over a long period of years.

"The Prayer." Text by Arthur Symons. Built upon a two-note motif; makes skillful use of modern dissonance.

"The Soldier." Brief dramatic snatches of familiar melody here interwoven into the polyphonic structure, these chiefly confined to quotations from popular English songs, such as "Rule Britannia," and "British Grenadiers." Still more effective is the composer's development of his own original four-part theme. The words are those of Rupert Brooke's sonnet, "If I should die, think only this of me." It is the song of a soldier about to die, and the tramp of the funeral march is never long absent from its accompaniment.

"Southland Sketches." Four pieces for violin and piano, based on Negro

themes. The two most popular are the *Andante,* a wistful and ingratiating piece; and *Allegretto grazioso,* a light piece of fluent melody. The concluding *Allegro* is brilliantly conceived.

"The Young Warrior." A stirring setting of a patriotic poem by James Weldon Johnson, written shortly after the World War, which was sung all over America and in Europe by the troops. Its fervid appeal—that of a young volunteer to his mother to think not of him but of the work he is to do—swept Italy in a flash, and the song was sung on many battlefields.

Other appealing songs are "In the Wood of Finvara" (text by Arthur Symons); and "Just You" (words by Madge Marie Miller) dedicated to and sung by Lucrezia Bori. (See also "The Negro and His Song," p. 186; and "Dvořák and Spillville, Forty Years After," p. 199.)

BUSONI, FERRUCCIO (1866–1924). Italian by birth, he spent many years of his life as a teacher and concert pianist. Among his compositions are masterly transcriptions of the Bach chorales, such as the "Sleepers, Awake!" (originally an old Dutch folk air); "In Thee is Joy" (which came from an Italian dance measure); "Rejoice, Christians," a melody heard and noted down by Luther (probably a serenade melody of olden times); and "I Call to Thee," which first appeared in the Martin Luther hymn collections of 1524. The four chorales mentioned as having been transcribed by Busoni, had all already been given inspired treatment in the

Chorale Prelude style by Bach. (See "The Pipe-Organ, King of Instruments: The Chorale Prelude," p. 126.)

BUXTEHUDE, DIETRICH (1632–1707). Born at Helsingborg, and died at Lübeck in Germany. He was the famous son of a famous organist. Succeeding Tunder as organist at Lübeck, he made his church famous by its remarkable series of evening concerts for which he wrote much "Abendmusik." These concerts he gave annually on the five Sundays before Christmas, following the afternoon service, including in them much beautiful music for orchestra, organ, and chorus. He had the words sung at all the five concerts bound together into books and sent to the homes of all the well-to-do citizens of the parish, these to be sent back with an honorarium. These are known as the first program-books in musical history.

CADMAN, CHARLES WAKEFIELD (1881–   ). Born in Johnstown, Pa. It was while in attendance on his duties as a critic for the Pittsburgh *Dispatch* that he had his first success as composer. His later intense interest in the tribal music of the American Indian led to many journeys to reservations, and to an employment of Indian themes and characteristics in many of his finest works. One of the first American composers to achieve the triumph of a Metropolitan Opera House presentation, he was also the first to write an operatic work designed for radio production. His serious works number into the hundreds, and include the lyric song cycle *Morning of the Year,* the spontaneous *Trio in D* for piano, 'cello, and violin, *Sonata in A* for piano, several important orchestral suites, four operas on Indian or American subjects (*Land of Misty Water, Witch of Salem,* etc.) and scores of charming songs and piano pieces. Mr. Cadman has also written much music for the films. For many years his home has been in California.

"At Dawning." Written to a text by Nelle Richmond Eberhart of Chicago, who has been Mr. Cadman's constant librettist. Mrs. Eberhart (born in Detroit but reared in small towns of Nebraska) was a teacher, at twenty, in a small Nebraska village at a time when weekly entertainments at the school were called "literaries." For the weekly "newspaper," the young teacher wrote a tiny "Serenade," the words of which, later found by Mr. Cadman in her scrapbook, became the text of this song.

"Land of the Sky-Blue Water." One of the set known as *Four Indian Songs* (which also includes "Far Off I Hear a Lover's Flute") which were the first results of Cadman's study of Indian tribal music. It owes its inspiration to airs collected by the late Alice C. Fletcher. Mr. Cadman's success with the Indian cycle led to his visit to Walt Hill (at the Omaha reservation in Nebraska), and a recording of over 200 Indian songs and flute pieces. In the "Land of the Sky-Blue Water" the composer has used, as introduction, an Omaha flute call; and for the theme of the song, an Omaha tribal song.

"Robin Woman" from *Shane-wis.* (First performance, Metropolitan Opera House, March 23, 1918.) Tells the story of an Indian girl, Shanewis, who, adopted by a wealthy American woman, is given a splendid education. Shanewis's Indian suitor, finding that she has been deceived by her patron's son, with whom she has fallen in love, kills him with a poisoned arrow. In the "Robin Woman" song—the best-known aria of the opera—Shanewis sings of an ancient princess of her tribe who was called by that name because she knew the language of the birds and could call them to her by her song.

Thunderbird Suite. An orchestral work of five parts, originally a part of the incidental stage music for a drama of the same name by Norman Bel Geddes. The scene is laid in the Blackfeet country in the West, and the theme includes references to tribal beliefs and ceremonies. The music is based on Blackfoot melodies highly idealized.

The Willow Tree. Opera in 1 Act (See also "From Greek Drama to Radio Opera"). Text by Nelle Richmond Eberhart; first performance from National Broadcasting Studios, October 3, 1932. Performance time, 23 minutes.

Cast: Donella, an Italian girl (contralto); Pietro, her father, a street-piano player (bass); Alison Travers, an American girl of wealthy family (soprano); and Gordon Stanton, son of manufacturer in whose plant Donella is employed (tenor).

Time: The present. Place: The shore of a small lake on a large private estate near an American seaport.

The Story: Gordon Stanton has won the love of Donella, a beautiful Italian girl in his father's employ, but, when the Travers family buys the adjoining estate, the blond loveliness of Alison Travers drives all thought of Donella from his head. One day, as Gordon shows Alison through the factory, Donella hears them plan to meet the next evening beside a large willow tree near the lake on Alison's father's grounds. Donella confides all this to her father and they plan to go to the tryst and spy on the lovers. Father and daughter arrive first at the appointed place and hide behind the willow tree. At the close of an impassioned scene between Gordon and Alison, Pietro dashes from behind the tree, attacks Gordon, and strangles him. As Alison faints, Pietro tosses the dead man into the lake, and he and his daughter flee from the spot.

The brief opera consists of eight "miniature" numbers. The "Mocking Bird's Song," "All Day Long I Dreamed of You," and the two concluding numbers are especially appealing. The Overture was originally written for an orchestra of 15 pieces.

The numbers are: Overture; scene (Donella and Pietro); "Tell Me No More" (Aria by Donella); "So I Am Here Before Him" (Recitative by Alison); "The Mocking Bird's Song" (Aria by Alison); "All Day Long I Dreamed of You" (Aria by Gordon); "This Is Love's Hour" (Duet by Alison and Gordon); and scene end ensemble (Alison, Gordon, Donella, Pietro).

CARPENTER, JOHN ALDEN (1876–). A lineal descendant of the John Alden of Plymouth fame, born in Park Ridge, Illinois. A graduate of Harvard University; while there, studied with Professor Paine. In Europe, he had lessons in composition from Elgar. Wrote settings of Tagore's *Gitanjali* (1914); orchestral music for use with ballet (see the story of *Skyscrapers,* p. 91); includes *Krazy Kat,* which drew its inspiration from a popular comic strip in the newspapers, and *The Birthday of the Infanta.* He has also written many other songs, a string quartet, a *Concertino for Piano and Orchestra,* and a number of smaller piano pieces.

Adventures in a Perambulator. A suite for orchestra (written in 1914), of typical American humor:

I. "En Voiture" introduces "My Nurse," "My Perambulator," and "Myself," themes representing these characters, which reappear constantly throughout the composition in varying forms. "My Nurse" appears promptly through the medium of two solo 'cellos. "My Perambulator" is heard in a motif from the celesta and the strings, over which the flute announces, by means of a gay little descending scale, "Myself." II. "The Policeman," short "intermezzo" suggesting the conversation between the policeman and the nurse. The remarks of the former are voiced by the bassoon, and the replies of the nurse by violins. III. "The Hurdy Gurdy" brings to the attention of the listener bits of familiar masterpieces as played by two xylophones and a harp, to the accompaniment of excited ejaculations from "My Nurse" and "Myself." IV. Here in "The Lake" there are heard swaying "little waves" from strings, flutes, and horns. V. "Dogs" of all kinds are heard in this movement, in which, toward the end, the old tune of "Where, Oh, Where Has My Little Dog Gone?" is used as the theme of a brisk little fugue. VI. "Dreams" brings a résumé of all the adventures.

"The Home Road." A patriotic song written in July 1917, when the World War was at its height.

CASELLA, ALFREDO (1883–   ). Born in Turin, Italy. A striking figure in international music circles, a leader among Italian nationalists, and earnest propagandist for Italian musicians. In 1915 he founded a National Society of Music in Rome. In *Italia* he has glorified the Italian folk atmosphere as did Denza in the popular *"Funiculi, Funicula."*

The Jar (La Giara). An orchestral suite from the music which Casella wrote during the summer of 1924 for the Swedish ballet. The story of both ballet and suite is a tale of rural life in Sicily. (See p. 91.)

Pupazzetti. (See p. 231.)

CHABRIER, ALEXIS EMMANUEL (1841–1894). Of French birth, Chabrier spent much time in Spain, where he made a special study of Spanish folk dances.

Rhapsody España. A brilliant and effective orchestral fantasy, based on two genuine Spanish dance melodies, the *jota* and the *malagueña.* It opens without melody, the rhythm of clicking castanets establishing the tempo.

CHOPIN, FREDERIC FRANÇOIS (1809–1849). Born in a Polish village about 30 miles from Warsaw, and died in Paris. His works, mostly for piano, include two brilliant piano concertos, three sonatas, and other large works, but it is through the very general study and playing of his shorter works that his name has come to be a household word wherever music is known. He was an ardent patriot and, though his body is buried in Paris, his heart is preserved in the Holy Cross Church in his beloved Warsaw.

"Berceuse." Like a series of exquisite variations. The accompaniment is a rocking chord pattern built entirely upon a single D-flat which is heard in each of the 70 measures of the composition. Above it the melody is presently adorned with the most florid, though delicate, arabesques.

"Butterfly Étude," Opus 25, No. 9. One of the 27 Chopin Études for piano, and a familiar pianistic "warhorse" of all artists and advanced amateurs. Several others of the Études bear auxiliary titles, such as "Harp," "Black Key," and "Revolutionary."

"Funeral March." The third movement of the Sonata, Opus 35. It opens with a relentless and insistent rhythm and a purposely monotonous melody, suggesting the sorrowful passing of a solemn cortège. The center section of the

March presents a sharp contrast in a cloyingly sweet melody, after which the first theme returns. This music is often played in an arrangement for military band.

"The Maiden's Wish," Opus 74, No. 1. This song, in mazurka form, is also famous in a transcription for piano by Franz Liszt, this work being, in reality, a series of three charming variations on the original air.

"Military Polonaise in A," Opus 40, No. 1. In the early days when Poland was an independent kingdom, it was a custom that heroes returning from a victory should pass in review before the king and court. The first recorded review of this kind was held in the former Polish capital, Cracow, in 1573, by Henry III of Anjou. From its essentially nationalistic character, the procession came to be known as the polonaise. "Military Polonaise in A" was written during the composer's sojourn at Majorca. So realistic are the martial rhythms and melodies that Chopin is said to have had an apparition that the walls of the room opened to allow the entrance of a phantom cavalcade of knights in armor, mounted on restive chargers. This so startled Chopin that he is said to have fled from the room, and that he remained unwilling, for days, to return to it.

"Minute Valse," Opus 64, No. 1. One of the shortest and most familiar of the numerous Chopin valses, is a charming work of simple construction, with swift passage work in the first section (and its final repetition) and a singing melody in the trio. Chopin played this Valse at his last concert in Paris, in 1848.

"Nocturne in E-Flat," Opus 9, No. 2. A graceful and elegant "nightpiece," written in 1832. It is frequently played in arrangements for violin, 'cello, and other solo instruments.

"Prelude in D-Flat," Opus 28, No. 15. Known affectionately as the "Raindrop Prelude," it was also written during the Majorca sojourn. It is a bit of program music, realistic in that it imitates the never-ceasing beating of the rain against the windowpanes; and impressionistic in that, without the aid of explanation, the ceaselessly reiterated tones suggest a definite mood of sadness and meditation.

COLE, ROSSETTER GLEASON (1866–). The eighth in direct line from ancestors who came to America from England in 1631; born in Michigan, where his father, though a merchant and farmer, spent his leisure hours as music director of the oldtime singing schools, directing the music of the local church, playing the organ and writing anthems that were published in volumes of church-organ music. Mr. Cole holds degrees from the University of Michigan, where he elected all the music courses offered in the courses of study. After study in Europe under van Eyken, he won a three years' free scholarship in the Royal Master-School for Composition in Berlin, under Max Bruch. He also studied conducting under Gustav Kogel and organ with Wilhelm Middelschulte. Since 1902 Mr. Cole has resided in Chicago, where he is active as a teacher, organist, lecturer, composer, and worker in all important musical lines. Since 1908 he has held the position of professor in charge of music in the Columbia University Summer Session in New York City.

His first composition was written in his senior year at college—a lyrical cantata, *The Passing of Summer,* for solos, chorus, and orchestra, performed by the University Musical Society (Michigan) in University Hall on the eve of his graduation. This performance is the only event of its kind in the annals of the University of Michigan. The cantata was later revised and published as Opus 14. Mr. Cole is also known for his *Choral and Church Music,* published as Vol. VI in "The Art of Music" series. His wife is known as the translator of the Marx *Interpretation of the Beethoven Piano Works.*

In 1913 the University of Michigan conferred a Master of Arts degree upon Mr. Cole "for services in the fields of teaching and composition"; and in 1930 he was made an alumnus member of the Michigan chapter of Phi Beta Kappa. He has served three terms as president of the Music Teachers' National Association; four terms as dean of the Illinois chapter of the American Guild of Organists; has for many years been director of the Theory Department of the Cosmopolitan School of Music in Chicago; and is a member of the MacDowell Colony at Peterborough, N. H.

In addition to works for organ, orchestra, and vocal ensemble, Mr. Cole is known as a writer of many successful songs, favorites among which are "Lilacs," "Love's Invocation," "Halcyon Song," "Your Lad and My Lad," and "In My Father's House are Many Mansions."

"Ashes of Roses." A frequently used chorus, arranged both for male and female voices.

Ballade for Violoncello and Orchestra (or Piano). One of the most important works for this instrument composed by any American, it had its first performance at a Minneapolis Symphony concert in 1909. Since that time it has been a favorite with all concert 'cellists. A strong declamatory melody (*Adagio*), fully developed, is followed by a vivacious middle part which leads into a partial reassertion of the slow theme, ending tranquilly.

Hiawatha's Wooing, the first serious work in the line of recitation with music to be published in America, is a setting of verses from Longfellow. The music is lyric, melodious, and harmonically rich.

Heroic Piece, Opus 39, for Orchestra and Organ. A brilliant and serious work; had its first performance with the Chicago Symphony Orchestra, Frederick Stock conducting, in 1924. This is one of the most important works for organ and orchestra in the repertoire. The *Piece* has also been arranged for organ solo, in which form it is magnificent.

King Robert of Sicily. A celebrated recitation with music, in a field to which Mr. Cole has made a significant contribution. It was given by the late David Bispham more than 500 times, being included in his repertoire for eight consecutive seasons. In his *A Quaker Singer's Recollections,* Bispham spoke of this as "the most satisfactory of these musical recitations . . . with the noble music of Rossetter Cole." The music is elaborate, in places very dramatic, and makes frequent use of two motives, a "King Robert" and an "Angel" theme. It is, in effect, a miniature opera, with opportunity to display every inflection of the speaking voice.

"Legend." The most important of Mr. Cole's published piano pieces, it has received much attention from the concert public and pianist.

Merrymount. A romantic opera in 3 acts, libretto by Carty Ranck, was begun in 1919 and finished in 1927. The orchestration was completed in 1931. The composer has himself made a summary of the plot:

"It is based on an historical incident in early New England colonial life (1625). Merrymount was the name of a cavalier group of gay, dance-loving, and care-free colonists in strong contrast to the stern and somber Puritan spirit of Plymouth Colony, close by. According to the librettist (here history ends) Roger, the young son of John Masterson, a stern Puritan deacon of the Plymouth Colony, has met in the forest glade Elspeth, lovely young daughter of Thomas Morton, leader of the Merrymount Colony, and is madly in love with her.

"When, at the command of his father, Roger refuses to give up Elspeth, the implacable John Masterson pronounces a curse upon the lovers and bids his son never to return to his home. Oliver, older

brother of Roger, also loves Elspeth, and helps to inflame his father against Roger. Act I ends with the old man's curse.

"In the second act, a picturesque Maypole dance is staged close to Merrymount, during which the wedding of Roger and Elspeth is to take place. The rustic wedding procession appears. Just as Paunch, a renegade priest of the Church of England, begins the ceremony, Masterson and Oliver tear off their masks (the dancers are all in masquerade costumes of animals and birds, and they mingle unnoticed among them), a band of Puritan soldiers rush in from the bushes that had concealed them, and the wedding is stopped. Confusion breaks loose, during which an unsuccessful attempt to shoot Masterson is made by Weetonah, an Indian squaw, who seeks revenge for the killing of her lord and master during a raid on an Indian village led by Masterson. The Merrymounters rush to their fort, pursued by the soldiers, Masterson hews down the Maypole with a broad sword, and it falls with a crash as the curtain drops.

"The action of Act III takes place in an open moonlit glade close to Merrymount. Masterson and Oliver are seeking the lovers who have eluded the soldiers. Elspeth is to be deported to England with the other Merrymounters captured in the raid. When the despairing lovers are finally overtaken, Roger passionately vows they shall never be separated and defends Elspeth against seizure by the soldiers. Oliver tries to beat down Roger's sword and is wounded. Then the old Puritan, furious at his young son's defiance, springs forward, sword in hand, to attack his own son. Roger sees Weetonah in the bushes about to fire upon his father. With a warning cry he springs in front of his father, receiving the bullet from the musket in his own body. Masterson, bending over his wounded son in an agony of grief and remorse, finds that the wound is not fatal. The old Puritan, shaken to the depths of his heart, calls upon God to let him make atonement. He places Elspeth's hand in Roger's as proof of his repentance. The end is happy, though a tragic atmosphere pervades much of the opera."

Psychologically, John Masterson is the central figure. Each act has an instrumental prelude which establishes the mood of its opening scene. Themes characteristic of the conflicting Puritan and cavalier ideals as well as of leading persons are used, somewhat after the leading-motive manner. All the lyrical portions are melodious, with several that approach the aria in their sustained sweep. Most of the opera is dramatic recitative, with intervening lyric moments. There is a sustained love-scene of great musical beauty in both the first and second acts. The climax of Act I is the tense scene leading to the father's curse. Act II has great variety—the lovers' scene, the boisterous gathering of the Merrymounters, the festivities at the Maypole, a rollicking drinking song, the Maypole dances (a morris dance, a boisterous turkey dance, and several daintier dances in old English style), a wedding chorus, and the thrilling scene as the Puritans disperse the Merrymounters. The

high musical moments of Act III are the duet of the despairing lovers, Elspeth's pathetic appeal for protection to the moon (guardian of lovers' vows), Roger's fierce defiance of Masterson's attempt to separate him from Elspeth; and after he is shot by Weetonah, his stern rebuke of his father's intolerance that caused the catastrophe. The composer has not hesitated to let the music be simple and melodious when the story seemed to demand it, or to let it be cacophonous and so-called "modern" when occasion required. The dramatic necessity has determined the style. On the whole, the music might be called moderately modern, but never atonal. Mr. Cole has arranged a *Merrymount Suite* for full orchestra, the thematic material being taken from the opera.

"Novellette" (G-flat Major). Mr. Cole's first published piece; has a fine singing melody over a lilting accompaniment, divided between the two hands. It was dedicated to Miss Fannie Louise Gwinner, who afterwards became Mrs. Cole.

Pierrot Wounded. A dramatic recitation with music, was written at the MacDowell Colony in June 1917, and is dedicated to Mrs. Edward MacDowell. It is a shorter piece than *Hiawatha* and *King Robert of Sicily* and deals with the last moments of a patriotic French poet who died in battle. One melody is used as a theme in *Merrymount*.

Pioneer Overture (*1818–1918*). Written in commemoration of the Illinois State Centennial, and dedicated to the memory of Abraham Lincoln. The music was composed at the MacDowell Colony, 1918. The music is pervaded by a more or less festival atmosphere, and its material is drawn largely from characteristic qualities of the typical western pioneer. The form in which the Overture is cast falls into three large divisions, consisting of prologue, main movement, and epilogue, each individual in character, but all bound together by certain common thematic material and an underlying programmatic relationship. The music is brilliantly scored.

"Rhapsody," for Pipe-Organ. Mr. Cole has here made use of an ingenious thematic device, in using the melodious pedal part of the principal theme as the main material for his secondary theme (rather slower and with shimmering registration). So far as known this is the first use of such a device in free composition. Persistent use is also made of the material of the principal theme, so that it is sometimes spoken of as a "rhapsody" on one theme.

Rock of Liberty. A Pilgrim Ode for Chorus and Orchestra. Had its first performances in connection with the Pilgrim Tercentenary, has continued in general favor, and has been heard in its entirety nearly 100 times since then, and in part countless times. It is vigorous, inspiring, powerful in appeal, and presents, in festive manner, the achievement of those upon whose early building our government has been erected. Four choral numbers from it, frequently used in concert and air programs, are the opening chorus "Lord God of Hosts," which continues the thematic material of the opening instrumental prelude; the gorgeous "Psalm of Praise"; "Patter, Patter, In and Out," for women's voices; and the closing chorus, "Hymn of the Union."

Sonata in D Major, for Piano and Violin. One of the notable examples of American chamber music. Its themes in the first and third movements are said to have been suggested to the composer by a two-day visit to the Wartburg Castle in Eisenach, Germany. The outstanding features of the Sonata are its playableness and its bewildering wealth of melody.

Symphonic Prelude for Orchestra. (Also arranged by the composer for Organ, under the title of *Fantaisie Symphonique*.) Widely known, it was given its first performance by the Chicago Symphony under Frederick Stock. It has been played by many other symphonic bodies. Notable for clear form, colorful melodies, and positive rhythms.

CORELLI, Arcangelo (1653–1713). Born in Fusignano, Italy. The greatest violinist of his time, and noted as a composer who did much to advance the art of concerted instrumental writing. For many years preceding his death, he lived in the Palace of Cardinal Pietro Ottoboni, in Rome. His concerts, given in the Palace each Monday, became the outstanding musical events of the city. He was honored for many years after his death by annual memorial performances of his compositions in Rome.

Christmas Concerto, No. 8. Written for harpsichord and "string band," before the advent of either modern piano or orchestra, for a Christmas performance at the Cardinal's Palace (1712). In the "Pastorale," or second movement, Corelli has introduced melody of aristocratic and dignified grace.

DAMROSCH, WALTER JOHANNES (1862–   ). Born in Breslau, Germany, the son of Dr. Leopold Damrosch, one of the pioneer musicians and conductors in this country. He received his earliest musical training from his father, then studied with Hans von Bülow, and others. In his early youth he came to America with his father, well known as conductor of orchestra and German opera in New York City. When just past 20, Walter Damrosch began his conducting at Newark, N. J., with the Newark Harmonic Society, and in 1885, at the death of his father, became assistant conductor and director of the German Opera Company of New York. For many years he conducted symphony and opera, also founding the Damrosch Opera Company for the introduction into America of the Wagner music-dramas. After an illustrious career of years as the conductor of the New York Symphony, Dr. Damrosch resigned in 1927 that he might give his entire time to music education. Since 1927 he has been the musical counsel for the National Broadcasting Company, where he has also rendered a valuable and unique service to music in America through his widely popular orchestral concerts of the air especially prepared for the youth of the land. It is estimated that each of these concerts is heard by an audience of over 6,000,000 people.

Always a patriotic citizen, Dr. Damrosch served during the World War, at the request of General Pershing founding the A.E.F. Band-Masters' School at General Headquarters, France.

Dr. Damrosch is also known as the composer of scholarly and well-liked works of wide appeal.

Canterbury Pilgrims. This incidental music for the drama of this name was composed in 1909 for a performance at Gloucester, Mass., by the Coburn Players.

Cyrano. This opera in four acts (the libretto by William J. Henderson, from the play by Edmond Rostand) had its first performance at the Metropolitan Opera House in 1913, with Pasquale Amato, Frances Alda, and Riccardo Martin singing the principal rôles. The opera follows closely the action of the play, the operatic version beginning at the Hotel de Bourgogne, where *La Clorise* is to be played. Cyrano is the "stainless knight" who thinks that he dare not woo his cousin Roxane, whom he adores, because of his ugliness. Possessed of a beautiful mind and heart, and a gift for writing, he helps Christian, her less-gifted lover, by writing his love-letters for him, and by singing original love-verses under her window. The courtship is successful and Cyrano sees the two married. Too late, when Cyrano is brought in from the battle-field dying, Roxane suspects the truth, but

Cyrano dies denying it, declaring that he leaves "without a stain upon his soldier's snow-white plume."

The music which accompanies the drama is very beautiful and effective. This was one of the first American operas to have the honor of performance at the Metropolitan.

"Danny Deever." This, one of the finest art songs written in America, tells the dramatic story of an English soldier stationed in India. The verses are from the *Barrack Room Ballads* by Kipling. The gruesome and realistic story of Danny Deever, "the regiment's disgrace," who is hanged because he shot a sleeping comrade, is told, by the Color Sergeant and Files, the sentry, through a series of questions asked by the one and answered by the other. At all moments the music faithfully follows the sentiment and episodes of the verses, creating a stirring atmosphere, brought to a thrilling climax.

Dove of Peace. This comic opera, composed in 1911 (book by Wallace Irwin) has had successful performances in both Philadelphia and New York City.

Electra. Dr. Damrosch composed incidental music for Margaret Anglin's production of the classic *Electra* of Euripides given by her at the Greek Theater of the University of California in 1915. In this, as in other incidental music to Greek drama, Dr. Damrosch utilized characteristic Greek modes, thus creating a charming and appropriate background for the text. In addition to the Euripides *Electra*, he composed incidental music for the drama of the same name by Sophocles (495–406

B.C.) for Miss Anglin's New York production in 1918. The music was written in 1917.

"The Looking Glass." This is a ballad to words by Rudyard Kipling.

Manila Te Deum. This inspired work was written for chorus and orchestra in 1898 in honor of Admiral Dewey's victory at Manila Bay.

Medea. The incidental music to this old Greek drama by Euripides was also composed in 1915 for Miss Anglin's California Greek Theater production, and is colored by the same historical associations.

"My Wife." A tender song dedicated to Mrs. Damrosch (who was Margaret Blaine, the daughter of James G. Blaine, the statesman), to words by Robert Louis Stevenson.

The Scarlet Letter. A grand opera on a text taken from the novel of the same name by Nathaniel Hawthorne. This was one of the first operas to take as its text an American novel.

DEBUSSY, CLAUDE (1862–1918). Born in St. Germain-en-Laye, near Paris, he was a fellow student at the Paris Conservatory with Edward MacDowell. (See also "Music of the Twentieth Century," p. 228.)

Apres-Midi d'un Faune. A unique orchestral fantasy (first hearing in Paris, 1894), entirely atmospheric in effect but built upon a fundamental three-part form. A faun awakens in a forest and endeavors to recall his dreams. He thinks that he was visited by nymphs but is not certain, and, as Debussy is said to have remarked, "the shadow of his vision is not more substantial than the shower of notes which fall from his precious flute." The main theme of the work (flute) is of subtle, elusive quality. It is immediately developed by oboe and clarinet and at the close of each phrase an exquisitely dainty *glissando* is interpolated by the harp. The second theme is slightly contrasted, and after a short development there is a return to the first theme, now played over and over, flute alternating with 'cello and accompanied by the harp.

The Children's Corner. A set of short piano pieces of highly descriptive character written in 1908 as a birthday present for the composer's daughter, it includes, besides several other clever bits of program music: "Little Shepherd," which, in its employment of whole-tone scale and improvisational passage work, suggests the whimsical playing of a shepherd's pipe; and "Golliwogg's Cake-Walk," in which Debussy glorifies the grotesque antics of a French rag doll.

Iberia. A series of three musical pictures of Spanish life. The first, *"Par les rues et par les chemins,"* brings a suggestion of the energy of life on the Spanish thoroughfares. The music is fragmentary in a manner found in some Spanish folk music, and is permeated with Oriental atmosphere. The second, *"Les parfums de la nuit,"* is as mysterious in its atmosphere as are many of the customs of age-old Andalusia. The third number, *"Le matin d'un jour de fête,"* suggests the sounds of dawning day, and finally, the procession which is a part of the festival celebration.

La Mer (The Sea). Three orches-tral sketches which are a richly imaginative portrayal of the forces of nature. The first section, "From Dawn to Noon at Sea"; the second, "Gambol of the Waves"; and the third, "Dialogue, Wind and Sea."

Nocturnes. (See "Chamber Music, Past and Present," p. 112.)

Pelléas and Mélisande. Of this, his only opera except for the one-act interlude *The Prodigal Son,* Debussy said: "I have been reproached because my melodic phrase is always in the orchestra, never in the voice. I tried, with all my strength and sincerity, to identify my music with the poetic essence of the drama. . . . I wished that the action should never be arrested, that it should be continued and uninterrupted."

The text of the opera (first performance at Opéra Comique, Paris, April 30, 1902), from a drama by Maeterlinck, is a mystical story, this atmosphere being constantly reflected in the music, which differs from that of the older Italian opera. There are 5 acts and 12 scenes. Mélisande is found by Golaud, the grandson of the aged king, while wandering in the forest. He takes her to the castle and wins the consent of the king to marry her. Later she meets Pelléas, and they find that they love each other. After many warnings, and a romantic scene, Pelléas agrees to leave. Mélisande begs that she may say farewell to him, and, as they meet near the fountain, Golaud thrusts Pelléas through with his sword. Though both have declared the innocence of their love, Golaud continues to doubt and not until her death does he realize that her child-like simplicity was but the reflection of the purity of her soul.

Mary Garden created the rôle of Mélisande, and also gave it the first American performance, Manhattan Opera House, New York City, February 1, 1908.

La Cathédrale Engloutie (The Engulfed Cathedral). This tone-poem relates an old legend told for many centuries by peasants who live on the coasts of Brittany. Ville d'Ys (City of Ys) was on a point of land connected with the mainland at low tide, but entirely separated from it when the tide was high. About it the good king had built a strong wall for protection against the ocean, and certain gates which led to the water were never opened save when the sea was calm. To make this protection doubly sure, the king always wore, about his neck, the cord upon which the only key to the sea gate was hung. His daughter, less interested in the fate of her father's subjects than in the admiration of a false suitor who was sent by an enemy of her people, came one night and stole the key while her father was sleeping. Then together, she and her lover opened the sea gate, thinking to admit the forces of the opposing armies. It was the water of the sea, however, which entered, and when, next day, the people on the mainland came to look out toward Ville d'Ys, it had vanished beneath the surging waves. The legend says that sometimes, on calm days, the steeple of the old church may be seen beneath the water, and that the bells of the church are heard as they are swung and rung by the restless water.

DE FALLA, Manuel (1877–   ). Born in the Spanish city of Cadiz. At 14 the Madrid Academy of Music awarded him the first prize for piano playing. Some time was spent in study in Paris where he was influenced by Debussy and Dukas. One of his most colorful works is based upon a certain phase of the story of *Don Quixote*. (See also "Music of the Twentieth Century," p. 232).

El Amor Brujo (Love, the Magician). Includes thematic material drawn from both native folk dances and gypsy songs of Spain. Arranged in a suite for orchestra, the numbers are as follows:

I. "Introduction and Scene," based upon a strongly rhythmic figure typical of Andalusian melody. II. "The Gypsies—Evening"; a tranquil oboe solo leads to *"Chanson du chagrin d'amour,"* the first of the Spanish songs which are featured in the work. III. "The Homecomer," a lively movement, features a solo for muted trumpet, which is followed by rapid scale passages and shimmering and *glissando* in wind, strings, and piano.

Jota, for Voice and Orchestra. One of *Seven Popular Spanish Songs,* it suggests all the characteristic features of the Spanish dance of the same name. There is a long dance prelude in three-beat measure; the melody is repeated in varied form as it might be were folk singers giving it performance in connection with a dance, and the voice part, when it enters, though of more flowing style, contains many of the unequal rhythms of the dance.

La Vida Breve (The Short Life).

This had its initial performance as a lyric-drama (2 acts and 4 tableaux) at Nice in 1913. The scene is laid in present-day Granada. Pealing church bells, shouting street vendors, and other street noises accompany the laughter of girls as Salud, the heroine of the drama, enters her home in the gypsy quarter. Salud and Paco profess undying devotion, but Sarvaor, the girl's uncle, distrusts Paco and threatens to kill him. Meanwhile, in another home in the city, Carmela, a wealthy girl, is celebrating her betrothal to Paco. The guests whirl in the dances which are accompanied by spirited singing and playing of the guitar. Presently Salud approaches the open window and watches the merriment. Then, as she begins to sing of unhappy love, Paco, already in the house, trembles with a sudden fear. A group of gypsies approaches the door, and Manuel, brother of Carmela, welcomes them, thinking that they have come to entertain the guests. Instead, they surround Salud who, after accusing Paco of unfaithfulness, falls dead in their midst. Her grandmother and the old uncle pronounce a fearful curse on Paco, and a wave of terror sweeps over the awed gathering, which stands silently as the curtain falls.

Three-Cornered Hat. Performed for the first time by the celebrated Russian Ballet at the Alhambra, London, July 23, 1919. The music was soon given prominence, in suite form, on the programs of leading orchestras. The subject matter for the ballet is derived from a novel of the same name by Don Antonio Pedro de Alarcon. The Corregidor (or Governor) wears a three-cornered hat as his badge of office. Come to arrest the miller, he begins a lively flirtation with the miller's wife. She entertains him with a graceful Spanish dance, fooling him so thoroughly that he tumbles over the bridge into the mill-stream. The laugh is thus turned against him, and, this accomplished, the miller's wife proceeds to help him dry his clothes. Meanwhile, the miller returns home, misunderstands the situation, and, for revenge, departs in the intruder's garments. In the music of *The Three-Cornered Hat* certain characteristic phrases occur at significant moments, making fantastic suggestion of *Leitmotifs,* and the comedy is enhanced by the contrast between the archaic mannerisms employed to impersonate the Corregidor and the simple beauty of those which suggest the country miller and his wife. In the Overture characteristic Andalusian song is heard as from behind the curtain, at first unaccompanied, save for the rhythmic clacking of the castanets and the clapping of hands. Essential elements of the music are the sharpness of the lively rhythms and the Oriental qualities of the melodies.

DE KOVEN, REGINALD (1859–1920). Born at Middletown, Conn. Educated in Europe, he took a degree at Oxford University, studied music at Stuttgart, Florence, Vienna, and Paris. He wrote, in all, 19 operettas, his masterpiece being *Robin Hood.* His grand opera, *The Canterbury Pilgrims,* based upon the tales of Chaucer, was produced at the Metropolitan Opera House in 1917. *"Oh, Promise Me."* This lyric is one of the best-known songs heard in the course of *Robin Hood*—but it was not written as a part of this work, and only interpolated for a single performance by Jessie Davis, one of the famous "Bostonians." It took the audience by storm, and ever since that night has been a regular part of the music.

Robin Hood. Completed in exactly three months, during the winter of 1889, while De Koven still lived in Chicago. It is based upon the story of Robin Hood and his Merry Men, who, in the early days, roamed through the Sherwood Forest of England. The abuses of the Sheriff of Nottingham brought about the activities of Robin Hood and his followers. The scene is laid in Nottingham in England, and important characters include, besides Robin Hood, Maid Marian, Little John, Will Scarlet, and the Sheriff. Delightful single numbers include the duet "Come Dream So Bright" (*Robin Hood* and *Maid Marian*), and the choruses, "Hey! For the Merry Greenwood," "A-Hunting We'll Go," the "Tinkers' Chorus," and "Come Away to the Woods."

DELIBES, Leo (1836-1891). For many years associated with the theaters and opera houses of Paris in the capacities of accompanist, and chorus-master. Later he became teacher of composition at the Conservatoire. Although he wrote many choruses and songs, his greatest talent was displayed in the creation of ballet music. His first commission of importance was for the writing of the music to *Coppelia* (See "Folk Dance and Ballet" p. 89). In 1877 he was made Chevalier of the Legion of Honor of France, and twelve years later was promoted to the rank of officer.

Lakmé, an opera in three acts. First performance, Opéra Comique, Paris, in 1883. The text tells of the love of Lakmé, the beautiful daughter of a Brahman priest, and the young Englishman who, an intruder in the private garden of the Temple, has remained to sketch the design of some jewels which he finds on a table. He is ejected from the garden by the wrathful father who finally thinks to drive him from the thoughts of his daughter by killing him. So Lakmé goes in the disguise of a beggar, to the marketplace, there to sing, in the hope that this will make the youth, who has been warned of his danger, reveal himself. The song she sings is the celebrated "Bell Song," in which is told the legend of the Pariah's daughter, accompanied by music of a definitely Oriental character. Gerald is thus lured to reveal his identity and is stabbed by the priest. Lakmé and her servant later nurse him back to health, but when his duty calls him back to his regiment she dies as the result of a self-administered drug.

Sylvia, a ballet, tells, through its music and accompanying pantomime, a tale of mythical times. The scene is before a rural Temple in olden Greece. A festival is in progress and the buffoons, the clowns, the dancers, and the musicians are ar-

CÉSAR FRANCK

BIRTHPLACE OF BRAHMS, HAMBURG

JOHANNES
BRAHMS

BRAHMS HOUSE,
BADEN-BADEN

ANTONIN DVOŘÁK

RICHARD STRAUSS

MAURICE RAVEL

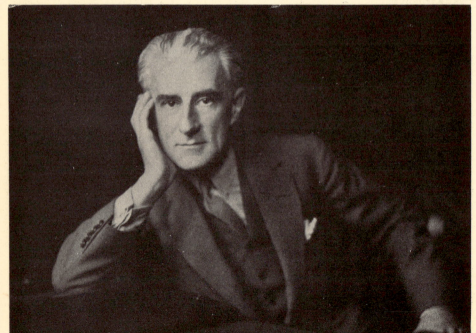

riving. The curtain rises upon the procession scene, where soldiers are trying to clear the space. The activities of all the many characters inspire the composition of much attractive music. Most familiar are the numbers known as "March and Procession of Bacchus," "Valse Lente," and "Pizzicato." This latter number, familiar to all music-lovers and amateurs, has been arranged for many instruments and many combinations of instruments. It is the dance of a young slave who strives, through graceful posturing and langorous glances, to attract the attention of one of the charming maidens, and owes its title to the manner in which the strings of the orchestra are played.

DE LISLE, CLAUDE JOSEPH ROUGET (1760–1836). The writer of the national air of France, was a Captain of the French Engineers. De Lisle was, in 1830, given a life pension by Louis Philippe, the King of France, because of his great gift to the nation. *The Marseillaise* was written in 1792. Knowing that the soldiers had no appropriate marching song, de Lisle, in a burst of fervent patriotic enthusiasm, wrote both words and melody in a single night, while the guest of the Baron de Dietrich, mayor of the city of Strassbourg. So agitated did he become through the force of his overpowering inspiration that he is said to have dashed down both words and music on the wall of his room that they should not be forgotten, then fell asleep with his head on his arms at a table. The song was first played in public on the following Sunday (April 29th) by the National Guard Band. On June 25th of the same year it was sung at a civic banquet in Marseilles, where it created a furore. It owes its name to the fact that it was used as a marching song by the volunteers from Marseilles as they surged into Paris and stormed the Tuilleries a few weeks later.

DELIUS, FREDERICK (1863–   ). Born at Bradford, Yorkshire, England, of German parents. One of the rare examples of an European composer whose creative inspiration was awakened in the New World. At twenty, he came to America, settling in Florida, where the beauties of the South and the singing of the Negroes set him to longing for the life of a creative musician. So he returned to Europe, going to Leipzig, where he studied with Jadassohn and Reinecke. Since 1890 he has spent much of his time in France, devoting himself to composition.

Appalachia. This work, a reminiscence of his days in America, is a set of Variations on an old Slave Song with final chorus for full orchestra.

Brigg Fair. This is one of two Dance Rhapsodies for full orchestra in which Delius—one of the first English composers to do so—broke entirely with German tradition so strong among the British musicians at the time, and in which he has made liberal use of English folk dance. The work is therefore, in truth, an English Rhapsody.

North Country Sketches. Here the composer has made remarkable use of the descriptive powers of orchestral instruments. The work is composed in sections, each suggestive of a season: "Autumn," "Winter Landscape," "Dance," and "March of Spring."

The Song of the High Hills. Composed in 1911, for orchestra and mixed chorus, reflects the composer's impressions of the Norwegian mountains.

DENZA, LUIGI (1846–1922). Born at Castellamare, a trading and fishing village near Vesuvius. Here it was that the funicular railway was built, and it was this that brought about Denza's greatest fame, though perhaps not his greatest art work, in his writing, in 1880, of the air "Funiculi, Funicula" to celebrate the building of the remarkable railway up the mountain side. The air was quickly taken up by the Neapolitans and had an immediate sale of nearly a million copies. It was translated into nearly all languages, and finally became known to the outside world as a Neapolitan folk song. Richard Strauss included it, to secure national atmosphere, in his orchestral suite *Aus Italien.*

"*Santa Lucia*" a boat song, or *barcarolle,* by Denza, is so frequently sung and so well beloved by the people of Italy that it is often referred to as an Italian folk song.

D'INDY, VINCENT (1851–1931). Born in Paris of French noble stock and was a student (piano) of Louis Diemer, and (harmony) of Lavignac and Marmontel. After his military service, he was a student of César Franck, of whom he became a violent

partisan. Willing to assume the humblest duties for the betterment of his nation's music, d'Indy wrote books, magazine articles, criticisms, and made personal visits to other countries in its interests. He won renown not only as a composer, but also as an inspiring teacher whose pupils number many of the outstanding artists of this century. D'Indy was interested in and influenced by liturgical music, and edited many seventeenth-century works.

"*Summer Day on the Mountain*" (See "Music of the Twentieth Century," p. 228).

DONIZETTI, GAETANO (1797–1848). Born in the village of Bergamo, Italy, made famous by Shakespeare's reference to the Bergomask dancers, in his *Midsummer Night's Dream.* For ten years an official and teacher in the Naples Conservatory, Donizetti's fame rests, however, neither upon this fact nor upon the success of his many sacred or instrumental works, but upon his brilliant and tuneful operas.

Daughter of the Regiment. Replete with gay vivacious songs, military drum calls, and trumpet flourishes. The scene of the opera is laid in the Tirol in 1815. Marie, the "daughter of the regiment," a foundling left upon the scene of battle, has been "raised" by the regiment, in special charge of Sergeant Sulpizio. She is loved by Tonio, a young peasant, who joins the troops in order to be near her. When he is accepted for service Marie is asked to sing for him. This she does, to stirring military accompaniment, the words of her song telling of the various exploits of her brave companions. Presently the Sergeant finds an opportunity to deliver to the Marchioness of Berkenfield a letter which had been addressed to her and left with the baby, years before. The Marchioness claims Marie as her niece and orders her to marry a count. When Marie rebels, she is told that the Marchioness is really her mother, to whom she owes obedience. This the girl agrees to. Her suppliance wins what defiance had not gained, and the lovers are allowed to wed amidst the joy of the adoring regiment.

Don Pasquale. A less familiar, but equally melodious opera is a delightful comedy. Old Don Pasquale is so angry with his nephew Ernesto, for daring to fall in love, that he threatens to disinherit him, and be married himself. Dr. Malatesta, a friend, tries to change the uncle's mind. Unable to accomplish this, he suggests his own sister as a bride for him. The suggested bride is not the doctor's sister, but Norino, the sweetheart of Ernesto. She agrees to the plot, and sets out to make life miserable for the old man. She calls him names, ridicules his appearance, spends his money and tells him how she will spend more of it when she has the authority, and ends up by allowing him to discover her making a rendezvous with Ernesto. Here the uncle and the doctor overhear the two lovers talking, and in his joy at escaping so capricious a wife, Don Pasquale gives the two his blessing and a promise of ample income. One of the loveliest bits of music in the whole opera is the "Serenata" sung by

Ernesto just before Marie joins him in the garden.

Lucia di Lammermoor. Opera in three acts, based upon Sir Walter Scott's *Bride of Lammermoor.* First appearance, San Carlo Opera House, Naples, 1835. Its success won for the composer his position as teacher at the Naples Conservatory. Old-fashioned as is the style of action, the solo melodies and the ensemble numbers rank among the finest in Italian opera.

Lucia, the heroine, has fallen in love with Edgar, the master of Ravenswood. Lord Henry, Lucia's brother, has acquired the title to the Ravenswood estates, through treachery, and now is angered by the news that the rightful heir has returned. When Lucia and Edgar meet, the next evening, in the garden, he tells her that he has been ordered to France on military duty. He wishes to go to Lord Henry and declare his love for Lucia, but she, dreading further treachery, will not allow it. During his absence Lucia is constantly urged to wed Lord Arthur Bucklaw. All of Edgar's letters are intercepted. Only when she is told that her acceptance of Lord Arthur will save her brother from ruin does she consent to it. No sooner has she signed the marriage papers than Edgar appears, and the singing of the principal characters—the famous "Sextet"—is one of the high points in the music. Lucia expresses her despair, Lord Henry his fears for his own future, Edgar tells of his faithful love and the reasons for his delayed appearance, and these voices, joined with those of other lesser characters form a remarkable climax. Edgar, in a furious rage at the trickery practiced upon him, finally calls down a curse upon Lucia and rushes away. Lucia goes mad, and while the wedding guests are still feasting, word is brought to the banquet chamber that she has slain her husband. She enters singing a happy song, as she now imagines that she is again with her lover. He, meanwhile, has been challenged to a duel by Lord Henry, and as he prepares for this, word is brought him of Lucia's madness. He now learns the whole story of the deceit which has been practiced upon them both and of her death, whereupon he rushes to the castle and takes his own life that they may be forever united.

DRDLA, Franz (1867-   ). A Viennese composer and violinist, Moravian by descent, a classmate of Ševčik, the violin virtuoso, and noted for his skill in writing fascinating miniatures for the violin. During his life as a student at the Vienna Conservatory, he won prizes in both composition and violin. He was for many years a conductor at the Volksoper in Vienna.

"Serenade." In this short but exquisite number, the theme for muted strings is introduced by a brief rhythmic phrase in the accompaniment. The theme is repeated four times in succession with slightly varied endings for each repetition. The mood is of an ardent character.

"Souvenir." This is a real musical remembrance, inspired by thoughts of the great masters. The story is told that Drdla, while riding one day on a street car past the Central Cemetery of Vienna, caught a glimpse of the monuments erected there to Beethoven, Gluck, Schubert, and Mozart. A lovely original melody entered his mind, and Drdla jotted it down on a street-car ticket. The bit of melody was later developed into the beautiful miniature so great a favorite with all violinists.

DUKAS, Paul (1865-   ). One of the most celebrated of the French musicians, an able critic, a teacher at the Conservatoire, and composer, is known for the writing of many orchestral works, and also for the opera *Ariane et Barbe Bleue*.

Sorcerer's Apprentice. A symphonic poem based upon a very old tale retold in verse by Goethe. The Sorcerer, on leaving for the day, has assigned to his apprentice certain duties which must be performed before his return. Among these is the filling of all the pans in the house with water from the nearby brook. The Apprentice, thinking to get the work done quickly by the means of magic, speaks a certain formula to the broom and orders it to carry in the water for him. This the broom proceeds to do. Soon all the pans and pots are filled and still the broom keeps thumping back and forth from the brook. When the Apprentice tries to stop it he finds that he has forgotten the magic word which will turn the wooden servant back into a broom. He cuts it in two, but then has two servants. Just at the moment the Sorcerer appears, says the magic word, and orders the broom into the corner again. The old tale says that the Apprentice ran away hoping in that way to escape punishment.

In the music, Dukas has made very clever use of the instrumental personalities of the orchestra. The bassoon is made to personify the broom, which clumsily thumps back and forth on its errands. When the broomstick has been cut in two, two bassoons personify the two wooden servants which continue the work. The first theme of the composition is of the type calculated to assist in the production of a mysterious effect. It is the second theme which tells the story of the broom. The return of the Sorcerer is announced by a broad blast from the trumpets, and trills from the wind instruments; and tremolo from the strings usher in the first theme which is again heard before the broom—on a downward sweep of rushing notes—runs back to its corner.

DVOŘÁK, ANTONIN (1841–1904). One of the two greatest Bohemian composers. His *Slavonic Dances* (composed as piano duets) opened the road to fame and aroused enthusiasm for a music so different from most music previously heard in concert halls. In 1892 Dvořák came to New York and became Director of the National Conservatory of Music.

Dvořák's chamber music comprises eight string quartets, several trios, and a piano quintet. Of his oratorios, his *Stabat Mater* and *Requiem* are best known. He wrote seven symphonies, and a variety of smaller numbers for piano, voice, and for various solo instruments.

In 1901 Dvořák was appointed head of the Prague Conservatory. (See Dvořák and Spillville, Forty Years After," p. 199.)

American String Quartet. The first movement is built upon three main themes, the first of which is a rhythmic statement of the simple triad, with additional emphasis given to the sixth tone of the scale. The second theme, in its falling inflections, recalls one of the outstanding characteristics of a genuine Indian song; and the third, and more suave theme, sung very softly, has also its suggestion of syncopation. In the second movement of the Quartet, Dvořák has introduced a lovely and retrospective air, in the minor mode. The third short movement is a set of variations upon a single theme, a syncopated melody which starts abruptly, without introduction, and later comes to a quiet close. The Finale (fourth movement) is a gay rondo which suggests a jolly folk dance of Bohemia, the Dvořák homeland. The opening theme (*vivace ma non troppo*) again employs the skips of a broken chord. In the middle section of the Finale (after the first and second themes have been clearly stated) there comes a sudden hush in the music, and here Dvořák has introduced an air which, in improvisational form, imitates a chorale. The lively mood soon returns and a climax is reached in the brief coda.

Carnival Overture. A brilliant work in strict sonata form, written in 1891, soon before his departure for America. At its first performance in Prague the *Carnival* was known as the "Bohemia.1 Carnival," but the first part of the title was dropped the following year at the composer's own recital in America. It suggests an elaborate sort of festivity, and is built upon three well-contrasted themes. The first is announced by the full orchestra. The second theme is quiet, and is introduced by the oboe. Presently the mood changes slightly, to that of a serene pastoral, the new theme being presented by the English horn, then repeated by the flutes, accompanied by muted strings.

"Humoresque." (See also p. 205.) The story goes that Dvořák wrote this for his own children, modeling it upon the air of "Suwanee River," which he disguised by clever alteration of rhythm and melody. The two gracious melodies arc frequently heard played simultaneously, in orchestral arrangements of the "Humoresque."

"Indian Lament" (Dvořák-Kreisler). This title was given by Fritz Kreisler to his exquisite arrangement for violin and piano of the melody from a *canzonetta* (little song) of the piano Sonatina, Opus 100, by Dvořák. It opens in G Minor, without introduction, the first theme being suggestive of tribal airs of the American Indian. The melody follows its rhythmic pattern in the phrases which follow, and the accompaniment is of simple chordal design. A second theme in brighter mood follows. The middle section (G Major) is also more elaborate, and there are brilliant effects of double stopping, but in each case the theme falls at the end of the phrase in true Indian fashion. A return to the minor key and the first theme complete the

piece, which closes, very softly, in violin harmonics.

New World Symphony (See p. 199). For the sake of unity, the composer has made reminiscent use in the *Largo* and *Scherzo* movements of the symphony, of the principal subject of the first movement; and in the Finale, there is a recapitulation of the principal material of all preceding movements.

First Movement (*Adagio*) E Minor, 4–8 measure. After a long, impressive introduction, in which the *pianissimo* string section is answered by the woodwinds, a sudden *fortissimo* leads to the first theme which is announced abruptly by two horns in unison, and then by the woodwind. This theme employs a device of syncopation (a peculiarity of Negro music similar to the "Scotch snap" of certain folk music of the British Isles) and the use of the five-toned scale. A spirited reply, from the violins is said to suggest the old camp-meeting favorite, "Didn't My Lord Deliver Daniel?" The second theme, from solo flute (G. Major), is from the air of "Swing Low, Sweet Chariot." (See p. 188). After the announcement of the second theme, a free fantasia and development section follows, and finally, the coda.

Second Movement (*Largo*) D-Flat Major, 4–4 measure. The first theme melody is, as introduced in the orchestral version by the English horn, the dominating characteristic of the whole movement. It is entirely within the five-toned scale (beginning on D-Flat), and is given out over an accompaniment of divided muted strings. Dvořák had labeled this movement *Adagio*, but while hearing it done once in rehearsal by Anton Seidl, he reached over without a word and changed the tempo indication to *Largo*, the rate of speed at which the great conductor was so wisely playing it. Muted strings reply to the first announcement of this theme, with a slightly altered version, and then two muted horns repeat, over and over, a small fragment of the melody. There is a sudden change to the key of C-sharp Minor, and after a brief transition, in hurried mood, the second, more vigorous theme is heard. This second theme is first played by flute and oboe. In the middle of the movement, there occurs a striking little episode, constructed out of a small *staccato* melody played first by the oboe, then passed from one instrument of the orchestra to another, with brilliant use made of trills and embellishments alternated between the choirs of the orchestra. An early return to the mood and material of the first theme in English horn, followed by a reply from the first violins, as at first, brings the movement to a close. The music ends *pianissimo* with a chord from the double-basses alone.

Third Movement (*Scherzo*) *Molto Vivace*, E Minor, 3–4 measure. This sharply contrasting music has an aggressive, eager first theme; an exquisite lyric air in E Major as the second theme (flutes and oboes); and an impetuous, sportive *trio*. The movement ends with almost barbaric flourish, the repetition of the *Scherzo* proper being followed by an elaborate *coda*.

Fourth Movement, Finale (*Allegro, con fuoco,*) E Minor, 4–4 measure. This movement, purely pentatonic, opens in march tempo, with great animation. The first theme, given out *fortissimo*, by the horns and trumpets, against *staccato* chords from the rest of the orchestra, is followed by a lesser theme, but one of great beauty, played by the clarinet over a delicate tremolo accompaniment. The English horn melody of the *Largo* and the first theme of the dashing *Scherzo* are again heard, and the Finale comes to a powerful close.

Quintet in E-Flat, Opus 97 (See p. 199). In the *Scherzo* is a strong suggestion of Indian dance rhythms and melody.

Romance for Violin and Orchestra, Opus 11. The slow movement, rewritten and published, from Dvořák's first string quartet (which remained in manuscript), written just a month before the composer's marriage.

Serenade for Strings. Composed of five units, the thematic material of which differs greatly in style and mood.

I. *Moderato,* E Major, 4–4 measure. Opens softly with a melody in the second violins, immediately answered by the 'cellos. II. *Tempo di Valse*. A graceful and alluring melody, presented first by the violins. This section of the *Serenade* has also a *trio* section. III. *Scherzo*. Opens with a playful melody played by the 'cellos and answered by the violins. IV. *Larghetto*. As its *tempo* indication suggests, of a somewhat quiet nature, and introduces a lyric melody of great charm. V. In the *Finale* the principal theme, given out by all violins, is notable for a peculiar syncopation. There is a return to the principal theme of the first section, after which the *Serenade, as a whole,* ends with a dashing flourish.

Sextet, Opus 48. Written with Slavonic feeling and ornamentation. Of the four movements, the first is constructed in the normal sonata form, and has three main themes. The second movement is a *dumka* (or Slavonic elegy) in D Minor, in which the first and last sections are, in fact, a dreamy polka. Notice should be made of the frequent five-measure phrases. The polka mood and melody alternate with an air in gypsy style. The middle section reflects the mood of a lullaby.

The third movement is a Bohemian *furiant,* a Czech dance of fiery character, in which there are frequent alternations of duple and triple measure obtained by means of syncopated accents placed over weak beats. The Trio is of remarkable delicacy.

The fourth movement or *Finale* is a set of six variations upon a mournful theme.

Sonatina for Piano and Violin. A number slight in style and subject matter, but colored by the composer's highly developed individuality, was written during the winter of 1893–94, when Dvořák was teaching in New York, and was dedicated to his children. (See "Indian Lament.")

"Songs My Mother Taught Me." One of the tenderest of Dvořák's "Gypsy Songs," it is like an improvisation. The voice part is written in 2–4 measure while the accompani-

ment is in 6–8 measure. The vocal air, which is as simple as a folk song, is enhanced in beauty by the counter melody with which the first portion of the accompaniment is featured.

Terzetto, Opus 74, for two Violins and Viola. Written in 1887, has four miniature movements, the first of which (with quiet first theme, and lively second theme of purely rhythmic character) merges suddenly, with a few modulatory chords, into the second, which the composer labeled *Larghetto.* The third, a lively scherzo, is followed by a *Finale* which is a miniature set of variations upon a single short theme.

EICHEIM, HENRY (1870–   ). Spent much time in the study of Oriental music, having lived, during 1915 and 1919, in the Far East. He was invited by Mrs. Elizabeth Coolidge to compose music for the Pittsfield Festival of 1921, and for this event he utilized as thematic material airs he had gathered during his Eastern trips. The result was a series of five Oriental sketches or studies, under the general heading of *Japanese Nocturne.* The motives used were heard by the composer in Ikao, Matsushima, Yokohama, and Tokio. The first performance on October 1, 1921, utilized a small orchestra similar to that sometimes heard in China. The work was later rescored for full orchestra. Other important works are *A Chinese Legend* (originally a ballet) and *Story of the Bell* (an Oriental impression).

ELGAR, SIR EDWARD (1857–1934). Born near Worcester, Eng. His father was an organist, violinist, and music-dealer, and also conducted choral and instrumental groups. He assisted his father at the organ, and upon the latter's retirement, took his place. Many of his earlier works had their first performances at the Worcester Festivals. Elgar is essentially a choral writer, and one of the first to break away from the German tradition so prevalent in England. He was knighted in 1904.

Dream of Gerontius. An oratorio written by commission for the Birmingham Festival, the text being taken from a poem by Cardinal Newman, tells the story of the dying Gerontius and his vision of the Guardian Angel and the throne of God.

Enigma Variations. A brilliant set, each variation of which characterizes one of Elgar's friends.

King Olaf. A cantata which is, in part, a setting of the Longfellow *King Olaf.*

Pomp and Circumstance. One of a set of six marches, and contains one of the most widely known march melodies of the world.

Pomp and Circumstance No. 1. Possesses a Trio section of rare beauty, and this is immortalized as the Chorale Finale in the Coronation Ode, used at the coronation of Edward VII, and known as "Land of Hope and Glory."

"Salut D'Amour." A popular trifle by Elgar, heard frequently and in many arrangements. Has made the name of Elgar known to thousands of amateurs by its distinctive melody.

Wand of Youth Suite No. 1. Written in 1869 when the composer was only twelve years old, and was designed to accompany an unacted play written by members of the Elgar family. Taken up many years later, and produced for the first time at a concert at Queen's Hall, December 14, 1907, it scored a huge success, partly because of its freshness and spring-like charm.

1. "Overture" (*Allegro molto*). A miniature in imposing style which presents a broad and dignified melody. 2. "Serenade" (*Andantino*). A lovely gem, the middle section of which sets forth an exquisite bit of melody. 3. "Minuet (Old Style)" (*Andante*). A dance written with such old-style manner and charm that Bach is suggested to the hearer. 4. "Sun Dance" (*Presto*). Characterized by two main themes, in their turn, brilliant and of singing delicacy. 5. "Fairy Pipers" (*Allegretto*). An idyl, the first theme of which, in thirds and accompanied by gently rocking chords, is followed by a second theme of fascinating loveliness. 6. "Slumber Scene" (*Moderato*). Characterized by great delicacy. 7. "Fairies and Giants" (*Presto*). Offers a vigorous theme played by the lower strings—the big bass drum evidently impersonates the giant.

Suite No. 2. This second "Wand of Youth" Suite, having the same origin as the first, was given to the public in its rejuvenated form at the Worcester Music Festival in 1908.

1. "March" (*Alla Marcia—Allegro moderato*). Might well have been named "March Miniature." It opens softly, the first theme in minor mode, gently clashing cymbals emphasizing the phrase accents. A con-

trasting second theme, in the major, is passed from choir to choir of the orchestra, with a curious running figure in the accompaniment. Both themes are then heard once more, with much shading from *fortissimo* to *pianissimo*. 2. "The Little Bells" (*Scherzino*) (*Allegro molto*). This piece is remarkable for its ethereal scoring. The introduction with its bells is followed by an exquisite first theme, a descending figure in broken thirds. The second section is more sustained in character, and is followed by an abrupt return to the first theme. 3. "Moths and Butterflies" (*Allegretto*.) There is here suggested a delicate contrast between the graceful, idle flutter of the butterflies, and the soft mysterious flight of the moths. Much prominence is given to the wood-wind. The first theme is given out by *pizzicato* strings, answered by the reeds. Phrases are carefully separated, giving an effect of great daintiness. 4. "The Fountain Dance" (*Allegretto comodo*). The rhythm suggested by the recurring figure in the 'cellos is of impressionistic character. The tempo varies erratically, as the wind, apparently, blows the water of the fountain. It closes *pianissimo*, with *pizzicato* and muted strings. 5. "The Tame Bear" (*Allegro moderato*). Judging from the plaintiveness of the opening melody, the Tame Bear has a heavy heart, and a heavy tread. When he growls he does so gently. Sounds of tambourine, syncopated beat of the drum, and snare drum on the off beat, suggest that it is doing a street show. 6. "The Wild Bears" (*Presto*.) This showy little piece, with

its hasty *tempo*, its tempestuous swirls of sound, its plaintive melodies, syncopated effects from the xylophone, wild rumbling grows from the basses, much use of the percussion instruments, is a climax to the second suite.

FAURÉ, GABRIEL (1845–1924). A pupil of Camille Saint-Saëns, and himself the teacher of many of the most prominent twentieth-century musicians. In 1905 he became the Director of the Paris Conservatoire. He was not only a great teacher, a composer of great distinction, but also a skilled organist. His compositions are notable for artistic and elegant simplicity of style. Fauré was a member of the Academie, and Commander of the Legion of Honor.

FLOTOW, FRIEDRICH (1812–1883). A pupil of Reicha, is noted for his facile melodies and for his keen sense of musical effectiveness.

Martha. First performance in Vienna, November 25, 1847. Had its origin in a ballet which Flotow had written for performance at the Grand Opera. There a work, *Harriet, or the Servant of Greenwich,* was needed at once, and each of its three acts was assigned to a different composer. The first act, which came to Flotow to arrange, was later developed by him into this charming opera.

Lady Harriet, maid of honor to the Queen, weary of the conventionality of court life, suggests to Nancy, her maid, that they attend the Richmond Fair—sometimes known as the "Mop Fair" from the fact that here, each year, it was the custom of servants, each of whom carried his implements of work with him, to seek new employment. Assuming the garments of servants as a disguise, and taking Lady Harriet's elderly cousin, Sir Tristan, along as a guide and protector, they allow themselves to be engaged as servants by two young farmers and accept the purse of money always given on such occasions to bind the bargain. Then when they think the joke has gone far enough, they find themselves unable to secure their release. They are taken to the home of Lionel and Plunkett. The young men arrive home and find that they have engaged very inefficient help. They try to teach the girls to spin, and there is here presented the "Spinning Song Quartet." Nancy rushes from the room, with Plunkett in pursuit. Martha—by which name Lady Harriet has allowed herself to be engaged —has attracted the attention of Lionel. She sings for him the old Irish air, "Last Rose of Summer," which so charms Lionel that he asks her to marry him. But she laughs at him. Left alone finally, the girls consult as to a way to escape. There is a tap at the window and they see Sir Tristan, who has come to rescue them. Some days later the young farmers attend the Queen and her court who have gone out to the hunt, and Lionel is amazed to see Lady Harriet there dressed as befits her rightful station. He again declares his love, but she pretends never to have seen him before. When he reminds her that, by law, she is his bound servant, she calls to the officers to arrest him. Before he is taken to prison he sends to the Queen a ring which had been given him many years before with the instruction to send it to the Queen should he ever be in trouble. The ring proves him to be the lawful heir to the Earl of Derby, and Lady Harriet now feels it proper to indulge her fondness for him. But even when she again sings to him, Lionel can only recall her cruelty. Nancy, however, has at all times been willing to accept the attentions of Plunkett. A year passes, and again the four friends attend the Richmond Fair, the renewed remembrances of which melt the cloud which has hung between Lionel and Lady Harriet, and the opera ends with all of the merrymakers singing the air of the "Last Rose of Summer," to which happy words have been joined.

FOSTER, STEPHEN (1826–1864). Born in Pittsburgh, Pa. As a child Foster spent many hours wandering along the banks of the river of his native city, listening to the Negro stevedores as they sang about their work. The old Foster home in Pittsburgh is now dedicated as a Foster Memorial, and Foster's piano is treasured in the Carnegie Institute there. Among his best-loved songs are the ever-popular "Old Folks at Home" (Suwanee River), "Old Black Joe," "Old Kentucky Home," "Come Where My Love Lies Dreaming," and "Uncle Ned." A Foster Hall has been built and dedicated to the preservation of Fosteriana by Josiah J. Lilly, on the grounds of his estate near Indianapolis. Here are assembled many original manuscripts, first editions, and other mementos of the composer. Another Foster shrine is the original of "My Old Kentucky Home" which remains as it was when Foster was a visitor in it, at Bardstown, Ky. A great amount of research regarding Foster and his music has been done by Harold Vincent Milligan, Foster's biographer.

FRANCK, César (1822–1890). Born at Liége, Belgium, by naturalization, a French musician. He stands as an intermediate, among French composers, between the classics and the modern French style. His first, private teacher was Anton Rejcha, a personal friend of Beethoven. At the Paris Conservatoire he won many prizes and distinctive honors. He was, for many years, the Organ Professor at the Conservatoire, and for 32 years, organist at the famous Church of Sainte-Clothilde.

Franck wrote in almost all fields of music, orchestra, chamber music, choral music, for organ, violin, and piano, and in the realm of opera. A devoutly religious man, many of his finest works are for the church and sacred use. A summary of his style and contributions to art would include the fact that through his influence other French composers were encouraged to develop their own personal idioms; that he was, in his writings, very polyphonic (he was often called the "French Bach"); that he used the chromatic scale greatly, and was almost incessant in modulation; that he delighted in throwing a shimmering and vague harmonic background about his melodic

thought; that he did things because they sounded well, rather than to follow rule arbitrarily; and that he used a new style of harmonic progression, what looked like chords on the printed page, being often a series of several independently and simultaneously moving melodies. He was also the teacher of many famous pupils.

Beatitudes. This, Franck's largest and most important choral work, which is a magnificent setting of a few poetic paraphrase of Christ's Sermon on the Mount, was completed in 1870, after ten years of writing. In it Franck used the device of a terrestrial chorus and a celestial chorus, and, throughout, the Voice of Christ is heard. The orchestral parts are wonderfully expressive. The monumental work closes in a grand hosanna.

Les Éolides, a symphonic poem in one movement, was inspired by a work of the same name by Leconte de Lisle, but it does not follow the literary work in its program. The chief theme is a short phrase of chromatic character used by Franck again, later, in his suite *Psyche* (a series of orchestral tone pictures on a mythical subject).

Panis Angelicus (Bread of Heaven). From a solemn Mass; is a simple song of religious emotion, and is of pure melodic type of sincere beauty. The separate song is frequently used in concert, and in devotional services under all creeds.

Prelude, Chorale, and Fugue for piano, also familiar in its orchestral transcription by Gabriel Pierné. In the *Prelude* (written in sonata form) a forecast of the fugue theme of the last movement is heard, its introduction here giving a cyclic character to the triptych. The *Chorale* (in three-part form) oscillates curiously between the keys of E-flat Minor and C Minor. A brief interlude carries the listener into the superb *Fugue*.

Symphony in D. The first performance of this symphony was in Paris, in 1889, shortly before the composer's death.

The first movement is unique in its construction in its persistent and repeated statement of the first theme, which is the same as that used by Liszt in *Les Préludes*. The symphony opens, without any preamble, with a statement of the theme (*lento*) by the 'cellos and basses in unison. The principal motif of the theme is very soon taken up by the wood-winds. The theme, in its entirety, is then repeated, in the same key, but much faster (*allegro non troppo*); and very soon again, slowly, in the key of F Minor, a third higher than the original key. It is then repeated *allegro* in the new key, thus having had four presentations. A short episodical section ushers in the lyric second theme, and the third, or conclusion theme.

The second movement (*Allegretto*) is written in the form of a scherzo, in three large parts, each of which is, in itself, a three-part form. The music gives prominence to the English horn, an instrument thought, at the time of the symphony's completion, to have no rightful place in such a work. The first section opens with a chordal introduction, which ushers in the first theme. The second theme is stated by violins. The second section opens with an agitated figure (violins). The second theme (clarinets) is flowing in character. The movement closes with a return to the very first theme, which is now combined with the other subjects.

The Finale opens with a brilliant outburst of chords, after which the first theme is heard (bassoons and 'cellos). The second theme is in the manner of a chorale, played by the brasses. There are heard in the coda, reminiscences of the themes from the first and second movements.

Variations Symphonique for Piano and Orchestra. The theme proper is preceded by an introduction (strings) and a piano solo passage of importance. The theme is given out by piano alone, then repeated by piano and orchestra. In the first variation the melody is played by violins and 'cellos while the piano adds embroideries. In the second, the piano carries the melody to the accompaniment of *pizzicato* chords from the strings. The 'cello next has the theme, and the piano a florid accompaniment. The fourth variation is by piano alone, after which the theme is passed to various instruments. Fragments from the opening piano solo passage are employed in interludes and in the brilliant coda.

Franck wrote in nearly all forms and for nearly all combinations of instruments. He made use of folk airs in some shorter works. Important works not discussed in detail include a mass for three voices; the *Redemption,* a symphonic poem for soprano solo, chorus, and orchestra; and many pieces of chamber music.

FRYSINGER, J. FRANK (1878–). Born at Hanover, Pa. Studied under Edgar Stillman Kelley, Richard Burmeister, W. Wolstenholme of London, and Ralph Kinder. He is a member of the Royal Guild of Organists (England) and F.A.G.O. His home is in York, Pa., where he is active as organist, teacher, and composer. Mr. Frysinger has had published over 200 compositions, most of which are for organ, favorite among which are "Gethsemane," "Laudate Domini," "Nocturne in G," "Scherzo Symphonique," "Toccata," and "Processional March."

GANZ, RUDOLPH (1877–). Born in Zurich, Switzerland. As a child he studied piano and 'cello; later piano with Busoni, and composition with Urban. Début with Berlin Philharmonic. Mr. Ganz was formerly conductor of the St. Louis (Mo.) Symphony and National Little Symphony Orchestras. He is now Director of the Chicago Musical College.

The Ganz compositions include very attractive pieces for piano; a *Konzertstück* for Piano and Orchestra, Op. 2 (1902) performed with many of the great symphonies; "Variations on a Theme by Brahms, for Piano; a male chorus, the "Cadets of Gascogne," from *Cyrano,* sung frequently by prominent glee-clubs; many songs, of which "Memory" is one of the popular numbers; and "What is Love?" written at the age of 17 and chosen by Humperdinck for the volume *Songs of the German People. Animal Pictures,* for both piano and orchestra, a series of 20 short pieces "for children who want to grow up and grown ups who can still be young," has called forth from A. Walter Kramer of the *Musical America* the remark that "Mr. Ganz has put more humor into these sketches than most composers give out in a lifetime. Each piece is a gem of musical invention, piquant in harmony. Mr. Ganz is a sensitive harmonist in everything he writes."

GERSHWIN, GEORGE (1898–). Brooklyn was the birthplace of Mr. Gershwin, and Brooklyn and Manhattan have been his only places of residence. His first success with composition in large forms came in his sensational *Rhapsody in Blue,* in which he uses the modern jazz rhythm as the basis of his expression of phases of American life. This work has been followed by a *Concerto in F* (resulting from a commission from the New York Symphony, 1925), and his theatrical *American in Paris.*

An American in Paris, a symphonic poem composed in Paris in 1928, tells an emotional narrative of a Yankee tourist. Although written in sonata form it is far from classic in atmosphere, and has five definite themes instead of the two customary ones. The *American* is introduced by a gay "First Walking Theme"; is amused by the French taxis (hear the Paris taxi horns in the orchestra); and goes into a café (alluring strains of *La Maxixe* from the trombones). He next passes a church and walks more slowly out of respect for the

service. The composer next per-
petrates a little pun, for the Yankee,
following the playing of the bridge
passage, as that part of the music
which connects the themes is often
called, is found to have crossed the
Seine. Here he has a conversation
with a charming young lady (hear
the sweet voice of the violin). He
thinks of home and it gives him the
"blues" and here the music breaks
into the noisy, cheery, and self-
confident "Charleston" with which
the work closes.

Jazz Concerto in F for Piano and
Orchestra was commissioned by the
Symphony Society of New York. Its
first movement is introduced by a
passage from kettledrums and other
percussion instruments, its main motif, a "Charleston" rhythm, coloring
the rest of the music. The principal
theme is given out by the bassoon.
The second section, an *andante,*
makes a strong contrast through its
broad, poetic atmosphere. The *finale*
is an orgy of rhythms and is written
in much the manner of a rondo.

Rhapsody in Blue, a jazz symphonic poem, is naïve and original
in all its elements. It opens on a long
portamento of the clarinet which
leads into a suave melody full of
twists and syncopations. The piano
enters with a quiet figure, then proceeds to elaborate it in cadenza-like
manner. A second, and more strident
and insistent figure enters, followed
by a third of crude and vital rhythm.
The agitation is then relieved by a
long solo passage from the piano. A
contrasting air of languishing charm,
an *agitato* passage, and a grandiose
coda bring the work to a close.

Second Rhapsody for piano and
orchestra was originally called
"Rhapsody in Rivets" and takes for
its basic theme a rhythmic motif suggestive of the "eternal tattoo" of skyscraper construction in the streets of
New York. This music is entirely
orchestral, the piano being used
merely as an important obbligato instrument.

GLINKA, MICHAEL (See "National
Characteristics in Russian Art Music," p. 19).

GILBERT AND SULLIVAN (See
Sullivan).

GLUCK, CHRISTOPH WILLIBALD
(1714–1787). For a time Court Musician to Maria Theresa. He made
continued efforts to reform opera and
bring about in it a closer relationship
between the text and the music. His
first successful opera, *Orpheus and
Eurydice,* and a later, *Alceste,* were
written with this in mind. In Paris
he had, as his royal patron, Marie
Antoinette, who had been his pupil
in her youth in Vienna.

Felix Mottl, a distinguished conductor, has arranged two important
orchestral suites of airs from Gluck's
operas.

GODARD, BENJAMIN (1849–1895).
A splendid viola player, and wrote
and arranged for orchestra.

"Berceuse" from *Jocelyn* (first performance in Brussels, 1888). A tuneful air of an exceptionally appealing
character sung by Jocelyn, the principal character, at the opening of Act
II.

GOLDMARK, KARL (1830–1915). A Hungarian composer whose works include the *Sakuntala* and *Springtime* Overtures, the opera *Queen of Sheba,* and a brilliant violin concerto. His *Rustic Wedding Suite* (sometimes spoken of as a symphony) aroused considerable interest, and the composer was called to many cities to conduct it. So often did this happen that, it is related, when he came one day to a certain city in which he was to conduct it that night, and arrived at his hotel with the orchestral parts of the cherished *Suite* under his arm, he registered as "Karl Goldmark and Suite."

Rustic Wedding Suite. First performance, March 5, 1876 (in Vienna); first performance in America by the Philharmonic Society of New York, January 1877, with Theodore Thomas conducting. It is in five movements.

1. "Wedding March." This is written in the form of a theme with twelve free variations and Finale, the first presentation of the theme being played by the 'cellos and basses, and suggesting, in its general character, the well-known "Adeste Fidelis." In the Finale the melody is first heard played by the entire orchestra, full strength, after which the instruments drop out, one by one, until at last the march in its original form is heard softly as though from a great distance. 2. "Bridal Song." A dainty bit of music, suggesting the song of the bride's friends. 3. "Serenade." A short prelude introduces a charming melody by two oboes, later developed by other instruments of the orchestra. 4. "In the Garden." This love duet

opens with a melody for clarinet (representing a soprano voice). A reply is made by the 'cellos and horns. 5. Finale—Dance. This jolly rustic dance is abruptly interrupted by a return of the clarinet melody from the preceding movement.

GOUNOD, CHARLES (1818–1893). Born in Paris; a graduate of the Paris Conservatoire and a winner of the Prix de Rome. Gounod excelled in writing for the voice, although his compositions include many works for orchestra. As a writer of orchestral accompaniment—as in his opera scores—Gounod has seldom been excelled.

"Ave Maria" (Bach-Gounod) (See Bach, p. 258).

Faust. Gounod wrote nine operas. *Faust,* a tragic work based upon the drama of Goethe, is only one of some 40 operas and operettas which bear this name.

Important characters are Faust, a philosopher; Mephistopheles, the evil one; Valentine, brother of Marguerite, the heroine; Siebel, a student; Wagner (Brander), another student; and Martha, Marguerite's elderly companion and servant. The scene lies in a German village of the eighteenth century.

A crowd has gathered in the village for the annual fair. The different groups are singing and visiting when Mephistopheles appears, the first exhibition of his mysterious power being the bringing forth of wine from the sign over the village inn. In this he toasts Marguerite, an act which enrages Valentine who offers to fight the stranger. The duel does not take place, however, and soon the crowd has forgotten the incident. Marguerite, who has been at church, passes on her way home, and is accosted by Faust, whose offers of attention she refuses. The next scene shows her simple doorstep upon which there lies the morning offering of flowers from Siebel and a casket of jewels which Faust—at the advice of Mephistopheles—has placed beside it. Tempted by the gems, Marguerite is won to Faust. Later, when she has been betrayed and deserted, Siebel remains faithful. She is denied the comforts of the church, but comes to pray before its doors at the moment when the troops return victorious, singing the famous "Soldiers' Chorus." Mephistopheles insults Marguerite by singing to her a horrible serenade, and in defending her honor, Valentine is mortally wounded. The opera ends with an impressive scene in the prison cell into which Marguerite has been cast for the murder of her child. Here Faust visits her, in deep contrition, while Marguerite, seeing the Evil One in the background, calls upon Heaven for protection. Angels appear and bear her soul away.

Aside from the "Soldiers' Chorus," the most popular single numbers in *Faust* are "Even Bravest Heart" (Valentine), "Flower Song" (Siebel), and "She Opens Now the Window" (Marguerite and Faust).

Funeral March of a Marionette. A humorous bit of story-telling music, in spite of its title, this *Funeral March* was improvised by Gounod while on a visit to London as a part of a "Suite Burlesque" for piano

which he expected to write. He never completed the Suite, but did set down the *March,* which is familiar as a light and interesting piece for orchestra.

The Redemption. A sacred work written in 1882, for the music festival at Birmingham, and dedicated to Queen Victoria, was always spoken of by Gounod as "the work of my life." One of its most devotional choruses is that which occurs as a finale to the second part, "Unfold, Ye Portals," a brilliant description of the ascension of the Saviour.

Romeo and Juliet. An operatic setting of the romantic tragedy of Shakespeare.

GRAINGER, PERCY ALDRIDGE (1882–   ). Born in Brighton, Australia, Grainger's first musical instruction was taken from his mother, who remained, to the end of her life, his main artistic influence. Later he went to Frankfurt-am-Main, Germany, where he was a student at the Hoch Conservatory. Still later he studied with Busoni. In 1902 Grainger made his concert début in London. In 1907 he was selected by Grieg to play the latter's *Concerto in A,* with the composer conducting, at the Leeds Music Festival. After the sudden death of Grieg, Mr. Grainger played as planned, with Sir Charles Villiers Stanford conducting. Greatly interested in all forms of folk art, Grainger has collected more than 500 records of folk song in Australia, the South Seas, Denmark, and England. Since 1915, he has considered himself a resident of the United States, which country he served in the World War as an enlisted soldier and instructor in Army music schools.

In his writings Grainger emphasizes melody as the root of all beauty in music, and in his compositions has created or developed many unusual musical features. He himself divides his work into two main divisions—folk-music settings and art music. In the first he wishes to be known as the servant of folk art. In his art music he never consciously uses any folk-music themes. Innovations set going by Grainger include a revival of the use of *passacaglia* form (see notes on "Green Bushes"), developments of large chamber-music groups, wordless choral writing (see notes on "Marching Song of Democracy"), elastic scoring, "Nordic English" in the markings in his music, and beatless music.

Grainger's name is a familiar one wherever music is played and studied. In addition to many large works, he has written scores of short and attractive compositions, several of which are perennial favorites.

Blithe Bells. This is, as Grainger expresses it, a free "ramble" by him on Bach's aria from one of the Secular Cantatas, the words of which begin, "Sheep may graze in safety when a goodly shepherd watches o'er them." The music is colored by the thought that Bach, in writing the melody in thirds that opens and closes the number may have aimed at giving a hint of the sound of sheep bells. The Grainger arrangement is written for 15 single instruments or for two pianos with orchestra.

Country Gardens. This popular number is also known as "Handker-chief Dance," as it was a custom of the old-time Morris Dancers to carry fluttering handkerchiefs as they danced. The melody of *Country Gardens* (which is heard frequently as a piano piece, as well as in the orchestral and band transcription) is made up of phrases from a very old Morris Dance tune to be found in the famous collection of Cecil Sharp of England. *Country Gardens* was first a sketch for room music—as were many other of his numbers most familiar in the piano setting—and later transcribed for piano. By "room music" Mr. Grainger means music for groups of musicians intended for performance in a large room or small hall. The work is an exhilarating combination of a contagious rhythm, a lilting melody, and tuneful harmonies.

English Dance. One of Mr. Grainger's contributions to art music, as he has himself classified his work, is not based upon folk music in any way, but is rather expressive of the vivacity and warmth of English music in general. It is one of Mr. Grainger's largest works, and is written for organ and orchestra.

Green Bushes. This is a *passa-caglia* on an old English folk song, and is scored for from 20 to 22 instruments (which may include two pianos). By many, this (and other of the Grainger folk settings) are incorrectly spoken of as being *variations* on the original airs. The *passacaglia* form comes from an early Italian dance similar to the *chaconne,* and takes its name from *pasar* (to walk) and *calle* (a street), therefore suggesting a tune played by itinerant musicians. It is usually a short tune of two, four, or eight measures. In a *variation* the repetitions of the given melody may be in either major or minor key, in altered tempo, or varied in any other way which the composer may desire. In a *passacaglia* the tune is always repeated but never varied, there are no changes in the mood, and no deviations from strict rhythm. Says Mr. Grainger, "This is a type of song come to us from the time when *sung* melodies, rather than instrumental music, held countryside dancers together." So, in his development of *Green Bushes* there are no pauses between repetitions of the melody, no changes of key or speed within the theme proper. The variety is provided by the voices and additions which are woven about the theme. This is an elaborate and brilliant work. It is interesting to note that the original melody was sung in the *mixolydian* mode, which corresponds to our major scale with a flat seventh tone (C D E F G A B-flat C). The use of this mode creates a quaint atmosphere in the music.

Handel in the Strand. A cheerful clog dance for piano and 2 or 3 strings or for massed pianos and string orchestra (also arranged for other combinations of instruments) which suggest a general hilarity. In the orchestral versions each instrument typifies a dancer and takes its turn in stepping into the dance.

Hill Songs 1 and 2. These compositions, listed by Mr. Grainger among his three largest works, arose out of thoughts about and longings for the wildness of hill countries, hill peoples, and hill music—such as that of the Scottish Highlands, the Hima-layas, the bagpipes, and so on. The writings of these followed upon experiments in writing "beatless music" and so here we find frequent example of lack of standard duration of beats, and moments in which the irregular rhythmic impulses of various parts occur independently of each other and at different moments.

Irish Tune from County Derry. A setting by Mr. Grainger (for piano, chorus, band, string-orchestra, or full orchestra) of one of the most exquisite melodies ever sung on Irish soil. It was collected by Miss Jane Ross, without title or text, but several titles have later been given to the tune, among them being "Farewell to Cucullain," and "Londonderry Air." Under the first title, Alfred Percival Graves wrote a poem to the air, in the form of a lament for an early Irish chieftain, and it is this title which Fritz Kreisler uses in his transcription for violin. The title of "Londonderry Air" comes about as the melody is found in its original state in the county of Londonderry in the north of Ireland, although it may first have been an English ballad tune transplanted to Ireland. It is also well known in its connection with the appealing words of the song "Danny Boy" by Weatherly; and in the song "Would God I Were the Tender Apple Blossom" by Fisher.

Jutish Medley. A setting of quaint airs recorded by Evald Tang Kristensen and Mr. Grainger while collecting folk songs in Danish Jutland. In it are preserved characteristics of the folk airs of the ancient Jutes, a powerful people of Northern Germany in the fifth century.

Lord Peter's Stable Boy. This was one of the first works done by Mr. Grainger after the tragic death of his mother, in April 1922. He and his mother had delighted, for years, to read aloud together from Danish folk tales, one of their favorites being the rhymed tale of "Lord Peter's Stable Boy," who is, in reality, "Little Kirsten," a loyal subject who dons male attire that she may serve at the castle. In connection with the tale, Grainger has used, in his setting, a ringing melody which he heard sung, while in Denmark, by a sturdy coppersmith. In his setting of this, for chamber music or orchestra, Mr. Grainger has made use of what he calls "elastic scoring," by which term the composer says he means that "as long as a satisfactory balance of tone is preserved, I do not care whether one of my 'elastically scored' pieces is played by 4 or 40 or 400 players, or any number in between."

Marching Song of Democracy. This is a buoyant composition expressing the on-march of optimistic democracy. It is in turn, heroic, exultant, energetic, and full of out-of-door spirit. The vocal parts are not sung to words, but to "wordless syllables" or "nonsense syllables," such as children sometimes use in their thoughtless singing. The composer explains his use of these by saying that he did not wish to pin the music down at each moment to such precise expression as words inevitably convey. The constantly changing rhythms are the result of experiment in beatless rhythm.

Molly on the Shore. The alluring rhythms and ever-fluent melody of *Molly on the Shore* (which is heard with equal frequency for string quartet—its original form—and as piano solo) have done much to establish the great popularity of the Grainger name.

Scotch Strathspey and Reel. The *strathspey* is a Scotch dance allied to the reel, which takes its name from the *strath* or valley of Spey, in the north of Scotland. Here the dance was formerly very popular. It abounds in many jerky motions (indicated in the music by dotted notes which produce the so-called "Scotch snap.") The reel is a rather more gliding dance. In Grainger's setting of some famous airs of the type, he has combined, in one part of his composition, seven authentic melodies from Great Britain, all of them of Celtic origin, and one at least, a sea chanty—all of them sounded simultaneously. The effect is that of a friendly babble of joyous voices.

Shepherd's Hey. This is a clever setting of an old English *hey* or country dance, of the thirteenth century. Some authorities say that the *hey* referred to the hedges, and that the dance was therefore longwise, as are hedge-rows. The melody here set forth is one still heard in many parts of England, and one which Cecil Sharp collected in at least four varying versions from as many country fiddlers. Grainger has used these variants effectively in his setting, which, though most familiar as a piano solo, was first written by him for 12 single instruments; then, somewhat later, for full orchestra.

Spoon River. This is an effective setting of an old fiddle-tune, or

American folk dance. It was heard, in its original form, at a country dance at Bradford, Illinois, in 1857, by a Captain Charles H. Robinson. When, in 1914, Edgar Lee Masters' *Spoon River Anthology* appeared, Captain Robinson, then nearly 90 years old, was struck by the likeness of the two titles. So he sent his manuscript of the old fiddle-tune to Masters, who, in turn, passed it on to Mr. Grainger. The melody is archaic in character, being so typically Scottish, or English, that it is thought to have been brought to this country by early immigrants from the Old World, and to have been preserved in its original style by descendants of those early settlers still to be met with in isolated sections of the Southern mountains. Two strains of a sturdy persistence are the foundations upon which the Grainger version rests. Around these Mr. Grainger has woven wistful melodies and harmonies of his own.

To a Nordic Princess. In this work, important not only as a masterly composition reflecting the pure style of the Nordic folk music, but also attractive from its sentimental associations, Grainger has massed a bewildering array of beautiful melody, gorgeous harmony, and rhythm. The work was composed for and conducted by him on his wedding night, at the Hollywood Bowl, as a tribute to his bride. This is an example of a piece that begins as chamber music (17 single instruments) and gradually, by the addition of more and more single instruments, is tonally augmented until the full orchestra is employed.

Tribute to Foster. Although the most familiar of the Grainger writings are instrumental, it is in his choral works that the composer takes his greatest pleasure. "One of my earliest impressions," says Mr. Grainger, "is that of my mother singing me to sleep with Stephen Foster's entrancing ditty 'Camptown Races' (or 'Doodah'), in which the words run:

'Camptown ladies sing this song:
    Doodah!
De Camptown race-track five miles
    long, Oh Doodah day!
I came down dah wid my hat cav'd
    in, Doodah! Doodah!
I go back home wid a pocket full o'
    tin, Oh, Doodah day!'

"In my *Tribute to Foster* I have wanted to give musical expression to these Australian memories and to my love and reverence for this exquisite American genius. . . . Thinking as I do of 'Camptown Races,' both as a dance song and as a lullaby, I have treated it in both styles in this composition."

Mr. Grainger has given Foster's tune first in its own originally lively manner, using the Foster words; then has followed this by a lullaby section mirroring a mood of memory of his mother's singing, in which the Foster tune is treated freely, and in which the solo voices are accompanied by "musical glasses" played by the chorus, bowed metal marimba, and other instruments. The original lively tempo is then resumed, and the piece ends with a "tail-piece" or coda which suggests forcibly a plantation teeming with rural dance music. Different airs seem to be emerging from the various cabins, until at last they lapse into silence.

The Warriors. Written in London and New York, between the years 1913 and 1916. Music to an imaginary ballet, but suggests no definite program, other than that the ghosts of male and female warriors of all times and places are supposed to be dancing. It is, in reality, an orgy of warlike dances, with interludes both amorous and festive in character. The original scoring is a brilliant one, for orchestra and three pianos.

GRANADOS, ENRIQUE (1869–1916). A native of Catalonia, Spain. He went down with the *Lusitania* while returning to the Old World after having conducted the first performance of *Goyescas* in America. *Goyescas*—the first Spanish opera to be given here in the Spanish language —is based upon three episodes which might have occurred during the lifetime of the famous painter Goya, who lived in Madrid during the early part of the nineteenth century. The Duchess of Alba (whose portrait by Goya is in the Hispanic Museum of New York) is the heroine of the action.

Suite of Five Spanish Dances. This typically Spanish music is not always based entirely upon real folk melodies, but their characteristics are employed.

1. "Villanesca." Picturesque music in which prominence is given to harp, celesta, and percussion instruments. 2. "Andantino." Opens with a *glissando* from the harp. It is characterized by crisp rhythms, and a continuous folk-style figure in the bass.

3. "El Pelele." Refers to a favorite amusement at Spanish peasant gatherings, when *el pelele* (the straw man) is tossed up in a blanket. 4. "Molto Andante." A mournful piece, with much use made of drums and cymbals. The drum beat falls upon the half-beat of each measure, and although the movement rises to an effective climax, it ends very quietly. 5. "Allegretto" (quasi moderato) brings the suite to a sprightly close.

GRIEG, EDVARD (1843–1907). Born in Bergen, Norway, and died in the same city. He is famed not only as a composer, but also as a patriot whose life was spent in making known to the world the beauties of the folk music of his native land. His music may be divided into three parts: that which uses Norwegian folk music as thematic material; that which is highly colored by folk music characteristics but which is entirely original; and that part made up of Grieg's larger art works. These include the *Piano Concerto in A Minor,* the sonatas for violin and piano, and a string quartet. Although he wrote more than 130 songs, he is best known as a composer for piano. At 30, Grieg was pensioned for life by his government so that he might give his whole time to composition. Many months of each year were spent at Troldhaugen, where, not far from his house, he wrote in a little Music House, now preserved by the community as a memorial to him.

External characteristics of his style are the strong influence wielded upon his works by old Gregorian modes, and the highly frequent use of unusual downward melodic progressions.

Ballade in G Minor. A set of variations, which constantly increase in difficulty and brilliance, written upon a quiet and tender little air of questioning mood.

"Bell Ringing." One of the most unusual of all the sixty-six *Lyrical Pieces* in which Grieg imitated the ringing of the church bells as they had sounded to him during a summer's vacation spent in a little village in Denmark. It is filled with the dissonances suggested by the overtones heard from the bells. The late Anton Seidl arranged it for orchestra.

Elegiac Melodies. Transcriptions for string orchestra by the composer of two of his own well-loved songs, the first of which, "Spring Tide," becomes "The Last Spring"; and the other, "The Wounded Heart," becomes "Heart Wounds."

"I Love Thee," written as a song setting to verses of Hans Christian Andersen, was sent as a love letter to his fiancée, Nina Hagerup, later his wife. Some time later Grieg made a piano version of the song which carries both melody and accompaniment.

"Norwegian Bridal Procession." The second of three piano numbers which constitute the suite *From the Life of the People,* tells, in music, of one of the picturesque customs of Norway. There, especially in the provinces, it is still the custom for the wedding party and the guests to go to church in a procession, either by boat, or on foot. If on foot, the procession is usually headed by a group of village musicians. In Grieg's music the rhythm of the drum is first heard, then soft strains of the melody, which is repeated many times. As the procession nears, both sound out more clearly. The middle section is full and clear, as though the wedding party might be passing directly by. Then it grows softer and softer, as if heard from a distance.

Peer Gynt Suite No. 1. The *Peer Gynt Suites,* of which there are two, are made up of incidental pieces written, at the request of Ibsen, for the latter's drama, *Peer Gynt.* The story, briefly, is that of Peer, the ne'er-do-well, who dreams of future glory for himself, and wanders over the earth, deserting all who love him. Åse, his mother, and Solvejg, his sweetheart, still believe in him, and their faith at last accomplishes his salvation.

1. "Morning Mood." Opens the first Suite and conveys the suggestion of the loveliness of the morning light as seen by Peer from a mountain top. 2. "Åse's Death." A brief and somber number, depicting the melancholy life of the forsaken mother, as well as her death. 3. "Anitra's Dance." A highly contrasting work, used in the drama at the point where Peer is welcomed to the tents of the desert folk and entertained by the sheik's daughter, is entirely Oriental in character, especially in its purposely monotonous bass. 4. "In the Hall of the Mountain King." Tells of Peer's adventure in the mountain cave to which he has gone to woo the daughter of the King of the Mountains. Here he is tormented and tortured by the imps.

Peer Gynt Suite No. 2. The extreme popularity of the first *Suite* led Grieg to arrange a second, among which are the following numbers: "Arabian Dance." Thoroughly Oriental in its melody, its rhythm, and in the instrumentation which is used in the orchestral version. The use of whole-tone and Oriental scales lend atmosphere, and the effective anticlimax, brings to prominence the persistent Arabian drums. "Solvejg's Song." Sometimes called the "Sunshine Song," as in it Solvejg sings of her faith that her lover will again return to her. "Cradle Song." Also sung by Solvejg, this is really Peer's death-song. It is of unusual construction in that its first part is made up of three-measure sections, two of which are sung, while the third, accompaniment only, completes the phrase.

Sigurd Jorsalfar. Incidental music written by Grieg for Bjornson's *Sigurd, the Crusader,* completed in 1872, and within eight days. The drama tells of Sigurd, a Norwegian hero of the Middle Ages, who led a Crusade to Palestine in the year 1152. Some time after its composition, Grieg assembled three of the pieces of incidental music and wrote them out as piano solos, and also in an effective orchestral version. These are "Overture," "Intermezzo: Borghild's Dream," and "Triumphal March."

"To Spring," one of the most familiar of the *Lyrical Pieces,* tells a story of life along the fjords. There, each spring, it is the custom to take the cattle to the higher mountain slopes where they can find food more readily. As there are no fenced fields, each flock must be watched by a herd-girl, and each of the animals wears a bell. The first measures of "To Spring" suggest the tinkling of the little bells, after which is heard the herd-girl's song.

Wedding Day at Troldhaugen. Tells in music of the traditional "race for the bride," as often carried out, on horseback, by enthusiastic friends of the bridegroom in Troldhaugen. Following this is a brief and quietly mysterious bit of music, said to suggest the solemnity of the church service.

GRIFFES, CHARLES T. (1884–1920). A native of Elmira, N. Y. He studied in Berlin, a pupil of Humperdinck. After teaching for a time in Berlin, he returned to America, where he was, until his death, a teacher at the Hackley School for Boys at Tarrytown, N. Y. He became interested in tribal music of the American Indian, and wrote a suite for strings in which he utilized Indian thematic material. He also wrote many distinguished works for orchestra, smaller instrumental groups, for the voice, and for the piano. "The White Peacock" for piano is one of his best-known works.

GRUENBERG, LOUIS (1884–). Born in Russia, he was brought to America when only two years old, and is always considered as an American. Studied piano in Europe, a pupil of Busoni. He was a prize-winner in composition of original works both in Berlin and America, having won, in New York, the Flagler Prize for the writing of a symphonic poem, *Hill of Dreams.* His best-known work is the music which he wrote to

O'Neill's play, *Emperor Jones,* which had its first performance at the Metropolitan Opera House, New York City, with Lawrence Tibbett in the principal rôle.

Emperor Jones. Tells the story of Brutus Jones, an ex-Pullman porter and fugitive from justice in the United States, who has reigned for two years over the savages in a section of the West Indies. Smithers, an old cockney trader, learns that the natives are to revolt, and informs Jones so that the latter may escape through the woods to the coast in an effort to reach a French gunboat. Jones tells Smithers of the silver bullet he has made to awe the natives, the only bullet that can kill him. He has five other shots in his revolver as he leaves. Beating of distant tom-toms tells him that the uprising has begun. When Jones reaches the edge of the forest he finds that the food he had cached there has disappeared. He becomes a prey to ghostly alarms as the tom-toms din relentlessly in his ears. He penetrates deeper into the forest, and, exhausted and overwhelmed by the blackness of the woods, is the victim of fearful visions. In these he again kills the man for whose murder he fled the States, thus shooting one of his precious bullets. Again he thinks himself taken to the chain-gang, and kills the guard. He sees himself on the auction block of old slavery days and shoots again. Finally all of his ammunition is gone save the magic silver bullet. He stumbles on, with the natives closing in upon him and beating the tom-toms constantly. A voodoo appears and all but hypnotizes him. At last,

worn beyond endurance, he cheats his pursuers by shooting himself with the silver bullet. The cumulative force of the music is tremendous. (See "Behind the Scenes with Lawrence Tibbett," p. 43; "The Negro and His Song" by Harry T. Burleigh, p. 186; and "Music the Greatest Joy" by Louis Gruenberg, p. 238.)

GUION, David W. (1895–   ). Born in Ballinger, Texas. A student with Leopold Godowsky at the Royal Conservatory at Vienna, he has done much to bring to the public ear the charms of American folk music, as found in the southwestern part of the country. Although he has written many works in the conventional forms, nothing he has done is so individual as his splendid treatment of the airs of such folk songs as "Arkansaw Traveler," and "Turkey in the Straw." His intimate musical treatment of the words of the "Home on the Range" has resulted in a ballad which is widely sung. His sacred song, "Prayer," is deeply touching.

HADLEY, Henry (1871–   ). An American orchestral conductor and composer, has made a careful study of the music of the Orient, and this study is reflected in his several suites. He has written four symphonies, many choral works, and operas.

HALÉVY, Jacques François (1799–1862). Real surname Levy. Had his training at the Paris Conservatoire, and won the Prix de Rome. From 1827 he taught at the Conservatoire and for over fifteen years was also chorus-master at the Opéra. He was a member of the Legion of Honor and secretary of its fine-arts section. His music is full of strong emotional contrast, remarkable musical characterization of personages, and displays high scholarship. His striking *La Juive* (The Jewess) was the last opera in which Caruso appeared before his fatal illness.

La Juive (See p. 51).

HANDEL, GEORG FRIEDRICH (1685–1759). Born at Halle, in Saxony. Much of Handel's study was done in Germany, but he also spent much time in Italy, and his writings reflect the lyric vocal quality of much Italian music. The latter part of his life was spent in England, where his royal patron, George I, was the same noble music-lover whom he had served in Hanover before fortune brought George to England to reign. The story of the Handel "Water Music," composed as a peace offering to the patron whom he had deserted in an earlier day, and which won him full forgiveness and a royal income, is an example of Handel's cleverness and diplomacy. He died in England and is buried in Westminster Abbey.

"Harmonious Blacksmith." This set of variations, written as one of the "Princess' Lessons," was originally for harpsichord.

Judas Maccabæus. This oratorio, written five years after the completion of the Messiah, uses as its subject the impressive Biblical story of Judas Maccabæus, the famous Jewish warrior. The first performance was in April 1746, and incidentally served to honor the victorious troops which were just then returning from the battle of Culloden in Scotland. The most familiar aria in the work is "Sound an Alarm," which Judas Maccabæus (baritone) sings to fire anew the courage of the Israelites as they go out to meet their enemy. This is sung in Part II of the Oratorio. In Part III, a messenger arrives bringing tidings of the success of the army, and those who have remained at home go out to meet Judas Maccabæus and his host, singing "See the Conquering Hero Comes."

"Largo." A popular melody by Handel, and played by many solo instruments and ensembles, was originally a tenor aria in the opera *Xerxes,* where it is known as the "Song of the Plane Tree."

Messiah. This oratorio, written in the space of 24 days, owes much to direct inspiration, and to the devout nature of the composer. It is in three parts, the first of which has to do with the longing of the world for the Messiah, and prophecies concerning Him. The second part tells of Christ's life and death; and the third part speaks of faith in Christ and in immortality.

It is written for chorus, *soli,* and orchestral accompaniment. This accompaniment is frequently taken over entirely by organ. It abounds in simple but masterly choruses; in others into which fugal development has been interwoven; in tender recitatives and impressive solos; and incomparable instrumental interludes. Among the most familiar numbers are the florid bass aria, "Who Do the Nations So Furiously Rage Together"; "He Shall Feed His Flock" (contralto) and "Come Unto Me" (soprano); "I Know that My Redeemer Liveth" (soprano); the chorus, "Surely He Hath Borne Our Griefs"; and the majestic "Hallelujah Chorus." (See p. 8.)

The Pastoral Symphony. An orchestral prelude to the chorus, "Glory to God in the Highest," it immediately precedes the soprano recitative, "There Were Shepherds Abiding in the Field," and is a tone picture of the Nativity. In it Handel has used an old Calabrian melody which he had heard played by the *Pifferari*—shepherd pipers—whose custom it was to throng the streets of Rome during the season of the Nativity, offering their musical homage to the festive season. At first the Symphony consisted of only a strain of this air, 11 measures in length, and called by Handel for the Italian shepherds, "Pifa." Later he added a second part on a loose bit of paper and fastened it to the original score. It is scored for strings only.

After 1784, performances of the *Messiah* were regularly given in Westminster Abbey, these on a huge scale with an orchestra and chorus of over 500 voices.

Saul. An oratorio dating from 1738. It follows the Biblical story of David and Saul. It is during the third scene, in which David is hearing, from the Amalekite, of the death of Saul and Jonathan (2 Sam. i. 15), that there is heard the celebrated "Dead March."

HANSON, HOWARD (1896–). One of the best known of America's contemporary composers, born at Wahoo, Neb. His father and mother of Swedish nationality, and both musical, his mother her son's first teacher. Dr. Hanson expresses gratitude for wise musical guidance to teachers in the Swedish Luther College of Wahoo, where he studied first piano, then 'cello, for eight years. A graduate of Northwestern University (where he studied composition under Lutkin and Oldberg) and the Institute of Musical Art in New York, a student with Dr. Percy Goetschius. At the age of nineteen, appointed Professor of theory and composition in the College of the Pacific, San Jose, California, and two years later made Dean of the Conservatory. A year later he was the winner of the Prix de Rome in composition. The Prix de Rome Fellowship was won with the symphonic poem *Before the Dawn* and a Prelude and Ballet. Three years later he became the Director of the Eastman School of Music at Rochester, New York. In addition to his executive work, and the conducting of classes in composition, Dr. Hanson has lent aid of a major character to the cause of American music education and American creative music. His American Music Festivals, held at Rochester, are outstanding events. Dr. Hanson has conducted many orchestral concerts in America and Europe, his latest task as international music educator being a mission accepted from the Oberlander Trust of the Carl Schurz Foundation, which sent him in January, 1933 to Germany and Austria to conduct the more important orchestras there in programs of American music. His compositions include, besides his earlier works,

Symphonic Rhapsody (1918), *California Forest Play of 1920*, and his prize works; two symphonies, four symphonic poems, a concerto for organ and orchestra, several widely used pieces of choral and chamber music, and a three-act opera *Merrymount*.

Lament of Beowulf. For mixed chorus and full orchestra, written in 1925. First performance at the Ann Arbor (Mich.) Festival in 1926. Received with enthusiasm by critics and music lovers in both Old and New Worlds. The music is based upon the latter portion of the old Anglo-Saxon epic. The mythical hero defended and delivered the Danish kingdom from the bog-monster, Grendel, and his ferocious mother. In it are preserved various legends of prehistoric times, some of which were also related in early songs. Fifty years after the extermination of the bog-monster and his mother, who had been wont to devour the guest in the great chieftain's hall, Beowulf, who has meanwhile inherited the kingdom, is again called upon to defend his people from a fiery dragon. He is again victorious, but dies from wounds suffered in the contest. His funeral pyre is erected upon a high bank near the seaside, and there, as the flames begin to roar, are sung the death-chant and the wailing songs of his friends. It is this last part of the story which Dr. Hanson has used. A short orchestral introduction ushers in the voices. The male chorus opens its refrain which is soon taken up by the women's chorus and later by the whole chorus and the orchestra, as the heroic themes are given out and

developed. That portion in which the wife and her maidens bewail their lot is intricately fashioned harmonically. A majestic climax occurs at the passage praising the hero, and the final plaintively intoned "Ah" of the eulogy, taken first by male voices and then by the women's choir and at last fading away into a doleful humming sound, is very imposing.

Merrymount. A three-act opera on a libretto by Richard Stokes, written as a commission from the Metropolitan Opera House of New York City. It has to do with an historic episode of the early days of the New England settlements, and stresses differing features of the story from those emphasized in the opera of the same name by Rossetter Gleason Cole.

Dr. Hanson's opera is decidedly lyric. The interest is centered on various arias and choruses which contain within themselves a definite and complete musical form such as is generally characteristic of the Italian opera. The story tells of the gradual change of character of the pastor of the Puritan flock from a stern ascetic to a half-mad fanatic. In the end, due to the violence of his emotions, he changes from a minister of God to a self-constituted bondsman of Satan. The harmonic technique used in depicting this process of character change attempts to work out in tone the basic underlying motives and emotions within the mind of the character himself. The musical background for the minister, therefore, changes gradually according to the change within the man's own nature. The character of the heroine on the other hand, which undergoes little fundamental change beyond the strengthening of her spirit through grief and struggle is revealed by a more constant type of harmonic and thematic material. The use of the chorus by Dr. Hanson might be said to bear a closer relation to the Greek idea than to the usual operatic conception. The opera also includes short Preludes to the first and second acts; a ballet in the third scene of the second act; and an orchestral interlude between the third and fourth scenes of the second act in which voices are employed for orchestral color.

Nordic Symphony. The earlier of Dr. Hanson's large works, it had its first performance by the orchestra of the Augusteo in Rome. There are three movements. Constructed in free classical form, the symphony is cyclical, the first movement containing the material upon which the entire symphony is based. This movement, strongly Nordic in character, sings of the solemnity, austerity, and grandeur of the North. The second movement, which is inscribed "To my Mother," is in marked contrast, peaceful in character, with the feeling of wistful sadness. The third movement, inscribed "To my Father," is rugged and fiery in spirit, and it is in this movement that the composer pays tribute to his love for the folk songs of Sweden, in several themes of folk-like character, one of which is an actual folk air.

The Finale, which follows the third movement without pause, begins with a reiteration of the opening theme of the symphony, and serves as a coda for the entire work.

Romantic Symphony. Requested by Dr. Sergei Koussevitzky for inclusion in the programs of the Boston Symphony's 50th anniversary year, and heard shortly after that in Rome. A work in which the composer aimed to write a work young in spirit, lyrical and romantic in temperament, and simple and direct in expression, in acknowledged contrast to the rather harsh type of modern realism. The work is in three movements.

HAYDN, JOSEPH (1732–1809). (See also "Mozart, Haydn, Beethoven: the Classic Symphony.") Born in Rohrau, Austria. Both his father and mother were musical. Haydn's earliest music lessons were given him by a relative, after which he was admitted to the boys' choir and choir school of Saint Stephen's in Vienna. The most important of his active years as an artist were spent in the service of Prince Esterhazy, who was his patron for about 30 years. On January 31, 1932, the present Prince Esterhazy had Haydn's remains reinterred in a mausoleum built especially to receive them, on the family estate at Eisenstadt, near Vienna.

The Clock Symphony. One of six symphonies which Haydn prepared on his second visit to London, derives its name from its second, or slow movement which, played *andante,* contains a lovely melody against a background that resembles, in its rhythm, the ticking of a huge clock. This descriptive clock-like background is given first to the bassoons and strings, and later to the flutes. The final impression of the symphony is that of a very delicate and exquisite composition, dainty and precise.

Creation. Haydn wrote nearly 1500 compositions, among them the two oratorios, *Creation* and *The Seasons,* 14 masses, and 30 motets. He wrote the oratorios following a visit to London in 1794, where he had heard some of the oratorios of Handel, these impressing him so greatly that he wrote his own great works in this form under the influence of the memory of that visit. It is said that he questioned a London conductor as to just how he should go about it, and that the answer he received was a gesture toward the Bible and the remark: "There! Take that, and begin at the beginning." This advice he followed literally in the *Creation.* It was planned to give the work its first performance in London on March 28, 1800. The score finally reached London on the 22nd of the month, with only six days left in which to copy out all the 120 odd parts. This the copyists did, and being complimented on their speed, one of them replied that "it was not the first time that the Creation had been accomplished in six days!" Most familiar to the general public is the baritone aria "Roaming in Foaming Billows," in which the highly descriptive accompaniment supplements the words of the text to a marvelous degree.

Emperor Quartet for Strings. Carries its unusual name because of the fact that one of its most important movements, the "Theme with Variations," is based upon the air of the Austrian national hymn which Haydn had written in 1797 and presented to the Emperor and the Austrian nation on the Emperor's birthday, February 12th.

The first variation presents the air in the second violin part, while the first violin plays a dainty *staccato* arpeggiated accompaniment, the other two instruments of the quartet being silent. In Variation II the melody is given to the 'cello, a counter-melody is played by the second violin, and the first violin and the viola play accompanying parts. The viola takes the theme in the next variation, the melody being slightly embellished. The fourth variation gives the now familiar air to the first violin. The movement closes with a brief *coda.*

Farewell (sometimes known as the "Candle") *Symphony.* Displays that happy geniality for which Haydn was so noted, and which won him the title of "Papa" Haydn. The quaint title was given the work, not because of its mood or any descriptive character, but because of the occasion for which it was written. It had been the custom, at Esterhazy, for all servants engaged for the castle to be able to assist, in some way, in the musical activities of the little court. Many months of the year were spent at the castle near Vienna, and the remainder in the city. Two stories are told of the troubles of the orchestra—one that they were about to be dismissed entirely; and the other that they wished the court to return to town after an abnormally long stay in the country. In any case, the attention of the Prince was desired, and Haydn set about to secure it by writing with unusual care, a symphony (F-sharp Minor), the first three movements of which proceeded in the conventional manner. The fourth movement only is involved in the little story. Its first theme is delicate and graceful, the second theme, slightly more sprightly in style. A brief *codetta* is added; but not concluding, the movement moves gently into a new episode in A Major, *adagio,* which is really a small three-part movement within itself. At the first cadence, in the first "part"—on the night of the first performance—the second horn and first oboe players blew out their candles, closed their music books, took their instruments, and quietly withdrew from the room. Twenty-three measures later the second oboist and another horn player withdrew; soon the double-basses, then the 'cellists, then all the players but the violinists and viola players left. At last only two violinists were left to finish alone, with a delicate two-voiced air. The players won their request.

Military Symphony in G Major. One of 12 composed by Haydn in 1795 for his London concerts (and under contract with Salomon) and, after the *Surprise* one of the most popular of all his works. It received its sub-title because of the prominence given to bass drum, cymbals, and triangle in its various movements, particularly the second and last. The "Minuet" of this symphony is especially attractive, and is here presented in three-part form—minuet, trio, minuet.

Surprise Symphony, (No. 6 of the set, and in G Minor). So named be-cause of the very entertaining second movement, the *Andante,* written at the Esterhazy castle, said to have been inspired by the Prince's frequent naps taken during the daily concerts. (See "Humor in Music," p. 134, and "The Romantic Idea in Music," p. 95.) Haydn was very fond of the melody of the *Andante,* and also used it as thematic material in his *Seasons,* in which, played by the piccolo, it represents a plowman whistling the air—"his wonted lay."

Toy Symphony. This unique work was written in 1788 at Esterhazy and is said to have been inspired by the composer's visit to the Fair at Eisenstadt. In it he has written parts for various toys, including drums, whistles, and toys which imitate the sounds of such birds as the nightingale, quail, and cuckoo. The little symphony is written in three movements. The Finale (*allegro*) is repeated twice, becoming each time faster and faster until, at the close, it is dashing along *prestissimo.*

HERBERT, Victor (1859-1924). A grandson of Samuel Lover of Ireland (who composed the airs of the songs, "The Low-Backed Car" and "Believe Me, If All Those Endearing Young Charms"), was born in Dublin. As a young man he toured Germany, Italy, and France as 'cello soloist, was first 'cellist of the Strauss Orchestra in Vienna, and of the court orchestra at Stuttgart. Coming to America he was for years first 'cellist at the Metropolitan Opera House, and also played with Theodore Thomas and Anton Seidl. His fame as a composer rests upon his light operas, which include *Babes in Toyland, The Red Mill, Naughty Marietta, Sweethearts, Mlle. Modeste,* and many others. He also wrote for male chorus, orchestra, and strings; and two important 'cello concertos.

Natoma. Herbert's only "grand" opera, based upon an historic tale of the early days of California. The scene is set in Santa Barbara. It is one of the few operas written to an English libretto. In it Natoma, the young Indian maid and companion of Barbara (daughter of the wealthy Spaniard Don Francisco), has lost her heart to Lieutenant Merrill of the Navy, who, in turn, loves Barbara. Alvarado, a young Spaniard, also loves Barbara and, in company with the half-breed Castro, plans to abduct her. The second act shows the public square of Santa Barbara where the people have gathered before the Mission Church to welcome Barbara as she returns from school. A dance begins and, to divert the general attention, so that they may carry Barbara off, Castro challenges anyone to dance with him the traditional dagger dance. Natoma rushes up, thrusts her dagger into the ground beside his, and the dance begins. At an opportune moment she springs forward, dashes his dagger aside, and with her own stabs Alvarado, who is just about to seize Barbara. The third act portrays the renunciation of Natoma, and her acceptance of the vows of the Church.

In the music to this opera, Herbert called upon many of the idioms of old Spanish music. The "Spring Song," which is sung by Barbara in the second act, is extremely joyous,

the accompaniment, bringing in many imitative suggestions of the sounds of Nature. The "Dagger Dance," the most familiar number of the opera, is barbarically simple, relying greatly upon a monotonous drum rhythm.

HINDEMITH, PAUL (1895–   ). Has risen most rapidly of all the German composers who have had their beginnings since the World War, coming first into international prominence at the Salzburg Festival of 1922, when his string quartet was played. Since then he has produced much chamber and vocal music. Although his writings are frequently unmelodic, he displays a smooth and facile technique, and an absolute mastery of the technique of instrumental writing. He has written four operas, the fourth of which, *News for the Day,* is a revival of the spirit of *opera buffa* from a modern viewpoint. His *String Quartet* is essentially modern in that it has no time signature, has very irregular rhythms, and is simply based upon a unit of speed for each quarter-note of value. His "We Build a City" (a bit of *Lehrstücke*) displays a chorus of children in dialogue with an older person. It recalls the "Morality Plays" of the Middle Ages in its characteristics.

HOLST, GUSTAV. For biographical notes and discussion of *The Planets,* see "Orchestral Suites," p. 101.

HOMER, SIDNEY (1864–   ). Educated in this country, and studied music in Boston under Chadwick,

ERNEST SCHELLING

FREDERICK
STOCK

OSSIP GABRILOWITSCH

FRANZ LISZT

RICHARD WAGNER

WAGNER'S HOME AT BAYREUTH

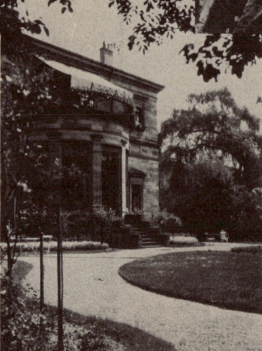

INTERIOR
OF EDVARD GRIEG'S
MUSIC HOUSE

GIUSEPPE
VERDI

and in the Munich and Leipzig Conservatories. He has written over 100 songs which have attained a wide and lasting popularity, including the ever-popular "Banjo Song." Others are the dramatic "Song of the Shirt," "Mammy's Lullaby," the gruesome "Pauper's Drive," "Sing Me a Song of a Lad That is Gone," "Uncle Rome," and "How's My Boy?" They are all songs of general appeal, of sincerity, and of real personality. Mr. Homer is the husband of Louise Homer, the celebrated contralto.

HONEGGER, ARTHUR (1892–). Though born in Havre, France, is considered as a Swiss composer, in spite also of his later close connection with French life and art. His mother and father were his first music teachers. When, at the age of nine, he heard the opera *Faust,* he decided to become a musician. At 13 he had already written two operas and some chamber music. At twenty he was admitted to the Paris Conservatoire where he became a student —along with Milhaud and Jacques Ibert—of Widor and Gedalge. This period of study was shortly interrupted by compulsory military duty in Switzerland, and upon his return to Paris he was a student in composition with d'Indy. Honegger is one of a group who organized themselves, in Paris, into a band known as the "Six," the purpose of which was to give concerts of their own compositions at home and abroad.

Honegger's musical traits include use of polytonality, the throwing into great prominence of brass instruments, a disdain for purely chordal writing, a feeling that dissonance in music is as important as concord, and the use of atonality. (See also p. 228.)

Chant de Nigamon. A symphonic work which was a student effort. Honegger presents a striking treatment of American Indian tribal themes. Tareah, the Huron, has reserved Nigamon and the other Iroquois to be burned alive. Fire is set to the fagots. When the flames begin to rise Tareah leaps across, mercilessly scalps Nigamon and his companions and slaps them with their own hair. Then the Iroquois begin their death chant—but when Nigamon lifts up his voice, the others stop to listen.

Three Indian themes are employed —a war song of the Hurons, a war song of the Iroquois, and an Iroquois song known as "The Warrior's Last Word."

Judith. Not an opera in the conventional sense. The music was originally incidental music written to accompany a play brought out in Switzerland. As an opera it is a succession of scenes briefly presented and not elaborated upon, and has to do with a Jewish legend of Judith and the head of Holofernes. Thus it is sometimes spoken of as a sacred opera. In it are heard many effective references to ancient music of the synagogues, especially in the first chorus of the women, and in the almost barbarous ferocity of the Assyrian soldiers. Honegger has been criticized for his manner of writing the "Warrior's Song" as, contrary to custom, the chorus of warriors does not file upon the stage in orderly fashion, singing stirring melodies and well-constructed four-part harmony. Instead, they rush on in realistic manner, shouting as real warriors might. His effects are dramatic in the extreme, both here and in the case of the wailing women within the walls, in the first scene.

King David. The way in which Honegger often makes reference to old forms of sacred music is in evidence in *King David* (*Le Roi David*), his most widely known choral work, a dramatic Psalm in 2 acts and 25 episodes. First used in connection with the text of René Moxas, in a dramatic work intended primarily for an Alpine open-air theater, it is more familiar in its form as an oratorio with Narrator, as arranged by the composer nearly four years later (1924).

Contemporary criticism of the first performances says, in part: "Honegger has been obliged to connect the various episodes with musical links. Viewed as a whole, the score seems a strange mosaic made from stones of the same color but different style. A section of the work is only expanded when a grandiose effect is required, for example, in the "Dance before the Ark," the longest section of the work. Otherwise, the varying fragmentray entries, fanfares, marches, and even psalms, rarely exceed 30 measures or so."

Pacific 231. This popular locomotive piece for orchestra had its first performance under Sergei Koussevitzky in Paris on May 8, 1924. In it, Honegger has given a musical description of power, and of an object —the locomotive—which had always interested him. On his journeys, twice a week, to his classes in the Paris Conservatoire, he had never failed to make a visit of inspection to the engine that pulled his train, and in his study at the present time has placed on the walls an array of photographs of his "majestic friends."

In this music the vigor of a compelling rhythm is the essential feature. There are three main themes, all used in counterpoint, the "locomotive theme" being always recognizable by its triplet form.

Unusual instrumental choices and uses are responsible for some of the unique effects produced, as, at the opening, when the hissing of weird harmonics in the strings suggest the restless escape of steam while the engine stands at rest. Then the vibrations of the cymbals and the heavy passages in the double-basses and 'cellos, with their extreme accents, as the big engine gets under way. The puffings of the locomotive theme, the accumulation of rhythms, the witty suggestions of revolvings of big and little wheels, the constantly increasing tempo and the unequal rhythmic division of notes—bring, gradually, the whole orchestral mass to its culmination in what the composer calls the "lyric moment" when the 300-ton train is finally hurtling through the night at a speed of 70 miles an hour. This prodigious volume, and the means by which it is achieved, are only equaled by the skill with which the musical "brakes" are applied and the engine finally brought to a stop, the moment it arrives at the station being dramatically expressed by a passage of broad and sumptuous chords.

Rugby, a symphonic scherzo. Honegger is, personally a lover of sports, and is well versed in the intricacies of the games as played at Rugby. While watching a championship game, he remarked that he could easily visualize the plays in music. A clever newspaper journalist came out, next day, with the statement that "Arthur Honegger is already at work upon an important symphonic work to be known as *Rugby,* which will be ready for performance in the near future." Honegger, amused, began to consider the possibilities of the idea, and when, presently, he had a definite invitation to write a symphonic work for the new Symphonic Orchestra of Paris for its first concert, set to work.

He has here suggested the various phases of the game, the escape of a player with the ball, the pursuits, and the frustrated efforts of the opponents. All this is done by means of two themes (each depicting one of the teams) these being used with geometric precision, sudden alternation of counterpoints in two or three voices, crashing polyphonies, quick stoppings and startings, and broken syncopated rhythms.

HUMPERDINCK, ENGELBERT (1854–1921). Born at Siegburg in the Rhine country, studied with Hiller, Rheinberger, and others, was the intimate friend and helper of Richard Wagner, and was for many years professor at Hoch Conservatory. Many of Humperdinck's writings are closely allied to the folk music of his fatherland. At times he used the folk tunes outright, and his orig-inal tunes are frequently modeled on the folk air. In addition to his operas he is known as a writer of much choral and orchestral music. His first close connection with opera came when he assisted Wagner at Bayreuth in 1880 and 1881 with the première of *Parsifal.* The first performance of his own *Königskinder* brought Humperdinck to America, where he conducted it in its world première at the Metropolitan Opera House.

Hansel and Gretel. This is, as the composer said, "for grown-ups with children's hearts" as well as for children. It is built upon a simple nursery tale. Humperdinck's sister, Adelheid Wette, who lived in Cologne, had arranged a little fairy play from Grimm for her own children for home Christmas celebration, and asked her brother to contribute some simple tunes for it. He became so interested in *Hansel and Gretel* that he made it into an opera, working at it slowly for three years as time and inspiration permitted. Richard Strauss gave it its first performance at the Weimar Opera, December 23, 1894, and at Munich a week later. The opera has three acts.

The "Prelude" (See "Famous Overtures," p. 106).

The characters in the opera are: Peter, a Broom-maker; Gertrude, his wife, and cruel stepmother of Hansel and Gretel; the Old Witch, who eats children and also turns them into gingerbread; Sandman, the Sleep Fairy; Dewman, the Dawn Fairy, and Children, Angels, and Peasants.

Act I. Scene, Cottage of Broom-maker, near the woods. The father and mother have gone to market leaving Hansel and Gretel at home alone. Hansel is making brooms and Gretel knitting. They soon tire of work and entertain themselves by singing and dancing an old folk air, "Susie, Little Susie." Gretel teaches Hansel to dance while they sing a gay folk tune. The mother returns, scolds the idle children; the milk-pitcher is accidentally overturned, thus losing all the food the poor family had left. The children are sent out into the woods to hunt wild strawberries. Peter, their father, now returns with his arms filled with good things to eat, and is horrified to learn that Hansel and Gretel are alone in the darkening woods, where they may be captured by the Old Witch who dwells there and eats children. As father and mother hurry out of the house in search of the children there is heard, as from the sky, the wild and weird melody of the "Witch's Ride."

Act II. In the Woods. In the depths of the forest Hansel and Gretel have been picking berries. Gretel makes a wreath of flowers as she sings. Now so dark that the children cannot find their way home or pick more berries, they lie down to rest. The Sandman comes, reaches over his shoulder into a bag which he carries on his back, and takes out a pinch of sand which he sprinkles over their eyes as he sings "I am the Sleep Fairy." But before they go to sleep Hansel and Gretel carefully sing their bedtime "prayer hymn,"

"When at night I go to sleep
Fourteen angels guard do keep."

Act III. Scene, Morning in the Woods. Hansel and Gretel are awak-ened by the Dewman, who sprinkles on their eyelids dew which he car-ries in the cup of a bluebell. They notice, not far away, a wonderful little house marvelously made of candy and gingerbread. All about it is a fence, made of gingerbread girls and boys. Hansel and Gretel begin to eat bits of the house as they break them off, but are frightened when there comes, from the inside of the house, a harsh call. Out pops the Old Witch. Hansel and Gretel are be-witched. Hansel is locked in a cage to be fattened and Gretel is ordered to get the oven hot. While the Witch's back is turned, Gretel seizes her wand and repeats the incanta-tion, breaking her brother's enchant-ment. The Witch orders Gretel to look into the oven to see if it is ready, but the clever girl pretends not to understand. When the Witch puts her own head in to show Gretel, both children push together, sur-prising her so that she falls into the oven herself. They shut the oven door quickly—such groans as the Witch makes inside! Soon the oven falls apart with a crash. Hansel and Gretel, who have rushed from the house, find that the spell has been entirely broken. The gingerbread posts have come back to life as happy children, and they all dance about joyously. Peter and Gertrude now ap-pear, the Old Witch is found to have been baked into a huge gingerbread cake, and the opera ends on the sweet melody of the children's "Prayer Hymn."

JAMES, Philip (1890–   ). His compositions have been performed by leading orchestras, sometimes under his own conductorship. Has conducted for various choral organizations, orchestras, and stage productions, at one time being musical director of some of Victor Herbert's operettas. Was made conductor and commanding officer of General Pershing's Headquarters' Band which so successfully toured the country for the Victory Loan.

In 1922 Mr. James founded the New Jersey orchestra and was its conductor for seven years. Mr. James has also been conductor of the Brooklyn Orchestral Society and has appeared as guest conductor of the Oratorio Society of New York, and the Manhattan Symphony, and the Pennsylvania Symphony of Philadelphia. In addition to his work at Columbia (where he was formerly a member of the faculty) and New York Universities, he has been active for the past four years in the radio field, conducting over 200 symphonic programs representing close to 3000 symphonies, tone poems, suites, concertos, and other items of all composers of symphonic literature.

In 1932 Mr. James won the National Broadcasting Company's first prize of $5000, in a contest which assembled 573 manuscripts from American composers. In this contest, five compositions were selected by a jury composed of Walter Damrosch, Stokowski, Stock, Serafin, and Sokoloff. These were, in turn, ranked by a national committee of award made up of 150 outstanding musicians of the country, who listened in by radio to the performances of the five winning works by the N.B.C. Symphony under the direction of Eugene Goossens.

Mr. James is now Conductor of the Bamberger Little Symphony, Associate Professor of Music at New York University, and Dean, School of Fine Arts (N. Y. U.), succeeding Percy Grainger.

Mr. James's published works include many attractive concert songs, piano works, and compositions for full orchestra and for many smaller combinations of instruments. They include "Songs of Night"; a *Concertino,* "The Nightingale of Bethlehem," on a legend of the Nativity by Frederick H. Martens; a *Stabat Mater* setting; *Kammermusik* for orchestra; "The Light of God," from a Nicodemian legend by Martens; *Judith,* a ballet based upon Jewish themes; a string quartet in modern idiom (composed in Venice); a suite for chamber orchestra—four movements—based on Greek scales, and many other works of importance.

Bret Harte. An overture in strict form and not a tone poem as the name might imply. It depicts the characters in Bret Harte's writings.

General William Booth Enters into Heaven. A rhapsody for male chorus, dedicated to Channing Lefebvre and the Down Town Glee Club of New York City. General Booth founded the Salvation Army in London in 1878, and "with an army of regenerated men and women picked from the gutters, saloons, jails, and brothels, the fiery General carried his crusade around the world." The text is by Vachel Lindsay.

The first line of the popular Salvation Army hymn, "Are you washed in the blood of the Lamb," is used as a parenthetical refrain throughout the poem. The music opens with a quotation from that tune in the small group of instruments which will be easily recognized as a "Salvation Army Band." Then follow the first theme, strong with dignity, and with its eloquent vocal refrain of "Are you washed," and the second theme, jazzy and vulgar. The first is Booth and religious sincerity, the second the crowd and its emotional conversion. The music which follows develops these opening themes with great ingenuity. More developments lead back to the jazz theme on "Hallelujah," the "Booth" theme again, and the entrance of the full organ as we come into "that holy land." As the figure of Jesus enters, the music acquires a devotional tenderness. But Booth's "queer ones" interrupt with an "unbalanced rhythm all their own." Then the transformation. The sick are made whole as their musical themes develop new forms. Again the jazz theme, this time combined with the old camp-meeting tune. After a tremendous climax shouting "Salvation," the real climax occurs in a passage of quiet rapture as Christ bestows the robe and crown upon his old soldier. A sudden loud burst and then, after the chorus and organ have held the chord of C Major against a dissonant clash in the other instruments, the work ends with the dissonances converted to the purer harmony. This is a choral composition of major importance.

Mass of the Pictures. In which each movement is suggested or inspired by some masterpiece of ecclesiastical printing or sculpture—such as the "Last Judgment," or Bellini's "Madonna," a work of spiritual beauty and strength—had its first performance by the Oratorio Society under Albert Stoessel in 1931.

Overture in the Olden Style on French Noëls. Constructed on French Noëls, two in number but of different character. These are *Venez, divin Messie*, which is the first in the composition, and *Rejouissez-vous, divine Marie.* Throughout the work the composer has studiously avoided anything like the modern idiom, and has simply given modern orchestral color and musical spontaneity to an overture in strict classical form, with the aid of two charming French carols.

Noëls or Christmas carols date far back into the Middle Ages. The word Noël is used continually in the ancient Christmas hymns and motets as a joyous exclamation. This particular kind of hymn was first cultivated in France or Burgundy, and was commonly sung there in very ancient times. While neither of the Noëls selected by Mr. James for musical treatment in his overture are among the very early ones, they are both excellent specimens. The first one, is known to have been performed annually at Beauvais and Sens, in the Twelfth century.

Station WGZBX. I. "In the Lobby." The first movement, in sonata form, is meant to portray the corridors of a large broadcasting station. After a few introductory measures the principal theme—a short, pert one, representing radio itself—is introduced. In the development one hears the various sounds peculiar to a radio station. From reception rooms come the noise and bustle of crowds, from audition rooms, fragments of voice trials. Occasionally the doors of near-by studios open and snatches of a Chinese or Indian program are heard, or talks and announcements intermingled with the rhythm of a jazz band. The movement is, in fact, a kind of radio "Grand Hotel." II. "Interference." The second movement, which is analogous to the symphonic scherzo, portrays the rather distressing moments caused by badly tuned receiving sets, blanketing of stations, static, etc. There are garbled scraps of announcements, heterodyne "squeals," the dots and dashes of a code weather report, and various other phenomena of "interference," aggravated and supplemented by static and fading. In this movement the voice of the Robot is introduced. He is reciting disjointed fragments of an announcement, crooning a phrase in the popular style. Finally, he bursts into wild, inhuman laughter, thus typifying the humorous side of mechanical reproduction of music. III. "A Slumber Hour." This movement expresses the quietude of a late evening broadcast. It begins with a majestic chord, built up tone by tone, followed by the chiming of a bell and solo passages for violin and violoncello. IV. "Mikestruck." The final movement is an exuberantly cheerful rondo, "Tempo di Jazz," suggesting the unquenchable enthusiasm of the "mikestruck" amateur, who finds the urge to express himself before the microphone.

JARNEFELT, Armas (1869–   ). A Finnish composer, a student at the Helsingfors Conservatory, and also a pupil of Massenet. Since student days conductor in many important Scandinavian theaters, and as head of the Helsingfors Conservatory. He is best known for his shorter works.

"Berceuse." A melodic work for violin solo, but transcribed for orchestra, constructed, principally, of a single theme. This, following an introduction in the minor mode, is stated three times, each time with differing instrumentation. A short coda *pizzicato* and *pianissimo* brings the piece to a close.

"Praeludium." Is very suggestive, in its instrumentation, of a dance into which one person after another steps until all are taking part. The particular feature of the music is the *basso ostinato* figure, plucked from the strings, with which it begins; and which is heard constantly, until the last note has been played.

JOHNS, Louis Edgar (1886–   ). A student in composition with Humperdinck. Professor of Music, Skidmore College, Saratoga Springs, N. Y. Compositions include *Lyrics from the Germans* (5 vols.); many notable works for piano, orchestra, chamber and choral groups.

KELLEY, Edgar Stillman (1857–   ). A native of Wisconsin, now a resident of Oxford, Ohio, where he holds a Fellowship for Composition at Western College. He is a graduate of the Conservatory at Stuttgart. His compositions include songs and other choral work, orchestral works, including *Two Moods of Nature* and *Macbeth Symphonic Suite;* music for the plays *Ben Hur* and *Jury of Fate,* and for a lyric opera, *Puritania.*

Aladdin Suite. This Chinese suite, for which much thematic material was collected in Chinatown in San Francisco, had its first performance in Berlin, the members of the Chinese Embassy attending in a body. After the concert they thanked the composer for his poetic treatment of their folk music. The first movement represents the "Wedding of Aladdin and the Princess," called by Mr. Kelly "a sublimated charivari" in which the oboes squawk, muted trumpets bray, *pizzicato* strings flutter, and mandolins twitter hilariously. The second, "A Serenade in the Royal Pear Garden," begins with a preliminary tuning of the Chinese lute of Samyin, after which it wails an odd lyric bit. The third movement, "The Flight of the Genie with the Palace," is a realistic portrayal of his struggle to wrest loose the foundations of the building. *Glissando* from upper harp strings and chromatic running passages from the violins, suggest the motion. The last movement, "The Return and Feast of the Lanterns," is written in sonata form and employs old Chinese airs.

Alice in Wonderland. Suggested by Lewis Carroll's fascinating fantasy, includes also several incidents from the sequel, *Through the Looking Glass.* The orchestral suite is made up of six numbers. Choruses appropriate to the story may also be used in connection with the orchestral numbers. The first performance was at the Norfolk (Conn.) Festival, June 9, 1919, with the composer conducting. The numbers of the suite are:

I. "Prelude." This is very brief, and opens with a fanfare, after which there is the announcement of "Alice on Her Way to Wonderland." II. "The White Rabbit." Looks at his watch, finds that he is late for an appointment with the Duchess, and scampers about, at length jumping down the rabbit hole. Alice follows him and the adventures begin. III. "The Cheshire Cat." Gives Alice his opinions from the bough of a tree and then vanishes in a smile. The Alice theme is heard again. IV. "The Caucus Race." The guests are dripping from a swim in the pool of tears resulting from sorrow over the Archbishop. The Dodo suggests a race. The music begins *lento,* then grows faster and more complex. V. "Forest of Forgetfulness." Alice has forgotten her name, her efforts to recall it being suggested by the fragmentary experiments with Alice's theme. At the close of the movement the theme is heard in its entirety. VI. "The Red Queen's Banquet." Opens with a fanfare, bringing the Suite to a close. A second fanfare announces the arrival of Alice as the Queen. Many things of a very strange nature happen, at the end of which Alice pulls off the table-cloth, bringing all the dishes down with a crash. The music follows the story closely.

New England Symphony, in B-Flat Minor, Opus 33. First produced at the Norfolk Festival, has been given a number of times at important European festivals and concerts. The four movements seek to portray the mood of the historic events that had to do with the early settlements on New England shores.

Pilgrim's Progress. Text by Elizabeth Hodgkinson. Mr. Kelley divides his composition into three parts. The setting was the feature of the fortieth anniversary festival of the New York Oratorio Society, directed by Dr. Walter Damrosch, in 1920, when it was sung by a chorus of 1500, accompanied by an orchestra of 150. Mr. Kelley entrusts the epic element to the "Dreamer," who here impersonates John Bunyan.

KRAMER, A. Walter (1890–). (See also "The Art of Transcription," p. 121). Born in New York, spent his childhood and youth in an unusually musical environment. His father, Maximilian Kramer, had come to New York in the eighties from Moravia in Austria and established himself as a musician and teacher, being, for many years, in charge of the music at the Horace Mann High School, and in the Stevens Institute of Technology in Hoboken. The son began his active study of music at the age of 11, after which he studied violin and viola with his father, and also gained much skill in transcription by arranging many familiar masterpieces for viola and violin so that he and his father could play them together. Later experience in ensemble work was gained through participation in the orchestral activities at the College of New York, and each summer, in playing first viola in the orchestra directed by Arthur Judson at Ocean Grove. In 1910 Mr. Kramer became connected with *Musical America,* of which he has, for a number of years, been editor. Two years and a half were spent in Europe.

Mr. Kramer has over 300 published compositions, many of them for voice, and in these he displays a sure knowledge of vocal requirements and a facile mastery in treating voice parts. All of his music is notable for harmonic richness, melodic line, artistic directness, and a faithful interpretation of the idea of the composition. He has written many successful works for women's voices (three- and four-part chorus), mixed voices, and male chorus, and some remarkably beautiful transcriptions for women's three-part chorus, which include *"Morgen"* (Richard Strauss); "To the Children" (Rachmaninov); "Lullaby," "Looking Back," "Where be Going?" "Don't Come In, Sir, Please." (Cyril Scott); *"Caro, caro, el Mio Mambin"* (Guarnieri); *"Bergerette"* (Recli); "Afar" (Gretchaninov); "Night and Dreams" (Schubert); "New Love, New Life" (Beethoven); "Four Swedish Folk Melodies"; and three songs, "The Maiden in the Alder Wood," "When I was Seventeen," and "To Fetch Some Water from the Spring" (Neptune).

"At the Evening's End." A sustained setting for medium voice of a Teasdale poem, free as to declamation and rich in nocturnal coloring. A basic motive, used in the opening prelude for piano, and recurring through the song, unifies it tellingly.

"Choral Prelude: Es ist ein Ros'
entsprungen" ("A Rose Springs Into
Bloom"). A transcription for violin
of the eighth of Brahms's little-
known "Eleven Choral Preludes for
the Organ," published after his
death. The tender melody lends itself
well to the violin. It is dedicated to
Fritz Kreisler who introduced it in
November 1932.

"Concert Prelude in D Minor,"
Opus 28, No. 3. An extended work
in severe style; opens with a pedal
recitative which is followed by a
vigorous Allegro in sonata form. The
work closes with a chorale-like
melody for full organ.

"Cypresses," Opus 47, No. 2. The
second of two preludes (the first is
entitled "Toward Evening") takes
its name from the trees in the garden
of the Villa Occioni in Asolo, Italy,
where the composer lived from
October 1923 to May 1924. The
melancholy feeling of those magnificent trees which one often finds in
Northern Italy impressed the composer deeply during the time of his
residence in this little village where
Browning had set his *Pippa Passes.*

Eklog, Opus 41. This is a brief
tone-poem, based on lines from
Theocritus's *Bion* which read, "Be-
think thee of my love and whence it
came." The music is a development
of a simple theme given out by the
violin on the G-string, and restated
later on the D-, A-, and E-strings.
First conceived as a composition for
violoncello and piano, Mr. Kramer
set it also for the violin. In this form
it attracted the attention of Fritz
Kreisler, who has performed it frequently in his recitals, and (in a
version for violin and orchestra)
with the New York Symphony Orchestra under Walter Damrosch in
1920.

"Elegy in G Minor," Opus 32, No.
3b. A somber melodious piece for
'cello, comprises a main *cantilena*
section for the solo instrument, and
a middle section *Religioso,* in which
the piano has a chorale-like melody,
interrupted from time to time by
phrases in the solo instrument.
"Elegy in C-sharp Minor" is a shorter
chamber-music work of the same
material as the "Elegy in G Minor"
for 'cello and piano, the main melody
given to the viola on its first statement, and to the first violin on its
repetition.

"The Faltering Dusk," Opus 44.
In folk style Mr. Kramer has set this
poem by Louis Untermeyer. Tense
and dramatic in tone, it has exerted
a decided appeal on all who have
heard it. It is widely sung.

"Humoresque on Two American
Folk Tunes, 'Suwanee River' and
'Dixie,'" Opus 30, No. 2. In light
vein Mr. Kramer has written a brilliant little piece for string quartet,
comprising an introduction built on
the opening phrase of Dixie, followed
by both "Dixie" and "Suwanee
River," and closing with a contrapuntal combination of the two.

"In Elizabethan Days," Opus 32,
No. 2. This is an old English dance
piece for violin, 'cello, and piano,
simple melodically, and written in
the strict form of an old pavan.

"Interlude for a Drama," Opus
46. This is an experimental vocal
composition without words, written
for medium voice, oboe, viola, 'cello,

and piano, composed for Eva Gauthier and performed by her in 1921. The composer has stated that the piece was suggested to him by Barrie's play *Mary Rose,* and that this music is to him that spoken of in the play as coming from the mysterious island. An edition for voice and piano is also published.

"The Last Hour," Opus 34, No. 6. Mr. Kramer's best-known song, with the distinction of having been retained in the repertoire of concert singers for almost twenty years. The poem is by Jessie Christian Brown. It is in free *arioso* style, with a touch of music drama in some of its phrases. It is also published in Vienna with a German text by R. St. Hofmann, one of the few American concert songs to be so honored.

Prelude and Fugue. This is a transcription for string orchestra of the "E-flat Minor Prelude" from Bach's *Well-Tempered Clavichord* and of the "F Major Fugue" from the same work. Mr. Kramer has transposed the prelude up to E Minor and the fugue down to E Major, so as to make the former more suitable to stringed instruments and the latter to complement the former appropriately as to tonality.

"Silhouette." This is a happy, yet deeply felt, movement for string orchestra in slow Viennese waltz rhythm, a tribute to the Austrian capital, symbolized not only in the nature of the music but in the words, "O City of the Emperors, Thou Beautiful One!" (*O Kaiserstadt! Du Schöne!*), which Mr. Kramer has used as a sub-title.

"Song Without Words," Opus 44.

Unlike most "songs without words" for instruments, this one, for violin, is actually what its name implies. It was first written as a "Song Without Words" for soprano voice and piano, the singer using the vowel "Ah" throughout. Shortly after its composition, Mr. Kramer made this violin version of it.

Symphonic Rhapsody in F Minor, for Violin and Orchestra, Opus 35. This is one of the few American violin concertos that has achieved publication. It is a concerto in one extended movement, occupying some seventeen minutes in performance. The main subject is the composer's own, but in the work he has used two Negro melodies, one the old Slave song "I'm Troubled in My Mind," and the other the spiritual "De Lord Delivered Daniel." There is a variety of technical elaboration for the solo instrument, and an extended cadenza. There are actually three sections, but the work is played without pause.

"Tracings." A striking poem by Bernard Raymund is here reflected in music that has for its underlying note an individual, dissonant, slow *arpeggio.* Over it the voice moves in free manner, telling the tale of a bygone day in a house no longer inhabited, recalling the "fingerprints on the window" of children now forgotten.

"Toward Evening," Opus 47, No. 1. (See also "Cypresses"). This, the first of two preludes in extended form, freely conceived, is based on a motto theme, F-sharp, E, B, which appears in various guises. It was written in 1922.

"Unto All Things Voice Is Given"

Opus 48, No. 2. A setting of a German poem by Cäsar Flaischlen, *Alle Dinge haben Sprache,* in the form of a vocal scena. It is an impassioned outburst suited best for dramatic soprano or tenor. The piano accompaniment is of orchestral character.

LA FORGE, FRANK. Born in Rockford, Illinois; had for his first teacher his sister, Ruth La Forge Hall. He studied with the late Harrison Wild in Chicago, and was, for 4 years, a pupil of Leschetizky. Composition studied under Labor and Navratil. Mr. La Forge's first world prominence was the result of tours as pianist and accompanist with Mme. Marcella Sembrich, with whom he toured Europe, Russia, and America. He has always memorized all his accompaniments, and today has a repertoire of over 5000 memorized song accompaniments. Other artists with whom he has been associated for a considerable period of time include Mme. Frances Alda, Mme. Matzenauer, and Mme. Schumann-Heink. As a voice teacher Mr. La Forge has created a unique place for himself in the musical world through the results of his scientific method of singing. Lawrence Tibbett, who made one of the greatest sensations ever created by a singer in the Metropolitan Opera House, has studied with Mr. La Forge since 1922; and other artists of the Metropolitan have worked in his studios. Mr. La Forge's songs have won recognition in all parts of the world, and are sung by leading artists. He has also written for organ and piano.

"Before the Crucifix." Sung by Schumann-Heink and other artists, is a deeply devotional song which has created a furore whenever and wherever sung.

"Come Unto These Yellow Sands." A setting of "Ariel's Song" from Shakespeare's *Tempest,* composed on the day that Mme. Sembrich engaged La Forge to be her accompanist and assisting artist—as the composer himself relates, a spontaneous expression of his joy at the beginning of this marvelous experience.

"Hills." Written in the La Forge "Retreat" on the St. Croix River in Canada, the musical interpretation of an inspired poem. The composer has achieved a delightful effect in his accompaniment to the words, "The far bells chiming," in which the pealing of the vesper bells is deftly suggested by the piano.

"In the Forest." A song written in the modern style, reveals the composer as a great lover of the glories of nature. The song is dedicated "To Laura," the composer's wife.

"Into the Light." A setting of an excerpt from Marie Corelli's "The Life Everlasting," allows much opportunity for dramatic effect on the part of the singer, and grateful harmonic effects from the piano.

"Little Star." Exceedingly popular and frequently heard, a clever setting of a lilting melody by Ponce, the Mexican writer. An unusual harmonic treatment greatly enhances the attractiveness of the melody. This number is also arranged for organ.

"On the Beautiful Blue Danube." A transcription of the famous Johann Strauss waltz (originally written as a male chorus, then re-

arranged for orchestra), which has met with much success as a concert number. Mr. La Forge has made two versions of his transcription, one an exceedingly brilliant work for coloratura, the other for lyric soprano.

"Pastorale." A unique setting of a text from Milton, an atmospheric song of rare beauty, suggesting delicately the improvising of a lonely shepherd, the whole-tone scale passages in the accompaniment being an impressionistic imitation of Pan's flute.

"Retreat." A setting of a text by the Princess Gabrielle Wrede, notable for long, broad phrases, for its skillful climax, and for the tender repetition of the final phrase, as though in retrospect.

"Song of the Open." A sea song, and in its pianistic accompaniment there are suggestions of the surging of billows; and, in the second and lighter part of the song in major key, of "foaming spray."

"Storielle del Bosco Viennese." An arrangement for voice of a well-known waltz by Johann Strauss. It was originally transcribed for Mme. Sembrich, who used it on many programs. The Italian poem which furnished the text is the work of Adolfo Betti, who was, for twenty-five years, first violinist of the celebrated Flonzaley Quartet.

"Wherefore do you droop?" Setting of a fragment from Shakespeare's *King John,* in declamatory style, and gives to the singer an opportunity for display of great vocal technique and style. The piano accompaniment aids in the creation of the dramatic atmosphere.

LEONCAVALLO, Ruggiero (1858–1919). Born at Naples. At 18 he had won the title of Maestro from the Naples Conservatory. Despairing of having any of his works printed by the publishers by whom they had been accepted, he wrote *I Pagliacci,* sent it to a rival concern, and became famous almost overnight. The opera had its first performance at La Scala in Milan on May 21, 1892. It is often coupled with *Cavalleria Rusticana,* as it is also of shorter than usual length. It has two acts. In America it has recently been coupled with Louis Gruenberg's *Emperor Jones.*

I Pagliacci (The Players). The opera opens with the celebrated "Prologue," sung by Tonio, who comes before the curtain to explain, as did the members of the Greek chorus, that actors too enjoy the same pleasures and suffer the same griefs as do other people. The scene is set in a small Italian village to which the strolling actors have come. The idea of a "play within a play" lends a novel interest. The players are to present a version of one of the old Harlequin comedies that have been familiar in Italy for generations. The stage is set up and the villagers come to enjoy an evening's entertainment. Nedda, wife of Canio, the manager of the strollers, has a rural lover, Silvio. Tonio, the clown, also admires her, and in his anger at being spurned, reveals to Canio the intrigue of the two lovers. As the play progresses, she is accused of disloyalty, and commanded to tell the name of her lover. This she refuses to do. The audience, seated before the little improvised stage, believes that all the tragedy they are witnessing is only enacted for their sake, and shout "Bravo!" Nedda seeks to divert Canio's attention, and not until he plunges a dagger into her heart do they realize that what they have been observing is an episode from real life. As Nedda falls, she cries to Silvio for help, and as he runs forward from the crowd he too is seized and thrust through with the dagger by Canio, who, turning to the audience, sings bitterly, "The comedy is finished!"

Beautiful choral numbers from this opera are the opening chorus "They're Here," with which the villagers greet the players; and the "Chorus of the Bells," a charmingly melodic song of true Italian beauty, sung by the villagers as they turn to go to the vesper service in the church.

LIEURANCE, THURLOW (1878–). (See also "Music of the American Indian," p. 148.) Born in Oskaloosa, Iowa. Has made notable contribution to the recording of Indian tribal music and rituals, as well as in writing much music based upon them. At 20 Mr. Lieurance served as chief musician in the 22nd Kansas Infantry in the Spanish-American War, and studied at the Cincinnati College of Music. He sang for a short time with the old Castle Square Opera Company, for the sake of learning something about opera and its production. He has visited over 30 American Indian tribes to record their music and customs, and many of these records are to be found in prominent museums and libraries of the country. Mr. Lieurance has been

given a complimentary degree from the Cincinnati College of Music, and was awarded the degree of Doctor of Music in 1931 at Fontainebleau. He has spent much time in harmonization, idealization, and exploitation of Indian art, and has written about 350 short works for voice and for various solo instruments or combinations, about one half of which are based either directly or indirectly on Indian tribal airs.

American Indian Rhapsody (Lieurance-Orem). Based entirely upon melodies collected by Mr. Lieurance. A very pretentious work, it became so popular with the American public that it replaced the customary overture on the Sousa programs during the seasons of 1918–19 and 1920.

"Aooah" (Pretty Leaf). Based upon a song of the Red Willow tribe of the Pueblos recorded by Mr. Lieurance in Taos, New Mexico, in 1913, and tells a true story of love in an Indian village. Aooah was the daughter of a pottery maker there, and so inspired the youth of the tribe that many quaint love songs and flute serenades were "made up" in her honor. The accompaniment, in picturesque fashion, imitates the Indian flute.

"By the Waters of Minnetonka." Based upon a Sioux melody, and in it is related the story of two Indian lovers, one of whom belonged to the Sun Deer clan and the other to Moon Deer clan. For this reason they were not allowed to marry. When they tried to escape from their families and flee together, they were pursued to the very edge of Lake Minnetonka (in Minnesota). Rather than

be captured, both plunged into the waters, where they drowned. To this day, says the old legend, the rippling waters of the lake still mourn them and murmur their names every day. The accompaniment suggests the murmuring of the waters.

"By Weeping Water." A tender mourning song, based upon both tribal melody and legend. It is said that the Falls of Minnehaha, in Minnesota, were once the scene of a bitter battle fought by the Chippewas and the Oneidas, and that, when the fighting was over, the water ran red with blood. Ever since that day, tradition tells us, the water of the Falls have sung a mournful lay, as though grieving for the dead heroes, and it became a custom with the women of the Chippewa tribe to go there each year, for several days, and mourn their departed dear ones.

"Chant of the Corn Grinders." Recalls both a Pueblo working song and the custom of the Indian women of that tribe to do all their work to the rhythmic accompaniment of song.

"Ghost Pipes." Tells of phantom chiefs "from long star trails," who come to hold councils as of old, and explains, according to the Indian's viewpoint, the presence of the colorless parasitical flowers often seen in the woods.

"Her Blanket" (Crow). The song of an Indian woman who tells of the weaving of her life story into her blanket, as is a custom with many tribes.

"Minisa" (Red Water at Sunset). A symphonic poem in six parts, portrays the moods and impulses of a romantic story of American Indians.

Indian themes are interwoven in all parts save the second. The new bridge (1932) across the Little Arkansas River at Wichita, Kansas, designed with Indian symbolism, has been dedicated as Minisa Bridge, one of the few monuments to native music in the United States.

"The Owl Hoots on a Teepee Pole" (to words by Frances Densmore). Unusual both in its interpretation of the Indian Medicine Man, and in its appropriate accompaniment, which depicts both Indian drum and rattle.

"Pa-Pup-Ooh" (Deer Flower). Another lovely courting song from the Red Willow Tribe of the Pueblos.

"The Sacrifice." A setting of a Vancouver legend. A young chief, on attaining his majority, was told that he must sacrifice to the fire his dearest possession. To the suprise of his friends, he dramatically threw to the flames his cherished flute, saying that with it there expired "the very music of my soul." The words of the poem are set to an idealized version of a Sioux flute call.

"Ski-bi-bi-la" (Indian Spring Song). A setting of a little charm or "wishing song" often sung by Indian children. With many of the Sioux it was a custom for the children to watch, toward the close of the winter, for a certain little gray bird, which they called "Ski-bi-bi-la." Of it they would ask, "Has spring returned?" To which the bird was certain to reply, "No, it has not returned." It would, however, at once fly swiftly back to the haunts of spring and bring to them the longed-for season.

"Sketch Book: 1931." Dr. Lieurance has here written an orchestral

interpretation of the Colonial Exposition in Paris. The impressions include "By the Fountains," "Mt. Vernon," "Ballet," "Moret," "Italians on Parade," and "Requiem."

"Wi-um." An idealization of a lovely melody Mr. Lieurance once heard a Pueblo mother singing to her papoose on the roof of one of the two communal dwellings in Taos. The song utilizes both the downward-moving air of four tones and a simple flute melody in six-beat measure.

MACDOWELL, EDWARD (For biography and discussion of several compositions, see pp. 190–8).

Four Sonatas. MacDowell wrote four magnificent sonatas for piano, in their order of composition, the *Tragica,* the *Eroica,* the *Norse,* and the *Keltic.*

Tragica. This work is said to have been inspired by MacDowell's sorrow occasioned by the death of Raff, his teacher. The first movement contains much lovely thematic material against which is contrasted a forceful agitation, particularly in the middle section. The second movement, a *Largo,* is characterized by pathos, sonority, and a remarkable nobility. The third movement is a *scherzo.* The fourth movement, a dramatic *finale,* brings the work to a triumphant climax which, immediately upon its culmination, is shattered. This, MacDowell portrayed by an abruptly descending passage in octaves, then ending the movement with a gentle reminiscence of the introduction.

Eroica. MacDowell wrote of this work to a friend, "While not exactly program music, I had in mind the Arthurian legend when writing this work. The first movement typifies the coming of Arthur. The *scherzo* was suggested by a picture of Doré showing a knight in the woods surrounded by elves. The third movement was suggested by my idea of Guinevere. That following represents the passing of Arthur."

The first movement might easily have been called a fantasy and allowed to stand alone. The *scherzo* is characterized by airy whisperings of great delicacy. The third movement is an impassioned and compelling love song. The last movement portrays the struggle of good against evil.

Norse. The third sonata, freer in form than those which precede it, and rich in personality. There is no *scherzo.* The work is dedicated to Edvard Grieg.

Keltic. Also dedicated to Grieg, is based upon the old story of Cuchullin, an early Irish king. MacDowell said: "The music is more a commentary on the subject than an actual depiction of it. . . . This fourth sonata is more of a 'bardic' rhapsody on the subject than an attempt at actual presentation of it, although I have made use of all the suggestion of tone painting in my power, just as the bard would have reinforced *his* speech with gesture and facial expression."

Two Fragments After the Song of Roland, for Orchestra. These are given the subtitles of "Saracens" and "Lovely Alda." "Saracens" is a picturing of the scene in which Ganellone swears to commit treason against Roland. Meanwhile, the Saracens feast amidst the flaring of pagan fires and wailing of sinister primitive music. "Lovely Alda" depicts the loveliness and grief of Alda, the wife of Roland, who died broken-hearted after the fall of her husband at Roncesvalles.

Twelve Studies for Piano. A series of small études, each of which, given a supplementary title, suggests a definite mood or happening.

Virtuoso Studies. These are 12 in number, for piano, and display varied phases of transcendental technique. Each is given a suggestive title. The set opens with the "Novelette," a gayly lilting bit of music. In the set is also the "Improvisation," "March Wind," and "Polonaise," a dazzlingly brilliant composition.

Indian (Second) Suite for Orchestra. One of the first attempts by any composer to idealize the tribal airs of the American Indian, is based upon authentic thematic material with which MacDowell became acquainted through the research records of Dr. Theodore Baker. For example, the "Love Song" takes its thematic material from an air of the Iowa Indians which utilized the five-tone or pentatonic scale. In using it MacDowell has only slightly altered the tribal melody (given to the flute, a characteristic Indian musical instrument). Response is made by the strings.

Woodland Sketches. This remarkable little suite of piano numbers, written in 1896 in the Log Cabin, contains the "To a Wild Rose" and "To a Water Lily," world "favorites," of which mention is made in "Everybody's Music," p. 7. Another "Sketch," "From an Indian Lodge,"

is dramatic and establishes, with its first chords, the atmosphere of a dignified Indian tribal scene. "The Deserted Farm," more tender in mood, tells a pathetic story of New England homes left to become desolate ruins by the "Forty-Niners." "From Uncle Remus," was inspired by the reading of Joel Chandler Harris's delightful stories, and depicts happy care-free life on the plantations.

MAGANINI, Quinto (1897–   ). Born in Fairfield, Calif., but has spent many years of his life in New York City. Studied with Barrere (flute), with Boulanger, and at the American Conservatory at Fontainebleau; and has been holder of both the Guggenheim Fellowship and the Pulitzer Scholarship. He is conductor of the New York Symphonietta which annually gives a series of concerts in which attention is given to the music of contemporary composers. Mr. Maganini has also given careful study to works of very early masters. His published original works include *Tuolumni, California Rhapsody* (for trumpet and orchestra); *A Cuban Rhapsody; Songs of the Chinese* (women's voices); and *Sonata* for Flute and Piano.

MALIPIERO, G. Francesco (1882–   ). One of the important twentieth-century composers of Italy, whose quartet for strings, *Stornelli e Ballata,* received the Coolidge Prize. Most famous of his works are the *Seven Canzoni,* seven episodes for theater, for voice, chorus, and orchestra. These are intended to be done in costume, and the various parts are connected by brief orchestral interludes. Other orchestral works are the *Impression of Nature* Suites, and the *Variations without a Theme*. His "Autumnal Poems," a set of piano pieces, are little masterpieces.

MASCAGNI, PIETRO (1863–). His musical training was largely received at the Milan Conservatory, and he was, in 1890, the winner of the Sonzogna prize with his one-act opera *Cavalleria Rusticana*. The same year he received the honor of the Order of the Crown.

Cavalleria Rusticana, a one-act opera, stands complete within itself, as to plot. It opens with an orchestral prelude of unusual character. Turridu is heard singing his tender song of love for Lola, to orchestral accompaniment, but from behind the curtain which has not yet risen. As the curtain rises there is shown the square in a Sicilian village, with the church and the home of Mamma Lucia, the mother of Turridu. It is Easter morning, and the people of the village are heard approaching, singing as they come. As they enter the church, Santuzza comes forward and calls for Mamma Lucia, to whom she confesses her distrust of Turridu and tells of his seeming desertion of her. Alfio passes, stopping for a moment to talk with the two women, and to confirm Santuzza's assertion that Turridu is still in the village, instead of having gone on his accustomed errands. It is Lola, Alfio's wife, whom Turridu first loved, who has again attracted his attentions. Turridu now enters the square and tries to avoid San-

tuzza, but she implores him not to desert her. Turridu casts her forcibly aside and follows Lola into the church. While they are there, Santuzza confides her suspicions to Alfio and he challenges the usurper to a fight. Before he leaves, Turridu bids farewell to his mother, begging her to befriend Santuzza whom he still loves. He rushes off, but not many minutes pass before there comes the news that he has been killed, and another tragedy of Sicilian life has reached its climax.

The two main sections of the opera are divided, though the curtain does not drop, by the playing of the popular *Intermezzo*. Other familiar pieces from the score are the opening chorus, "Blossoms of Oranges," and the Easter chorus, "Let Us Sing Our Lord's Wondrous Story."

MASON, DANIEL GREGORY (1873–). He comes of one of the best-known musical families in the United States. He is a grandson of Dr. Lowell Mason, a nephew of Dr. William Mason, and a son of Henry Mason, founder of the Mason and Hamlin Company. Graduated from Harvard in 1895, he studied music with Nevin, Chadwick, Whiting, and others in America, and with Vincent d'Indy in France. He has received the honorary degree of Doctor of Letters from Tufts College, and that of Doctor of Music from Oberlin College and the Eastman School of Music. Recognized as an authority on the music of Brahms, Dr. Mason received, in 1932, a grant from the Oberlaender Trust, of the Carl Schurz Memorial Foundation and spent many months in Europe studying source material on Brahms and his music, in preparation of a centennial analytical study of all the Brahms chamber-music works, the most complete study of this kind ever undertaken. Through his many valuable books, his critical and analytical essays on musical subjects, his delightful and scholarly lectures, his composition, and his teaching, Dr. Mason wields a profound influence upon the musical thought of the nation. He is MacDowell Professor of Music at Columbia University.

In addition to the compositions discussed below, Dr. Mason has written many other charming works for piano, voice and chorus, for large and small chamber-music groups, and for orchestra.

Chanticleer Overture. This festival overture for orchestra, which had its first performance by the Cincinnati Orchestra under Fritz Reiner in 1928, has been heard more than 30 times since, and is in the repertoire of leading orchestras. Its motto—"I do not propose to write an ode to dejection, but to brag as lustily as chanticleer in the morning, standing on his roost, if only to wake my neighbors up"— is from Thoreau's *Walden.* The principal theme of the overture is based on the cry of the cock. Associated with the main theme are two others, one given out immediately by the wood-winds, and another, a little later, by four horns. All three themes are expressive of great joy. Following a development and climax in which the full orchestra participates, the music diminishes until only the strings, here played *pizzicato,* are

sounding. The "hen" motif is then introduced by the solo bassoon. A short middle section in quiet mood —muted strings and solo horn—is brought into direct contrast by a lively return to the animated mood of the opening measures. The overture closes with the cry of the Chanticleer, amid a brilliant and joyous swirl of sound.

Country Pictures (Op. 9). Written at Easthampton, Long Island, during the summer of 1908, one of the loveliest sets of tone-poems for piano ever written on American soil. Of them Josef Hofmann wrote Dr. Mason, soon after their publication, "Your music is all expression. No *notes* without meaning . . . a happy combination of modern music and good music." The six pieces are published in two sets. "Cloud Pageant" (Vol. I, No. 1). Opens mysteriously (*Andante non troppo*), depicting, with poetic imagery, the changing aspect of the summer sky. The theme presently takes on a sturdier character (*tempo di marcia lento*), as though portraying the stately movements of the clouds across the heavens. Fantastic shapes of the dissolving cloud-banks are suggested by a delicate cadenza which is interpolated before the strongly chordal climax with which the piece closes. "Chimney Swallows" (Vol. I, No. 2). A vivid delineation of the restless rhythm of birds in flight, a problem for the fingers as well as for the fancy. A contrasting melodic middle section is followed by a gradual return to the restless mood of the opening measures. "At Sunset" (Vol. II, No. 1). A brief idyl of rare charm, displays the composer's skill as a colorist. "The Whippoorwill" (Vol. II, No. 2). A tone-poem of consummate beauty and delicacy which is a clever imitation of this night-bird's warbling, combined with a melody improvisational in character. The composer has told of the source of his inspiration, thus: "One evening, about twilight, while playing softly in my barn-studio at Easthampton, I was charmed by the sweet and persistent singing of a whippoorwill in the woods behind me. Over and over it sang its brief call, always in the key of E-flat Minor; and presently I began to improvise softly on my piano, trying to see into how many keys I could go without marring my agreement with the gentle songster." "The Quiet Hour" (Vol. II, No. 3). A brief composition, its mood one of intimate contemplation. "The Night Wind" (Vol. II, No. 4). The closing number of the suite, opens *presto agitato,* the brief introduction being followed by changes in dynamics, swirls of sound produced by the use of brilliant alternating octaves and dashing scale passages, and occasional combinations of irregular rhythms. A tender middle section provides but a momentary contrast before the "night wind" returns to its earlier mood, the piece providing a dashing climax to this charming set of pieces.

("The Quiet Hour" and "Chimney Swallows" have been arranged by the composer for string orchestra with flute and two horns, and in this version were performed at the American Composers' Concerts in Rochester, in the spring of 1933.)

Divertimento. For two pianos, four hands; also arranged for quintet of wind instruments, and for symphonic band. As the title suggests, it is intended for entertainment. The first movement, "March," is built upon a melody of delicate, grace. The trio, the central part of the piece, turns momentarily to a more tender and tranquil mood, and here the formal beauty of the work is stressed by the canonic treatment given to the melody. But very soon there is a return to the persuasive rhythmic gayety of the "March" proper. "Fugue," the second movement of the *Divertimento,* is based on a jolly theme constructed and developed in traditional manner. After a climax of considerable complexity and dynamic power, the work closes with a reminiscence of the quieter mood of the opening measures.

Fanny Blair (Opus 28), a Folk-Song Fantasy for String Quartet. Had its first performance by the Detroit String Quartet in March 1929. *Fanny Blair* is a free composition based on a folk song of the same name, of which Cecil J. Sharp says, in his *One Hundred English Folk Songs,* "The tune is a curious one. The singer varied both the seventh and third notes of the scale, sometimes singing them major and sometimes minor, in a most capricious way, so that I can only give the tune in the form in which he most frequently sang it."

This fluctuation from major to minor in the melody is responsible, in part, for the plaintive character of the early statement of the theme in this Fantasy. Here it is treated in triple measure, and in two-bar phrases. Throughout its development the theme retains its simplicity, but is varied in mood, and the work ends with a spirited coda characterized by canonic treatment. The composer's choice of the folk melody as thematic material illustrates Dr. Mason's spoken conviction that the most beautiful music consists in a lyric expression of romantic feeling.

Passacaglia and Fugue (Opus 10), for Pipe-Organ. Through the balance and concentration of its structure, and dignity and beauty of its thematic material, this is one of the most noble examples of "absolute" music done by a contemporary composer. It opens with a brief prelude, based upon thematic material drawn from the passacaglia proper, which leads quite promptly to a *fortissimo* statement of the main eight-bar theme in D Minor (four sections of two bars each), given out by the organ pedals.

There are 13 variations, and the development follows closely the traditional manner of embellishment of a ground bass. Variations I to VII maintain the theme in unaltered form in the pedals, while the counterpoint grows with each thematic repetition in brilliancy and intensity. New rhythms are added in variation VI, and a figurated form of the theme bass appears in the seventh. Variations VIII and IX take the theme into lighter registers of the organ, the former being played entirely on the manuals. Variation X (theme in the soprano) begins to build toward the climax; variation XI continues the melody in clear-cut chords, accompanied by a lively figure in the pedals. An expansion of the cadence in XII (the theme now returned to the bass) leads to the climax. A final and culminating variation (XIII) is played full organ, *maestoso*. This leads without pause to the double fugue, the first theme of which (D Major) is derived from thematic elements of the passacaglia melody. The second theme is, presently, combined with the first, and the two are skillfully developed together. The final page of the composition is an abrupt reversion to the passacaglia theme proper, which, given a final variation in the major key, forms a stately and effective *coda* to the entire work. This work has been arranged for orchestra by Ottorino Respighi.

Prelude and Fugue (Opus 20). For two pianos, or for piano and organ, this was originally for piano and orchestra, and in that version has been widely played by John Powell and other concert pianists, with the Boston, New York Philharmonic, Philadelphia, and Chicago orchestras. In the original version, the orchestra opens with a fateful motif to which the piano answers with a tender motto of sensuous beauty, the *Prelude* being entirely concerned with this contrast. The *Fugue* is constructed in three main sections, the tragic mood of its theme being foreshadowed by melodic passages in the *Prelude*. The first theme is stated in the lower register of the piano, during the first section, is heard in contrary motion in the wood-wind of the orchestra in the second section, and later from 'celli and other strings. The third section, with its polyphonic part-weaving and its rich harmonic structure, brings the work to a triumphant climax, with a final orchestral presentation of the theme in inverted form and in *stretto*. Toward the close the theme of the *Prelude* is heard in combination with that of the *Fugue*. This work is a splendid example of Dr. Mason's skillful use of orchestral tone color in contrast with that of solo instruments.

Russians. A song cycle (text by Witter Bynner) for baritone and orchestra, or piano, is an outstanding success, and has already been sung in concert series of the Boston, Philadelphia, Detroit, Chicago, St. Louis, Cleveland, and New York Orchestras. It is remarkable for the suavity of its composition, the gorgeousness of its barbaric melodies, the force of its dramatic rhythms, and its masterly accompaniment.

Scherzo for Orchestra (Opus 22). Composed by Dr. Mason as a movement for his *First Symphony*. Later, feeling that the unity of the symphony had been achieved without inclusion of the *Scherzo*, Dr. Mason issued it as a separate orchestral number, and also made it available to pianists in a two-piano (four-hand) arrangement. The first theme, given out by the horns at the very beginning, is a very old melody from the Gregorian plain-chant, and has been used over and over by composers of all ages, including Mozart (in the *Jupiter Symphony*), Bach (in the *Well-Tempered Clavichord*), and d'Indy (in his *E Major Quartet*). Combinations of rhythms, a clever use of the three-note motif given such prominence throughout the score, and variety of mood—whimsical at first and lyric at the end—make this a work which is effective when and wherever it is performed.

String Quartet in G Minor on Negro Themes (Opus 19). Dedicated to the Flonzaley Quartet, given its first performance by them in New York, Dec. 30, 1919, this is among the American works most frequently played by the major quartets of the day. In three movements Dr. Mason has made use of authentic Negro songs as thematic material, and his marvelous skill in completing, developing, and combining these expressive melodies—together with an unyielding regard for harmonic beauty—has made their vivid appeal universal rather than narrowly provincial. The first movement opens with a brief introduction (in G minor) to the Negro song "You May Bury Me in the East" which is the burden of the theme. Here there are employed the raised sixth step and the curious oscillation between major and minor cadence which give to the air much of its peculiar plaintive flavor.

The second movement is an example of the alternation of slow and quick themes in à single movement. The first theme is the melody, "Deep River," here stated without preamble by the first violin. In its second state (*allegro scherzando*)—this quicker portion of the same movement taking the place of the traditional separate *scherzo*—the melody is given out by the second violin. Throughout this movement Dr. Mason has displayed the qualities of which he himself wrote in an article on "Folk

Song and American Music" (*Musical Quarterly*, July 1918), when he said: "What is needed in the composer who would deal with such material, then, in addition to a tact that enters into its spirit, is a synthetic imagination capable of rounding out its incompleteness, of tracing the whole of the curve it suggests, of developing into full life what it presents only as a germ."

The second theme of the movement (viola), employing "Deep River" as an accompaniment, is entirely original.

The third and closing movement employs three other Negro songs— "Shine, Shine," "O, Holy Lord," "We'll Die in the Field"—as well as a touching reminiscence of "Deep River," the spirit of which seems to permeate the entire movement.

Symphony, No. 1, C Minor. Dedicated to E. J. de Coppet, the founder of the Flonzaley Quartet, this was begun at Boffres, Ardeche, France, in July 1913, and finished in Paris the following spring. It has been played by prominent orchestras, including the Philadelphia, New York Philharmonic, and Detroit orchestras. The work is in three movements.

The first movement (*Largo sostenuto*, 3–4; and *Allegro moderato, risoluto;* C Minor) states in the introductory *Largo* the three motives from which the entire symphony develops. The first motif is a pondering, almost melancholy subject (flutes and clarinets), the first five descending chromatics being used in combination with a counter phrase in the bassoons. The second motive foreshadows the energetic phrase (unison strings in triple rhythm) which become the first theme of the opening *Allegro* and also the main theme of the entire symphony. The third motif is an upward moving, questioning melody, stated first by the solo violin, and soon repeated by the oboe. This becomes the second main theme of the movement.

The second movement (*Larghetto tranquillo*, D-flat Major; *Andantino commodo*, A Major, 4–4) gives over its first part to a new and lyric theme, first sung by the English horn against a quiet background of strings. This is later developed by the entire orchestra. As this dies away, a single trumpet sounds a call (a variant of the second central theme of the symphony), which is presently continued and repeated by other solo instruments over a murmuring accompaniment of muted strings and harp. It comes at last to its complete form as played by the violins and first oboe, accompanied by horns, clarinets, harp, and other strings. All of this section is pastoral in mood. Later the music becomes more animated, the agitation increases, until a climax (full orchestra, *fortissimo*) is reached. Tranquillity then returns and the movement ends peacefully.

The third movement (*Allegro molto marcato*, C Minor, 5–4 and 6–4) opens with the unruly theme of the Finale (a new version of the central theme of the symphony) given out by four horns in unison. The other chief themes of the first movement play their parts here, the quieter second theme being now in the violins, its first three notes now in falling, instead of rising, motion.

The pondering motif of the first movement is now heard from the flutes and clarinet, accompanied only by the tapping of the kettle-drums. The last word, however, is given to the main motif, which is now solemnized into a broad chorale of superb beauty.

Symphony, No. 2, A Major, Opus 30. Completed in 1929. This work is an example of musical expression of simple and spontaneous emotion, of strength and shapeliness of structure, of continuity of style and eloquent intensity. The symphony is orthodox in the succession of its movements which are four in number. It had its first performance by the Cincinnati Symphony under Fritz Reiner, and has since been played by the Chicago and New York Philharmonic orchestras. Dr. Mason, in writing of the symphony (Jan. 24, 1932) said, "In this symphony I have tried out an innovation in structure. Instead of writing for the first and last movements two separate and self-complete pieces, each with its own themes, I have telescoped the whole symphony in such a way that the Finale is a recapitulation of the themes stated in the first movement. These themes do not undergo development according to the classic tradition; in place of a development there are inserted the slow movement and the scherzo. The whole work thus gains, I hope, in unity and in concentration."

The main characteristics of the four movements are as follows:

I. *Maestoso,* A Major. The first and main theme, is based on a motive of three descending chromatic notes. The second theme, played by solo horn, is meditative in character. Toward the close of the movement, a concluding theme enters, over a pedal point on E. II. *Andante Sostenuto,* C Major. Without pause, passages for solo violin and solo clarinet lead into a slow movement of deliberate melody and subtle beauty. This is a lyrical movement, simple in structure, and built upon three treatments of a single long melody. III. *Vivace scherzando,* C-sharp Minor; Trio: *Allegretto quasi pastorale,* D-flat Major. As the music of the scherzo rushes on, fragments of themes from the first movement are heard, at times rhythmically altered and distorted. A trio of folk-song simplicity and charm arrests the movement for a moment, but there is immediately a return to the scherzo movement which leads soon to a cadenza for solo violin and to a persistent rhythm for kettle-drum over which the movement gradually dies away. IV. *Lento largamente: maestoso,* D Major and A Major. The main theme of the symphony (three descending chromatic notes) are now heard again, but slowly and *pianissimo,* from trumpets and trombones. There is also a suggestion of the persistent kettle-drum rhythms from the scherzo. The materials of the first movement are next reviewed, in jubilant mood, after which the melody of the slow movement is played in a glorified and broadened form. As this dies away the main theme re-enters, now over a pedal point on A, and the symphony closes in an elegiac mood.

Variations for String Quartet on a Theme by John Powell. The theme being one used by Mr. Powell in his "Sonata Noble." The contemplative theme, given out by Dr. Mason in the first violin (*Andante con moto*), is unusual in its odd three-bar phrases. There is a series of seven variations and, at the close, a highly individual coda, in which cadenzas are provided for first violin, viola, and 'cello. Particularly striking are variations V, VI, and VII. The *Variations* have been played by the Flonzaley, Gordon, and Roth quartets, and at the South Mountain festivals at Pittsfield.

Sonata in G Minor for Piano and Violin, Opus 5 (Dedicated to Edouard Dethier). Has long been a popular piece of chamber music in America and in England. No one has written for the two instruments or combined them in a more sympathetic or masterly manner than has Dr. Mason here, and such distinguished artists as Mr. and Mrs. David Mannes have found in this work emotional power and sincerity which attract the steadfast interest of all audiences. The *Sonata* follows the traditional three-movement pattern, the first movement being *Allegro moderato;* the second beginning and ending *andante tranquillo, non troppo lento,* with a comparatively more brilliant middle section; and the third, marked *allegro vivace,* makes a sparklingly gay and effective climax. The violin part is of sonorous beauty, and gives to the violinist ample opportunity for display of both his technical and interpretative powers. The piano part is entirely satisfying.

Songs of the Countryside (Opus 23). For soprano and baritone soloists, chorus, and orchestra. A song cycle written in 1926 to five poems by A. E. Housman. Its central theme is woven about the conflict between love and war. The cycle lends itself effectively, by reason of its unity of mood and central theme of dauntless youth facing the grim approach of death, to treatment as a miniature drama of struggle between ardent love of life and the man-made forces of destruction. Each poem is given an individual setting of appropriate forcefulness, and yet all merge into a balanced and unified whole. The cycle uses the folk idiom, and is one of the finest of American or modern choral works.

"Silhouettes" (Opus 21). Three short piano works. Each of the tone-poems, within its few pages, presents a definite mood, and each bears the impress of scholarly workmanship.

No. 1, in A Major, is an example of poetic use of a lovely melody. The work is in simple three-part form with coda. No. 2 (F-sharp Major), in swaying three-beat measure. The simple melody is surrounded by rich but subtle ornament. On its repetition it is placed in high register and enriched by imitative echoes and by shimmering *fiorituri.* No. 3, in C Minor (*Tempo di marcia*) is dramatically conceived as a march commencing *pianissimo misterioso* and ending, after a clangorous trio, with the full resources of the piano in a brilliant climax, after which the trio theme, over a long pedal point, brings a broodingly reminiscent conclusion.

MASSENET, Jules (1842–1912). One of the most facile of the modern French composers, with many successful operas, oratorios, ballets, and orchestral suites. At the Paris Conservatoire he won high honors and then won the Prix de Rome, which gave him three years in Italy. Much of his later work shows the Italian influence. A member of the Academy of Fine Arts and the Legion of Honor of France.

Alsatian Scenes. Produced in Paris in 1882, many years after Massenet's return from army service in Alsace. The suite is composed of four short sketches. The composer left a definite program:

1. "Sunday Morning." "The village streets are deserted, all the houses are empty save for the ill or the aged. The church is full, and the resounding music of sacred hymns is heard as one passes." 2. "At the Tavern." "The joyous life and gay companions of the wee tavern on the main street, its little windows framed about with lead." The music (*allegro*) depicts a gay dance scene, the music opening with a well-accented solo (3–4 time) from the tympani. 3. "Under the Lindens" (*Adagio sostenuto*). Here the strings are all muted. From the wings of the stage as the music is being played, comes the sound of a clock striking six. Massenet says, "The same village . . . but with the great silence of evening . . . and all at the edge of the fields a long avenue of linden trees. Hand in hand, a couple of lovers,

she gently thoughtful, while he murmurs, 'Do you love me today?' " 4. "Sunday Evening" (*Allegro moderato*). "Evening, all the world at its doors, the young people dancing to the rhythmic folk songs of the country. Eight o'clock! The sound of a drum (tambourine) and a song— Alsace! It is time for retiring—a parting roll of drums—mothers calling to their children."

"Meditation" (from *Thaïs*). The scene of the opera *Thaïs* lies in Thebes, Egypt, and the nearby deserts. The plot is from a very old story. "Meditation" is closely associated with the moment of Thaïs's decision to leave her revelries and enter a life of religious service, and is first heard in the opera in Scene One of Act III, at the moment of Thaïs's conversion; again as she disappears in the desert; as an eloquent entr'acte before the third scene of Act III; and at the final moment when she expires.

MENDELSSOHN, Felix (1809–1847). At the age of 17, when he wrote his *Quartet in B Minor,* for strings, Mendelssohn had already displayed great genius. His "Overture" to *Midsummer Night's Dream,* written in his early youth, was inspired by readings from Shakespeare. In August 1835 he was made director of the famous Gewandhaus Orchestra, and during his short life he did much to bring about the world-wide recognition of the genius of Johann Sebastian Bach.

Elijah. This oratorio was first heard at Birmingham, England, in 1846. Mendelssohn had, from his early youth, considered Elijah one of the most romantic characters in the Bible, and felt inspired to give a profoundly devotional setting to the incidents connected with his life. Important single numbers in the work include the brilliant "Hear Ye, Israel" (soprano); "Oh, Rest in the Lord" (contralto); and "Lift Thine Eyes," which is sung to Elijah by the trio of angels as he flees from the vengeance of Jezebel, the wicked queen. "He Watching Over Israel" is the setting of the promise that the Lord "neither slumbers nor sleeps."

Fingal's Cave Overture. Written in strict sonata form, recalls Mendelssohn's visit to the Hebrides Islands off the coast of Scotland. There he visited the cave and immediately afterward wrote to a friend: "In order to make you realize how extraordinarily the cave affected me, I must tell you that the following came into my mind there," and he then continues by adding a sketch of the slight musical theme from which the whole work is developed. A month later he was in London and wrote again that "the Hebrides story builds itself up gradually." First performed in London, 1832.

"Songs Without Words" (See also p. 96). These charming works for piano, are said to have been written in part by Mendelssohn's almost equally talented sister Fanny. Most familiar are the graceful "Spring Song," the "Spinning Song," with its incessant whirring rhythms, and the sturdy "Hunting Song," with its galloping rhythm.

Midsummer Night's Dream. This incidental music to the Shakespeare comedy had its beginnings in the "Overture" written when Mendelssohn was little more than a boy. The entrance into Fairyland is suggested by means of four stately chords. The music which follows suggests the dancing of the fairies. At its close there are again heard the "magic chords." The "Nocturne," written many years later, is played between the third and fourth acts of the play. The "Scherzo," is used as entr'acte music to both first and second acts. The "Wedding March," played as the Duke, Hippolyta, and the lovers are ushered on to the stage, is a popular and familiar number.

St. Paul. Mendelssohn's first oratorio, contains "But the Lord is Mindful of His Own," a magnificent, though simply constructed, aria for contralto; and "Be Thou Faithful," a setting of the words spoken by Paul when he said farewell to the people of Ephesus.

Italian (A Major) Symphony. A result of Mendelssohn's Italian sojourn in 1830–31, first performance in London 1833. In a letter to his family, written from Rome, Mendelssohn says, "The 'Italian' Symphony is making great progress. It will be the most mature thing I have ever done. The last movement, *Presto,* will be the gayest. For the slow movement I have not yet found anything exactly right, and I think I must put it off for Naples."

The first movement (*Allegro vivace,* A Major, 6–8) is constructed along formal lines. The second movement (*Andante con moto,* D Minor, 4–4) has frequently been called the "Pilgrims' March." The third movement (*con moto moderato,* A Major, 3-4) is characterized by a minuet rhythm. The final movement (*Presto,* A Minor, 4-4) is a gay *saltarello* (a Roman or Sicilian dance of the fifteenth and sixteenth centuries). Previous to his writing of this movement, Mendelssohn had witnessed a Roman Carnival, which doubtless influenced its composition.

MILLIGAN, HAROLD VINCENT (1888-   ). Formerly president of the American Guild of Organists, he is now the organist at the Riverside Church in New York City. Mr. Milligan has made valuable contributions to the history of American music in his arrangements of songs by early American composers; and in writing a carefully authenticated biography of Stephen Foster. He has also written a number of very singable anthems.

His works for organ include "Elegy," "Idyll," "Prelude on a Traditional Melody" (*Mooz Zur*), and "Russian Rhapsody."

MOORE, DOUGLAS STUART (1893-   ). Born at Cutchogue, Long Island. His father was the publisher of the *Ladies' World,* one of the earliest of the American woman's magazines; and his mother was the editor. Mr. Moore had his education in Brooklyn, at the Hotchkiss School for Boys in Connecticut, and at Yale, where he earned two degrees and where he was a pupil in composition with David Stanley Smith and Horatio Parker. For four years he was director of music at the Art Museum at Cleveland, Ohio. He then won the

Pulitzer Traveling Prize in Music with his *Four Museum Pieces.* He is now Associate Professor of Music on the Joline Foundation at Columbia University, N. Y. Mr. Moore's later studies in composition have been with Vincent d'Indy, Ernest Bloch, and Nadia Boulanger. He is also a member of the MacDowell Colony at Peterborough.

In his music, at appropriate moments, Mr. Moore displays a delightful sense of humor and whimsy, vivacity, great lyric beauty, a fine gift for colorful orchestration, and an ability to write truly individual modern music without artificial dissonances.

In addition to the compositions discussed below, Mr. Moore's larger works include a "Sonata for Violin" (1929); a symphonic Poem, *Moby Dick* (1928), in which he establishes the atmosphere of the ever-restless sea through characteristic dissonance; and incidental music to Shakespeare's *Twelfth Night* and *Much Ado About Nothing.*

"Comedy Overture" on an American Air (Sweet Adeline) given in its first three performances as *Babbitt.* Composed during the summer of 1931, and immediately heard from major orchestras, endeavors to do justice to the figurative character of *Babbitt.* The music is in classic form and opens with a short introduction. Presently there is heard a reference to "Sweet Adeline"—an alluring popular melody of other days. "Into the overture," says the composer, "I have tried to put a few ideas about a much maligned figure of American life. I have tried to put into it some

of the joviality, the sentimentality, and pathetic striving after 'higher things,' of the man that Mencken refers to as the *homo boobiensis.*"

Four Museum Pieces. A suite, written first for organ, then arranged for symphonic orchestra. It was composed while Mr. Moore was in Cleveland, and the pieces were inspired by the pictures and objects which he saw daily in the Museum there. The separate numbers are: 1. "Fifteenth Century Armor." A quaint march, in which is depicted a joust of other days. 2. "Madonna of Botticini." In which the devotional spirit and exquisite serenity of the subject are suggested by means of skillful use of plain-song melody. 3. "The Chinese Lion and the Unhappy Flutist." Here Mr. Moore reveals his inimitable ability as a writer of program music. The short number, in true scherzo style, tells the brief story of a persistent flutist who awakens the lion by his constant performance, and who is effectively silenced by the lion's terrible roar. 4. "A Statue by Rodin." A contrasting number of forceful character, inspired by the statue "Man of the Age of Bronze."

Pageant of P. T. Barnum. A colorful orchestral work written at Peterborough during the summer of 1924, portraying in music certain qualities of American character which abounded in the life story of the great showman. The music had its first performance by the Cleveland Orchestra under Sokoloff during the 1925–26 season, and was heard the next year in New York. Making an instant appeal to audiences through its lyric

and thoroughly human qualities, it has been played repeatedly since then by major orchestras, and under such conductors as Sokoloff, Damrosch, Goossens, Hanson, Hadley, and Schelling. The music seeks to portray the glamour and beauty, the genuine sentiment and spontaneous humor of American life. The suite is in five parts, each of which is a musical picture of one of the most interesting episodes or personages connected with the life of Barnum:

1. "Boyhood at Bethel." P. T. Barnum, the famous showman, was born in 1810 at Bethel, Conn., and in this section of the suite Mr. Moore has suggested the characteristic environment of the youthful hero, with its fiddle dance music, New England bands, and its inheritance from early Connecticut hymnology. The composer is authority for the statement that the zestful rhythm of the opening "calliope" theme was inspired by the lines from Vachel Lindsay— "I am the Calliope, Calliope, Calliope, willy, willy, willy, wahoo." The statement of the first theme is followed by a brief *fugato* treatment from the strings, after which derivatives from it form a *basso ostinato* against the second theme, a "brass band" melody. During the ensuing development section, there is heard a direct quotation (in the flutes) from the ancient hymn "There is a Happy Land," after which all three themes are combined in contrapuntal fashion. *"Joice Heth."* Joice Heth was a Negro woman, said to be 161 years old, and the first nurse of George Washington, of whom she related many intimate anecdotes. Barnum bought

and exhibited her for money. Joice Heth and her monologue are suggested in colorful manner by recitative and themes from Negro spirituals. The music is in three-part form. The pathetic melody of "Nobody Knows de Trouble I've Seen" (in original five-tone scale) is given first as a solo and then with harmonies also in pentatonic scale. Joice Heth then delivers her monologue, after which its melody is combined with that of the old Negro spiritual. 3. "General and Mrs. Tom Thumb." An animated bit of music in which are set forth characteristics of these famous midgets whose rise to notoriety came through the efforts of Barnum. There is a clever burlesque upon certain passages in the Tschaikowsky "Overture 1812," with its fiercely booming cannons. In "General and Mrs. Tom Thumb" one of the suggested instruments for performance, in the percussion group, is a cap-pistol which—when the orchestral performers have been able to secure and use it, as has been once or twice impossible owing to stringency of local civic law—yields an effect hilariously funny. The early bombastic melody of "General Tom Thumb" is presently contrasted with a theme suggestive of his wife in the melody of an old-fashioned waltz, presented, however, in truly modern fashion. The piece concludes with a re-entrance of the General in a miniature fanfare. 4. "Jenny Lind." Commemorates the singing of that famous artist of other days, the "Swedish Nightingale," at her first concert at Castle Garden, New York City, in 1850, when she came to America for a tour under the Barnum management. The movement opens with a romantic harp introduction, after which Jenny Lind (impersonated by the flute) sings a tender air characteristically Scandinavian, both in melody and interval. Soon the violin takes up the melody and the flute adds brilliant embellishments in the style of a coloratura soprano. The piece ends in a passage of quiet beauty. 5. "Circus Parade." Closes the suite with a humorous and realistic imitation of a Barnum parade, with its exhibitions of noisy animals, the creak of circus-wagon wheels, and raucous steam calliope. The music is notable for a special ingenuity, the carefully monotonous *ostinato* of the rumbling wagon wheels, the calliope just off pitch, and the ponderous swing of the elephant's tread. In a strikingly unusual restatement of principal themes, each is presented as a phrase in melodic and solid choral style, and each phrase is separated from what follows by a brilliant interlude from the percussion. Toward the end the calliope and the tune of "Old Dog Tray" carry the day, and P. T. Barnum passes from view, as he would like to, in a blaze of circus glory.

Symphony of Autumn (1930). A short three-movement work, unprogrammatic in style, which follows strictly classic lines, and which seeks to depict autumn as it is known on eastern Long Island. The first movement opens with a horn call, and contains a "motto" heard with frequency throughout the movement. The second movement, the theme of which, suggested by the rhythmic song of the katydids, has a middle section of rarer charm. Here there is a soft and artistic blurring of two tonalities—a solo 'cello playing in A-flat Major against an accompaniment in A-flat Minor. The third and last movement is alluringly gay, and written mostly in irregular 5–8 measure. The first performance of the symphony was given by Dr. Howard Hanson (to whom it is dedicated) in Rochester, N. Y., April 1932.

MOUSSORGSKY, MODESTE (1839–1881). Prepared at first for a military career, he became intensely interested in the national music of Russia, and was largely instrumental in the banding together of "The Five."

Boris Godunov. (See "Favorite Choruses from Opera," p. 49.)

Khovanchina. Often spoken of as "a musical folk-drama," is, like the same composer's *Boris Godounov,* based upon certain Russian historic events. The score of the music was not completed at the composer's death, and was revised, completed, and orchestrated by Rimsky-Korsakov. An attractive passage is the entr'acte, which comprises the 51 measures played by the orchestra at the opening of the second scene of Act IV. Galitsin, about to be led into exile, and guarded by a troop of cavalry, crosses the public square on his way. The bells of the church, Vassily-Blayeny, are tolling mournfully. As the troops pass by, comments are heard from the onlooker. The music is touchingly appealing, both in tone quality of the instruments which are playing, and in the rhythm of the music.

MOZART, WOLFGANG AMADEUS (1756–1791). Born at Salzburg, Austria, the son of Leopold Mozart, who was vice-chapelmaster there at the Court of the Archbishop. Among his greatest works are numerous symphonies, operas, masses, and works of almost every type for voice, piano, and every solo instrument. His last work was a *Requiem,* which, though ordered for another, he declared he was writing for himself. Mozart died in Vienna, December 5, 1791. More than 60 years later a monument was erected on the probable site of his grave by the city of Vienna. (See also "Haydn, Mozart, Beethoven, and the Classic Symphony," p. 92.)

Concerto in D for Violin and Piano (or Orchestra). Dates from 1775, but after a century and a half of time, it keeps untarnished its felicity and transparent elegance, its gentleness and gayety, although, from the middle movement on, there are momentary withdrawals into a more melancholy mood. Instead of a high-spirited rondo, the final movement (*Andante grazioso*) has frequent moments of pensiveness.

"Alla Turca" (Turkish March). Originally the closing movement of a piano sonata written in 1779, is now frequently heard in orchestral version. It is given this unusual title because of the character of the bass, in which, it is said, Mozart imitated the rhythmic beatings of Turkish drums, cymbals, and crescent.

Cosi fan Tutte. Written during the latter part of Mozart's life, this is a work of much charm, in which humorous situations abound. The many ensembles are brilliant and enjoyable, and the *arias* for the chief characters show the composer's usual masterly treatment. The work recalls the old-style *opera buffa,* by which is meant an opera always more or less comic in which much of the light or playful dialogue is spoken.

"Cradle Song." One of the loveliest of all lullabies, has been said to possess a "divine melody." One of its most exquisite features is the lingering phrase with which the song closes.

Don Giovanni. (First performance in Prague in 1787.) A setting of a famous story in which the statue of a murdered man accepts an invitation to eat with the murderer, appears, and drags the guilty man down to Hell. The "Overture," frequently heard as a concert piece, was written on the eve of the first performance. Mozart had passed a happy evening visiting with friends, who warned him that his overture was not yet ready. Mozart began to work about midnight, and, kept awake by his wife, who told him entertaining stories, he had the work finished by three o'clock in the morning. Next evening, with the sheets of music paper still wet from the copyists' ink, Mozart directed it without rehearsal and won a storm of applause. The "Minuet" from the same opera suits the stately movements of the courtly dancers of the eighteenth century.

Magic Flute. Mozart's most celebrated opera, is based upon an old folk tale of the magical power of music. (See also *Schwanda.*) In this opera, with its impossible situations, are introduced scenes of fantastic beauty, fantastic horror, genuine humor, and delicate grace and beauty.

Tamino and his companion, the birdman, are each fortified with magical musical instruments, the one a magic flute and the other a set of chimes, with which they may exert an influence great enough to rescue them from all perils as they journey in search of Pamina, daughter of the Queen of the Night.

When Mozart began work on the music he had so many interruptions that Schikaneder, who had invited him to write it, established him in a tiny garden house near the theater. As with *Don Giovanni,* the "Overture" was not written until the last moment. Contrary to his usual custom, Mozart included in it no themes from the opera itself, but made of it simply a piece of enchantment which should introduce the audience to the story it was to hear. It opens with three long-drawn chords, symbolic of magic words; then dashes into a gay fugue, the subject of which is first given out by the clarinets, followed by the cornets, and, in turn, by almost every instrument of the orchestra.

Marriage of Figaro. An opera very similar in plot to the *Barber of Seville* by Rossini, written at the command of Emperor Joseph II of Austria. The "Overture" is a gem. The rollicking little figure played by the violins at its beginning, in unison with the bassoons, soon reaches to all the other instruments, who join in the jollity as though they were, instead, dancers joining in a romp.

Mass, No. 12. Mozart wrote, in all, 15 authenticated masses. The "Gloria" (in C) from this one is a work of great dignity and wonderful effect. Its first theme is built upon a simple ascending arpeggio. *"Kleine Nachtmusik"* (Night Music). For strings only, this might well be called "serenade" as it so clearly suggests outdoor entertainment at night. There are four movements, an *allegro,* a minuet with trio, a romance, and a finale.

"Overture in Italian Style." A spirited work written just after Mozart's return from Paris at the age of 24, resembling the style of the Italian theater symphony of the seventeenth and eighteenth centuries. It opens with a vigorous *tutti* in which an ascending triplet figure is given much prominence. The second, or slow section, features a gentle subject for violins alone, although they are presently joined by the other strings and accompanied by the bassoons. Then the flutes sing the air. A modified form of the first *allegro* completes the "Overture."

Jupiter Symphony. The last of three symphonies written by Mozart during the space of six weeks, in the summer of 1787, was given its title because of the loftiness of its musical ideas, and the nobility of its proportions.

The first movement (*Allegro vivace*) opens with the announcement of the main subject in C. This—given out in unison—may be thought of in two parts, the first in the type of a fanfare, and the second a reply (from the strings). The first is given out vigorously, and the second gently, in a questioning manner. At the ninth measure the full orchestra plays it triumphantly, accompanied presently by a descending figure in the strings. After the first theme has been sung

several times, the music modulates to the key of G and the second main subject is heard, in persuasive style, from the first violins. Later it is echoed by the violas and 'cellos. The closing subject of the first section of this movement is sometimes spoken of as a *codetta.* There follows the development section, in which there is an abrupt modulation to the key of E-flat; after which, beginning with the closing theme (or *codetta*), the main subjects are played with variations of rhythm, structural treatment, transposition into different keys, and varied instrumental coloring. The recapitulation, with which the movement closes, brings back all themes in the main key of the symphony (C Major).

The second or slow movement is an example of melodic ornamentation not without depth of expression. In the main theme is heard an example of persistent syncopation which is imitated with variations further on in the movement. The second theme is given out by the oboes and bassoons.

The graceful minuet, or third movement, is in regular three-part form, and attention is called to the canonical writing (in which oboes, bassoons, flutes, and violins follow one another in repetition of the first theme) toward the close of the first main section. Notice may also be made of the persistence of the repeated cadence, and of the sequential modulations, in the trio, or second large section.

The fourth movement is a marvel of technical construction and in use of contrapuntal devices. The first subject is taken from a Gregorian melody. It was evidently a favorite with Mozart and other composers, as he used it in others of his works, in the *Credo* of his *F Major Mass* (1774), in the *Sanctus* of the *C Major Mass* (1776), in his *B-Flat Symphony* (1779), in his *Sonata in E-Flat* for Violin and Piano (1785). Handel also used it in the chorus "Then Round About"; as did Bach, in the "E Major Fugue" of the *Well-Tempered Clavichord;* Schubert, in his *Mass in E-Flat;* and Mendelssohn, in his *St. Paul,* his *42nd Psalm,* and in two of his symphonies. A second subject contains a unit which is much used later in the movement. The first theme returns to become the subject of a five-voiced fugue, in which the theme is played, in turn, by the second violins, the first violins, the violas, the 'cellos, and by the flutes and oboes in unison. The third theme, a short ascending phrase immediately imitated in the basses, is then heard, while the persistent canonical development of the first theme continues. A subordinate fourth subject is later heard, with many imitations. Still another theme soon enters, this fifth little air completing the subjects with which Mozart constructs his masterly fugal Finale. The development section is brief, followed by a Recapitulation. Then comes the coda which is one of the most remarkable examples of contrapuntal complexity in all symphonic literature, for here he makes a simultaneous statement of all five themes, theme 1 in the first violins, theme 3 in the seconds, theme 5 in the violas, theme 2 in the 'cellos, and theme 4 in the doublebasses.

NEVIN, Ethelbert (1862–1901). Born in Edgeworth, Pa., one of the early American composers to achieve prominence. His early musical study was done in Boston, after which he was the student (in Berlin) of Karl Klindworth (a celebrated pupil of Chopin) and Hans von Bülow. Later years were spent in Florence and Venice, Italy. His composition is mainly devoted to songs and short works for the piano, including his "Sketch Book," "Water Scenes," and "Venezia."

OFFENBACH, Jacques (Jacques Levy). (1819–1880). Took the name by which he is best known from the German town in which he was born, Offenbach in Hesse. He studied for a while in Paris, but much of his ability as a writer came from associations with other musicians. During his life he was a successful manager of musical events, a skillful violinist, and a popular rather than a scholarly composer. In addition to appearances on the Continent and in the British Isles, he made one concert tour in America.

"Barcarolle." From *Tales of Hoffmann* (see also p. 8), a fantastic opera in three acts, a prologue, and an epilogue, based on the Poe-like stories of the nineteenth-century German writer, E. T. A. Hoffmann. The scene of Act II lies in Venice, in a palace overlooking the lagoons of the Grand Canal. Hoffmann is enamored of Guiletta. As an atmosphere entr'acte before the rising of the curtain, the "Barcarolle" is heard softly from the orchestra. The notable feature of this music is its rocking rhythm,

which suggests the movements of a Venetian gondolier.

As the curtain rises, the melody is taken up and sung as a duet by Guiletta and Niklausse as they disembark from a gondola. Later, as the Act closes, they depart over the moonlit waters, again singing the refrain, snatches of which reach the listener's ear after the boat has passed from sight.

PADEREWSKI, IGNACE JAN (1860–). Born in Poland, he was a student at the Warsaw Conservatory, and of Leschetizky, the celebrated Viennese teacher of piano. Of his works the opera *Manru* is the largest. It is as a virtuoso pianist and as a patriot that he is best known. His first concert in America was given at Carnegie Hall in New York on November 17, 1891. During the World War he gave up music entirely for efforts in behalf of his native land and its war relief. In addition to the raising of large sums of money, he offered to the United States the services of an army of 100,000 Poles and 50 trained officers. Returning to Poland from the United States, as soon as conditions made this possible, he was there elected Premier on January 26, 1919, and 30 days later the Allied Council at Paris recognized the Polish Republic under his guidance. Paderewski continued as Premier until 1920. Since then he has again concertized, maintaining homes both in Poland, and at Morges, Switzerland.

"Minuet in G." This popular number, a conscious imitation of the quaintly courteous, classic music of

Mozart, Haydn, and Beethoven, was composed, it is said, as the result of a friend's insistence that no one could now write in the manner of Mozart, and now forms the most famous unit in a charming series of *Six Concert Humoresques.*

PARKER, HORATIO W. (1863– 1919). Born at Auburndale, Mass., and was a student first of his mother, then of Emery, Orth, and Chadwick in Boston; and with Rheinberger and Abel in Munich. In 1893 he became director of the School of Music at Yale University. In 1911 he won the $10,000 prize, offered by the Metropolitan Opera Company for an American opera, with his opera *Monā,* based upon a libretto by Brian Hooker. The opera tells a story of the times of the Druids, in early Britain. Four years later, the same two artists won another prize of the same amount offered by the National Federation of Music Clubs, with their opera *Fairyland.* Parker's finest work is displayed in his oratorio *Hora Novissima* (The Last Hour), which he wrote in 1894.

PONCHIELLI, AMILCARE (1834– 1886). Born near Cremona, Italy, a student at the Milan Conservatory, and had a long and distinguished career of writing for the stage. His best-known work (although he wrote many ballets, operas, and some sacred music) is *La Gioconda.* He was, for years, director of music at Bergamo Cathedral.

"Dance of the Hours." From *La Gioconda* (an opera based upon Victor Hugo's drama, *Angelo*), occur-

ring in the second scene of Act III. The "Dance" is devised by Alvise for the entertainment of his guests, and symbolizes the struggle of the powers of light and darkness. When used as a ballet, the 24 dancers are always dressed to impersonate the Hours of Day and Night.

POWELL, JOHN (1882–   ). Born in Richmond, Va., and a graduate of the University of Virginia. Known as a pianist and composer, he was a student for five years with Leschetizky. He has toured widely in both the Old and New Worlds. In his compositions he has made striking and effective use of the idioms of the music of the Negro. (See also "Virginia Finds Her Folk Music," p. 167.)

Sonata Virginianesque for Violin and Piano. First performance in Vienna, 1908. It is in three movements. The first, "In the Quarters," after a slow introduction, depicts the Negro making merry. Unrestrained gayety and humor lilt through the racy themes which are based upon Negro dance-songs. The second theme is very characteristic, and is still sung to the words, "Done pawn my wife, done pawn my chile, done pawn my di'mon' ring." The development section reverts to the gloomy motif of the introduction, which is developed to a tragic and barbaric climax, after which the recapitulation takes its course merrily to the end of the movement. "In the Woods." Very different in mood and presents the young Negro on his way to see his sweetheart. The first melody is a lyric one, the second deeply contemplative. "At the Big House." Shows the Negro making music for the dancing of his master and thoroughly enjoying the gayety of the whites. The movement is in rondo form and the themes are based upon old Virginia reel tunes derived from the music of "Sir Roger de Coverley" and other English country dances. The melodies, though vigorous, are refined and graceful and imbued with that gracious warmth and charm so characteristic of "Ole Virginny." The *Sonata* was introduced to American audiences by David and Clara Mannes.

Negro Rhapsody. Mr. Powell has made a very careful study of the music of the South, in its various phases, and had very definite and interesting ideas as to the origin of Negro song. Of the melodies which he has interwoven into his very successful *Negro Rhapsody* he says, "Some years ago, when I was working on my *Rhapsody,* I happened to visit friends in Richmond, and through the door that led from the kitchen to the room where we were sitting, there came the sound of someone humming. There was something so primitive, so passionate, so subtly stirring, about the muted minor cadences, and the pulsing tom-tom beats of this humming, that I could not put my mind to anything else. Quietly, at last, I tiptoed to the pantry, and there was black Pauline, piling glasses on a tray, and humming or singing softly at her work. When she saw me she was so startled that she let slip her tray, glasses and all. At last, after a great deal of adroit coaxing, I got her to tell me what it was she was humming: what was this thing of primitive allure that had reached and invited me, on the other side of the door. Her song had been her own version of a common gospel hymn, called 'I Want to be Ready.'

"Now, as she shifted from her own version and sang the hymn proper, a great many things became evident. She had consistently converted the original major intervals into the minor, completely changing the character of the tune, and on top of that she had added to each cadence a wild little tom-tom-like tail beat that had not come into the original at all. Finally, what do you suppose the tune of the 'hymn proper' turned out to be? It was the tune of 'Sally Get Your Hair Cut Short,' a street-song of 30 years before. By weaving this commonplace tune over with unconscious embroideries out of her own Negro background, Pauline had created a 'spiritual' of stirring beauty. I have used Pauline's spiritual for the second climax of my *Rhapsody,* and to me it represents a great deal. It stands as the epitome of the colored race, seizing haphazard upon stray elements of an alien culture, and making them over into an entirely new and different expression of their own."

Natchez-on-the-Hill (Three Virginia Country Dances). This piece is a setting of three traditional Virginian fiddle tunes: "Natchez-on-the-Hill," "The Hog-eyed Man," and "The War-whoop." All three are authentic old dance-tunes in particularly fine versions and unusually well-preserved. They came to Mr. Powell from Mrs. John Hunter, just as she used to dance to them, when—as Miss Polly Boston—she heard them played by her grandmother in Louisa County, Virginia.

The tunes are remarkable for their charm of local color, their ear-taking melodiousness, their foot-compelling lilt, which are irresistibly captivating to all.

The tune "Natchez-on-the-Hill" is one of a large group of variants deriving from the old (probably Tudor) English country dance, "Old Mother Oxford." The name recalls an interesting and forgotten bit of last century history, when the Mississippi was the frontier of this country and conditions there were similar to those in California somewhat later.

The form of the composition approaches that of the rondo: A-B-C-B-A, with a short coda. In his setting, Mr. Powell has added nothing extraneous, but has confined his efforts to emphasis of those qualities inherent in his material.

PROKOFIEV, SERGEI. A twentieth-century Russian composer, best known for his immensely clever burlesque opera, *Love of Three Oranges,* which had its first performance in the New World, at the Chicago Auditorium (Chicago Opera Company), December 30, 1921, the composer directing. The "three oranges" are three princesses who are imprisoned by a wicked sorceress. The Prince is ill, and his physician orders his magician to prepare a masquerade in the hope of inducing the gloomy invalid to laugh. Every effort is in vain and at last he is told that he may not be happy until he has fallen in love with three oranges. The prophecy is fulfilled when he is finally taken to the strange castle where a cook guards the three oranges in which the princesses are hidden. He cuts open one of the monstrous pieces of fruit and out steps a beautiful girl. Both she and the second princess to emerge from an orange die, but the third is revived, and as she returns the Prince's love, the curse is lifted, and all "live happily ever after." The most interesting pieces of instrumental music in the score are the "Waltz Scherzo," which accompanies the dancing of the devils at the masquerade; and the "March and Scherzo."

Classical Symphony. The first movement is written daintily, and in strict sonata form; the second is, in character, as though it might have been written by Mozart himself; and the third movement is a gavotte.

PUCCINI, Giacomo (1858–1924). Came of a distinguished musical family. Rare talent displayed at an early age won for him the active sponsorship of the Queen of Italy and a pension which enabled him to study at the Conservatory of Milan. His writings, mostly in the field of opera, are filled with beautiful melody. His best-known works include the operas *Le Villi, Manon Lescaut, La Bohême, Tosca, Madame Butterfly,* and the posthumous *Turandot.*

La Bohême. Had its first performance in the Teatro Regio, Turin (Italy), February 1, 1896, with Toscanini conducting. To the writing of it Puccini gave his deepest devotion,

and he succeeded in creating picturesque, spontaneous atmosphere, and a clear portrayal of character and situation, as well as music of a highly appealing character. There are four acts.

The characters: Rudolfo, a poet (tenor); Marcel, a painter (baritone); Colline, a philosopher (bass); Schaunard, a musician (baritone); Benoit, the landlord (bass); Alcindoro, aged lover of Musetta (bass); Mimi, a maker of embroideries (soprano); and Musetta, a friend of Mimi (soprano). Time and Scene: Student life in Latin Quartier of Paris, 1830. The source of the libretto is Murger's novel, *La Vie Bohême* (Bohemian Life), the plot differing frequently from the original in fact, but not in spirit.

Act I. Scene, in the Attic, Christmas Eve.

With no fire and no food, Rudolfo alternates in attempts to write and to keep warm. Marcel alternately paints and blows upon his fingers. Colline enters, followed by Schaunard, who has come into enough money to buy fuel and food for them all. Their hilarity is interrupted by the crafty landlord who comes to demand his rent.

The money presently divided evenly among the four comrades, all but Rudolfo start for the Café Momus to celebrate. He, lighting a candle, begins to write, when he hears a timid knocking at the door. Mimi, an attic neighbor, enters, key in hand, begging a light for her candle. At leaving, she accidentally drops her key just as both candles are extinguished by the draft from the open door. While groping for the key, Rudolfo touches Mimi's hand, and this calls forth his celebrated aria, "Che gelida manina" (Your little hand is frozen), and "Racconto di Rudolfo" (Rudolfo's Narrative). Mimi, in turn, tells of her humble occupation and of her longing for the beauties of nature in "Mi chiamano Mimi" (They call me Mimi). Called to the window by the voices of his comrades, Rudolfo suggests that Mimi accompany him for the evening's merry-making, and the act closes with the duet, "O, soave fanciulla" (O, lovely maiden), part of which is sung as the two descend the attic stairway.

Act II. Scene, open Square, Café Momus at one side. Adjoining shops on the Square are filled with a gay, vivacious throng, street vendors, Punch and Judy. General confusion reigns. Rudolfo and Mimi join the "Bohemians" at a table set before the Café. While revelry is at its height, Musetta (Marcel's former sweetheart) and Alcindoro appear. Musetta, hoping to attract Marcel's attention, sings her famous waltz song, "Quando me 'n vo soletta per la via" (As through the streets I wander). She joins the gay party at the table after sending her escort on a fruitless errand. The friends depart, leaving the entire bill for Alcindoro to pay on his return.

Act III. Scene, outside an Inn near the city gate of Paris. This sad scene is relieved by the fickle gayety of Musetta and her quarrels with Marcel. Rudolfo has come to mistrust Mimi's love, and in the chill and bitter night, Mimi, now very ill, bids

him farewell. At the same time the angry tones of Musetta and Marcel are heard, and the scene ends in the quartet, "Addio, dolce svegliare" (Farewell, sweet love).

Act IV. Scene, the attic. Marcel and Rudolfo mourn their lost loves in the duet, "Ah! Mimi, tu piu" (Ah! Mimi, Thou False One). Mimi is brought to Rudolfo's doorstep in a dying condition, by Musetta. The comrades make her as comfortable as possible on the bed, and go out for medicine. Colline, leaving to pawn his coat for funds, sings the celebrated "coat" song, "Vecchia, zimarra" (Garment, antique and rusty, a last good-by). Rudolfo comforts Mimi, who starts to remind him of the song he sang to her at their first meeting, but breaks off in coughing. Pathos and restrained delicacy accompany the final death scene. "The death of Mimi," said Puccini, in a letter to his publisher, "with all that leads up to it, is very touching."

"One Fine Day." Sung by Butterfly, the little Japanese heroine in *Madame Butterfly*. The plot of the opera, built upon a story by the late John Luther Long of Philadelphia, which was later dramatized by David Belasco, tells a tale of life in the "flowery kingdom." It is simple and direct, its pathos tenderly echoed in the music. The opera is in three acts. In the first there is shown the wedding celebration of Butterfly and the American, Lieutenant Pinkerton. The second act displays the loyal faith of Butterfly as she awaits the return of Pinkerton from America. The third act is filled with tragedy, as Butterfly realizes that she is deserted, and dies by

her own hand. "One Fine Day" is sung at the opening of Act II, when, while others doubt, Butterfly sings of the fine day when the great ship shall be seen upon the horizon and her lover will return to her.

RACHMANINOV, SERGEI (1873–). Best known to the public as a concert pianist, and as the composer of the ever-popular "C-Sharp Minor Prelude." Born in 1873 in Novgorod, Russia, he spent many years as a student in St. Petersburg and Moscow, his teachers being Siloti and Arensky. His published works include songs, short numbers for piano, two concertos for piano and orchestra, an opera, chamber music, a symphony, and shorter works for orchestra.

The Island of the Dead, Opus 29. An elegiac poem for orchestra which aims to suggest in music the same mood and scenes depicted by the artist A. Böcklin, of the storied isle, a burial place for centuries, in the Bocche of Cattaro on the coast of Dalmatia. The painter was so captivated by the beauty of the spot, and with its ancient traditions, that he was impelled, through the years, to paint six pictures of it. The picture, which shows a soul's journey, in a ferry, to its last home and life is characterized by great dignity and solemnity, these being intensified by the dark shades cast by the somber cypress trees.

In his symphonic poem, Rachmaninov has suggested the same feeling of oppression and deep grief, and the sublimity of the occasion. The music has three sections. The first is in 5–8 measure and slow tempo. Fea-

tures of this section are a monotonous wave-like motion imparted by a continued *legato* figure for harp and muted 'cellos; a persistent muffled drum beat; the tremulous figures from flutes and the shuddering downward-moving chromatic passages which suggest the winds blowing through the cypresses. The middle section is somewhat livelier and more agitated, building up, by use of new themes and tempos, a huge climax, from which it returns to the original key and mood, as though depicting the return of the now empty boat to the lonely hillside from whence it came.

RAFF, JOSEPH JOACHIM (1822–1882). Born at Lachen, on the Lake of Zurich in Switzerland, but spent much of his life in Germany, dying in Frankfurt. He was happy in the friendship of many great men, including Liszt, von Bülow, and Mendelssohn. He was the teacher of Edward MacDowell.

"Cavatina." Familiar both as a violin solo and in various arrangements, this is a lyric gem familiar to an unusually large public.

RAVEL, MAURICE (1875–). (See also "Music of the Twentieth Century," p. 228.) Ravel's music is often descriptive. He makes much use of the exotic Eastern scales, and, in some instances, uses archaic dance forms.

Mother Goose Suite. Based upon the old legend of "Beauty and the Beast." The music was written as a piano duet, then arranged as ballet music for use with a stage spectacle. Now it is most familiar in its form of an orchestral suite. It is scored for small orchestra with the addition of many appropriate percussion instruments. The first number, "Pavane of the Sleeping Beauty," is a brief tone-picture. The second number portrays the wanderings of Hop o' My Thumb, who strewed crumbs behind him to show himself the way back home. These were eaten by the hungry birds, and Hop o' My Thumb was left to wander alone in the darkness of the night. The muted violin here suggests the indecision of the little boy, and violin harmonics, aided by brief passages from flute and piccolo, which suggest the cries of birds. The third number, "Empress of the Statuettes," suggests the busily bobbing figures of the statuettes that have come to life, and who now sing, and play on their lutes and viols, as the Empress bathes. Here Ravel has employed the five-tone scale in combination with the whole-tone scale, producing a distinctly Oriental effect. In the fifth number, "Beauty and the Beast," Beauty is symbolized by a graceful waltz melody, and the Beast by an unhappy phrase from the contra-bassoon. The suite closes with "The Magic Garden," a bit of dreamy and elusive music.

"Valse." This music, sketched during the World War, and completed in Vienna in 1920, was at first given as a ballet. The music is really a succession of waltzes, at first sensuous and languorous, then playful and piquant, sentimental, showy, and strenuous.

RESPIGHI, Ottorino (1879–   ). Born in Bologna, Italy. He was a pupil of Rimsky-Korsakov. (See also p. 103.)

Ballata delle Gnomidi (Ballad of the Gnomes). This work had its first performance at the Augusteo in Rome in April 1920. The music is a free fantasy based upon a poem by Carlo Clausetti.

Fountains of Rome. A tone-picture of four of the ancient fountains which are so closely allied with the history of Rome. The first, "La fontana de Valle Guilia all' alba' " (The Fountain of Valle Guilia at Dawn), suggests pastoral scenes common to all Italian cities. The music also suggests the coming of the light, and the many faint or weird sounds of Nature that often accompany it. The second, "The Triton Fountain at Morn," with its joyous fanfares, recalls the troops of naiads and tritons which seem to dance between the jets of water in this old fountain. "The Fountain of Trevi at Midday." The solemn first theme, which is shifted from wind instruments to the brass, is an announcement of the approach of Neptune's chariot across the water. The trio section is gay and triumphant and after it the mood of the opening measures returns. A coda, in which the echo of horns is heard, carries the music directly to the opening of "Villa di Medici Fountain at Sunset," in which there is heard a suggestion of vesper bells and a hymn-like melody.

Pines of Rome. Here the composer has taken Nature as a point of departure in order to recall memories and visions. The century-old trees which are such a feature of the Roman landscape become symbolic of important events in Roman life. 1. "The Pines of the Villa Borghese" (*allegretto vivace*). Depicts children at play in the pine-grove of the Villa, mimicking the soldiers who frequently pass, the birds that sing near them, and singing and playing the Italian equivalent of "Catch Me." 2. "The Pines Near a Catacomb." Permeated with the characteristics of the old Gregorian modes. From the depths of the catacombs seems to come the air of one of the early psalms which the Christians were obliged, in early days, to sing secretly, if at all. 3. "The Pines of the Janiculum." Produces the effect of distance, setting a scene for the singing of the nightingale for which Respighi has used the mechanical record of a nightingale, as he is said to have felt that music written by any composer would lack something of the spontaneity and flexibility of the real bird's song. 4. "The Pines of the Appian Way." Recalls the marching of the old Roman army along the historic highway.

RIMSKY-KORSAKOV, NICOLAI (1844–1908). Born in the Russian province of Novgorod, educated at the governmental Naval College, and spent some years of his early life at sea as a naval officer. As one of "The Five," he became intensely interested in use of Russian folk lore and music as a basis for a national "school." This is exemplified in such compositions as his *Symphonietta* for orchestra, Opus 31, in which he employs such Russian airs as "In the Shade

of the Garden Strolling," "Ah! See the Old Pear-Tree," and "Over Fields, Over Meadows." In addition he was one of the most gifted of all musicians in the technique of orchestration, and left a group of well-trained students.

Caprice Espagnole. One of the most brilliant pieces for orchestra written by any modern composer; is divided into five distinct divisions. Within the limits of the piece, Rimsky-Korsakov has provided solo music for each instrument or choir of the orchestra. The first of the five sections, "Alborado" (which in this connection has to do with music played at dawn, in honor of an official, a custom of Old Spain), opens with a flourish, the entire section having a strongly military flavor, at the same time being embellished in characteristic Oriental manner, and set in Spanish rhythms. Part two, "Variations," is a set of elaborate variations, upon a quaint Spanish folk air. Here many instruments are given ample opportunity to display their possibilities in the solos, duet, and quartet passages with which the variations abound. Part three, again entitled "Alborado," is thematically a repetition of the first part, but is remarkably different in effect because here Rimsky-Korsakov has provided an entirely different instrumentation. Part four, "Scene and Gypsy Song," a series of florid cadenzas, in effect, carries the music into the finale, a Spanish fandango which, through further use of embellishments, Oriental scale passages and intervals, sharp *staccato* and *pizzicato,* chromatics, and dashing rhythms, brings the music to a dashing close.

Golden Cockerel (Le Coq d'Or). (See "National Characteristics in Russian Art Music," p. 19.)

Sadko. A fascinating opera, both musically and pictorially, a setting of one of the oldest of all Russian river folk tales. Here Sadko, who spends many hours of each day playing sweet music upon his *gousli* while sitting on the river bank near Novgorod, is presented with immense wealth by the God of the River. In return Sadko promises to come often to play for him. Instead, Sadko becomes forgetful while sailing the seas in pursuit of still greater riches. Upon one occasion he invites a party of merchant visitors from various lands to tell him of their home lands. The popular "Song of India" is the story of the merchant from India. Sadko is finally shipwrecked and thus taken forcibly to the palace of the king of the Waters, far under the sea, there to play for the dancing of all the guests. He is offered his choice of the king's daughters as his bride, but she, when he has made his choice, guides him again to the shores of his beloved river.

Scheherazade (See p. 87).

"The Snow Maiden" (*Sneguroshka*). A four-act opera with prologue, an allegory of the triumph of the Sun and Spring over the snows of Winter, tells of a legend and custom old in the history of all Slavic peoples. Snowmaiden, the daughter of the King of Winter, comes to dwell with mortals. The warmth of her love for the shepherd youth melts her away, while the peasants, gathered to celebrate the departure of winter and its snows, sing praises to the Sun.

ROGERS, JAMES HOTCHKISS (1857–). Born in Fairhaven, Conn. but has spent most of the time since 1883 in Cleveland, O., where he was organist and music-critic for the *Plain Dealer* for many years. His compositions embrace various branches of music, his delightful songs being favorites with all concert-goers. His "When Pershing's Men Go Marching" was one of the few patriotic art songs of the World War days. He was a pupil of Haupt, Loeschorn, Guilmant, and Widor.

ROSSINI, GIOACHINO (1792–1868). For a time director of the Italian Theater in Paris, and Royal Composer, exerted a profound influence upon the whole operatic world by the character of his writings. Although much of his life was spent in France, he was born in Pesaro, Italy, to the officials of which he willed money to establish a conservatory of music.

Barber of Seville. Rossini wrote this complete work in thirteen days, keeping his librettist constantly at his side. The opera, the scene of which is laid in Seville, tells of Rosina, ward of the mean and suspicious old Doctor Bartolo. The Count Almaviva comes, with a band of hired singers, to serenade her, then lingers near her home. Figaro, the Barber of Seville, passes, and the Count plots with him to arrange a meeting with Rosina. Meanwhile, the old Doctor has given strict orders to his servants that no one is to be admitted to the house save Basilio, the music master. The Count proceeds to impersonate him, and while he is present in the house, the real music master arrives. Recriminations follow, but in the end, the Count, with the help of the ever-present Figaro, wins the hand of Rosina, and the old Doctor accepts the situation as best he can.

The music of the opera is particularly delightful and merry.

"Cujus Animam." A tenor aria from Rossini's oratorio, *Stabat Mater,* follows the opening chorus of this majestic work. The same text has been the inspiration of many composers, among them Palestrina, Pergolesi, Haydn, and Dvořák. The work was written in 1832 shortly after Rossini had completed *William Tell,* and was composed for the Spanish minister, Don Valera. Rossini was taken ill before he could complete the music, and a friend did the last four numbers. Ten years later Rossini wrote four new settings to replace these, and in this completed form, *Stabat Mater* had its first performance in 1842.

William Tell. This, Rossini's last work for the stage, had its première in 1829. William Tell, the Swiss patriot, defies Gessler, the tyrant who sought to make him bow to the hat that had been set up in the marketplace of little Altdorf. Tell has come down into the village, bringing his small son with him. Halted upon his refusal to make the required obeisance, he is told that he will be freed if he will shoot an apple from the head of the little boy. Tell is successful in his shot, but as he relaxes from his kneeling position, a second arrow falls to the ground, and this, he replies when questioned, was for Gessler, should he have failed and hit his son. Tell is then placed in a boat to be taken over the lake to the prison. While on the way a great storm arises, and amidst the sounds and dangers of the thunder, lightning, and rain, Tell jumps ashore and escapes.

The music throughout the opera is intensely dramatic. Most familiar is the *William Tell* "Overture," a work which falls naturally into four main divisions, each of which is a description of some phase of Alpine life. Part I, entitled "Dawn," suggests the sunrise over the mountains. Part II, "The Storm," is an extremely realistic piece of music. "The Calm," is a *pastorale,* in which is heard the *Ranz des vaches,* or mountain air, so frequently heard from Alpine horns in the Alps of Switzerland. In Part IV, Rossini brings the work to a dazzlingly brilliant close.

RUBINSTEIN, Beryl (1898–   ). A native of Georgia, studied in America with his father and with Alexander Lambert; and in Europe with Jose Vianna da Motta and Ferruccio Busoni. His American professional début was made in 1916. A London début was made in 1925. He has been piano soloist with the New York Philharmonic, Cleveland, Detroit, Philadelphia, San Francisco, and London orchestras. Since 1921 Mr. Rubinstein has been connected with the Cleveland Institute of

Music, of which he is now Director, and he has been given honorary degree of Doctor of Music by the Western Reserve University. His major compositions include two string quartets (C-sharp Minor and D-flat Major); *Scherzo, and Suite for Orchestra;* a clever "Sonatina in C-sharp Minor for Piano," written in modern idiom; a number of piano and violin solos, orchestral pieces, and songs. In 1931 Mr. Rubinstein acted as American Chairman of the Piano Section of the Anglo-American Music Conference in Lausanne, Switzerland.

SAINT-SAËNS, CAMILLE (1835–1921). A prominent French musician for over seventy years. Played piano recitals in Paris at the age of ten and astonished his audiences by playing them without notes—an unusual occurrence in those days. Gounod, who was born in the same quarter of Paris, was a life-long friend, and was also his teacher. He visited the United States at the time of the Panama-Pacific Exposition, as conductor. His government showered him with honors, including membership in the Legion of Honor. For many years he spent his winter months in Algiers, across the Mediterranean, and it was there that he died in 1921.

Danse Macabre. This "dance of death" is a telling, in music, of a medieval legend of Hallowe'en, at which time, it relates, the skeletons may leave their graves for the few hours between midnight and dawn, and dance to the music provided by Death, the Fiddler.

At the opening of the composition, the ominous hour of midnight is heard sounded loudly in repeated harp tones. Then Death stalks forth, and tunes his fiddle to a diminished, rather than a perfect fifth, as a sinister portent of what is to follow. The rattle of the xylophone suggests the arrival of the ghostly dancers; a flute announces the dance (G minor, 3–4 time); and Death begins to play. The heavy pulsations of the waltz tune—which is a grotesque caricature of the *Dies Irae* (Latin hymn of Death)—are accented by the clacks of the xylophone. The second and contrasting theme is a more serious air, suggesting night and the loneliness of the grave. The themes are interwoven as the dance becomes more agitated. Suddenly the cock crows (oboe). The revelers are heard dispersing hurriedly, Death plays a last weird strain, and the dance ends with two chords for wood-wind, and strings *pizzicato.*

"My Heart at Thy Sweet Voice" from *Samson and Delila.* This contralto aria, sung to Samson by Delila during the second act of the well-known Biblical opera, is anticipated and suggested throughout the overture and preceding act by means of frequently and cleverly interwoven bits of its melody or accompaniment. In the scene of which the aria is a part, Delila has brought Samson to the Vale of Sorek, where, on the terrace outside her dwelling, she tries, by means of alluring words of love, set to a beguiling melody, to win from him the secret of his marvelous strength. Added appeal is given to the melody by the unusual and skillfully constructed accompaniment.

Phaéton and *Le Rouet d'Omphale.* Symphonic poems, founded upon Greek myths. Phaéton, the son of Phoebus, became so arrogant that he fancied himself able to drive the chariot of the sun across the sky in his father's place. He soon displayed his inability. The blazing chariot swerved from its course, bringing the danger of the burning of all vegetation to the earth. So it is necessary for his father to hurl a thunderbolt upon him. The opening of the music suggests the galloping of the horses attached to the chariot through the constant repetition of a figure in the strings. The appearance of Phaéton is announced by a suave and noble theme from the horns. The furious drive of the rhythm is cut short by the crashing of the thunderbolt. The work closes with a reminiscence of the opening measures, and chords, *pianissimo.*

In *Le Rouet d'Omphale* Saint-Saëns has conceived the music in three distinct parts. The first part depicts the power of Omphale's fascination over Hercules. In the second part Hercules, who has been drawn into bondage, is heard groaning and moaning as he is forced to spin with the women. Part III portrays the ridicule of the spinners, at the vain efforts of Hercules, and throughout the piece the rhythmic hum of the whirling spinning-wheel forms the subtle background for the flowing melodies.

Suite Algérienne. Upon the title page of this music Saint-Saëns wrote the sub-title: "Picturesque Impressions of Voyage to Algiers." Two of the most attractive numbers of the suite are the "Reverie du Soir" (Reverie of Evening) and the vivid "Marche Militaire Française." The music is subtly suggestive of the rather Oriental atmosphere of the old city, the "Reverie" being a contemplative bit of music in romantic style. A tiny cadenza follows the climax, after which there is a brief return to the melody of the opening measures, a sequential development of it, and a quiet close.

The "Marche" records the impressions of the composer upon visiting the old French Fort Blidah, one of the interesting sights of a trip through the Mediterranean. Many of the devices of the native bands are imitated in the jaunty music, and there is much sounding of brass and clashing of cymbals, military flourishes, and fanfares of bugles. One part of the composition features a persistent droning of the basses, this an imitation of the drones of the native bagpipes of the Egyptian soldiers.

"The Swan." In his *Carnival of the Animals,* of which "The Swan" is the thirteenth part, Saint-Saëns wrote music intended to amuse his friends. In it he gave individual treatment of many of the orchestral instruments. The composer liked it so much that he himself transcribed it for almost every solo instrument of the orchestra. "The Swan" was written as a 'cello solo with accompaniment from two pianos, the second piano providing additional atmosphere by its harp-like chords which fall upon the accented or stressed beats. Throughout the piece only one musical subject is heard. This is sup-

ported by a suave and undulating figure in the accompaniment.

SALTER, MARY TURNER (1856–). Best known by her dramatic "Cry of Rachel." Mrs. Salter (the wife of Sumner Salter) has written two groups of children's songs and several song cycles, including the "Sappho Lyrics," the "Japanese Cycle," "The Lover of Damascus," and "Love's Epitome."

SALTER, SUMNER. As composer, editor, organist, and teacher, Mr. Salter has wielded a profound influence upon the music of America. For many years he was in charge of the choral music of Williams College at Williamstown, Mass. His original choral works, and his masterly arrangements include such works as his "Te Deum," "Jubilate," "The Lord is my Light." Mr. Salter won the *Étude* song-prize by his setting of "The Sword" by Michael Barry.

SCHELLING, ERNEST (1876–). Born at Delaware, New Jersey. Has for many years, conducted Children's Orchestral Concerts in New York. He studied with Paderewski. His two best-known orchestral works are *Impressions of an Artist's Life* and *Victory Ball,* a fantasy inspired by the post-War poem by Alfred Noyes which tells of the fevered gayety of the survivors of the World War, and of a ball given soon after the armistice, at which the "shadows of dead men" are watching. Some of the "shadows" are angry that they seem to be so soon forgotten. The dancing continues, at one time interrupted by

the ghostly march of the Scotch Pipers who were killed in the War, as they pass through the room, unseen but felt. (See also "Stories in Sound," p. 85). Sounds outside the ballroom remind the dancers that the aeroplanes still wheel overhead.

Mr. Schelling was himself in the War and wrote this music soon after its close. Of it he says: "I have used two army calls—the "Call to Arms" and 'Charge'—which ominously usher in the War Vision; and at the very end I have used 'Taps.' The work is a perfectly free fantasy, with, however, a certain amount of thematic development. I had occasion, during the World War, to hear the Scotch Pipers, and to observe the extraordinary effect their music had on the troops; and at the end of the work I have tried to make the whole orchestra a huge bagpipe, perhaps most pagan and primitive form of music." The piece is scored for full orchestra, and bears the inscription, "To the memory of an American soldier."

SCHOENBERG, ARNOLD (1874–). Born in Vienna. Experimentation has characterized much of his composition. He has completely abandoned tonality, making use of the chromatic scale in a set order known as the "twelve-tone series." He makes the interval of a fourth, rather than that of a third, the basis of his chord building, and has, in many other ways, created an entirely individual type of music. His early works include a string quartet and the *Gurrelieder.* Later works include *Pierrot Lunaire,* many tone poems and orchestral pieces, a string quartet, and pieces for piano. He has frequently employed the "Sprechstimme," a use of the voice which is neither singing nor speaking.

Gurrelieder. Like *Pierrot Lunaire* a cycle of songs, was written between his opus no. 4 and no. 5, and published, much later, without opus number. It is based upon a cycle of ballads by Jacobsen, a Danish poet, and is divided into three parts, in the first and second of which are ballads for soprano, alto, and tenor, after the style of the *Lied,* each being connected organically with the others by means of orchestral preludes, interludes, and postludes. In the third division, a male chorus is added, and at the very close, a mixed chorus. Just before the chorus the composer inserts a dramatic episode for speaking voice and orchestra.

The story is of the deathless love of King Waldeman for Klein-Tove, whom he sees for the first time when he visits Castle Gurre. Disaster comes to the lovers, and Part I closes with the sorrowful message that Tove has been killed by the jealous queen. The second part contains but one song, the king's complaint and rebellion against God. Part III features the 12-part chorus for male voices, this being followed by the pathetic song of the jester who publicly bemoans his lot. "The wild chase of the summer wind," in this part, was scored by the composer much later than the rest of the work, in his later manner, and so offers, within the one composition, an effective contrast of Schoenberg's changing styles.

SCHUBERT, FRANZ PETER (1797–1828). Born in a village near Vienna, in which city he died, the descendant of sturdy Moravians and the son of the town schoolmaster, who was also a good musician. He attended the Imperial School and was later a student with Antonio Salieri. His marvelous natural gifts were displayed at an early age by his composition of a piano sonata for four hands (still played) and several small songs. Schubert left a rich heritage of songs, orchestral and piano music, and dramatic works.

"Ave Maria." A setting of Sir Walter Scott's "Hymn to the Virgin" as found in Canto III of his *Lady of the Lake.* Here Ellen Douglas is singing, to the accompaniment of the harp of the minstrel Allan Bane, a prayer for protection during the night. The melody has been widely used for both voice and instruments, having been transcribed for many instruments and combinations of instruments.

"Ballet Music" from *Rosamunde.* Written as incidental music to an opera by von Chezy, a romantic work which survived only two performances. The music was then laid away by Schubert in his famous cupboard, from which it was taken, many years after his death, by historians who were searching among his effects for material concerning him and his music.

"The Brooklet." In this song the accompaniment suggests very clearly the never-ending murmuring of the shallow water of a brooklet as it ripples along over its stony bed.

"The Erl King." Spaun, a school-mate of Schubert at the Imperial School, tells in his diary of the writing of this song: "I went to see Schubert this afternoon and found Franz in his room in a very wild state of excitement over Goethe's ballad of the Erl King, which he had just seen for the first time. He had only read it through once or twice when he had an inspiration to set it to music, and he was still pouring the music down on paper when I arrived. Indeed, it was already done but a bit of filling in of the accompaniment. And all of this had taken less than one hour!" (See "Song and the Accompaniment," p. 27).

"Hark! Hark! the Lark!" Written in a public garden near Vienna, to which the composer and some friends had gone for refreshment. On the table lay a copy of Shakespeare's *Cymbeline.* Schubert picked it up, chanced to read the verses which tell of the coming of dawn, and was at once inspired to set them to music. The friends ruled staves upon the back of some bills-of-fare, and the music was set down at once. Both this and the "Erl King" were transcribed for piano in brilliant manner by Franz Liszt. (See "The Singer and the Song," p. 34).

Marche Militaire. First written by Schubert as a piano duet. Later it was arranged as a concert solo by Carl Taussig, the celebrated and gifted Liszt pupil, in which form it has become familiar to concert-goers around the world. The march comprises a stirring chordal introduction, a lilting and martial first section, two trios, an immediate return to the first march melody, and a brilliant coda.

"Moment Musical" (in F Minor). One of a series of short numbers by which Schubert has endeared himself to generations of music-lovers. Written for piano, a rhythmic two-measure introduction precedes the lively first theme. Frequent use is made of embellishment, of contrasting *legato* and *staccato,* and of a purposely monotonous and persistent bass which accentuates the constant rhythm. The main part of the little piece is made up of three genial themes, each of which is repeated; the first and third being in the prevailing key of F Minor, and the second in the contrasting key of A-flat Major. Then follows a graceful development section, and a brief and lightly moving coda built upon fragments of the main theme.

"Serenade." One of the most tenderly expressive of the Schubert songs. A serenade is a lyric and romantic evening song, and takes its general characteristics from the sentimental songs of the Troubadours of Provence.

Unfinished Symphony. This symphony, begun by Schubert as an acknowledgment of courtesies paid him in 1822, when he was elected to honorary membership in musical organizations of Linz and Graz, is called "Unfinished" from the fact that only two movements and a few bars of the third were written. These were evidently put aside with the thought of later completion. They were never finished, nor was the music ever played until over forty years later, after the composer's death, when it was found by Sir George Grove among a pile of forgotten manuscripts laid away in an old cupboard and treasured for many years by Anselm Huttenbrenner, and musical friend of both Schubert and Beethoven. Both movements are written in strict classical form.

The first movement, with its refinement and gentle themes, opens abruptly, with no introduction, on a gracious melody for the low basses. This is followed almost immediately by the first theme proper, a curious undulating figure in the violins, over a bass in persistent rhythm. There presently enters, through the instruments of the wood-wind section, a melody of the utmost grace, accompanied by a figure derived from the first theme. Modulations bring the listener to the celebrated second theme, a melody of alluring beauty, played by 'cellos. This melody is repeated many times in transposed and altered forms. A free development follows, the melodies being passed from instrument to instrument rapidly and with increasing agitation. A massive restatement of themes, displaying freshness of treatment and a skillful technique, and a short but impressive coda bring the first movement to a close.

The second movement is a colorful and fitting companion to that which preceded it. After a two-measure introduction, the violins present a quiet melody, which is presently followed by a tender, yearning air played by the clarinets against a syncopated accompaniment in the

strings. The *Unfinished Symphony* is considered to be one of the most perfect examples of pure music in the world.

"*Who is Sylvia?*" An exquisite setting of the love song from Shakespeare's *Two Gentlemen of Verona,* written on the same evening, and on the same bills-of-fare which served as score paper for "Hark! Hark! the Lark." In the play the words of the song have been written by Thurio, one of the lovers of Sylvia, and is sung by him and a group of hired musicians in the hope of winning her favor. This is an art song of the strophic type.

SCHUMANN, Robert (1816–1856). His studies at the University of Leipzig, undertaken at the age of 18, were in the school of law. He later overcame the disapproval of his parents and took up music study seriously, becoming a pupil of Friedrich Wieck, whose daughter Clara—some years later—became his wife. Schumann not only wrote significant music, but did conspicuous work as a critic and as a patron of young artists. He served for some years as director of the Leipzig Conservatory.

Quintet (E-Flat Major). The work, which has four movements, opens with a brilliant and massive succession of chords from the piano. The melody thus announced is doubled in the strings. The lyric melody with which the first movement is associated is first presented by the piano, and then, in turn, by each of the stringed instruments.

The second movement, written as

a slow march (*In modo d'una Marcia*) is in sorrowful mood, the principal melody, in the minor, being first given out by the violin. A contrast in mood is accomplished by the second theme, after which the first theme is again heard. Both are then developed, and repeated in varied keys and rhythms. The movement is, in form, a rondo.

The third movement (Scherzo) develops effectively a series of rapidly moving scale and note patterns. There are heard, in the coda, reminders of the opening theme. Another characteristic of the Scherzo is the frequent use of syncopation. The Finale is an immensely brilliant movement built, in the main, upon a simple, but sturdy theme.

"Scenes from Childhood." A collection of 13 delicate miniatures for the piano, intended not as music for children to play but rather as mature recollections of the moods and experiences of childhood, served to bring Schumann effectively into the notice of the concert-going public of his native land. When many of his fine and larger works had failed of great success, the immediate appeal of these gems, as played by Clara Schumann, gifted wife, won for him a large following. Each small number is named by the composer, giving a hint of what he had in mind when he wrote them. (See "The Romantic Idea in Music," p. 95, and "Everybody's Music," p. 7.)

"Two Grenadiers." A setting of a poem by Heinrich Heine, written in 1840, relates the conversation of two veterans of Napoleon's army of 1812 as they learn, upon their arrival at the frontier from the unsuccessful campaign against the Russians, that disaster has come to their native land and that Napoleon is now a prisoner. The verses are lent an added interest when it is recalled that Napoleon was, in 1810, in Düsseldorf, the home city of Heine, who was about 13 years old at the time, and that the youth thus had a personal acquaintance with the spirit of the French soldiers.

The song opens in minor mode, a military atmosphere being immediately suggested by means of a short and snappily martial rhythm in the accompaniment. The imagination is stirred by the imitation of a resounding drum beat in the opening strains ("To France there traveled two Grenadiers") and by the downward direction of the sorrowful ending to the same phrase. The conversation of the two soldiers is allied to music of a recitative style, with few note changes, while in the accompaniment is a restless repetition of a simple four-note pattern. With the last two stanzas, there enters the broad and thrilling strains of the triumphant "Marseillaise," which brings the Schumann song to an eloquent close.

SCRIABINE, Alexander (1871–1915). A musical revolutionary, born in Moscow. He was a student with Balakirev and Arensky at the Moscow Conservatory, where he later became a teacher of piano. He wrote three symphonies. In his *Poem of Ecstasy* he uses eight themes. A typical feature of Scriabine's writing is in his use of a "magic chord," created by use of harmonics or overtones. In his *Prometheus,* which had a profound influence upon the work of contemporary composers, he employs a huge chorus and orchestra, and also wrote a part for color organ.

SKILTON, CHARLES SANFORD (1868–). Born in Northampton, Mass., and graduated from Yale in 1889. After study at the Berlin Hochschule he spent several years as director of music in Winston-Salem, N. C. (College for Women). He went in 1903 to the University of Kansas, where he is Professor of Music, and where he was, for many years, Dean of the School of Music. Mr. Skilton, winner of several prizes (including the Music Teachers' National Association Prize, 1897) and many honors, is a member of the MacDowell Colony at Peterboro, N. H. His works include a Pueblo Indian opera, *Blue-feather;* music to the *Electra* of Sophocles for Women's Chorus and Orchestra, developed from choral odes for a performance in Greek of *Electra* written for and given by the senior class at Smith College (Northampton, Mass.), when the composer was only a junior in college; Suite, *East and West,* for small orchestra, written especially for Barrere's Little Symphony; "Three Indian Sketches" for piano; and many shorter works for piano, voice, and violin.

From Forest and Trail. A series of 12 short and colorful numbers for three-part women's chorus, (words by Charles O. Roos) featuring many phases of nature. The titles include "Ghost Pipes"; "Red Bird," in which a flute melody from Chippewa tribal music is used; "Birch," in the middle section of which a colorful melody is accompanied by a clever suggestion of the monotonous Indian drum; "Forest Trail," in which both text and music reflect Indian characteristics.

The Guardian Angel. Mr. Skilton's second oratorio was written in 1919, and brought to performance and publication in 1926 by the Kansas Federation of Music Clubs. The story is founded upon a legend of the mountain district of North Carolina, and centers about the old Moravian settlement at Winston-Salem. It tells of a little daughter of the village who, wandering away from her playmates while they picked flowers in a meadow, entered the nearby forest, forbidden to the children. As darkness falls, she lies down to rest under a low bush, sure that her father will come for her. Three times she is awakened by a sweet voice which calls now near, then far away. Each time as she is about to answer, thinking it may be her mother, a hand is laid over her lips and she is gently pushed back to her resting place under the bushes. In the morning a rescue party finds her, and only then does she learn that it was a panther's voice that roused her in the night, and that it was the watchful care of her Guardian Angel which saved her life.

The Prelude opens with a Moravian Children's Hymn, the theme of which is heard frequently throughout the work. In the Prelude, the melody is used canonically, leading directly into the first choral number.

There are, throughout the work, many reverent choruses, both for adults and for children. The melody of the opening "Children's Hymn" is occasionally used as a beautiful obbligato to another chorus and is sung by an unseen chorus behind the scenes. There is a vivid instrumental Intermezzo, and another instrumental number serves as a prelude to the second part of the work, and suggests an atmosphere of uncertainty and fear. An interpolation of the Moravian hymn, "He shall give His Angels charge over thee," is sung by children's voices in unison, accompanied by mixed chorus and tenor solo. There is an inspired setting of the Biblical text, "Suffer little Children," and a magnificent Thanksgiving Chorus, "Jesus makes my heart rejoice." The accompaniment is, throughout, beautiful and appealing. The Intermezzo from Part I was intended to be a *scherzo fugue* that should suggest the playing children.

Kalopin. An American Indian Opera, using as a libretto a poem by Virginia Armistead Nelson, telling of a historic incident among the Chickasaw and Choctaw Indians near the Mississippi River in Tennessee. This opera won a David Bispham medal given by the American Opera Association of Chicago in November 1930. The first performance was at Nashville, Tenn., for the annual meeting of the State Federation of Music Clubs, where it was presented in concert form.

The opera is built about the legendary causes of the "New Madrid Earthquake" of 1811, which, the Indians said, was punishment sent them by the Great Spirit because Kalopin, the youthful chieftain of the Chickasaw tribe, took a bride from another tribe. Mr. Skilton has treated this as an allegory representing the overwhelming of the Indians by the white race, as the Indian village was overwhelmed by the flood and the earthquake. In the opera the composer has used the device of *Leitmotif* (or characteristic theme), and many of the more important of these are based upon tribal airs. Certain scenes are also developed about passages from the composer's "Two Indian Dances" and his *Suite Primeval*.

Principal characters are Kalopin, Chief of the Chickasaws; Culleoka, who loves him, and Osceola and Nashola, her father and brother; Tallula (Chocktaw), whom Kalopin loves; and Biwier and Pantotoc, medicine men.

Midnight. A work for women's chorus.

"Shawnee Indian Hunting Song" (originally Piano and Violin). Based on a Shawnee melody, and used by the composer as the basis of his "Hunting Chorus" in *Kalopin*.

Suite Primeval. For both string quartet and full orchestra, in two parts, the first part (often designated as "Two Indian Dances") including the "Deer Dance" and the "War Dance"; and the second part including "Sunrise Song," "Gambling Song," "Flute Serenade," and "Moccasin Game." The "Two Indian Dances" were originally written for string quartet and given their first performance by the Zoellner Quartet in January 1916. That same year the composer arranged them for full or-chestra. The "Deer Dance," in the middle of which occurs a passage in 2–4 measure accompanied by the drum beating 3–4, portrays the an-nual memorial service of the Rogue River Indians of Oregon.

Mr. Skilton says of the music: "The opening strain is a lament sung by the chief singer without drum accompaniment; after sufficient repe-tition of this, the chief makes a speech in praise of the departed, which is briefly suggested by the cadenza. The dance begins at the 2–4 section, some dancers putting on the skins and horns of deer and other animals, while others, in the garb of hunters, pursue them in and out among the spectators, who stand in a semicircle, men and women alter-nately marking time with the left foot. The young men sing a rising third in the tenor, and the old men a falling one in the bass, combining with the melody and 3–4 drum-beat to make a curious primitive en-semble. The 'War Dance' is a Cheyenne melody."

The "Two Indian Dances" are in the repertoire of the major sym-phonies of America, and are heard on the broadcasting systems of Eng-land, France, Japan, Germany and the United States.

Of Part II, most of the Indian melodies employed were sung to Mr. Skilton by George La Mere, of the Winnebago tribe. (a) "Sunrise Song." A Winnebago melody sung as an act of morning worship in the spring of the year. In the orchestral version, the graceful air is given first to the 'cello, then to all first violins, and lastly to the viola. (b) "Gam-bling Song." Draws its musical ma-terial from the Rogue River Indians, and is characterized by two simple themes. (c) "Flute Serenade" (from the Sioux). Employs a tender air heard five times, first, as in the orig-inal, played by flute. It is later re-peated, as though by the pensive In-dian lover, in higher key, but still by flute; then by all wood-winds, and again as flute solo. At all times it is embellished with delicate trills, rhythmic figures, gently murmuring flourishes which reflect the main theme, and by *pizzicato* chords from the strings. (d) "Moccasin Game." Tells, in music, the story of a primi-tive gambling game, in which the Indian passes a marble or other small object rapidly under one or more of the pieces of moccasin he has spread upon the ground before him.

Sun Bride (or "Bluefeather"). A musical recording of an old Pueblo Indian legend. The libretto is by Lilian White Spencer. The work was written in 1928, and had its world première over the air from the studios of the National Broadcasting Com-pany, New York City, April 17, 1930. This was the first opera by an American composer to be presented in this manner.

The Witch's Daughter. Mr. Skil-ton's first oratorio, written at the Peterborough Colony in 1918, the first serious treatment of Salem witch-craft in music (the text from a poem by John Greenleaf Whittier). Had its première in St. Louis, Mo., where it was sung by the Pageant Choral Society, accompanied by the St. Louis Symphony.

American Indian Fantasie for Organ. Composed for Pietro Yon. In 1932 the work was adapted by the composer for 'cello and orchestra.

Ticonderoga, a Cantata for Male Voices. Robert Louis Stevenson's poem, a ghost story of the French and Indian War, vividly retold in music.

SMETANA, FRIEDRICH (1824–1884). Born in the Bohemian village of Leitomischl, dedicated his talent and ability to the composition of musical tributes to his fatherland. These include a remarkable series of six symphonic poems which he grouped under the general title of *My Fatherland*. (See "The Symphonic Poem," p. 109.)

Moldau. The second of these symphonic poems, of which the composer wrote: "Two springs start their courses in a shady Bohemian forest: one is warm and sparkling, the other cool and tranquil. Their clear waters, that run so gayly over stone and pebble, unite and sparkle in the morning sun. The rapid forest brook, rushing on, becomes the River Moldau, which, as it takes its course through the fields and valleys of Bohemia, grows into a mighty river, flowing through thick forests wherein the joyous clanging sound of the hunter's horn seems to approach the listener. It pursues its way through meadows and farms. A rustic wedding is being joyfully celebrated with music and song and dance. The water nymphs disport themselves by moonlight in the river's glittering waters, in which are reflected towers and castles as reminders of the de-parted glory of chivalry and martial fame. At St. John's Rapids the stream winds its way through the foamy rapids of the cataract and through a deep and narrow rocky cleft into the broad river-bed, along which it rolls majestically on to Prague, welcomed on its way by the venerable Vyšehrad, and disappears in the distance from the composer's vision."

The Bartered Bride. An opera based upon an old Bohemian folk tale. In it the composer has employed much folk music, and many of its characteristics. It tells a story of Jenik, a peasant who loves the daughter of a rich man. Her father has arranged a wedding, through the marriage broker, between her and another man, the son of Micha. Marenka, the heroine, refuses to discuss this until she learns that Jenik is the long-lost son of Micha. She therefore gleefully signs the marriage contract with a "son of Micha," and Jenik soon appears to claim both bride and marriage settlement. The Overture to this lively drama is permeated with folk atmosphere. The first theme is taken from parts of two old Bohemian dance airs, and the second theme, anticipating the opera proper, is a version of the love duet melody heard as Marenka and Jenik declare their affection for each other.

SOUSA, JOHN PHILIP (1856–1932). No more popular name than that of John Philip Sousa has appeared in music during the past fifty years. He made many world tours; played before, and was decorated by, scores of monarchs; wrote over 350 compositions, ranging from cantata to opera, and his 140 marches won for him the enviable title "March King." Honors were heaped on him from the days when he and the Marine Band used to assemble at the Barracks in Washington and ride to the White House on a street car, until his last night on earth, when he was being honored at a banquet in Reading, Pa. It is appropriate that a strain of his best-known march, "Stars and Stripes Forever," is carved on his tombstone in the Congressional Cemetery at Washington.

SOWERBY, Leo (1895–   ). Born in Grand Rapids, Mich., 1895. Graduated from the American Conservatory of Chicago, where he now teaches theory and composition. Studied with d'Indy and Percy Grainger. He won the Fellowship of the American Academy in Rome, and the Eastman School Publication Award. Mr. Sowerby is also known as an organist.

"Comes Autumn Time." An organ tone poem, in which two themes of contrasting character symbolize the phases of the two seasons. The first suggests a gust of autumn wind. An episode as capricious as a zephyr is followed by the second theme, which, accompanied by a droning *ostinato,* suggests a pastoral day in the Fall.

"Madrigal." This is an instrumental madrigal for organ which follows the true conception of the old vocal madrigal. The form is simple.

Prairie. A symphonic poem suggested by Carl Sandburg's "Prairie."

The composer says of the music that it "is constructed in such a way that sections seeking to interpret the moods of the poet's 'red sunset,' 'shore of night stars,' 'wave lines of dawn,' 'threshing crews,' follow one another in succession without break or special line of demarcation."

Prelude on a Palestrina Motet. A choral fantasy built upon melodic fragments from Palestrina. The first subdivision of the main theme is of four-measure length, the second of six-measure length. The composer has used an adaptation of sonata form. An episode in the nature of a carillon lends a mystical atmosphere to the work.

SPEAKS, Oley (1876–   ). Born near Columbus, Ohio, for many years a soloist in prominent churches of New York. Has written oratorios and more than 200 songs, of which "The Lord is My Light" and "On the Road to Mandalay" are prime favorites. The latter song is a realistic setting of the poem by Rudyard Kipling.

STRAUSS, Johann (1825–1899). Familiarly known as the "Waltz King." At nineteen he had his own orchestra. He played before kings and queens of Europe, and at his death was honored by burial in the famous Musicians' Corner of the Vienna Cemetery. He composed in all over 400 waltzes, and many tuneful operettas.

Beautiful Blue Danube. The world's most famous waltz, takes its title from a rhythmic poem by Karl Beck, which, accidentally heard read by Strauss, inspired in him an appropriate musical theme. The waltz was first written as a male chorus, and sung in Vienna with only moderate success. Its great fame came after Strauss had rearranged it for orchestra. It is, in reality, not a single waltz, but a collection of eight small ones.

STRAUSS, RICHARD (1864–). The son of Franz Strauss, a Munich horn player, he succeeded von Bülow as conductor at Meiningen (where Brahms had also served). His compositions include a *Symphonie Domestica,* seven great symphonic poems, and operas. The symphonic poems are *Macbeth* (completed 1887), *Don Juan* (1888), *Death and Transfiguration* (1889), *Till Eulenspiegel's Merry Pranks* (1895), *Thus Spake Zarathustra* (1896), *Don Quixote* (1897), and *Ein Heldenleben* (Life of a Hero) (1898). *Salome* is the story—told in operatic version based on Oscar Wilde's drama —of the Biblical tale of the daughter of Herodias, who danced before the King for the head of St. John the Baptist. *Der Rosenkavalier* is a comedy with music, in three acts. *Elektra* and *Egyptian Helen* are other Strauss operas.

Till Eulenspiegel. The exploits of Till Eulenspiegel, who may, or may not, have been an actual person, are supposed to have taken place in about the fourteenth century. Till is represented in Strauss work by a grotesque theme, which at once introduces the comical element into the music. The chief episodes in the music are Till at the marketplace, as priest, and Don Juan; the troop of worthy Philistines; and Till as a merry and insolent liar. His activities bring him before the judge. He lies three times, even when the judge threatens, and is condemned to be hung. An epilogue follows.

Ein Heldenleben. There are, in this music, six quite distinct sections: 1. the "hero" theme; 2. the hero's adversaries; 3. his consort (a duet of great intensity); 4. the battlefield, upon which the hero is called to defend his ideals and defeat his enemies; 5. a reference to his works of peace; 6. the hero, having won serenity and calmness, retires from the world. In the fifth section, Strauss makes reference, through quotation, to 23 of his own compositions.

STRAVINSKY, IGOR (1882–   ). The son of a Russian opera singer, born near the city of St. Petersburg (now Leningrad), in Russia. Rimsky-Korsakov became his teacher and exerted an intense influence upon his career. Stravinsky is known for his unconventionality in method of expression. His major works include a "Concertino" for sting quartet; a *Symphony of Psalms* for orchestra and chorus; *Fireworks,* a brilliant fantasy for orchestra which Stravinsky wrote in honor of the marriage of the daughter of his teacher, Rimsky-Korsakov, to a fellow student; *Pulcinella,* a ballet with song, based upon musical passages from the Pergolesi scores; *Renard,* a burlesque for male voices and chamber orchestra, the text of which is founded upon old Russian folk tales; *Œdipus Rex,* which the composer calls a two-act opera-oratorio; and *Navra,* a one-act opera buffa after Pushkin.

Fire Bird. Ballet and suite for orchestra, based upon a Russian folk tale of an ancient enchanted castle. Ivan comes to the castle while hunting by night, and there beholds a bird of remarkable plumage. He captures it in the act of plucking a golden fruit from one of the silver trees, but releases it in answer to its urgent entreaty. As a token of gratitude, the Fire Bird presents him with one of its feathers, which has a magic power. Ivan is warned by the thirteen princesses who come from the castle of the presence of a horrible monster, Kastschei. He, they tell him, turns all travelers into stone images. Protected by the magic feather, Ivan learns the secret of the monster's power, breaks the magic egg, the monster dies, the castle vanishes, the petrified travelers are restored to life, and he weds the most beautiful of the princesses. The music of the *Fire Bird* Suite follows the action of the legend closely.

The Nightingale. (See p. 221.)

Sacre du Printemps (Rites of Spring). (See p. 90.)

Petrouchka. This ballet and suite of the jealous puppets tells of a wooden doll, Petrouchka, a clown who loves the dainty ballerina of the Showman's troop. She is also loved by the Moor, whom she prefers. While the carnival is at its height Petrouchka runs out into the street, pursued by the angry Moor. Petrouchka is killed. The excited crowd is calmed by the Showman who explains that these are just wooden dolls, and to emphasize this picks up the dangling wooden body of Petrouchka for all to see. Although the crowd is satisfied, Petrouchka has his revenge, and when the Showman seeks to re-enter the tent and stuff the doll into his box, the clown's ghost appears above the booth leering at him, and frightens him away. "Danse Russe," with which the suite opens, is given full orchestra, *forte,* being built upon a two-measure theme. This is repeated abruptly, four times in succession, after which the theme is passed, measure by measure, from instrument to instrument, while harps and piano furnish a strongly rhythmic accompaniment.

"In Petrouchka's Room," a tiny one-measure phrase introduces the scene. It is followed by rhythmic groups in which musical allusions are made to the different personages in the "cast." "Grand Carnival" suggests the jolly confusion of one of the historic Fairs for which Russia was so famous. "Dance of the Bear and the Peasant" suggests the antics of the tame dancing bear which entertains the visitors at the Fair. The music moves clumsily, as the bear would move. "Dance of the Coachmen and the Grooms" emphasizes, through its purposely clumsy rhythms, the peasant-like stolidity of some of the dancers. A *basso ostinato* from tuba and trumpet, heavy chords from the strings, and swirling figures from clarinet and horns, characterize this music. The suite ends with a gorgeously brilliant dance, "The Masqueraders."

Story of a Soldier. Pantomime with orchestra, displaying the composer's unique methods of gaining rhythmic variety and musical acceleration by placing the strong pulses of the music together. To accomplish this he frequently uses consecutive measures in which the meter markings are 5–4, 4–4, 3–3, 5–4, 3–4, 9–16, and so on. Herein Stravinsky has used chords without regard to melody, and sometimes without regard to tonality.

STRICKLAND, LILY (Mrs. Courtney Anderson). Born in South Carolina, and in many of her very popular and successful songs has reflected the Southern idiom to so great a degree that some of them have already come to be spoken of as "folk songs." Following her marriage to Mr. Anderson, Miss Strickland went with him to the Far East, and during their nearly ten years of residence there, spent much time in careful study of the folk and religious music—including the dances—of India, Indo-China, Egypt, Burma, Java, Tibet, and Japan. Much of the information and lore thus absorbed has been used by the composer, since her return, in giving authentic color to recent compositions. (See "Music of the Orient," p. 221.)

Miss Strickland's "Lindy Lou" was written during a spell of homesickness for the South. "Dreamin' Time," "My Arcady," and "Ma Li'l Batteau," of the *Bayou Songs* are on the concert programs of many artists. For many of her songs, Miss Strickland also writes her own words, under various pen names. "From the High Hills," "Down South" (collections of songs), "At Eve I Heard a Flute,"

and "My Love's a Fisherman," are given repeated hearings. Miss Strickland, since her return from the Orient, has written: *Dance Moods* (12 Oriental dance forms and annotations, of which drum rhythms as well as scale-modes are authentic); *Dance of Shira,* a ballet used by Ted Shawn at the New York Stadium, in other places in America, and in Europe; and other ballet numbers of wide familiarity. Among choral works, Miss Strickland's *St. John the Beloved* has achieved a wide popularity, as has *White Hawk,* a dramatic song cycle of Indian tribal life. Her first operetta, *Jewels of the Desert,* is enhanced in attractiveness by its Eastern spirit; and a symphony for full orchestra entitled *Carolina* employs Negro spiritual melodies as thematic material.

SULLIVAN, SIR ARTHUR (1842–1900). A distinguished English conductor and composer, trained as a choir boy in the Royal Chapel, at the Royal Academy, London, and at the Leipzig Conservatory. For many years he served as organist in large churches of London, and frequently served as conductor for the larger festivals. In collaboration with W. S. Gilbert he wrote a series of almost 20 of the most sparkling operettas ever written, these being often spoken of as the "Savoy Operas" from the fact that they were, at first, presented at the Savoy Theatre in London. Sullivan's "Lost Chord" is his best-known short work.

Mikado. This operetta, written in 1885, is thought by many to be the masterpiece of the series. In it Gilbert's humorous—sometimes nonsensical—lyrics are joined to music fully as humorous and delightfully melodious. The scene is set in Japan and the time "the past."

The Prodigal Son. First of the Sullivan oratorios, was written for the Worcester Festival, England, in 1869. It is a short work based on the Biblical parable. "How Many Hired Servants of My Father," a tenor aria from the oratorio, is of exceptional beauty.

TARTINI, GIUSEPPE (1692–1770). The founder of an important school of violin-playing in Padua, Italy, was also the originator of many improvements in the construction and technique of the violin bow. Tartini wrote some sacred music, but is more familiarly known for his viol studies which rank in importance with those of Bach. Tartini was one of the earliest violin virtuosi.

"Air with Variations." One of Tartini's most brilliant works, written in a style popular with composers of his day, is founded upon a lilting gavotte by Corelli.

"The Devil's Trill." From Tartini's *Sonata in G Minor,* is one of famous "war-horses" of all concert violinists. The composer is said to have dreamed that the Devil appeared to him and played to him a piece of bewitchingly beautiful music. Several days later, while still under the influence of his strange dream, he wrote this brilliant and technically complicated work.

TAYLOR, DEEMS (1885–). Born in New York City, where he received his education (New York University), has made large contributions to the history of American music through his work as a music critic and editor, his compositions, and as radio announcer.

King's Henchman. Given at the Metropolitan Opera House in 1927 (libretto by Edna St. Vincent Millay), is based upon old English legends. It tells the story of Aethelwold, henchman of King Eadgar, who journeys to Devon to learn whether Aelfrida, daughter of the Thane of Devon, is fair enough to be a queen. The henchmen and his servant arrive in Devon on All Hallows Eve, and being weary, lie down under an oak tree to sleep. Aelfrida enters the wood, as she wishes to practice certain traditional charms which, she is told, will bring her a lover. No sooner has she spoken the incantation, than the moonlight shows her the sleepers under the oak. Believing that Aethelwold has come as the direct answer, she kisses and so awakens him. He, still true to his master, tries to flee the wood, but Aelfrida calls him back, and he sends his servant to tell the king that she is not of beauty fit to be a queen. He will therefore stay in Devon and wed her. One night, the king arrives for a friendly visit with his former henchman. Aethelwold then tells his whole secret to his wife, charging her to retire and do what she can to hide her charms from their visitor. Aelfrida, dazzled by the thought of the station to which she might have been raised, dons her loveliest garments, and her jewels, and enters the room. Her husband, then overcome with grief at his deception of his king, kills himself by plunging a dagger into his heart.

Through the Looking Glass. This Suite for orchestra, given the subtitle "Five Pictures from Lewis Carroll," is played without pause. The different divisions of the work are entitled "Dedication," "The Garden of Live Flowers," "The Jabberwocky," "Looking Glass Insects," and "The White Knight." Written in 1919 for strings, wind instruments, and piano, and in this scoring performed by the New York Chamber Music Society. Three years later the composer rescored the music for full orchestra.

Peter Ibbetson. Commissioned by the Metropolitan Opera, had its world première at the Metropolitan Opera House on February 7, 1931. Is based upon a novel of the same name by George du Maurier, Mr. Taylor himself arranging most of the libretto. It is bilingual, and there is no wait between any of the three acts, the music being continuous. In the music Mr. Taylor has made liberal use of French folk music. Throughout, the story is dreamy and romantic. Unique stage devices are employed. In the earlier part of the work, while Peter is telling Mrs. Deane of incidents from his childhood in Paris, the story is being enacted at the rear of the stage, in pantomime. Later, when he is asleep, and dreaming of past pleasures, the dream is enacted in the same way.

THOMAS, Ambroise (1811–1896). A French composer born in Metz, studied at the Paris Conservatoire where he won many prizes, including the Prix de Rome. In 1871 he was appointed Director of the Conservatoire, a post which he filled with distinction until his death.

Mignon. First performance at Opéra Comique, Paris, November 17, 1866. Tells the pathetic story of a girl stolen from her home in Italy by a band of wandering gypsy players. Her father, disguised as a minstrel, has sought her in many lands, and when at last they do meet, they do not recognize each other. One day Mignon refuses to dance for the entertainment of a party of passing actors. When threatened by the gypsy chief she is befriended by Wilhelm, a young student who later asks her of her home. To this she replies in a lingering and questioning manner— "Knowst thou the land?"—in which she muses about her recollections of it in an aria of wistful sentiment. The opera libretto is based on Goethe's *Wilhelm Meister.* "Polonaise" (I am Titania) from the same opera, is a brilliant aria for soprano (Act II, Sc. 2), sung by Philina at the conclusion of a successful performance of *A Midsummer Night's Dream* by the assembled players.

"Air of the Drum Major." Even Thomas's comic opera *Le Caid,* the scene of which is laid in an Algerian village, this is a dashingly brilliant aria for bass. In it, Michel, the self-important young drum-major, tells of his own great importance, in a humorous and boastful manner.

TSCHAIKOWSKY, Peter (1840–1893). Born near the ancient and historic Russian city of Nizhni-Novgorod (now Gorky), the son of a superintendent of a copper mine in the Ural Mountains. Although his first musical instruction was given by his mother, Tschaikowsky was first intended for the law, and at the age of ten was sent to the School of Jurisprudence. There he entered, also, the choral classes and continued the study of piano. Later he attended classes at the St. Petersburg Conservatory of Music. In 1891 he conducted his *Sixth* (*Pathétique*) *Symphony* at the opening of Carnegie Hall in New York City. Tschaikowsky is noted for much richly colored orchestral music, including six magnificent symphonies, and as a writer of opera, ballet music, chamber music, and music for piano, violin, and voice.

"Andante Cantabile." From *String Quartet No. 1,* Opus 11, composed in February 1871. Was written at Kamenko, where the composer was at work on an opera *Undine* (which he destroyed two years later), and is based upon an exquisite Russian folk air which Tschaikowsky overheard a workman sing. The original air, "Johnny on the Sofa," recorded by Rimsky-Korsakov in his collection of *One Hundred Russian Folk-Songs,* is sung partly in 4-4 and partly in 5-4 measure, as is the opening melody of the "Andante Cantabile."

The second theme is played by the first violin over a delicate *pizzicato* figure in the 'cello which is repeated for many measures.

Concerto in B-Flat Minor, for Piano and Orchestra. One of the most brilliant of all concertos written for this instrument. The chief subject of the first movement is a melody which Tschaikowsky is said to have heard sung by a blind beggar at the village fair in Kamenko. The waltz-like theme of the tender second movement, presented in animated tempo by the violas and 'cello is that of a French folk air, "Il faut s'amuser, danser, et rire," which the children of the Tschaikowsky family had always liked to sing. In the third movement there is much syncopation, of a decisive and Oriental character.

The first performance of the *Concerto* was by Hans von Bülow (to whom it was dedicated) and the Boston Symphony, October 25, 1875, and it is said that the first cablegram ever sent from America to Moscow was that which told Tschaikowsky of the brilliant success of this concert.

Italian Caprice is an Orchestral Fantasia. A souvenir of several months spent in Rome in 1880. It pictures the typically varied scenes of an Italian carnival. In it are heard folk songs sung upon the open streets; bugle calls of the Royal Cuirassiers, cavalry men whose barracks stood near the composer's hotel; and vivid suggestions of street dancing. The piece opens in a decisive manner with a fanfare from the trumpets (*Andante un poco rubato*). The melancholy mood of the first subject, which follows, given out by the strings, is soon lightened by piquant folk airs which are introduced. The *Caprice* ends in a dashing tarantella.

Marche Slav (or "Russian-Serbian March"). Composed in 1876 at the invitation of Nicholas Rubinstein (brother of the famed pianist, Anton Rubinstein), who conducted its first performance in November 1877, at a benefit concert given to aid soldiers wounded in the Turko-Serbian War. In it three main themes are introduced and developed. The work opens, with four measures of rhythmic drum-beat. There follows, immediately, the mournful air of a Serbian folk song, "Glittering sun, you do not shine the same." This melody, accompanied by persistent beating of the drums, and repeated with many embellishments and by different instruments, is presently followed by a startling fanfare from which the music moves to the brighter folk air typifying the courage of the Slavic soldiers. This is played by a quartet of wind instruments, then by a quartet of trombones. The third theme is that of the hymn of the former Russian Empire, "God Preserve Thy People," heard first in the bass, then by all strings in unison and, after a change of key, from the full orchestra.

Nutcracker Suite, for Orchestra. Made up of eight short numbers taken from the music written, by invitation, for a ballet of the same name to be given at the St. Petersburg Opera House. It follows the fairy tale by Hoffmann, in which Marie, who has received for Christmas a number of beautiful dolls from different lands, and other charming toys, creeps back once more, before going to bed, to see them and her Christmas tree. She finds that the toys have come to life, and that they are having a struggle for supremacy with the mice, who have come to rob the tree of its goodies. The Mouse King is about to win, when the Nutcracker—a Prince who has been put under a horrible spell—comes to life, and drives them away, after which he conducts Marie into fairy land, where she sees the lovely dancing of the flowers. The numbers of the Suite are:

1. "Overture Miniature." A tiny classic in true sonata form. 2. "Marche Miniature." Suggests the procession of the toys about the Christmas tree. It opens with a tiny fanfare (clarinet). The first theme (trumpet and horn), is answered by the strings. A short Trio presents a gay little melody (wood-wind and strings) with its reply (bassoon and horns). There is a return to the first theme, the beauty of which is now enhanced with dainty arabesques. 3. "Dance of the Sugar Plum Fairy." Owes much of its charm to its dainty rhythmic character, and to the composer's use of the celesta, the bell-like tones of which, both in solo and cadenza, add delicacy to the sparkling music. The celesta Tschaikowsky had just heard in Paris, and here used for the first time, in his fascinating impersonation of the sugar plum fairy which comes to life off the Christmas tree. 4. "Trepak" (Danse Russe). Written about an old folk air of Russia, sung to the accompaniment of much foot-stamping and clapping. It opens *fortissimo,* full orchestra, the first theme being given out by the violins at a lively pace and with the accents placed on the second, instead of the first beats, of the measures. The flutes answer, and then many other instruments enter, singly, and in pairs, as though impersonating dancers. The music, of a wild, almost primitive character, is characterized by many *staccato* skips, and by mo-

notonous rhythmic drone from kettle-drums and tambourines. The dance concludes in the manner of a round in which the melody is passed about among the various instruments. 5. "Danse Arabe." In the ballet supposed to be danced by Marie's Arabian doll. Opens with a slow melody on muted strings, with drone bass accompaniment. Features of the music are the irregular rhythms, much use of double-thirds, and the Moorish character of the soaring melody. 6. "Danse Chinoise." Only 32 measures long, beginning with a rhythmic four-measure Introduction. The melody is then heard played by flutes and shrill piccolos, with many embellishments, to an accompaniment of bassoons and *pizzicato* double-bass. The clever imitation of Oriental din closes abruptly. 7. "Danse des Mirlitons." Or dance of automatic toys, features a trio of flutes. 8. "Waltz of the Flowers." Suggests the fairy land to which the Prince Charming takes Marie. Notable features of the music include the harp cadenza which is a part of the long Introduction, the arabesques which decorate the main theme heard in the second section of the "Waltz."

Overture 1812. Written and first performed in 1882, commemorates Napoleon's invasion of Russia (1812–1813) and depicts with picturesque brilliancy the famous Battle of Borodino, September 7, 1812, when nearly 80,000 soldiers were killed or wounded.

The theme of the introduction of the *Overture* is the old Russian anthem, "God Preserve Thy People,"

which is played by the lower strings. There is presently heard the beat of drums and fanfare of horns and wood-winds. This section is followed by the main movement of the piece, in which the army of Napoleon is suggested by fragments of the *Marseillaise.* The gayety of a Russian feast-day is suggested by a folk-song air from ancient Novgorod. The fighting continues, the strains of whichever air is prominent giving the clue to the victor. Finally, in the coda there is heard a recapitulation of the first theme, the thundering of the national anthem of Russia, and the peal of bells from the Kremlin Tower, signifying the final victory over the invaders.

This music was written in response to an invitation to compose an orchestral work for use in Moscow at the dedication of a large cathedral. The music was first played out-of-doors on the open Square before the Kremlin, and at that time the bells of the Kremlin actually took a part in the general din with which it closes.

"Valse" from the *Sleeping Beauty Ballet and Suite.* This celebrated ballet, built upon the old fairy tale of Perrault (which is also suggested in Ravel's *Beauty and the Beast,* in Wagner's use of the "magic fire" which Wotan places about Brünnhilde, and in music by other composers), is set to scenes arranged by Vsievolovsky, the director of the old Imperial Opera. This colorful "Valse" is heard in Act I. It begins abruptly, with a swinging phrase in lively tempo. The waltz theme proper is heard some time later after a brief

interlude in which the *one*-two-three of the waltz rhythm is carefully accentuated.

Symphony, No. 5. Tschaikowsky wrote in all, seven symphonies, this number including the *Manfred Symphony* which takes its program from Byron. Most familiar is probably the *Fifth Symphony in E Minor,* written in 1888. This work is remarkable for its unity, produced by Tschaikowsky in several ways, principal among which is his constant use of the rather somber opening phrase of the first movement, there given out by the clarinets and accompanied by the lower strings. This is repeated in the second movement, where it receives special emphasis, has a subdued reappearance near the end of the third movement, and is drawn upon for thematic material in the fourth and final movement of the symphony. The first theme proper of the opening movement is a much livelier air, taken from a Polish folk song here given out by the solo clarinet and solo bassoon. The second theme is a soaring syncopated melody in short phrases, given out by the strings alone. The movement ends, full orchestra, in a tremendous climax.

The second movement begins in the same general key and mood as that of the close of the preceding movement, and low in the orchestral registers. It rises gradually to upper registers and to the key of D Major, in which this second movement is written. There then emerges a lovely singing melody for French horn, soon repeated, in imitation, by the oboes. After a short interlude, the 'cello plays it, and is followed in turn by various other instruments which display tiny ornamental figures derived from it, and enhanced by embellishments. The new second theme is presented by the oboes, followed by the development section, and presently, after a dramatic pause, by a third repetition of the French horn melody on the G-strings of the violins in unison. The movement ends *diminuendo* and *pianissimo*.

The third movement, which the composer has labeled, simply, "Valse," called forth a great deal of comment at its first performances, as many critics felt that a waltz had no place in a symphony. It presents a new theme of superlative beauty, which enters abruptly, without introduction, as a violin solo. Toward the end of the movement the Polish folk air from the opening movement is restated. It is here given in three-beat rhythm instead of in fours, as at first.

The fourth movement, or Finale, has a long and slow introduction, and immediately there is heard the same melody as that which opened the symphony, now played (by all violins and 'cellos) in the key of E Major, instead of E Minor, as at its first hearing. The main subject of this movement is characterized by a curious downward progression, very *staccato* and very rapid. Toward the end of the movement the trumpets again announce the air of the introduction, in the spirited march which closes the work.

Sixth Symphony (Pathétique) in B Minor. Tschaikowsky's last great work, had its first performance at the symphony concerts of the Imperial Musical Society of St. Petersburg, on October 16, 1893.

The piece had its first performance under the title, *A Programme Symphony*. Later the name of *Pathétique* was suggested by the composer's brother, and immediately accepted. Three weeks after the first performance, November 6, Tschaikowsky died of cholera.

The first movement has an opening theme (presented by muted strings) heard, later, in three separate octaves in unison; and finally, *adagio mosso*, as a clarinet solo.

The second movement, which called forth much comment at its first hearings, was the first ever to introduce five-beat rhythm into a symphonic composition. It follows in its rhythm the character of a folk dance, especially in the second part. The first part of the melody presented unusual difficulties to the orchestral players of the Continent at the first rehearsals and was the cause of many amusing incidents. In the Trio section of this movement a monotonous drone effect is created by the constantly beat tone of the tympani which accompany the melody heard from the strings.

The third movement, in march rhythm, opens brilliantly, in an utterly joyous mood. The main theme is of a curious rhythmic figure and the second, and very prominent theme, played by clarinets and horns, is of a strangely stirring character.

The fourth movement, Finale, is, contrary to usual custom, a slow rather than a brilliant movement. It is, as Leopold Auer, the distinguished Russian violinist, and friend of Tschaikowsky, has said, "an *Adagio lamentoso*, a kind of funeral song, and it almost seemed as though the composer had anticipated his sudden end, notwithstanding that he was in perfect health and full of vigor." It is from this intensely pathetic movement that the symphony takes its name.

VERDI, GIUSEPPE (1813–1901). Born near Busetto, in Italy, was inspired to take up the study of music by his intense admiration for the tunes played by the village organ-grinder. At ten he had mastered the intricacies of the little spinet which his father bought for him, and was able to take charge of the organ in the village church. Verdi's greatest interest in music, when he was grown, centered in opera, to which he contributed over 30 works. He is also honored for the beauty of his *Requiem*, which he wrote in 1874 in honor of the Italian patriot, Mazzini.

Aïda. Written to commemorate the completion of the Suez Canal, and given its first performance at Cairo in Egypt in 1871, was commissioned by the reigning Khedive of Egypt, who, with its first performance, also celebrated the completion of the new opera house. The composer spent much time, before he began the actual writing of the music, in search of authentic background from Egyptian history. The scenes reproduce the old Egyptian cities of Memphis and Thebes. The time is that of the Pharaohs. Aïda, the daughter of the Ethiopian ruler who is warring against the Egyptians, has been captured. As a slave, she has concealed her identity, and serves Amneris, the daughter of the king. Rhadames, the captain of the Egyptian troops, loves her, but is about to be forced to marry Amneris, the king's daughter. Rhadames and the troops return victorious from battle, their triumphant procession before the king and the court being one of the most magnificent and impressive scenes in any opera. Among the new prisoners of war, Aïda recognizes her own father. He begs her not to divulge his identity. They meet on the bank of the Nile that evening. He begs her to use Rhadames's love for her as a weapon to aid her own countrymen, that she may learn from him the plans that are being made for further invasions. This Aïda does, though reluctantly, but the military knowledge which she receives is never used. Amneris, jealous of Rhadames, has followed him and overheard all of the confidences. Rhadames is thrust into prison and sentenced to a living death. To save him, Amneris offers to marry him. Upon his refusal she angrily agrees to his entombment, and the stone is lowered into place above him. Aïda, faithful unto death, has secreted herself in the stone tomb, and the two lovers die together.

Favorite arias from the opera include "Celeste Aïda," sung by Rhadames in the opening scene; "Return Victorious," sung by Aïda in the same scene; "O Native Land," sung by Aïda in Act III, during the scene on the banks of the Nile; and "The Fatal Stone" and "Farewell, O Earth," sung in duet form by Rhadames and Aïda in the final scene. Other famous music is that provided for the accompaniment of the ballet in the second act.

Rigoletto. This popular opera is adapted from Victor Hugo's play, *The King Amuses Himself.* The curtain opens upon a court scene. Rigoletto, the Duke's jester, has a beautiful daughter whose existence he had hidden from his dissolute master. The Duke is heard planning intrigues with a countess, which brings upon both the Duke and his servant the curse of the Count. Meanwhile, the Duke, posing as a student, has won the heart of Gilda, the jester's daughter. The latter is caused to assist in Gilda's abduction, although, being blindfolded, he thinks it is the Countess he is helping to steal from her home. Upon his recognition of the deception practiced upon him, and his daughter's peril, Rigoletto realizes that the curse has fallen upon him. Gilda, who now knows the identity of her lover, is still faithful to him. Rigoletto engages an assassin to kill the first person who enters the house; then plans that the Duke shall be lured there by the blandishments of the murderer's sister. She, however, pleads with her brother for his safety, which, he tells her, he can grant only in the case that another victim is found for him by midnight. Gilda overhears this conversation, and sacrifices herself, by presenting herself at the door in boy's clothing, where she is stabbed. Rigoletto, coming to claim the body of the Duke, is given that of his daughter in a sack. While rejoicing over his successful vengeance, he hears the voice of the

Duke. Amazed, he opens the sack, and finds the dead body of his own daughter.

This gruesome story has inspired much fine music, including the ever-popular quartet. In it Rigoletto and his daughter Gilda sing while standing outside the house, observing the Duke's love-making to Maddalena. Each of the four characters, in singing, expresses his or her own emotions at the time and the musical result is this dramatic ensemble. A popular aria is "La donna e Mobile," which the Duke sings in the early part of the third act, and which he is again singing when heard by Rigoletto, who had thought him dead.

Trovatore, Il (See "Favorite Choruses from Opera," p. 49).

Simone Boccanegra. (See also "Behind the Scenes at the Opera with Lawrence Tibbett," p. 43.) First performance in March 1857. The hero is the father, Simone Boccanegra, who, from being a corsair, has become a *doge.* The libretto was taken from a Spanish play of the same name written by the author of *Il Trovatore.* The work had its first American performance on January 28, 1932, with Lawrence Tibbett in the title rôle. The time of the action is in the fourteenth century. The score now used in productions is one which Verdi made about 20 years after the first performances.

WAGNER, Richard (1813–1883). (See "Wagner and Music Drama," p. 52.)

Flying Dutchman. The legend of the Flying Dutchman (see p. 53) who is cursed and compelled to sail the high seas for eternity unless, during one of his periodical visits ashore (each seven years), he can find a woman who is willing to sacrifice herself for him, is the basis of this, one of the most popular of the Wagner music-dramas. The scene of the first act is a bay in Norway, where Daland, a Norwegian sea-captain finding shelter there from the storm, encounters the ghostly sailor and his spectral crew. The Dutchman talks with Daland and, learning that he has a daughter, offers him a huge sum of money if he may be permitted to woo her. Contrary to his better impulses, Daland agrees to this, and the next act shows Senta (Daland's daughter), who is already familiar with the old legend, singing of it to her maids and friends as they spin together. Upon arrival of the boats, she accepts her father's suggestion of marriage. The Dutchman becomes remorseful and decides that he cannot accept so great a sacrifice. Senta, however, loves him more than life, and, to save him, casts herself into the sea. The curse is broken, the phantom ship disappears into the sea, and the spirits of the Dutchman and Senta are seen ascending to Heaven.

Lohengrin. A romantic opera, based upon the legends of the Holy Grail. Elsa, with her brother Godfrey, have inherited the kingdom, and are left as orphans under the unwise care of a wicked guardian, Frederick of Telramund. He appears at the annual outdoor court of the king and claims their heritage, the Duchy of Brabant. Godfrey has meanwhile disappeared, and Elsa, left alone, calls to Heaven to witness her innocence when Frederick accuses her of the murder of her brother. She prays for a champion, and the answer comes in the person of a strange knight, who, drawn along the River Scheldt by a swan, asks her hand in marriage. Only one condition is interposed. She is not to question him as to his name or former dwelling. This Elsa gladly promises, but on the eve of her wedding, when Frederick and his jealous wife, Ortrud, accuse him of being a magician, and in other ways influence her, she loses complete confidence. The wedding takes place, but when she and her knight are left alone, Elsa chides him for his lack of utter faith in her. He, trying to prevent her from asking the only question which may not be answered, is attacked by Frederick, who rushes into the room. Frederick is killed. The open court is again convened, the knight defends himself for the killing of his enemy, and reveals his own identity as Lohengrin, a Knight of the Holy Grail. The swan appears, but as the knight kneels in prayer, it sinks beneath the waves and in its place there rises the long-lost brother upon whom an evil spell had been cast by Ortrud. He comes again to protect his sister, and a dove descends from Heaven to guide Lohengrin on his return journey.

Die Meistersinger. This three-act comedy has for its central character the old cobbler, Hans Sachs. (See also pp. 44, 53, 107, 135.) Walter, a noble youth, visits Nuremberg and learns that Veit Pogner, the goldsmith, is to bestow upon the winner of the approaching singing contest the hand of his beautiful daughter, Eva, whom Walter loves as soon as he beholds her. Beckmesser, the town clerk, also desires her, and seeks to eliminate Walter from the contest. Beckmesser serenades Eva by night with his own garbled version of Walter's original song, which he has stolen from its temporary resting place in the cobbler's shop. This song Walter has received in a dream, and although it does not altogether fit the somewhat over-strict rules of the mastersingers and their guild, it wins the prize, and Pogner gives him the hand of Eva after Hans Sachs has hung about his neck the coveted medal of St. David.

Parsifal (See pp. 53 and 107).

The Ring (See p. 54).

Tannhäuser "March." A brilliant and tuneful march, one of the most spectacular numbers from the Wagner music-dramas, is also popular in its arrangements for band and orchestra. In the opera it is part of a scene which is set in the stately hall of the Castle Wartburg in the Thuringian Mountains. Thuringian knights and nobles are making ready for the song contest, the prize for which will be given the successful contestant by Elizabeth, the lady of the manor. With the opening strains of the march, the doors of the great hall open and the court enters in gorgeous array, singing as they come, in praise of poetry and song, and of Hermann, their noble patron.

WEBER, CARL MARIA VON (1786–1826). Born at Eutin, Germany, one of the greatest forces in the developing of truly national German opera. He studied in Salzburg, the pupil of

Michael Haydn, the brother of the more celebrated Joseph Haydn. Among his most famous works are a brilliant *Konzertstück* for piano and orchestra (completed on the very day upon which the opera *Der Frei-schütz* had its première), and three operas, *Der Freischütz, Euryanthe,* and *Oberon.* Weber was famed as composer, pianist, and conductor, and died in London, where he had gone to conduct the first performances of *Oberon.*

Der Freischütz (Free-shooter, or Magic Huntsman). The first of the romantic operas of Germany, and has to do with an old tradition among German huntsmen, that whoever is willing to sell his soul to Zamiel, the Demon Huntsman, will receive in exchange seven magic bullets which will always reach the mark intended. The story centers about two true-hearted lovers living in a forester's cottage on the edge of a German forest. The music, in which the composer has interwoven many melodies of spontaneous charm, suggests the delights of the place, as well as its weird associations with local legend. A strongly marked religious element gives to the music of some scenes a semi-sacred character. The opera had its first performance in Berlin on June 18, 1821. The Overture, long a favorite as an independent concert number, is the first operatic prelude in which a composer freely made use of important melodies from the body of the opera itself. It opens with a melody played by the horns (an air which has been incorporated in many hymnals), after which is heard a passage which suggests the sinister appearance of the Demon Huntsman and other scenes of terror from the opera. The Overture closes, however, in joyful manner, the thematic material being taken mainly from the aria of Agatha, the heroine, "We shall meet in joy at last!" which she sings as she sees her lover approaching.

Euryanthe Overture. From the opera of the same name, has long outlived the work for which it was intended as a prelude. In it Weber introduced many lovely melodies, and effects thought very "modern" in his day, such as harmonics for muted violins and tremolo of violas. The work is developed in the manner of a classic sonata, the first theme being treated contrapuntally and, at last, both themes being restated in the original key of the Overture. A lively coda brings the work to a close.

Invitation to the Dance. A distinguished concert waltz written by Weber as a relaxation while working on *Der Freischütz,* and dedicated to his wife, was composed during the summer of 1819 at a little country place, Hosterwitz, near Pillnitz, in a house (now carrying an inscription) in which the Webers lived for several summer seasons. The first concert piece for piano to exploit the rhythm of a dance, and written with the expressed purpose of appealing to the imagination of its hearers, the *Invitation* owes its early popularity to the fact that Franz Liszt, the brilliant pianist, played it in his concerts throughout Europe. "The slow opening measures," said Weber, "suggest the meeting of the dancers, the gentleman's invitation to dance, and the lady's assent. There is their conversation—his voice low in the bass, hers a treble." The waltz which follows the "invitation" is a bit of lively and graceful melody. The music closes with a return to the slow measures of the introduction, and easily suggests the thanks of the gentleman and his partner's gracious reply.

Oberon. The fairy opera written by Weber at the direct invitation of Covent Garden, London, was the composer's last great work. It was written to an English libretto, which inspired the German composer to take more than 100 lessons in English, that he might fully understand its subtler meanings. It had its first performance April 12, 1826. Eight weeks later, Weber died, the end being hurried, it was thought, by his unusual exertions. It is based upon a very old and romantic story of Huon of Bordeaux, said to have been sent by Charlemagne to visit the Caliph of Bagdad. The elf king, Oberon, was said to have given Huon a magic horn as a safeguard while on his adventures. By blowing this he might at any time summon Oberon and his fairy helpers. The Overture, frequently heard independently from the opera, opens with a call from the magic horn. There follows a rush of little notes, symbols of the fairy folk and, after a pause, the gay music sometimes known as "Charlemagne's March." The gracious love melody sung by Rezia as she beholds a rescue ship approaching, is finally heard—the air by which many people best know this charming work.

WEINBERGER, Jaromir (1896–). Completed the course of study at the Prague Conservatory, and at the age of 20 entered the master classes of Max Reger at the State Conservatory in Leipzig. He was also a student in composition with Jaroslav Kircka. He taught composition for a short time (1922–1923) at Ithaca, N. Y., Conservatory. Returning to Prague, he became greatly interested in operatic music. His "Folk Opera" *Schwanda*, in two acts and five scenes, though only a moderate success at first, became a tremendous success in its second year, and within its first four years of life was translated into 14 languages, and given more than 2000 performances on 120 stages.

Schwanda, the Bagpiper of Strakonitz. (Text by Milos Kares; first performance, Prague; first American performance at Metropolitan Opera House, Saturday afternoon, November 7, 1931.) The libretto has its origin in a Czech variant of a favorite legend concerning the miraculous power of an inspired magician. Old Bohemia had known it as a successful play for which Weinberger's teacher, Kircka, had written some incidental music. To this merry tale in which comedy abounds, Weinberger, his head full of native Czech rhythms and melodies, set his attention. The resulting opera is a combination of many lyric and dramatic situations; merry, melodious, and skillfully written music; scenes of such unique humor that in them one finds a modernistic view of Hell, where the Devil sits playing solitaire and the Headsman sits chewing gum, and in which are seen such modern equipment as typewriters, tabloids, electric elevators, and an electric call board from which the Devil summons his demons. There are, besides, many enticing stage pictures; charming ballets; a spontaneous and graceful musical score, in which are heard in turn learned fugues, exhilarating polkas, exuberant *furiants,* and exquisite lyric melodies. The composer has shown an ability similar to that of Humperdinck in setting simple tunes ingeniously. Among the intriguing melodies are those of Schwanda's aria, "Ich bin der Schwanda"; Babinsky's Ballad; Dorota's "Auf uns-'rem Hof daheim" and "Dornen auf den Wegen"; Schwanda's "Wie kann ich denn vergessen"; the Polka; and the "Odzemek"; and such humorous music as the bit when the Devil plays on Schwanda's pipes and the orchestra plays a brief version of the Polka set simultaneously in B-flat Major and F-sharp Minor.

The cast of characters: Schwanda, the Bagpiper; The Sorcerer; Dorota, Schwanda's wife; The Queen; Babinsky, a Robber Chieftain; The Judge; The Executioner; The Devil; The Devil's Disciple; The Devil's Captain; First Halberdier; Second Halberdier.

In the Overture are heard themes from the songs of Dorota and Schwanda.

Act I, Scene 1. To Schwanda's farmyard come troops, hunting a notorious robber. Dorota tells them that no one has passed that way and they leave. Babinsky, the object of their search, slips down from a tree in which he has been hiding and at once plans to win Dorota from her husband. When Schwanda arrives,

Babinsky paints a glowing picture of the Court of Queen Ice-Heart, telling him that there his bag-pipe music will gain him fame and great reward. Schwanda agrees to accompany his tempter and, during the temporary absence of Dorota, they leave. Dorota resolves to follow Schwanda.

Scene 2 (Opens with "Danse Tragique.") The Court of the Queen, who has sold her heart to the Sorcerer for a diamond scepter. Schwanda's merry music brings happiness and laughter to the gloomy spot. The Queen kisses Schwanda and declares that she will marry him. Dorota just then appears, and the Queen then orders that Schwanda be beheaded.

Scene 3. Public Square before the City Gate. Schwanda is about to be executed and the Headsman waits as Schwanda's last request—that he be allowed to play once more upon his bagpipe—is granted. The bagpipes cannot be found, and the Headsman raises his ax to strike— but a broom has been substituted for it. Babinsky hands the pipes to Schwanda, who at once begins to play. His music sends the Queen and her court back into the city, leaving on the Square Schwanda, Dorota, and Babinsky. To Dorota's reproaches, Schwanda answers that if he ever kissed the Queen, "may the Devil take me to Hell on the spot!" There is a roll of thunder and a flash of lightning, and Schwanda sinks from sight into the earth which opens under his feet. Dorota rejects Babinsky, who then promises to bring Schwanda back to her.

Act II, Scene 1. Schwanda, in Hell, refuses to play for the Devil, and is about to be tortured. Babinsky appears and offers to play a game of cards with the Devil, staking his own and Schwanda's souls against one-half the Devil's kingdom. The Devil wins, but is caught cheating and so becomes the loser. The now generous robber offers to restore the one-half kingdom he has won, and Schwanda begins to play on his bagpipes, setting the Devil and all the imps of Hell dancing to the strains of his magic Polka. Schwanda and his rescuer are restored to the upper world in an electric elevator.

Scene 2. Schwanda and Dorota are reunited and the happy couple sing a rapturous song in which they are joined by a chorus of their delighted neighbors, relatives, and friends. The scene closes with a dance.

WILLIAMS, Vaughn (1872–   ). One of the most important of the contemporary British musicians, an individual in his use of the elements of British folk song. In his *London Symphony* he attempted to record many of the sounds of the metropolis at various times of the day or night. Underlying the whole work there is an atmosphere of modality suggestive of the early history of music on the British Isles. The first movement suggests life near the Thames, at dawn, with "Big Ben" chiming the hour. The scene moves to the busy Strand, and all the songs, sights, and sounds of this section of London are suggested in the music which follows. The second movement portrays Bloomsbury, in the twilight of an autumn day. In the third movement the composer has made suggestion of the motion of the waters of the Thames, along which, on a holiday evening, there are heard gay sounds as though from a county Fair. The final movement deals with the unfortunate of the city, then returns to the mood and sounds of the opening measures of the entire work, with "Big Ben" again striking the hour.

Hugh, the Drover. A modern opera of English life, the scene of which is laid in an English village in the days of 1812.

Index

INDEX

411

INDEX OF ILLUSTRATIONS

NOV 29 1990

JUL 31 1995

JAN 25 1998